Alien Encounter

Science Fiction
Alien Encounter

Edited by
FRANK N. MAGILL

Derived from Library Editions
Published by Salem Press, Inc.

SALEM SOFTBACKS
Pasadena, California

Some of this material has appeared previously in
Survey of Science Fiction Literature.

First Printing

PUBLISHER'S NOTE

MAGILL SURVEYS form a series of integrated study guides designed to provide sources for augmenting classroom work in the Humanities. These guides offer ready-reference information about authors and their works and are structured with classroom requirements in mind.

Magill Surveys are intended to take the student far beyond the immediate assignment. *Alien Encounter*, the first science fiction volume in the series, presents the student with essay-reviews discussing seventy-five literary works which deal with this theme. Each article offers publication information, a list of the principal characters, and a two thousand word analysis as it appears in *Survey of Science Fiction Literature* (1979). These discussions emphasize the major thrusts of the original work and the reasons for the author's achievement or limitations in his or her undertaking. Thus, the student may gain extensive background information about a number of works dealing with the theme of alien encounter while concentrating on in-depth study of a particular work.

The original introduction to this volume offers an overview of the ways in which different authors have used the meeting between human beings and intelligent beings from a planet other than earth to achieve their literary goals. Using this volume as a guide to study the theme, a student will find stimulating ideas for directed reading, classroom discussions, and term papers.

The original material reproduced in *Magill Surveys* has been developed through consultation with and contributions by hundreds of professors and scholars throughout the United States and abroad. Its authoritativeness is attested to by the thousands of academic and public libraries where the basic works from which this material is drawn will be found. The student who wishes to go beyond his assignment will find here ample means to satisfy his desire.

CONTENTS

CONTENTS

CONTENTS

List of Contributors

Rosemarie Arbur
Richard Astle
Douglas Barbour
Neil Barron
Clifford P. Bendau
Peter Brajer
Peter Brigg
Donald R. Burleson
Thomas D. Clareson
Judith A. Clark
Grace Eckley
Wilton Eckley
Charles Elkins
Ina S. Faye
Beverly Friend
Vl. Gakov
Stephen Goldin
Stephen H. Goldman
Eileen K. Gunn
William H. Hardesty III
Jane Hipolito
Dorothy K. Kilker
Merrell A. Knighten
Donald L. Lawler
Russell Letson

Sam J. Lundwall
Michael W. McClintock
Patrick L. McGuire
Willis E. McNelly
Richard Mathews
Walter E. Meyers
Katherine M. Morsberger
Dirk W. Mosig
Al Muller
Brian Murphy
Keith Neilson
Maxine S. Rose
Franz Rottensteiner
David N. Samuelson
Harvey J. Satty
Kathryn L. Seidel
Ray C. Shiflett
Kathleen Sky
Brian Stableford
A. James Stupple
Charles W. Sullivan III
Frank H. Tucker
Jack Williamson
Gary K. Wolfe

INTRODUCTION

In Poul Anderson's *The High Crusade*, hostile aliens from a far-off star land in fourteenth century England; the townspeople at first take them to be devils, but they very quickly learn otherwise, and meet the aliens' force with force. The Englishmen take over the spaceship and set out to conquer the cosmos. Anderson is on solid historical ground in showing this remarkable medieval accommodation to the idea of beings from another planet: indeed, thinkers of the time would have found it more remarkable had the universe not been full of intelligent life. For them, God's creation showed the principle of plenitude—the great chain of being was filled with life on every level. Milton later reflects this notion when he has Adam ask Raphael about "other Worlds, what Creatures there/Live, in what state, condition or degree" (*Paradise Lost*, VIII, 175–76). From that time to this, we have continued to ask the question, and science fiction tries to answer it.

The selection of stories reviewed here defines the alien in a way traditional to science fiction: as an intelligent being from a planet other than Earth. Meeting such creatures, the ultimate "other," is a subject of real importance to the genre. As the writer Thomas M. Disch says, "the encounter with alien forms of life" is a theme that "more than any other defines sf." And the reason for this importance is apparent: the theme of alien contact attracts writers because it adapts so readily to a wide variety of purposes—because it can act as a vehicle for many messages. The number and richness of those messages are illustrated in this book.

First, a writer may choose alien contact as a theme out of a spirit of playful inventiveness, as a "thought-experiment" that explores the variety of life-forms the universe may contain. Stories like this succeed or fail on the soundness of their science, both on our present knowledge of physical reality and on legitimate extrapolations of what we know. For example, a memorable story of this kind resulted from a nonfiction article in *Astounding* (May–June 1939), L. Sprague de Camp's "Design for Life." De Camp argued that intelligent life, wherever it evolved, would fall within a comparatively narrow range of shapes and sizes—say, from a small dog to a large bear. Ten years later, Hal Clement's *Needle* appeared, a novel based on the author's disagreement with those limits. Clement argues, in the form of fiction, that an intelligent alien could weigh as little as four pounds. From de Camp's initial challenge to the inventiveness of writers, a very fine and convincing novel resulted.

Later, Clement began with the idea of a very strange planet, one whose diameter and gravitational pull varied widely. Suppose, for example, that the shape and rotation of the planet produce a gravity at its equator three times that of Earth, but seven hundred times Earth's at the poles. On a world like this, what sort of creatures would evolve? How, for instance, would something as mundane as trade be carried on? For the answers, see Clement's *Mission of Gravity*.

Some of the very best of "hard" science fiction has arisen in exactly this way, from the desire to follow an idea to its logical conclusion, or in a manner just the reverse, from finding a conclusion impossible on Earth and devising the conditions that lead to it. Suppose the conclusion to be the existence of human-sized mammals capable of true flight; what conditions could produce such a society? First, a very dense atmosphere would be needed, which would require a planet with a mass far in excess of that of Earth. But if the planet is to be much larger than Earth, it must be less dense, or its gravity will be too great. If, therefore, the writer wants a large but light planet, it must lack the heavier elements. Such a planet is the setting of Poul Anderson's *War of the Wing-Men*, in which the very environment that allows intelligent flying mammals condemns them to a stone-age culture.

As might be expected, rigorous adherence to scientific knowledge in stories like these produces aliens both uniquely different yet gratifyingly plausible. While Hal Clement and Poul Anderson are acknowledged masters at stories of this kind of alien contact, other satisfying examples may be found in Larry Niven's *Ringworld* or in Niven and Jerry Pournelle's *The Mote in God's Eye*.

The theme of alien contact has other uses, too: it is unexcelled as a vehicle for telling us something about ourselves, for seeing human society from a fresh and sometimes disturbing perspective. The meeting with another intelligent species can be seen as a test of our definitions of humanity: how much do appearances count for and how much do abilities matter? These are questions probed in H. Beam Piper's *Little Fuzzy*. The aliens may present a challenge against which we measure our most prized qualities. Stories of this sort are represented by Jack Vance's *The Last Castle* and *The Dragon Masters*, and by Edgar Pangborn's *A Mirror for Observers*. Looking at the aliens, we may see our own flaws—either present ones, as shown by the Nazi-like aliens in Egar Rice Burroughs' series of Carson of Venus, or the flaws which current tendencies will produce, like the intense specialization of the Selenites in H. G. Wells' *First Men in the Moon*.

Ever since the Houyhnhnms of *Gulliver's Travels*, alien societies have served to satirize human folly, as we contrast the poverty of human desires with societies that are morally superior. Science fiction has supplied many notable examples of this method: after striving against all odds to preserve his life on Mars, the human hero of Rex Gordon's *First on Mars* finds his struggles mocked by the Martians, whose acceptance of the universe has taken them beyond desire itself. Their passivity reminds one of the Tralfamadorians of Kurt Vonnegut's *Slaughterhouse-Five*, whose acceptance of fate teaches Billy Pilgrim a way to live with the memory of the fire-bombing of Dresden. The humans concerned with getting and spending in Philip K. Dick's *Martian Time Slip* seem grasping and shabby compared to the much more primitive Martians, who nevertheless command powers that humans cannot match. The locale need not be another planet: the aliens of Zenna Henderson's *Pilgrimage* and *The People* are here on Earth, but their tolerance and goodwill are often tested by humans who lack those same qualities. In John Boyd's *The Rakehells of Eden*, star-faring humans cannot even recognize a utopia when they see it, and their attempts to remake the alien planet in the likeness of Earth show us, as do all the stories in this category, an unflattering face of humanity; they show us how far short of our aspirations our actions often fall.

There is a third use for alien contact stories, one which takes its form from parallels in our own history. Earlier ages saw something like meetings with intelligent alien societies when explorers encountered peoples previously unknown to them. And those meetings were often bloody: the collapse of a civilization before the onslaught of vigorous, ruthless strangers, as in the barbarian invasions of the Roman Empire, or the crushing of a more primitive society by a technologically superior culture, as in the colonization of North and South America, provides us with a possible scenario for a future meeting with aliens. Pessimistic writers can argue, with much historical justification, that the violence of past encounters with our own kind furnishes little hope for greater tolerance in meetings to come. One of the strongest traditions in alien-contact stories began with thoughts such as these: as Frederik Pohl notes, "H. G. Wells told us that the essence of first contact might be invasion and exploitation (in *The War of the Worlds*), on the highly defensible assumption that since that had been the way it had usually been in earthly affairs, interplanetary affairs would likely be the same."

Abetted both by other writers such as Kurd Lasswitz (*Two Planets*) and by the myth of the warlike god after whom the planet was named, Wells began the tradition of the invading Martians. We see similar invaders from other planets in works like John Varley's *The Ophiuchi Hotline*, Robert A. Heinlein's *The Puppet Masters*, and Keith Laumer's *A Plague of Demons*.

In other stories, the hobnailed boot is on the other foot, and humans become the invaders. On several occasions, Ray Bradbury points out similarities between the American Indians and the Martians of his *Martian Chronicles*. And Bradbury was not the last writer to use the theme of alien contact to warn us against repeating mistakes of our past: if one does not recognize a romanticized portrait of the Vietnamese in the oppressed aliens of Ursula K. Le Guin's *The Word for World Is Forest*, even the most inexperienced of readers should see a satire of the American military in her picture of their oppressors. More generalized, but not less effective, is the first part of Harry Harrison's Deathworld Trilogy, which shows very graphically the response that human hatred and fear call forth on an alien world. So firmly fixed in the public consciousness is the idea of interplanetary invasion (as Hollywood demonstrates) that it can itself be burlesqued, as in Fredric Brown's *Martians, Go Home*.

Finally, there is a peculiarly modern use of the alien-contact theme, one possible only in a post-Darwinian society. Since the publication of the theory of evolution, different and disturbing questions have been explored in science fiction: if evolution is seen as a process resulting in survival of the fittest, if a red-toothed, red-clawed Nature has allowed Man to replace the dinosaurs, then what will replace Man? If the human race is a momentary episode in the history of the universe, how important can we be? Works such as H. P. Lovecraft's *At the*

Mountains of Madness stress heavily the transience and insignificance of humanity, a theme elaborated on at length in Olaf Stapledon's *Star Maker*. What is the next stage of evolution? Our replacements may not come on spaceships ready for battle—they may already be in our midst, as are the aliens of Chad Oliver's *Shadows in the Sun*, or being nurtured by us, as are the strange children of John Wyndham's *The Midwich Cuckoos*. Even if those who supersede us spring from our own seed, that is not necessarily cause for rejoicing: Joe Haldeman's *Mindbridge* suggests that the telepathy and the group consciousness of the aliens lie in the human future, too, but other stories are not so hopeful: the bat-winged, devil-tailed Overlords of Arthur C. Clarke's *Childhood's End*, despite their technological powers, are not the real aliens—the immaterial, composite being that Earth's children become is more inconceivable to us in its motives and actions than is a spider or a sea anemone.

As these stories imply, discussions of the ends of humanity easily shift to discussions of the purpose of humanity. When questions of teleology are raised, one has begun to speak of religion; small wonder, then, that alien contact in science fiction has generated direct treatments of religion—of the purpose, the fulfillment, even the ascension of godhood of both individual and race. Variations on the theme are numerous, from the attractions of primal innocence of John Boyd's *The Pollinators of Eden* to the awed contemplation of the universe in Gregory Benford's *In the Ocean of Night*. How will contact with the alien affect us? In Robert Silverberg's *Downward to the Earth*, the extraterrestrials embrace the Earth narrator as part of their godlike consciousness. And what about the aliens themselves? Their existence immediately raises theological questions: are they sinful or sinless? If sinful, are they damned or redeemed? Are they devils or angels? James Blish's *A Case of Conscience* gives one answer, C. S. Lewis' *Out of the Silent Planet* gives another. Even the title of Gregory Benford and Gordon Eklund's *If the Stars are Gods* suggests the ease with which divinity enters the theme of alien contact.

The human response to the variety of challenges that aliens present is itself varied; as we have seen—as science fiction has shown—it may be the force that is sparked by fear. Or it may be love, as Fritz Leiber portrays in *The Wanderer*, and Philip José Farmer in *The Lovers*. But whatever the response, chances are that it will have been foretold in science fiction.

Aliens have many uses: for hundreds of years these fictional creatures have been serving us well—to entertain us, to expand our minds, to point a signpost to the future, and most important, to show us ourselves from a different perspective. In teaching us, in pointing out our follies, in testing our virtues and chiding our vices, they hold the mirror up to human nature. And that, as Hamlet said, is the purpose of art.

Walter E. Meyers

Alien Encounter

THE ANDROMEDA STRAIN

Author: Michael Crichton (1942-　)
First book publication: 1969
Type of work: Novel
Time: 1967
Locale: Nevada and other parts of the United States

An account of the crisis created by the return to Earth of a contaminated sampling satellite in which a team of scientists working in a secret installation attempt to identify and counteract a substance or creature which causes human blood to clot into powder

Principal characters:
> DR. JEREMY STONE, a bacteriologist, lawyer, and top government adviser
> DR. PETER LEAVITT, a clinical microbiologist and epidemiologist
> DR. CHARLES BURTON, a pathologist
> DR. MARK HALL, a surgeon
> MAJOR ARTHUR MANCHEK, Project Scoop duty officer
> PETER JACKSON, one of the two survivors in Piedmont

When the excitement of reading *The Andromeda Strain* has worn off, one becomes aware that despite the gripping action, what one remembers most clearly is the presentation of classified or little-known information about the biological horrors which the contemporary science-government complex is either prepared to meet or is itself in the process of creating. The plans and facilities which Crichton documents are a seamless blending of what exists now, what Crichton deduces exists but is top secret, and what he speculates must be the plans and facilities that will be necessary to meet such crises. While the Andromeda event itself may be fictional, Crichton has gone to every conceivable length to give the book the texture of a chilling historical reconstruction; the resulting mixture places *The Andromeda Strain* beside John Brunner's *The Sheep Look Up* as the most frightening example of an "imminent catastrophe" novel in science fiction.

The novel begins when a Scoop satellite, sent into orbit to search for foreign organisms, is being routinely picked up by van from the Arizona desert. The discovery that the satellite has been opened by the local doctor, killing all but two citizens of the tiny community of Piedmont and then killing the recovery team, causes Scoop duty officer Arthur Manchek to call a "Wildfire Alert," a secret contingency plan involving a five-level underground laboratory in Nevada, where a preselected team of scientists assembles to attempt to identify and counteract the substance or organism. The problem is complicated by a series of human and mechanical errors, each of which greatly increases the danger to the research team and to the West Coast of the United States. Because Crichton has announced his own presence as the omniscient narrator by signing the acknowledgements section (in which many real senior scientists and military figures appear), he can warn us when a false trail is taken without explaining at the time why it is dangerous or nonproductive.

The detailing which dovetails real science and politics with the crisis and sets up the texture of the novel can be seen in the explanation for the Wildfire Project itself. As Dr. Jeremy Stone is being driven to an aircraft to rush him to the underground installation, Crichton breaks off the narrative to flash back to the roots of Stone's advocacy of the project. A real paper on the likelihood of extraterrestrial "invasion" being viral or bacterial led Stone to form a caucus on the subject and eventually to write directly to the President of the United States to initiate the project. Twenty-two million dollars were then spent on the underground laboratory, including the installation of an underground nuclear device which would automatically detonate three minutes after the laboratory became contaminated unless countermanded by a special procedure. In addition, Stone's team developed a Life Analysis Protocol, a sequence of tests thought necessary to identify any living thing, and it was arranged that Wildfire could order a Directive 7-12, called Cautery, a thermonuclear bomb to sterilize the site where the "invaders" had landed. Because of Hudson Institute conclusions on the high risk of thermonuclear holocaust from Cautery, the President retained veto power over it.

As if the Wildfire Protocol (resembling, as it does, existing facilities and options to counter biological warfare) had not sufficiently unnerved the reader, Crichton then has Dr. Stone read a file on Project Scoop, whose seventh satellite had brought the contamination to Earth. It is only at this moment that Stone, a leading and trusted member of the scientific-political establishment, becomes aware that a series of military satellites has been orbited with the specific intent of finding new and deadly organisms for biological warfare. This leads to some frightening descriptions of the half billion dollar per year American Chemical and Biological Warfare program, whose major installation, Fort Detrick, Maryland, covers thirteen hundred acres, cost over one hundred million dollars, and produces the ghastly weapons of future war. By the time Stone finishes the Scoop summary he is aware that Wildfire was built to conform to military thinking and, indeed, with an eye to its possible function as an adjunct should Scoop produce something more powerful than its masters hoped.

Over and over again, Crichton reveals the hard, calculating, mechanical planning of the political and military masters of science. Vividly unusual images abound such as the fierce, army-trained German Shepherds who guard Wildfire throwing their heads forward in a silent bark, their laryngectomies having given them all bite and no bark; or the extraordinary efforts to sterilize and decontaminate the scientists by burning away the epithelial layers of the skin with ultraflash.

As *The Andromeda Strain* progresses Crichton performs brilliant *tours de force* in his effective explanations of the complex scientific discoveries the team is making; these digressions seem part of the work, and do not lower the tension of the narrative. They discover that the organism kills in differing fashions and that it has a biologic structure unlike any form of life known on Earth. By the time one has come to the deadly and unexpected conclusion of the novel, a great deal of biology has been communicated without impeding the rush of the four days of desperate struggle to overcome a hostile organism that kills in seconds.

The most chilling aspect of this plunge into a nightmare that could happen tomorrow is the role chance and the subconscious play in a sequence of events that is supposed to be as computer-precise as technology can make it. The crisis begins when a small-town doctor opens Scoop VII instead of reporting it. The town happens to have an aspirin-eating Sterno drinker whose survival produces a vital clue. Wildfire fails to get messages, including the word that Cautery has *not* been carried out, because of a piece of waste paper that sticks in a teletype machine printout. Time after time the scientists, partly stymied by fatigue and trapped by the weaknesses of their personalities, fail to see the meaning of something they have discovered or observed. Crichton systematically points out each of these moments but always waits to reveal their importance.

When the Andromeda Strain is finally understood, it is by a burst of intuition beyond the logical processes of the scientific method. A failure in the sealing gaskets traps Burton in a contaminated area and Stone remarks to Hall that Burton is "scared to death." Strangely enough Burton does not die immediately and Hall wanders away obsessed with the connection between the remark and the frightened baby who survived Piedmont. When he cannot reason out the problem he blunders off to relieve the nearly intolerable tension by seeing Leavitt, whose hidden epilepsy has erupted in a *grand mal* seizure and left him unconscious. It is while checking Leavitt that Hall's mind wanders slightly to the outside world and an image from daily life pops forward as the answer to the whole puzzle. The frightening idea that important discoveries are often made randomly and accidentally is extremely chastening, and Crichton forces the point home with a final twist ending that leaves Hall's correct solution almost worthless.

The only flaws in *The Andromeda Strain* are the unlikely premises behind Wildfire, and the melodramatic ending. Despite all the care and precaution supposedly lavished on the Wildfire Protocol, the team operates short one man from the beginning because no alternates have been named. Indeed, it is unlikely that such a priority project would not have a lower-echelon staff trained to perform most of the Life Analysis Protocol on call at Wildfire, rather than have to wait for people to assemble from across the United States. It is even more unlikely that the Wildfire team would never have practiced the protocol together or even have seen the facility. It is also unlikely that any teletype message sent over such a select secret priority network could be left unacknowledged by a special function station on emergency alert.

However, these weaknesses in the logic of *The Andromeda Strain* can be dismissed on the simple grounds that no planners ever foresee the unforeseeable. Indeed, this is the subject of the novel, for the Wildfire Protocols are a conscious attempt to attack a problem with the minds of its team as open as possible to any unbelievable and unexpected biological invader. When the challenge is posed, human beings with human flaws, but with the unique supralogical capabilities of the human mind, attack it. The exhilaration of following deductive skills in the esoteric world where science, technology, and politics exert their relentless directives and offer deadly alternatives is the reward for reading Michael Crichton's *The Andromeda Strain*.

Criticism:

Bova, Ben. "The Role of Science Fiction," in *Science Fiction, Today and Tomorrow*. Edited by Reginald Bretnor. New York: Harper & Row, 1974, pp. 5-6. Bova gives a succinct analysis of Crichton's *Andromeda Strain*.

AT THE EARTH'S CORE

Author: Edgar Rice Burroughs (1875-1950)
First book publication: 1922
Type of work: Novel
Time: Approximately 1903-1913
Locale: At the Earth's core

Two explorers in a mechanical digging conveyance burrow to the hollow interior of the Earth where they have a series of adventures

Principal characters:
  DAVID INNES, a wealthy young mine-owner
  ABNER PERRY, inventor of the mechanical subterranean prospector
  DIAN THE BEAUTIFUL, princess of the tribe of Amoz
  THE MAHARS, the rulers of Pellucidar

In a discussion of the work of Edgar Rice Burroughs, there should be room for a few words about publisher Frank A. Munsey. Apparently interested more in money than in anything else, Munsey experimented with several magazine formats in the late nineteenth century, and eventually developed the one that was later to be the vehicle for the Golden Age of science fiction — the all-fiction pulp magazine. Science fiction had appeared often in the pages of the pulps before Hugo Gernsback came along, much of it in the magazines published by Munsey: *Munsey's*, *Argosy*, *Cavalier*, and especially *All-Story*. And in the second decade of the twentieth century, Edgar Rice Burroughs was the star of the Munsey enterprise.

Burroughs' first novel was *Under the Moons of Mars*, which ran as a six-part serial in *All-Story* in 1912; when *Pellucidar* appeared in 1914-1915, it was his seventeenth. In that span of about three years, Munsey printed the following works by Burroughs: *Tarzan of the Apes* (*All-Story*, 1912), *The Gods of Mars* (*All-Story*, 1913), *Nu of the Neocene* (*All-Story Weekly*, 1914), *The Warlords of Mars* (*All-Story*, 1914), *The Mucker* (*All-Story Cavalier Weekly*, 1914), and *At the Earth's Core* (*All-Story*, 1914). And these were, of course, in addition to those Burroughs placed elsewhere. Richard A. Lupoff, one of his biographers, estimates that in 1913 alone, Burroughs wrote over 400,000 words of fiction.

The popularity of this very prolific writer underlines the fact that, although it was not called science fiction, the form was very much in evidence well before the birth of *Amazing Stories*. When Edgar Rice Burroughs wrote *At the Earth's Core*, the central idea of that story had appeared in fiction several times during the previous hundred years. The heroes of *At the Earth's Core*, David Innes and Abner Perry, discover that the earth is hollow; after passing through five hundred miles of crust, they emerge into Pellucidar, the concave inner surface of a hollow sphere seven thousand miles in diameter. Above their heads hangs a miniature sun which gives never-ceasing light and heat to this world within a world.

Burroughs' setting, "hollow-earth," had several precedents, but the wide-spread popularity of the hollow-earth theory began in 1818 with the activities of Captain John Cleves Symmes, an American army officer. Symmes proposed that openings at the poles gave access to five hollow concentric spheres within the globe, and he pursued his imaginative conception through letters to professors of science at universities on two continents, and in a petition to Congress for an expedition to search for the opening. His ideas reached the public in full form with his 1826 book (coauthored with James McBride), *Symmes Theory of Concentric Spheres*.

The first embodiment of the idea in fiction was *Symzonia*, a novel of 1820 by "Captain Adam Seaborn" (the name may be a pseudonym of Symmes himself). The novel, or at least the idea behind it, was known to Edgar Allan Poe: his hero sees the polar opening in "The Unparalleled Adventure of One Hans Pfaal" (1835), and the theory behind the novel is hinted at both in "MS Found in a Bottle" (1833) and in the unfinished *The Narrative of Arthur Gordon Pym*. Perhaps Poe's stories suggested the setting to his most famous admirer, Jules Verne, whose novel *Journey to the Center of the Earth* (1864) takes place in a vast underground expanse entered through an extinct volcano. Although Verne's setting is an immense cavern rather than the interior of a hollow sphere, he populates it with flora and fauna extinct on the surface, a detail to reappear in Burroughs' handling of the theme.

Several American works also utilized the hollow-earth notion; one example is William Bradshaw's *The Goddess of Atvatabar* (1892), which is set in an underground land lit from the interior by a small sun, rather than depending on light reflected through the openings at the poles. The idea of a hollow earth remained popular, through John Uri Lloyd's *Etidorhpa* (1895) and Charles Willing Beale's *The Secret of the Earth* (1899), right up to Willis George Emerson's *The Smoky God* (1908), printed the year before Robert E. Peary's expedition to the North Pole found no opening.

Very likely inspired by an amalgam of sources, Burroughs, then, drew his setting, adding to it the touches of his own inventive imagination. But Burroughs seldom showed absolute originality; his strength lay, rather, in a competent use of the themes and techniques which the tradition of popular adventure fiction made available to him. Although in 1913 he was in only the third year of his professional writing career, he already had a firm hold on the few simple devices of plot and character that were to make him widely read and enjoyed to the present day. His hero, David Innes, is once again a young man of inherited wealth and technical background. His resolution and resourcefulness carry him through a series of adventures, in the course of which he meets, falls in love with, is separated from, and finally is reunited with a young woman of beauty and high birth whose energy and daring match his own.

The story is written in the first person, a point of view consistently favored in almost all of Burroughs' stories, and it opens with the typical framing device: a traveler tells of meeting Innes in the Sahara, and frankly states that he does not expect the reader to believe his story. Like all such devices, the frame serves to fulfill two seemingly antithetical purposes: it establishes an atmosphere of verisimilitude at the same time that it makes little claim to the reader's credence. The point of view, the way of beginning, and the episodic adventures that follow are all familiar to readers of Burroughs.

But several details deserve separate attention. First, Burroughs has almost never been noted for a deft use of humor, chiefly because so little that is humorous occurs in his stories. Tarzan, on the whole, is a pretty moody fellow, and John Carter's adventures are lightened, if at all, only by a grim irony or two. The lack of humor is easy to explain; it derives from the author's characteristic choice of narrator — the stock figure whom Isaac Asimov has termed "the big lug," a capable but inarticulate man, who seldom looks within himself to analyze his emotions. The typical Burroughs hero accepts what fate sends, often struggling to survive yet lacking the sense of incongruity from which so much of the comic springs. In novel after novel, the hero's love for the heroine comes as a surprise to him, although it has been clear to the reader for chapters. The characters have powerful emotions, but they lie beneath the level of conscious thought until, having matured, they break upward to their owners' attention.

At the Earth's Core is different; rather than being shaped in the usual mold, David Innes is not only aware of his romantic plight, he can joke about it. For example, through a good part of the novel, Innes aids Dian, the daughter of the chief of Amoz, in her escape from Jubal, the Ugly One. Jubal has marriage by capture on his mind. After slaying Jubal in single combat (albeit reluctantly), Innes approaches Dian, confident that he has won her love and respect, or at least her gratitude. When he is greeted with contempt, Innes turns to the corpse of Jubal and says, "May be that I saved you from a worse fate, old man." David Innes is one of the most fully developed and successful characters that Burroughs created.

A second triumph of characterization in *At tne Earth's Core* is the race of Mahars. The Mahars are avian reptiles, six to eight feet tall, descended, Perry tells us, from the "rhamphorhynchus of the Middle Olitic." They communicate with one another in some way not understood by the humans in the story; nor do the Mahars understand that humans communicate with one another. Believing that humans have no speech, the Mahars look on them as moderately intelligent animals, which they herd for food, or keep around as slaves for simple tasks.

In another way, the Mahars seem surprisingly modern: they are a race of females who reproduce parthenogenetically. Ages ago, we are told, the Mahars came under "the intelligent and beneficent rule of the ladies." With the males tending to warfare, science and learning became the sphere of the females, until one of them discovered a chemical means of fertilizing eggs.

With males no longer necessary, they ceased to exist. Reptiles though they may be, the Mahars are one of the few all-female races in fiction to form a scientific and technological society either in early or modern writing.

All does not end happily for either the adventurers or the human natives of the Earth's interior. Although the Mahars are overthrown, David Innes' triumphant return to the surface is spoiled by a traitor. A captive Mahar is substituted for Dian, and Innes steps onto the surface of the Earth accompanied by a female other than the one he had expected. Burroughs, given to writing series of adventures utilizing the same characters and settings, was not one to allow a worked-out society to be wasted on a single novel. Consequently, *At the Earth's Core* ends with Innes preparing to return to Pellucidar, and the outline of a sequel already visible on the horizon. Setting a new plot in motion at the very end of the book was a technique Burroughs consistently employed with the John Carter series. Indeed, readers of magazines in which his work was appearing almost monthly had come to expect Burroughs' adventures to follow one another in rapid succession.

It is easy to find defects in much of Burroughs' work: the Tarzan stories show a sameness of plot that quickly becomes repetitious; *The Land That Time Forgot* begins with a preposterous series of coincidences; even in the Martian novels, John Carter tends to repeat himself, and the series must depend on exotic setting and bizarre characters for its appeal. But in *At the Earth's Core*, we find real and likable characters, romance that is not dated, and suspense that still captivates; here is Burroughs doing his very best with those materials which he always uses well.

AT THE MOUNTAINS OF MADNESS

Author: H. P. Lovecraft (1890-1937)
First book publication: 1964
Type of work: Novel
Time: 1931
Locale: Antarctica

   A scientist attempts to discourage further exploration of Antarctica lest certain alien entities be disturbed, with dire consequences for the sanity and survival of mankind

   Principal characters:
        WILLIAM DYER, the narrator, a geology professor at Miskatonic University and head of the Antarctic expedition
        FRANK H. PABODIE, an engineer
        LAKE, a biology professor at Miskatonic University
        ATWOOD, a meteorologist and physics professor
        DANFORTH, a graduate student
        GEDNEY, a graduate student in Lake's party
        THE ELDER ONES, the revived alien entities and their kin
        THE SHOGGOTH, their monstrous and unmanageable creation

   This novel is a *tour de force* that must be read and reread in order to be savored fully. It works at several levels, and it is intended to do so. In order to understand both the style and the substance of the narrative we must realize that H. P. Lovecraft believed that an effective depiction of imaginary marvelous events must be presented in the manner of a well-contrived hoax, striving for the utmost verisimilitude and realism in every detail except the bizarre event itself. Furthermore, the characters must be subordinate to the awe-inspiring and fear-inducing occurrence, never overshadowing it; they must react to it as normal flesh-and-blood persons would if they encountered such an outrageous violation of natural law in real life. They certainly do so here.

   Lovecraft presents us with a report supposedly written by a geologist warning against further expeditions to Antarctica. The narrative does indeed read as if it had been written by such a scientist, because it abounds in technical and scientific data and terminology — reflecting the author's impressive erudition in matters of geology, biology, archaeology, and paleontology — and because it lacks flashy "action" scenes and the description of trivial incidents unlikely to find their way into a *bona fide* report of this kind. There is no dialogue whatsoever. Nevertheless, characters such as Dyer and Danforth come alive, their plight eliciting our sympathy, and their courage compelling our admiration.

   The plot, as it unfolds in Professor Dyer's narrative, has a special twist, best understood when one remembers that for Lovecraft a work such as this should call forth an affective reaction in the reader (ranging from awe — not untinged with fear — to terror and horror), rather than be a didactic tool for the exposition of ideas. The Miskatonic University expedition to Antarctica, of which Dyer was the leader, uncovers some strange triangular striated markings, actually alien footprints over 500 million years old. Professor Lake takes an air party in search of further evidence, and discovers a colossal mountain chain. He establishes a base on the foothills. Here, after some drilling, he finds a subterranean cave, and in it a number of barrel-shaped, star-headed alien beings, well-preserved fossils from the immemorial past. A storm develops, and contact with Lake's party is lost.

When Dyer arrives with rescue forces, he finds the camp in a shambles, its equipment strangely tampered with, and the bodies of all but one of the men and all but one of the dogs in Lake's expedition lying about. Dyer and the student Danforth fly through a pass in the mountain chain and discover the ruins of a cyclopean city on the other side, as well as an even more titanic range of mountains in the distance. They land and explore part of the city, entering its subterranean realms, and by examining a series of wall carvings unravel the history of the race responsible for the awesome metropolis — the same as that represented by the "fossils" discovered by Lake. They also encounter fresh traces as well as gear missing from Lake's camp, and it soon becomes obvious that the creatures had awakened and disposed of the biologist and his party. But rather than destroying savagely, they had evidenced the curiosity of scientists, dissecting human and canine specimens, and taking them along as representatives of their species.

Up to this point the reader has been shocked to realize that the alien beings have indeed come back to life and treated man as man would treat a biological specimen. But now Lovecraft displays his narrative genius in a brilliant twist of the plot. He makes the reader empathize with and even feel compassion for the creatures by disclosing their aeon-long struggle against other alien beings. He follows them as they fight against disturbing life forms of their own creation, tracing the history of their civilization from its zenith to its nadir and then apocalypse. "Poor devils!" exclaims the narrator, admiring their courage, intelligence, and tenacity. "They were men!" And then, when the reader has relaxed his guard, Lovecraft suddenly confronts him with the hideous thing of which the monsters are afraid, the amorphous protoplasmic nightmare of the shoggoth, which destroys the elder beings who had been its creators, and sends the two protagonists on a frantic flight to escape the nightmarish being. They do escape, and flying back over the mountain range Danforth glimpses even greater horrors that lie beyond the farther titan mountains of madness — horrors that permanently shatter his sanity. And now the shaken Professor Dyer, who had originally intended to keep such horrors secret, is forced to reveal them in the desperate hope of preventing further exploration of the accursed region, with its latent threats to sanity and the very survival of the human species.

As with many of Lovecraft's later works dealing with his fictional concept of a universe peopled even beyond its dimensional confines by intelligences of unthinkable antiquity, *At the Mountains of Madness* immerses the reader in a world view in which mankind is the most recent, the most transient, and the least significant of life forms in the whole scenario of Earth's history. Like the story "The Shadow out of Time" (1936), this novel presents a pseudohistory of our planet involving the early advent, burgeoning, and cataclysmic decline of intelligences whose civilizations spanned stunning periods of time and vanished at periods so remote in Earth's past as to defy even being called "fabulous" in any common understanding of that word. As represented by Dyer and Danforth, man, a mere terrestrial newcomer by comparison, learns of the dim and awesome prehistoric tenancy of the Old Ones, yet is made to feel a profound sense of empathy with his predecessors. The grandeur of the crumbling city is mute testimony to the greatness of the Old Ones; yet it is exceeded by the sense of horror inspired by the sprawling protoplasmic shoggoths below, in realms as dark as Coleridge's "caverns measureless to man." Indeed, it is this continuity with an unimaginable past, this implication that a detestable and now greatly magnified vestige of that past still lurks below after countless aeons to menace overly inquisitive human beings — it is this shocking linkage that gives the novel its unforgettable horror.

There is also another kind of continuity: with Lovecraft's other works. Dyer and Pabodie have read the *Necronomicon*, that ancient tome kept under lock and key at Miskatonic University, and they know that the discoveries at the Lake camp are disturbingly reminiscent of *Necronomicon* references to elder beings who once held dominion on Earth and even created human life as a jest or a mistake. The dreaded book, of course, plays a centrally important role in many other Lovecraft tales, as does Miskatonic University itself. Further, Dyer and Pabodie are aware of the similarities between the Antarctic discoveries and certain matters of prehistoric folklore mentioned by their Miskatonic colleague Wilmarth. Readers of Lovecraft will recognize this colleague as the same Wilmarth who has had a frightful encounter, in "The Whisperer in Darkness" (1944), with the Winged Ones, another prehuman race. And in the pseudohistory provided by *At the Mountains of Madness*, these Winged Ones, or Mi-Go, drive the Old Ones from northern lands and there establish themselves. Great Cthulhu has not been unknown to the Old Ones, and the Plateau of Leng, on which the city of the Old Ones stands, figures in other Lovecraft works. Moreover, the realm of the *farther* mountain range, beyond the Plateau, even links the Antarctica story to the dream fantasy world of *The Dream-Quest of Unknown Kadath* (1943). The Antarctica novel, perhaps as much as anything in the Lovecraftian *oeuvre*, supports the view that most of Lovecraft's stories may be seen as chapters in one enormous novel.

In terms of craft, *At the Mountains of Madness* offers much to admire. As in other works, Lovecraft here shows his admiration for classical models, as he emulates the Greek theater in keeping violence "off stage." Lovecraft deliberately places Dyer, through whose eyes the reader must witness the events of the novel, at a spot far removed from the scene of the tragic revivification of the Old Ones, so that the reader's link with the carnage is only through radio communication. As revelation after revelation is made, followed finally by silence, the reader shares Dyer's sense of tantalizing mystery. One is reminded of *The Case of Charles Dexter Ward* (1941), in which the reporter of the action is a diarist who has been placed with a contingent of the party *not* present at the scene of violence, and able only to report shots and cries heard from a distance. Lovecraft is masterful at employing narrative devices in such a way as to effect a certain distance between the reader and the sources of horror, so that the reader participates imaginatively, filling in the details for himself, or merely continuing to feel a sense of wonder about them.

Stylistically, this novel is Lovecraft at his mature best. Critics since Aristotle have regarded the effective use of metaphor as a mark of the capable writer, and Lovecraft's use of metaphor is striking. The imagination is moved by his description of the "horizon-grazing" midnight sun of Antarctica. The description of iceberg mirages as "battlements of unimaginable cosmic castles" not only stirs a sense of dark beauty and builds the requisite mood, but also effectively foreshadows the novel's coming events. When Lovecraft says that the pass through the mountains to the Plateau of Leng has "malignly frowning pylons" he exhibits his remarkable feeling for the sentient nature of place. Indeed, here as in many other Lovecraft stories, one almost feels that the place, the setting, is a character in itself. Lovecraft was not content merely to tell a story; he insisted on telling it artfully, weaving his somber web of mood and atmosphere with striking and lingering efficacy by skillful use of language and imagery. The effect is like the painting of some dark and disturbing canvas, and indeed the novel's narrator often heightens this impression of prose landscape by comparing the scenes around him to the strange paintings of Roerich.

The novel has a strong psychological appeal, touching deep emotions in the reader. Lovecraft himself was haunted all his life by a vague but persistent sense of "adventurous expectancy," a feeling that immediately beyond one's grasp, beneath the prosaic world of appearances and normalcy, lay substrata of wonder. And who can fail to feel, with Dyer and Danforth as they enter the immemorial city beyond the mountain range — a city of this very Earth but untrod by human feet — the excitement of discovery, mingled with awe at the implications of the place for Earth's history and man's motelike place in it? The novel stacks awe upon awe, horror upon horror. The Old Ones and their crumbling citadel are overshadowed by the piping shoggoths, whose immensity fills the cave-riddled mountain range to the very peaks, and these horrors in turn pale in comparison with the unnamed things lying beyond the farther mountain range and only dimly glimpsed, only fearfully guessed at. Whatever wonders there are, there are always more, just beyond clear discernment.

At the Mountains of Madness stirs deep-seated capacities for attraction and repulsion; the reader may shudder at the experiences of Dyer and Danforth on the accursed Plateau while at the same time yearning to be in their shoes. The reader is left, paradoxically, both with a heightened sense of human adventurousness and a curious sense of the unimportance and evanescence of humankind. As is the case with all great artists' works, these sensations, along with other impressions left by the novel, grow in potency with rereading.

BILL, THE GALACTIC HERO

Author: Harry Harrison (1925-   )
First book publication: 1965
Type of work: Novel
Time: Sometime in the future
Locale: The planet Phigerinadon II, a spaceship, and the planets Helior and Veneria

The story of how a simple farm boy, Bill, drafted into the space navy, becomes a "hero" through a series of improbable, comic adventures

> *Principal characters:*
> BILL, a simple farm boy
> DEATHWISH DRANG, a drill instructor
> EAGER BEAGER, a Chinger in the disguise of a human
> FUSE TENDER SIXTH CLASS TEMBO, a Reverend of the First Church of Reformed Voodoo

Perhaps under the impact of the social revolutions that swept America in the 1960's, and of the increased consciousness which resulted, much science fiction published in that decade underwent important changes. The most obvious of these, of course, was the growth of what was eventually called the "New Wave," but even prior to such a revolutionary period, many writers were indicating something of their own social awareness in their work. The dangerous visions of the late 1960's were muted ten or even five years earlier, but the visions were nonetheless present, even in such an apparently innocuous novel as Harry Harrison's *Bill, the Galactic Hero*.

On first reading, the novel is nothing more than a rattling good yarn, a space opera filled with typical Harrisonian good humor, satire, *panache*, and marvelous puns. It is a funny book, with gag after gag cascading from Harrison's typewriter. Who but Harrison would have the *chutspah* to refer to planets as "distant Distantia or far off Faroffia"? *Bill, the Galactic Hero*, in other words, is drenched with action, fast-paced plot, improbable characters, hilarious situations, and — what is finally most important — more than a modicum of social commentary.

What is the novel about? It tells of just plain Bill, a technical fertilizer operator from down on the farm, who is shanghaied into the Empire's Space Corps to fight against the lizardlike Chingers. Bill's adventures on the good ship *Christine Keeler* and on the aluminum-clad planet Helior, and his battles against the Chingers on a jungle planet that curiously resembles Vietnam, comprise the rest of the novel. Its headlong, pell-mell pace never slows, and the novel ends as he recruits his younger brother Charlie into the hell he has known for twenty years simply to get a month cut from his own enlistment time.

Space opera? Yes. Thud and blunder among the stars? Certainly. But if the novel was nothing more, it would almost certainly be quickly forgotten. Yet *Bill, the Galactic Hero* has been in print almost constantly since its original publication in 1965 and was one of the first books selected for the Equinox SF Rediscovery Series. Thus, there must be something more to the novel than a surface reading indicates. It is a tribute to Harrison's skill that the additional elements which make the book memorable are so well woven into the texture of the story's action-adventure-humor format that they do not obtrude or shout MESSAGE on every other page. These additional elements consist of a thinly concealed satire of standard science fiction techniques, as well as of particular science fiction works. The novel is also distinguished by its depiction of war as the ultimate absurdity, and by its lampooning of the military mind in terms so strong that at times *Bill, the Galactic Hero* resembles the black comedy of Joseph Heller's *Catch-22*.

Harrison's satire of science fiction takes off from Robert Heinlein's famous paeon in praise of the infantry, *Starship Troopers* (1959), which was quite controversial in science fiction circles, since some readers, including Harrison, felt that Heinlein prettified war. But to counter Heinlein directly would certainly not make a novel, and a direct attack might be considered by some science fiction fans as *lèse majesté*. Thus, Harrison made his infantryman, Bill, a dolt, and put him through a series of misadventures intended to implicitly poke fun at Heinlein's pretentiousness. Harrison's weapons were the rapier thrusts of ridicule or the stiletto jabs of satire. Who could seriously credit Heinlein's assertion that only those who had once served in the military forces had the right to vote when faced with Harrison's apotheosis of all drill instructors, Petty Chief Officer Deathwish Drang?

> He was wide-shouldered and lean-hipped, while his long arms hung, curved like those of some horrible anthropoid, the knuckles of his immense fists scarred from the breaking of thousands of teeth. It was impossible to look at this detestable form and imagine that it issued from the tender womb of a woman. He could never have been born; he must have been built to order by the government. Most terrible of all was the head. The face! The hairline was scarcely a finger's-width above the black tangle of the brows that were set like a rank growth of foliage at the rim of the black pits that concealed the eyes — visible only as baleful red gleams in the Stygian darkness. A nose, broken and crushed, squatted above the mouth that was like a knife slash in the taut belly of a corpse, while from between the lips issued the great, white fangs of the canine teeth, at least two inches long, that rested in grooves on the lower lip.

If you can't beat 'em, Harrison seems to say, laugh 'em to death, and thus disposes of *Starship Troopers*.

To his undeniable talents as a storyteller, Harrison adds his keen sense of the ridiculous. The horrible seven-foot-tall lizardoid Chingers — "Would you want your sister to marry one?," a military poster shrills — turn out to be a seven-inch-tall peace-loving and intelligent species who believe that war is against their religion and who will fight only in self-defense. And why does the Empire fight the Chingers? Well, the "Chingers are the only nonhuman race that has been discovered in the galaxy that has gone beyond the aboriginal level, so naturally we have to wipe them out." We fight the Chingers, one character maintains, because we have always fought the Chingers, but Harrison later develops the acidulous concept that human beings fight because they are not a civilized species: quite simply, humanity is a race that likes war.

· Harrison's sense of the absurd never fails him, whether it be in the description of the Purple Dart with Coalsack Nebula Cluster, which resembles an inverted, jewel-bedecked toilet seat, or in the very name of His Imperial Majesty's dreadnaught of space, the *Christine Keeler*, honoring the young lady whose amorous episodes brought about the resignation of a British cabinet minister in the early 1960's. In fact, the very excesses of the absurdity provide Harrison with still one more target — bureaucracy itself, as typified by Helior, the Imperial planet, the ruling world of ten thousand suns. Helior more than slightly resembles Isaac Asimov's Trantor, the chief planet of the *Foundation* series, but instead of centering about the great galactic decisions that Hari Seldon is concerned with in the Asimov books, Harrison asks small questions: If Helior, like Trantor, is a planet which, over a period of thousands of years, has been reconstructed into a world completely covered with metal, where does the planet's oxygen come from? And what do they do with their garbage in this spherical, multidimensional, futuristic version of the Pentagon? Asimov never bothered with such ordinary things like oxygen and trash, and Harrison pokes great fun at Asimov's excessive seriousness by having the trash stored in filing cabinets while oxygen is shipped in from agricultural planets in exchange for Helior's carbon dioxide. Logical but insane, Harrison maintains. Finally, Bill solves Helior's garbage and trash problem with the brilliant stroke of having it space-mailed, at government expense, to names selected at random from old telephone books garnered from other planets.

Harrison's brilliant comic inventiveness slides into mordant, corrosive satire with his sketch of the underground with which Bill innocently becomes involved. The Empire's bureaucrats mistake the lost, identityless souls who literally live hundreds of levels below the surface of Helior for a true subversive group. The consequent infiltration of this "underground" by dozens of members of the Galaxy Bureau of Investigation — the G.B.I. — provides Harrison with scope for some very pointed satire. The episode culminates in the long-postponed revolution instigated by the G.B.I. *agents provocateurs*. The agents disappear and Chauvinistisk Square is empty save for Bill, who has been duped by double-agent, counterspy Gill O'Teen. Harrison obviously wishes the reader to wonder if the only "Communists" feared by the F.B.I. during the 1950's were the hundreds of F.B.I. agents who subscribed to the Daily Worker, and whose subscriptions may have kept that paper alive.

Yet Harrison almost always cloaks his anger with humor; in doing so, he resembles many of the science fiction writers of two decades ago who covered their social awareness with humor, indirection, suggestion, hint, or allusion. Not all of them were as successful as Harrison, usually because their stories became lost in didacticism. Harrison, however, insists on action — ridiculous action, to be sure, but action nonetheless. This characteristic marks Harrison as a writer who learned his trade writing for John W. Campbell's *Astounding-Analog*. Yet Harrison shared the fears of many other science fiction writers in the gloomy aftermath of World War II: that the threat of nuclear annihilation might lead, at the very least, to the depersonalization and dehumanization of the entire race. Ray Bradbury spoke of this concern in *Fahrenheit 451*, as did Harlan Ellison in "A Boy and His Dog" twenty years later. Harrison's fears, incarnated throughout *Bill, the Galactic Hero*, center about the character of Bill himself.

Bill is anything but a galactic hero. He is a simple farm boy, totally innocent, completely uncorrupted. He is one of a class of heroes whose members include such disparate characters as Melville's Billy Budd, Voltaire's Candide, or Vonnegut's Billy Pilgrim. All approach the world with a wide-eyed clarity of vision unbesmirched by the mire in which they soon find themselves. In fact, one of the strongest appeals of Bill as a person is the way he retains his innocence in the face of incredible violence, insanity, and absurdity. Neither Deathwish Drang nor the cruelties of the training base, Camp Leon Trotsky, can corrupt him. He bends, but does not break, as he becomes a Fuse Tender Sixth Class, unskilled, aboard the good ship *Christine Keeler*, and his confidences revealed secretly to the chaplain are shattered by the chaplain in his alter ego as laundry officer, who has somehow or other lost six hundred jockstraps in the wash. Bill even retains his innocence when he learns that the Emperor of ten thousand worlds, "The father of us all" before whom he had groveled, was nothing but an actor.

Bill's loss of innocence is instead a gradual, crumbling erosion, as Harrison subtly transforms him into a veritable *miles gloriosus* concerned only with survival. Bill kills his Chinger friend, Eager Beager, simply to survive, and finally blows off his own right foot to avoid certain death in combat on the Vietnam-like jungle planet Veneria which circles the sun Hernia. Harrison makes Bill's transformation broadly comic as he elicits the reader's sympathy for the improbable galactic hero, blending some genuine pathos with the rich comedy.

In the end, *Bill, the Galactic Hero* may not be one of the most distinguished science fiction novels of all time, yet it remains a sterling example of how a skilled craftsman can transform the most banal of science fiction devices into a multitextured work that is both serious and comic.

CARSON OF VENUS

Author: Edgar Rice Burroughs (1875-1950)
First book publication: 1939
Type of work: Novel
Time: The mid-twentieth century
Locale: Venus

   The romantic adventures of Carson Napier, a twentieth century American, who combats Venusian totalitarianism and wins the heart and hand of a beautiful Venusian princess

> Principal characters:
> > CARSON NAPIER, heroic American aviator
> > DUARE, Carson's beloved princess of Venus
> > MINTEP, Duare's father
> > MEPHIS, Venus' most powerful Fascist
> > MUSO, Mephis' secret ally
> > TAMAN, leader of the Venusian resistance to Mephis
> > ZERKA, Carson's anti-Fascist protectress

   Edgar Rice Burroughs wrote five novels about Venus fairly late in his career, between 1931 and 1941. In the Venus series Burroughs relied on many of the stock characters and situations he had been using and reusing since 1912, when he introduced John Carter of Mars and Tarzan of the Apes to a receptive world. Again there is a hero who makes both war and love superlatively; again there is a beautiful, virtuous princess in interminable need of rescue from dangers all over her planet; again there is an exotic alien setting which hero and heroine courageously explore during their perilous search for happiness and self-fulfillment. But despite the presence of these familiar, even dreary formula elements, the Venus novels are essentially different from Burroughs' other writings. In several significant respects they are more original, more mature, and more thought-provoking than anything else he wrote.
   The strengths of the Venus novels are especially evident in *Carson of Venus*, the third and by far the finest book in the series. In *Carson of Venus* the series' protagonist, a twentieth century American aviator named Carson Napier, confronts and defeats the most malignant forces on Venus, and in so doing finds the home which he and his beloved Princess Duare had failed to find throughout the two preceding volumes. This happy story has the most coherent, controlled, and consistently intelligent plot of the series. It has an intensity rarely seen in Burroughs' usually episodic style, with events building to a thoroughly dramatic climax and resolution. Here the themes, attitudes, and values which govern the five Venus novels are brought to a full, clearly focused development. The meaning of all that happens to Carson and Duare becomes clear — a startling meaning, because it directly challenges some basic assumptions of Burroughs' other writings.
   Burroughs seems to have conceived his Venus series as a contrast to his

Mars series. Although Carson Napier is Venus' greatest warrior and truest lover, he expresses these heroic talents in very different ways than does John Carter of Mars. Carter is consistently the superhero, an idealized figure who easily does what ordinary people can only daydream about. Carson is everyman, a quintessentially average guy, who attains heroism only because events force him to do so. Burroughs gives him names which underline his ordinariness. He is a hero who appears ridiculous to himself and everyone else when he adopts glamorous, grand aliases of the sort which Carter repeatedly acquires. Carson prefers to be called by his first name or by the simple term "Homo," for, as he realizes in *Carson of Venus,* he represents plain humanity. Carson narrates his adventures in the colloquial style of the common twentieth century American, not the rather archaic, bombastic "heroic style" he often assumes. Moreover, unlike the enthusiastically bellicose Warlord of Mars, who learns to love long after he has learned to fight, Carson is a heroically gentle man who avoids violence whenever he can, and who saves his princess by virtue of his wits, not his muscles.

Carson's primary mission on Venus is to debunk and destroy much of what Carter stands for on Mars. Carter, embodying mankind's idealized hopes for itself, perpetually struggles to establish absolute, permanent control over Mars, the symbolic battleground of mankind's hopes and fears. He is a superman, whose descendants and allies are the first members of Mars's new master race. To Carson, however, all authority figures are suspect, theories of master races are dangerous nonsense, and only extremely foolish and seriously deluded people can believe the claims of would-be dictators. Every incident in *Carson of Venus* dramatizes a challenge to dictatorial authority. In the novel Carson defies one caste-ridden tyranny after another: the cave-dwelling Samary, whose Amazonian women brutalize their terror-stricken mates; the Fascistic Zanis; and finally, Duare's own Vepajans. Carson admires and helps only democratically minded Venusians, such as Taman and Zerka, who seem heroic to him because they, too, combat despotism.

The planet on which Carson discovers and asserts the common man's heroism contrasts strikingly with Carter's arid, almost dead Mars. Under its thick cloud cover, Burroughs' imaginary Venus is a mostly oceanic world, dotted with lushly vegetated islands. Various weirdly alien flora and fauna flourish on these islands, but the Venusian people, a homogeneous race except for a few birdmen, closely resemble Earth's human beings in their biology, their costume design, and especially their psychology. They are, in fact, figments of Burroughs' satiric imagination, and each of their island communities caricatures a particular set of human follies and delusions. Living as they do on separate, isolated islands beneath dense clouds, with few technological means of correcting their very limited and distorted perceptions and no philosophical incentives to do so, the Venusians naturally know extremely little about real life. Burroughs' readers share the initial amusement felt by Carson, the space-age Gulliver who tries to convey his larger knowledge to them. But amusement quickly becomes alarm, dismay, and outrage, for over and over, on island after island, the Venusians' obstinate refusal to change their ways unleashes tremendously destructive, despotic forces in their societies. By the time Carson gets to the communities and events described in *Carson of Venus*, the true function of Burroughs' Venus is unmistakable — to dramatize the causes, character, and consequences of totalitarianism.

Venus' significance begins to emerge in *Lost on Venus*, the second novel in the series. In this book Carson and Duare encounter two civilizations which clearly symbolize aspects of totalitarianism. Morov's dictator is a sadistic vampire, who drains the blood from his living subjects and has such a powerfully hypnotic will that even Morovian corpses do his bidding. Burroughs follows this sensationalized image with another which is more subtle, but no less devastating — the scientific "utopia" of Havatoo. Havatoo is Burroughs' version of the "brave new world" which results from uncritical belief in scientific breeding. For the people in Havatoo, biology is destiny in every sense. After generations of selective breeding, they have achieved a perfectly efficient, totally rational, rigidly stratified civilization in which everyone is assigned a suitable place to live and a job to do, and from which all physically, morally, and intellectually deficient persons are excluded. The Havatooans have no dictator and need none, because their eugenic theory dictates every element of their lives. As they apply its principles they become dispassionate, almost mechanical murderers, decreeing death for Duare because she is physically defective (having been born in a foreign country) and finding Carson, with his individualistic instincts, a loathsome atavism. Carson and Duare turn the Havatooans' technological expertise to their own advantage, getting from them the airplane and fuel they need to escape to another island. In the fourth and fifth volumes of the series they combat the sterile intellectuality and demonic scientism of systems like the Havatooans' all over Venus.

Carson of Venus presents two more fascinating anti-Utopias. The Samary reverse sexual stereotypes in a way that Burroughs obviously intended to seem distasteful, with grotesquely strong cavewomen thoroughly dominating comically passive cavemen. In this female chauvinist society, biological gender is destiny, and, as in Havatoo, biological determinism results in social despotism. As Carson and Duare learned the value of spontaneity, passion, instinct, and individuality in Havatoo, so the negative example of the Samary persuades them both to abandon all sexual chauvinism. Carson deplores but cannot alter the whining cavemen's conviction that might makes right. He does far better in dealing with the larger, infinitely more dangerous manifestation of the same theory in the Zani revolution. As their name indicates, the Zanis correspond exactly to Hitler's Nazis. Burroughs' searching, brilliantly satiric analysis of Nazism is the finest political criticism he ever wrote. His critique of the Nazis is all the more remarkable for having been composed in 1937, when Nazism was a young, relatively unnoticed phenomenon.

The Zanis have two principal characteristics: brutal ferocity, and the same smug assurance of their own utter perfection which distinguishes Burroughs' other anti-Utopians. But as Burroughs presents them, their behavior is almost as ridiculous as it is terrifying. Shrieking "Maltu Mephis!" ("Heil Hitler!") at every opportunity, the Zanis reverently stand on their heads whenever their puny Beloved Mephis appears, and they march in a peculiar hop-skip-and-jump step which gets them practically nowhere. Most tellingly, Zani education is done with mirrors. In a clever evocation of Plato's Allegory of the Cave, Burroughs locates Zani schools inside darkened theaters, where the pupils face the rear walls and see only the mirrored images of their actor-teachers. While Burroughs mocks the Platonic theory of the ideally "philosophical" state in Havatoo, he adopts Plato's theory of despotic psychology to explain the Zanis. Implicitly, through his allusion to the Allegory of the Cave, and explicitly, through the direct comments of Carson and other anti-Fascist characters, Burroughs declares that the root of totalitarian bluster and cruelty is extreme fear, insecurity and ignorance.

Although the Zanis epitomize the worst in the pervasively distorted Venusian thinking, Venus holds another and greater threat for everyman. The climax of *Carson of Venus* occurs not when Carson and Duare bomb the Zanis to extinction, but later, when they face and defy the more attractive but much more deadly Vepajan ideology. Vepaja, a community of tree-dwellers lives by a centuries-old complex of customs. Vepajans eschew the crude biological and pragmatic rationales of other Venusian Utopias, and see themselves as the guardians of Venus' purest, most civilized traditions. The values which the Vepajans defend include several which concern the sanctity of the family — the authority of the father, the inviolability of virginity, society's duty to protect the innocence and safety of its women. One of the most intriguing aspects of Burroughs' Venus series, and of *Carson of Venus* in particular, is that here Burroughs challenges these values, on which he had based the heroic codes of his most popular protagonists, Carter and Tarzan. From Carson's individualistic, commonsensical perspective, unthinking adherence to any custom, however hallowed, is as dangerous and leads as surely to despotic abuse as the attitudes and practices of the Morovians, Havatooans, Samary, and Zanis. As Carson could forge his heroic identity only by modifying the pattern set by Carter of Mars, so he must break some of Carter's most cherished taboos in order to establish his and Duare's home on Venus; indeed, he becomes "Carson of Venus" precisely because he outgrows the values of Carter of Mars, and lives with Duare on his own terms.

Because the search for a home is the basic theme of the Venus series, the reader relates to these books quite differently from the way he views the Mars stories, which center on the development of a superheroic personality as conceived in essentially escapist daydreams. In the five Venus novels humanity comes home to itself. Everyman, personified by Carson Napier discovers the heroism inherent in his ordinariness, and defeats the despotic delusions which make any planet hellish. The Venus books express the mature Burroughs' realistic hopes and fears for the popular culture he had spent a lifetime addressing. His message remains urgently relevant to our twentieth century world.

A CASE OF CONSCIENCE

Author: James Blish (1921-1975)
First book publication: 1958
Type of work: Novel
Time: 2049-2050
Locale: The extrasolar planet Lithia and the United States

Earth visitors to Lithia find in the Lithians, an unfallen race, a challenge to Christianity and an opportunity for fusion bomb production, while a Lithian raised on Earth finds here many challenges to Earth's ethics and to reason

Principal characters:
> FATHER RAMON RUIZ-SANCHEZ, a Peruvian Jesuit priest and Earth team biologist
> PAUL CLEAVER, Earth team physicist
> MARTIN AGRONSKI, Earth team geologist
> MIKE MICHELIS, Earth team chemist
> CHTEXA, a Lithian metallurgist
> EGTVERCHI, Chtexa's son, reared on Earth
> LIU MEID, female laboratory chief for Ruiz-Sanchez
> LUCIEN LE COMTE DES BOIS-D'AVEROIGNE ("H. O. PETARD"), Earth physics theorist and politician
> HADRIAN VIII, Pope, of Norwegian birth

James Blish's extremely well-plotted novel *A Case of Conscience* develops themes of utopia-dystopia, of egotism as a destructive force, of ethics *versus* religion. It clarifies the way a system shapes the thinking of the individual and, in a crisis, withdraws its support and forces the individual to act on his own. As indicated by the title, which comes from James Joyce's *A Portrait of the Artist as a Young Man* (1916), the ultimate power is in the individual.

Father Ruiz-Sanchez, Cleaver, Agronski, and Michelis form an exploratory party of Earthmen commissioned to determine whether the extrasolar planet Lithia, fifty light years away, will serve as a suitable port of call for interplanetary travel. Inhabited by twelve-foot reptilian people of nonaggressive, strictly reasoning nature, lush with persistent drizzle and built on rock (lithium) more potentially rich than the Church's rock of St. Peter, the planet seems to be a sort of Eden. Remarkably advanced in some types of technology, the Lithians have a shortage of iron and an abundance of natural gas, a Message Tree as super-radio, and static electricity. Governed only by an unwritten common understanding, they have no religion, no crime, no amusements, no politics. Lithia is Utopia.

Leaving Cleaver ill from a plant-spine wound, Father Ruiz-Sanchez, the consciousness of Book I, suffers only a minor twinge of conscience in abandoning Cleaver to visit Chtexa's home, thus foreshadowing his general lack of concern for people. What he learns from the noble Chtexa completely alters his view of the universe, but it confirms his view of literature. While neglecting the work of the Church on Lithia, he has been reading Joyce's *Finnegans Wake* (1939), a banned book; and he ponders and solves, in the Honuphrius passage, a case of adulterous conscience involving a priest. Only one short conceptual leap is then necessary: if a book can be written by the Adversary and subsequently banned, and if through the understanding of it the Adversary can be outwitted, then a planet can be created by the Adversary and, if the planet is banned, the Adversary can be defeated. The first, however, is Church policy regarding books; the second about Satan restates the Manichaean heresy — a case of conscience which, in his extreme parochial egotism, Ruiz welcomes.

The Earth commission council reveals Earth's conflicting ideologies. Cleaver, the physicist and imperialist-militarist, proposes to convert the planet into a thermonuclear laboratory and arsenal of fusion bombs for the United Nations. Michelis, the chemist and secular humanist, objects to forcing the Lithians to slave labor and urges an exchange of information with them. Agronski, the geologist and ordinary man, sides with Cleaver. Ruiz, the biologist and theologian, urges a quarantine of the planet because it is a "creation" of the Adversary.

As a biologist the priest is staggered by the process of recapitulation which the Lithians go through *outside* the mother's womb, with eggs laid in the abdominal pouch, birth in the sea, amphibian-to-kangaroo-like development on shore, and emergence from the jungle as homeostatic and homeothermic adults. As a theologian he sees that the Lithians obey Christian precepts perfectly without a Christ and live in complete harmony with everything in their world, as humans did before the Fall. As creatures of logic, they live by axioms — a set of "givens" — with no apparent giver. He sees the planet as a rebuke to the Church's aspirations to promote reliance on God and calls it a trap created by Satan. Of the four Earth visitors, only Ruiz finds his system shattered by this new knowledge of ontogony; for his Church has outlawed Manichaeanism.

With Chtexa's parting gift of a beautiful vase containing a fertilized egg — his own child — the ethical and scientific superiority of Earth will be tested. On Lithia the offspring faces the environment without parental protection (which itself seems both a sin and a crime to Ruiz) and develops a moral code tested by the rigors of their varied environments; they return to society as adults to practice the code, and it works well. On Earth the offspring are protected while growing and are given a moral code which, when the children are thrust out on society, they must test in a world which mentally, morally, and physically seems to be governed not by the code but by survival of the fittest; in other words, the code does not work. Ostensibly, rearing a Lithian on Earth should combine the best of both worlds; but Cleaver's shadow falling over Ruiz's on the departing spacecraft indicates the contest will be between the military and the ethical. Egtverchi, son of Chtexa, subsequently draws his following from the youth of Earth who have no workable code for their living conditions.

As Book II opens, civilization has gone underground since the international shelter race of 1960-1985, a reaction to the threat of nuclear war. The Corridor Riots of 1993 resulted from resentment of the shelter economy and provided an excuse for the United Nations to set up a world state with places such as Greater New York as "target areas," and only a few of the wealthy and powerful are privileged to live above ground. The war-scare economy, having gone underground, has defeated itself; even with international government, it cannot support the cost of reconstruction above ground. This, in the Holy Year 2050, is dystopia.

The priest, wrapped in clouds of theological debate and more concerned with his own soul than the welfare of his foster son Egtverchi, goes to Rome expecting to be tried for heresy. At home the unemotional and perfectly scientific Dr. Liu Meid as foster mother of Egtverchi fails to provide any of Earth's own touted human warmth and emotional support. Egtverchi's computerlike mind, as he matures, reveals his orphanage; he has no loyalty either to Lithia or to Earth. Michelis, often the consciousness of Book II, sees these problems but has no clear doctrine of his own; before he can decide to act, a United Nations commission — the epitome of bureaucratic self-interest and ineptness — passes Egtverchi for citizenship. Ruiz, instead of affixing human responsibility for Egtverchi's psychological displacement, helplessly and characteristically interprets the United Nations action as inevitable for a creature under the protection of the Adversary.

Citizenship gives Egtverchi a country to deny. He destroys a coming-out party given him by Lucien le Comte des Bois-d'Averoigne (a scientific writer known as H. O. Petard) and exposes the count's politically powerful guests variously compromising themselves in private cells for sexual perversion. Despite Earth's arrogance as demonstrated on Lithia, its differentiated systems, in a principle of action-reaction, continually generate events no one, and no system controls. Egtverchi's wrecking the party forces the count to flee and to resign his political operations; but it provides the impetus for his retreat to scientific experimentation, where he becomes the great scientist-magician proper to his heritage. At the party, also, Egtverchi superbly displays his understanding of the anarchically useful monstrosity of his appearance. More than ten feet tall, a reptile walking like a man, with grinning jaws and wattles swiftly changing color, small dinosaurian arms with clawlike hands, a balancing tail, and a tenor voice, he cunningly contrasts his sensational size and distinctiveness with an entourage of ten uniformed automatons. So also the disaffected youth of the world will follow him; and in his subsequent news broadcast, Egtverchi brilliantly exposes and condemns Earth's fraud and failure.

In his next broadcast, urging his audience to write protests against anything that irritates them and to sign his name, Egtverchi emerges as a great revolutionary leader. With the shelter economy, one fourth of Egtverchi's sixty-five million audience are insane, and one third join his forces. Earth's commercial system assures that the sponsors refuse to cancel his program, a financial windfall; and the United Nations as government, instead of rising to meet a crisis, thrusts responsibility for handling Egtverchi onto Michelis and Liu. Moreover, the United Nations has secretly sent Cleaver to Lithia to construct a fusion power plant and, having made an immoral decision, wants Ramon as opposing expert on Lithia disavowed by his Church before they announce the Lithian plans. Egtverchi is clearly right in his last dramatic newscast when he renounces his citizenship and declares himself — like Stephen Dedalus in Joyce's *A Portrait of the Artist as a Young Man* — a citizen of no country but that of his own mind. He urges his followers to do likewise, and he vanishes.

With the state revealed as corrupt, Blish offers a view of the Church in action; here again the institution thrusts responsibility upon the individual. Pope Hadrian VIII, a Norwegian, extends Joyce's satire on Hadrian IV who gave England control of Ireland and extends Frederick Rolfe's pope in *Hadrian the Seventh* (1904). To the Pope, Ruiz explains Egtverchi as a Colin Wilson "Outsider" — "a preacher without a creed, an intellect without a culture, a seeker without a goal," morally interested and contemptuous of morals. Instead of formal excommunication for Ruiz, the Pope has decided he is the man "to bear St. Michael's arms," to be the chief antagonist of Satan and to banish the Adversary from Lithia. A bit Machiavellian and crafty like the Emperor Hadrian of Rome, he knows Ruiz was derelict in duty on Lithia; but neither does he exhibit any papal wisdom. With the suggestion that Ruiz try exorcism, he banishes Ruiz from the Church until Ruiz shall win this battle against Satan.

The fate of society is thrust upon three persons: Michelis, Cleaver, and Ruiz. All must act according to their allegiances. The human solution fails when Egtverchi speaks to his father by way of the Message Tree and the Count's new circum-continuum radio; Egtverchi, having been cast out of Lithian society, refuses to obey Lithia's Law of the Whole. In the riots left in his wake, the innocent Agronski, least indoctrinated of all the Earth's commission, is killed. This implies the converse — that personal egotism, a personal belief, gives power. But with Egtverchi and Lithia posing a stand-off between the United Nations and Ruiz, Blish does not permit the novel to degenerate into a simple confrontation between church and state, though he does show all institutions reduced to the efforts of one person. As the United Nations' problems mount, with riots between its forces and Egtverchi's raging in the streets, only one United Nations man takes action. When Egtverchi is found as a stowaway on a ship bound for Lithia, the United Nations man appeals to Liu, Ruiz, and Michelis to deal with him by way of the Count's new observatory on the Moon.

Either an error in Cleaver's experiment combined with the Planet's natural gas, or Ruiz's simultaneous exorcism, may cause the planet's explosion; the ending is intentionally ambiguous. Cleaver, in destroying all humanity on Lithia, would have unknowingly worked a devil's triumph, Ruiz would have worked God's triumph. But the solutions are equally destructive. Egtverchi had denounced man's fear of death as a form of insanity, so the grief at the close is not from a loss of Egtverchi but rather a loss of what might have been: the humanistic goal of cooperation with a planet that could teach us much. The external problem of Lithia is destroyed but the internal problem of what to do with Earth remains. Ruiz as an agent has shown the Church to be inhuman. The ethical system has failed, and religion's part in it remains obscure except as man believes he is its agent. Every decision remains an individual case of conscience.

Criticism:

Ash, Brian. *Faces of the Future*. New York: Taplinger, 1975, pp. 185-187. Ash calls *A Case of Conscience* a novel marked with "religious overtones."

Mullen, Richard D. "Blish, van Vogt, and the rise of Spengler," in *Riverside Quarterly*. III (August, 1968), pp. 172-186. This article gives a close analysis of the novels written by Blish, showing how themes and wording suggest the influence of Spengler.

CHILDHOOD'S END

Author: Arthur C. Clarke (1917-   )
First book publication: 1953
Type of work: Novel
Time: 1975-twenty-second century
Locale: The Earth and the planet of the Overlords

Under the restraining hand of a group of devil-like aliens, man develops into a hivelike race suited to become part of another alien entity

> *Principal characters:*
> RIKKI STORMGREN, Secretary-General of the United Nations and intermediary for the Overlords during the first years of their rule
> GEORGE AND JEAN GREGGSON, a representative couple during Earth's "Golden Age," whose children show the first signs of metamorphosis
> JAN RODERICKS, a stowaway on an Overlords starship
> KARELLEN, the chief of the Overlords guarding the Earth

When it first appeared, Arthur C. Clarke's fifth novel, *Childhood's End*, drew critical attention to commercial science fiction. A "classic" after only a quarter of a century, it is still a highly readable account of man's aspirations and limits and illustrates how a concept of sufficient grandeur can overcome considerable literary and scientific flaws.

A short Prologue, written from the viewpoint of rocket scientists of the United States and the U.S.S.R., reveals that plans for imminent spaceflight have been thwarted by the appearance of alien spaceships in the sky over fifty major cities. These aliens are the Overlords, whose distant presence, electronically aided, will end human violence within the next fifty years and bring about a Golden Age.

When the Overlords finally disclose their appearance, they resemble the medieval image of Satan. This in itself is less threatening to mankind than the eventual Utopia which will remove every challenge in life. With no hope of matching the Overlords' technology, there is little inspiration even for the community of artists and intellectuals who have segregated themselves on the island of New Athens. But the people offer interesting subject matter for the Overlords, who are trying to isolate what distinguishes men from them and unite man with other races they have guided to maturity. When human children begin dreaming of far-off planets and alien conditions, it is clear that man's metamorphosis has begun.

When their children are taken away from them, the citizens of New Athens foresee the end of their world. As a result, they destroy themselves and their island. However, one man survives by defying the Overlords' ban on human space travel. He stows away on a starship and eventually sees the world the Overlords have converted into their home, replete with infernal gloom, low gravity, and an atmosphere enabling them to use their wings to fly. After also seeing what may be a tangible manifestation of the Overmind, he returns to Earth only to witness its final destruction. The children are converting the Earth into the energy needed for their journey to join the Overmind. The survivor broadcasts a description of this event from the Moon; *en route* to another assignment, the Overlords listen and brood.

Much of Clarke's fiction (*Sands of Mars*, *Prelude to Space*, *Earthlight*, *Islands in the Sky*) soberly depicts the near future growth of man's science, technology, and territorial domain, for which he has been an untiring prophet and propagandist in nonfiction as well. But his most popular and probably most enduring stories and novels transcend such rationality and extrapolation, and raise questions about man's ultimate destiny. From the fairy-tale adventures of *Against the Fall of Night* to the immensely popular book and movie, *2001: A Space Odyssey*, he has appealed successfully to his audience's religious or mystical side, without significantly alienating more scientifically and historically minded readers.

Childhood's End illustrates Clarke's ability to deal with both the traditional spaceflight as a metaphor for progress and the panoply of scientific and technological developments leading to the end of individualism. The human technology of the novel is capable, for example, of reliable oral contraceptives (not yet perfected in 1953), methods for proving paternity, perfected air transport, as well as such advances as electronic newspapers, undersea laboratories, plastic taxidermy and even a mechanized ouija board. Given time, man might be able to achieve the Overlords' level of technology, with its noninjurious pain projectors, three-dimensional image projectors, cameraless television, timeviewing devices, inertialess drive, interstellar travel and planet transforming powers.

Although such progress is praiseworthy in Clarke's later Utopia, *Imperial Earth*, in *Childhood's End* it is unsatisfactory; mere technology furthering peace and comfort will not bring about the millennium. The best members of the human race, self-exiled in New Athens, find their artistic and philosophical creativity stifled by the Overlords' superiority and the incomprehensible potential that the metamorphosis is creating in their offspring. In fact, all the human characters act as if they know their day has passed; they are simply marionettes on a puppet stage, whose actions will not matter in the ultimate scheme of things.

Stormgren, despite his role as the chief link between the races, is depicted in melodramatic posturings of minimal significance. He tries to persuade a religious fanatic of the futility of his protests against the Overlords, even when that has already been made clear by the Overlords' technology. The bulk of his story concerns his kidnaping by gangsters and inevitable rescue by Karellen. His final act is a childish plot to find out, before he dies, what the aliens really look like. In the original novelette version, "Guardian Angel" (1949), Clarke went so far as to hinge the entire story on Stormgren's glimpsing of an enormous tail.

The novel spares us that revelation, but the actions of subsequent characters are even less ambitious. Rupert Boyce, hosting a party near the beginning of Book II, is satisfied with showing off his "possessions," a wildlife preserve and a projector that makes his image giant size to greet his guests. The high point of the party is a séance, at which Jean Greggson falls into a trance and produces a code number which is later identified as belonging to the Overlords' adopted home star. For the remainder of Book II, she and her husband George worry a lot, while their Overlord adviser assures them that everything has a rational explanation, and their children drift away from them.

Only Jan Rodericks has ambitions which transcend the limits set by the guardians. Yet his adventure as a stowaway is merely a romantic, storybook act, to which it is difficult to believe that the Overlords would object. Only after his flight and the sightseeing which soberly demonstrates to him both the limitations of science and the finality of the metamorphosis of the human race, has Jan reached a level of maturity comparable to that of the Overlords. Yet it is a maturity that he has little time or inclination to enjoy. Clarke's style and vision only do justice to the grandeur of the novel's theme through Jan's tragic recognition.

If the actions of individual humans seem ridiculous, it is at least in part because they have no significant choices to make; the metamorphosis is out of their hands. Yet the reader, in identifying with them, must decide whether to see the change as tragic or joyous. Time has already dated the realistic components of the novel, making the choice more obviously symbolic now than it was originally. Shall we seek to continue our scientific and technological growth, following the relatively slow and tortuous path of evolution and history; or shall we seek a radical discontinuity, a metamorphosis into another form, a mystical unity with one another and with whatever we regard as God? Although we may not consider the second alternative a realistic future possibility, it has ruled the lives of countless individuals throughout the history of man.

The philosophical and aesthetic success of the novel depends largely on the reader's coming to grips with the ironic structure of the imagery. If this were simply a tale of metamorphosis, with aliens acting as midwives, there would be no need for the aliens to take the particular form which Clarke has given them. He is not only explicit as to the Satanic shape of the Overlords; he even goes to great lengths to establish the significance of that imagery. Their home planet is infernal in appearance; it even has been adopted and transformed, as was the world of Milton's fallen angels. Unable to thwart the will of their Master, they do Its bidding, striving to understand the how and why of each metamorphosis, as if hoping to master the technique itself or somehow undermine it. Their progressive unveiling and the modification of their messages to mankind as their original statements prove false or inoperative, further reveal their resemblance to the Father of Lies.

Yet their "modifications" of the truth can also be seen as the progressive approximations of science (forbidden knowledge has long been associated with the Devil, even in horror movies for skeptical audiences). As a further extension of the scientific and technological path on which man, particularly western man, is launched, the Overlords provide the novel with the only real alternative to sinking back into childishness or barbarism. Indeed, this is in a sense the Overlords' story. Only they, most visibly Karellen, are present from beginning to end, while generations of humans are born and die. Their elegiac tone lingers on after the Earth has winked out of existence, and Jan Rodericks, the last of his kind, has given way to a version of his race transformed out of recognition as humanity. Theirs is the "evolutionary cul de sac" open to man, from which ESP, spiritualism, and mythological allusions cannot extricate him.

It is understandable that readers prefer the fate of mankind ordained by the narrative, given the age-old resonance of the God and Devil images in the West — the home of empirical science — and the much older attraction of a universal oneness given meaning by a force beyond ourselves, delivering us from the need to make individual decisions. But the imagery with which the Overmind is rendered, the boiling mental volcano on the Overlords' planet, the merciless destructiveness of the organized children, even the hive-mind concept, are not really any more positive than the cosmic loneliness of the Devil, in symbolic or naturalistic guise.

Incidental imagery in the novel tends to support widening perspectives and a three-stage hierarchy which places the Overmind at the top and man at the bottom. In relation to power, Stormgren rules the human masses, Karellen dominates him, and the Overmind is Karellen's master. Stormgren is like a beloved pet to Karellen, an image echoed by the mourning of the Greggsons' dog for his own young master, lost in dreams. The disruption of the gangsters foreshadows the suicide of New Athens and the annihilation of the Earth. A séance foreshadows the children's dreams, which provide a link to a future beyond the end of the novel. Stormgren's "ascent" to Karellen's ship leads to Jan's flight to the Overlords' world and then to the final departure of both the children and the Overlords. But these are simultaneously images of limitation. The frustration of the rocket scientists in the Prologue is echoed by Karellen's edict that "the Stars are not for Man" and by Jan's final realization of the essential if not literal truth of that edict, since the "children of man" are quite different from their progenitors.

The final transformation of the children into a symbiotic, superorganic form of life is foreshadowed by various kinds of togetherness, which become progressively more compressed. The fifty starships hovering over world capitals turn out to be projections of only one, and the power of Karellen subsequently breaks up a mob demonstration and a gangsters' "conference." The Greggsons gather at a party and then form part of a colony dependent on its individual members; their dissolution as a family stands for its failure, and the island's loss foreshadows the final disruption. But perhaps the key image of compression is Karellen's entrance in Book II. Descending from his ship with trusting children in his arms, he counts on the image to recall Jesus' encounter with the young. But even that association is pregnant with foreboding, since Jesus warned his followers they could not enter the Kingdom of God unless they became as little children.

Olaf Stapledon, whose *Last and First Men* (1930) and *Star Maker* (1937) were an inspiration to Clarke, has never achieved popularity because he would not or could not render his vision in novelistic terms on a human scale. Clarke has succeeded, to some extent, in yoking the cosmic and the human levels, but the compromise is a fragile one, an illusion subject to effacement if the reader pays attention to detail. The human characters are not up to the adventure on which they are launched, by no choice of their own. The equation of the "breakthrough" with ESP and spiritualism and the tortuous explanation of the supposedly "universal" Devil image as a memory of the future do not stand up to close examination. In spite of the assurance of both man and the Overlords that everything has a rational explanation, their naturalistic framework is dwarfed by the morality play opposition of alien forces with its foregone conclusion.

Despite these flaws, a structural imbalance, and a style which vacillates between historical chronicle and uninspired narrative, rising to distinction only with the climax and diminuendo at the end, *Childhood's End* continues to delight and challenge readers. In part this may be due to a historical accident. The "children" of the 1960's reminded us how near the surface of our "technological society" the forces of the irrational lie are, and how easily they may come to be seen as preferable to the more recent tradition of "progress." In part, the novel's appeal comes from its contrast of cosmic and human levels and their identification with mystic and scientific ways of thought. At best, however, it succeeds in evoking haunting images which resonate with our sense of how fragile the human race is, and how evanescent may be its dreams of glory, as well as the tools with which it attempts to make them come true.

THE DEATHWORLD TRILOGY

Author: Harry Harrison (1925-   )
First book publications: Deathworld (1960); *Deathworld II* (1964); *Deathworld III* (1968)
Type of work: Novels
Time: An indefinite future
Locale: Three imaginary planets

Three works in which soldier-of-fortune Jason dinAlt contends with the lethal environments and dangerous politics of three bizarre planets

> *Principal characters:*
> JASON DINALT, a gambler
> KERK, leader of the Pyrran
> META, a Pyrran woman
> MIKAH SAMON, a religious fanatic
> IJALE, a slave woman
> TEMUCHIN, warlord of the nomad tribes on Felicity

Pyrrus is a world so deadly that in order simply to survive, one must be trained from birth instinctively to recognize and kill anything hostile. Pyrrus is a heavy gravity planet, apparently at war with mankind, where native life forms evolve and mutate, becoming more deadly each day that one survives. In addition to unending war, the planet is plagued with volcanic activity and extremes of temperature. Harry Harrison presents three such "deathworld" planets, which test the ingenuity, strength, and intelligence of his main character, Jason dinAlt. The novels in the trilogy are about survival in the physical sense, as situations, environments, plants, animals, and people actively attempt to kill Jason. The three *Deathworld* novels are exciting adventures depicting the hero's ability to survive and to overcome immense odds.

Since science fiction heroes take many shapes and forms and enjoy diverse abilities and technological advances, it is surprising that Harrison chose to give his main character only sporadic telekinetic powers and limited native intelligence. Jason is cast initially in the role of a successful wandering gambler, a sophisticated type drifting from casino to casino in search of a challenge which will make his life meaningful. The deathworld planets provide a background against which he can pit all his talents and discover his worth. Each planet has its unique dangers and obstacles to overcome; each is the setting for a game whose stakes are Jason's life.

Deathworld, the first novel of the trilogy, begins when Jason dinAlt receives a message capsule in his suite on the casino planet Cassilia. He knows no one who could be aware of his identity, so he prepares to welcome his visitor by hiding his gun under a pillow on the couch. His visitor is Kerk from the planet Pyrrus, and he resembles a heavyweight wrestler. Thinking that Kerk must be sent by the police or by an old enemy, Jason insists that he remove his gun. When he attempts to enforce the request by drawing his own weapon, Kerk outdraws him with superhuman speed. With the barrel of his enormous gun pointed directly between Jason's eyes, Kerk impatiently explains his proposition. Kerk must raise three billion credits by morning; gambling is the only way to do it. Having looked into Jason's past exploits, he offers him a bankroll of twenty-seven million credits to play with. Anything over the three billion which Jason wins is his to keep. Should he lose, Kerk will kill him.

The theme of risking one's life is repeated throughout the trilogy. Life must be put on the line in order to live fully. Fascinated by the large sums of money, the urgency, and by the remarkable Pyrran man, Jason agrees to the gambling venture; he gambles and wins. The management is not exhilarated by his good luck and attempts to prevent his departure. Kerk intervenes to help Jason collect his winnings; the two shoot their way to freedom, stop later for a quiet meal, and then battle their way off the planet.

Over Kerk's strenuous objections, Jason then decides to go to the Pyrran planet to see what he has risked his life for and to see what kind of place breeds men like Kerk. On the journey he meets Meta, a Pyrran woman who moves and thinks with the same speed and precision as Kerk. She is the pilot of the sole Pyrran spaceship, which is transporting the cargo paid for by Jason's gambling venture. The cargo turns out to be guns, ammunition, and military supplies with which to fight the hostile planet Pyrrus. During the long trip, Jason and Meta gravitate towards each other and finally become lovers; but as soon as the journey ends, both Kerk and Meta become singleminded in pursuit of their objective. Meta no longer pays attention to Jason, leaving him perplexed and angry.

The reason for the Pyrrans' caution is that the planet Pyrrus is deadly. Even the crew of the spaceship, who are far superior physically to Jason, must be unloaded like cargo in armored cases; they have been away too long, and need to be brought up to date concerning the latest dangers facing man. Jason is injected and innoculated against all the microbiological dangers, and forced to go through classes with the Pyrran children. In a simulated environment, he is drilled to perfection to respond instinctually to danger. At the end of many months of training, however, he realizes he will never become proficient enough to survive unattended.

Meta's rejection, together with his dependent position, prompts Jason to investigate the history of the settlement. Just as he begins to understand the Pyrran character and to uncover taboos surrounding the mysterious war, the city suffers another attack and Jason inadvertently causes the death of a Pyrran. Imprisoned, he awaits the return of the spaceship to take him away from Pyrrus. During his confinement, he learns that there are settlers who live outside the armored city, and that only limited trade and communication between them and the city dwellers is allowed. Jason then bribes a guard and escapes into the wilderness, where he meets the settlers, who, he learns, are hated by the city dwellers because they have learned to live with the planet. A state of war exists between the two groups, and the outside settlers, who have been cut off from the benefits of technology, ask Jason for his help and return him to the city.

Realizing that the city dwellers' problem is their own hatred of their environment, amplified and turned back against them, Jason organizes the outsiders to capture the spaceship. The control of offworld access will force the city dwellers to listen. The raid is successful and Jason dramatically demonstrates the truth of his discovery. Reluctantly, the city Pyrrans accept Jason. Meta realizes Jason's true worth and they are reunited.

No sooner is Jason accepted into Pyrran society, however, than he is kidnaped and then shipwrecked on "Deathworld II." In the second novel of the trilogy he faces a planet cut off from civilization, a world whose culture has lost most of its technological heritage. *Deathworld II* takes Jason on an evolutionary journey, beginning with his capture and nomadic slavehood. He advances up the evolutionary ladder by being captured by a more "advanced" group. He gains privileges by demonstrating his knowledge of proprietary scientific secrets and makes his escape, only to be captured again by another group still higher on the ladder. In hopes of finding the means to contact his Pyrran friends, he begins seeking the highest level of technology on the planet. As time passes, Jason tires of being passed from one power group to another and decides to change the medieval social structure by consolidating all the scientific knowledge in the hands of one group and introducing advanced technology. In spite of his successful campaign he is seriously wounded and only at the last moment rescued from certain death by the arrival of his Pyrran companion Meta.

In *Deathworld III*, the Pyrrans battle the nomadic inhabitants of Felicity, a heavy gravity planet containing enormous mineral resources. Although the natives fiercely defend themselves from outside exploitation, Jason decides that the Pyrrans need a new challenge, and ought to invade the planet. It takes more than stamina and physical skill, however, to overcome the resistance of Felicity's inhabitants; the Pyrran strategy of overwhelming the barbarians by sheer strength fails. With the help of his shipboard computer library, Jason recalls the experience of the Mongolians in attacking the Chinese civilization, and tricks the barbarian warlord into conquering the more civilized lowlands. Jason's recognition of the historical precedent yields him the final victory, and the conquerors are assimilated.

In each of the three deathworlds, Jason appears to be the underdog, weak, slow, and ill-adapted to the environment. But he comes prepared with knowledge, experience, and the determination to overcome all obstacles. As a gambler, he has learned to stretch the odds; he risks his life and wins.

At times Harrison is a better, more subtle writer than appears on the surface of his action-packed stories. His subtlety is most evident in the character of his disparate heroes, and is particularly evidenced by the developing nature of Jason dinAlt himself. To understand this development, we must remember that these novels were written for John W. Campbell, Jr., when *Astounding-Analog* dominated the science fiction magazine field. Harrison worked very closely with Campbell and, in fact, edited a collection of the Campbell's provocative and sometimes controversial editorials for book publication. Campbell had a rather restricted notion of what constituted a hero, and authors often tailored their lead characters according to the editor's specifications. Usually two-dimensional men who have their greatness thrust upon them, Campbell's heroes often solve problems by studying them from a unique viewpoint.

Harrison began the *Deathworld* series by creating Jason in the image that Campbell desired. Thus, in *Deathworld I*, Jason is the apotheosis of the Campbellian hero: at odds with society, he is trapped in circumstances he can neither understand nor comprehend. If he accepts the situation as defined by the almost superhuman Pyrrans, he will very likely die. Only when Jason refuses to take at face value the continuing war being fought by his captors does he begin to see the possibilities for survival. Surely this situation was typical of many stories printed by Campbell, and Harrison's treatment differs little from the Campbellian prototype. However, even in the first book, Harrison violates one of Campbell's unspoken edicts: Do not give the hero a love interest. Jason falls deeply in love with Meta, a situation that rarely occurred in standard *Astounding-Analog* fiction. Yet Harrison makes this happening crucial to Jason's growth, and his consequent development as a person depends upon this circumstance as well as upon Jason's increasing ability to look "otherwise" at the situations he finds himself in.

Harrison once remarked that he got terribly tired of Jason in *Deathworld II* and *Deathworld III*. The more he considered the devious yet "heroic" person he had invented, the more he became aware of Jason's essentially paradoxical, exaggerated nature. At this point, Harrison's irrepressible sense of the ridiculous took over, and to rid himself of the last vestiges of Campbellian "jasonism," he created a new "hero" in his 1965 novel, *Bill, The Galactic Hero*. Bill is such a bumbling idiot and the book about him so hilariously funny that no reader would ever again be able to take Campbell or Jason seriously. Therefore, the *Deathworld* series can be viewed as the culmination of the development of the classic science fiction hero, leading directly into its opposite, the creation of the anti-hero.

However, Harrison is far too good a craftsman to let his notion of the ambiguous hero get in the way of telling a story. All three novels are filled with action and suspense guaranteed to hold the reader's interest, although they are not equally successful: Harrison's interest in *Deathworld III* seems to flag and the plot becomes somewhat laborious at the end. *Deathworld IV* turned into *Bill, The Galactic Hero*, and science fiction finally proved that it could laugh at itself after the penny-dreadful seriousness of the first three books, which, if they lack the brilliant comedic invention of Harrison's later work, are still well worth reading, if only as period pieces.

DIMENSION OF MIRACLES

Author: Robert Sheckley (1928-   )
First book publication: 1968
Type of work: Novel
Time: The present
Locale: Earth and several alternate Earths

A satirical picaresque novel about a man who, having journeyed to the Galactic Center to collect his prize for winning an intergalactic sweepstakes, has no idea how to return to his own Earth amid a multitude of possible Earths

> Principal characters:
> TOM CARMODY, Everyman in search of his home
> THE PRIZE, an object/animal/being capable of shapechanging
> MELICHRONE, a god
> MAUDSLEY, a contractor, builder of Earth
> CARMODY'S PREDATOR, a thing with the sole purpose of eating Carmodys

Robert Sheckley's books refuse to be categorized. Are they fantasy, science fiction, Zen philosophy, or the work of a sane madman? There is no one answer. The only choice is to say that whatever they are, they are the best in that field. It is easy to make comparisons to other art forms to explain Sheckley: he is Magritte, he is Dali, he is surrealism in prose form. But his is a surrealism with rules. There is a beginning, a middle, and an end — a framework — but what happens within that framework is pure Sheckley. *Abandon preconceived notions of reality, all you who read here* is the watchword of any Sheckley novel. Sheckley's writing is not, however, experimentation for experimentation's sake; it also entertains, and allows the reader a glimpse into a very intriguing mind.

Dimension of Miracles is the "simple" story of a simple man in search of his homeland — a topic familiar since ancient times. In this case the hero is Tom Carmody, who is informed that he has won first prize in the Galactic Sweepstakes; caught up in the joy of winning, he fails to take into account what such a prize might entail. He is told that the prize has value, but nowhere is he told what sort of value that might be. The Prize is a *yenta*, a whiner, and a half-baked philosopher, but it must have some value — it is, after all, a prize. Sheckley makes the point that our civilization is too prone to consider prizes — be they material gain, fame, or being named best in class — as an end in themselves rather than as a possibly dubious honor that might prove to be more trouble than it is worth.

After being given his Prize, Carmody is told he must find his way home on his own — and not merely to a point in time and space, but to a point in several possible dimensions. There are many Earths. Which one is Carmody's Earth? And which Earth does he really want? Carmody seeks an answer from the autochthonous Melichrone, but finds that he too needs answers. A god who

has tried all aspects of godliness, who has been worshiped by countless billions, and who has created both Heaven and Hell, he has grown bored with it
all; Melichrone wonders what a god's ultimate purpose is in life.

Carmody comes up with an answer. Because Melichrone has been a god of
one planet, in one section of space, he has internalized his godhood. Now, to
have purpose, he must externalize his power — and the only way to do that,
Carmody explains, is to aid others outside his own world, which is, in reality,
himself. Carmody is external to Melichrone, needs help, and is, therefore,
Melichrone's purpose in life. Unable to get around the skewed logic of all this,
Melichrone agrees to help Carmody. Logic taken to its most absurd conclusions is the hallmark of a Sheckley book. So skilled is he at this art that after
working his way through the dizzying prose, the reader finds himself convinced, for the length of the book, that the author's *reductio ad absurdum* is
indeed the height of logical thought.

Melichrone's aid takes the form of sending Carmody on to Maudsley, the
world contractor. But before he allows Carmody to leave, he warns him of
impending doom: a Carmody predator is after him because he is the only Carmody. The theory is that all creatures fit into the chain of life as the eaters and
the eaten. All things have their predators, but such predators are native to the
habitat of the eaten. Carmody, by removing himself from his home, had also
removed himself from the sphere of his natural predators — and so it was
necessary for the Universe to create a predator especially for Carmody: a Carmody eater. The predator is very wily, knowing all the tricks a Carmody might
use to avoid him; and, worst of all, the Carmody eater is hungry. There is but
one Carmody, just as there is but one Carmody eater.

Duly warned about his predator, Carmody goes to Maudsley in hopes that
the latter can remember the contracting job — Carmody's Earth — done for an
elderly chap with a beard and long nightgown. Maudsley does remember the
job, and with some shame. He cut several corners on the job and cheated his
customer, the God of Earth. But God accepted Maudsley's flawed creation and
even stated he would turn the flaws into something useful — his people would
have something to wonder about, something to puzzle their minds with, and,
not being gods, they would come up with many explanations of the inconsistency of the world, thus giving them something to do with their lives. God and
Maudsley had between them invented science.

Maudsley agrees to construct a machine that will take Carmody back to the
Earth (or one of them), but while waiting for the device to be completed Carmody has his first brush with his predator. Cleverly disguised as a girl in
distress, a hero-scientist, and a rocket ship all at the same time, the predator
almost succeeds in eating Carmody. The description of the incident is pure
space opera. Sheckley masterfully dissects the genre and points out all of its
absurdities, while Carmody falls for the predator's ploy. Only the quick action
of the Prize and Maudsley saves Carmody from his fate. The Prize has some

use, after all.

Maudsley explains further the laws of predators and warns Carmody that he must in the future be extremely cautious. The predator will strike again and again, and since it is Carmody's fate to be eaten, the predator will more than likely win in the end. Carmody's only hope is to find his own world — the only place that does not need a Carmody predator. Maudsley points out that Carmody has an additional problem: will he be able to tell if the Earth he is on is *his* Earth? Maudsley's machine can take him to Earth, but only to *Where* Earth. Where Earth is only the first of the three W's involved in finding Carmody's Earth; the second W is When and the third is Which. The Earth Carmody will find on the first try is bound to be the wrong one, but Maudsley will give him a letter of introduction to someone who can help him with the temporal problems. Carmody is not amused by the limitations of Maudsley's help, but anything is better than doing nothing at all to get home.

The first Earth is definitely the wrong one — or possibly the right one at the wrong time. It is the Cretaceous Period on a world with talking, intelligent dinosaurs, and is not Carmody's idea of his world at all. He meets a dinosaur named Borg and engages in a very carefully constructed discussion of the future without telling the creature that in his Earth dinosaurs have been extinct for some sixty million years. One wrong step in this conversation could go badly for Carmody. He doubts very much that Borg would enjoy hearing the truth and might get violent.

Carmody's predator next appears in the guise of an IRS representative, but this is too obvious — even Carmody knows that IRS agents are predators.

Carmody's next contact proves to be the head of the Galactic Placement Bureau, one Clyde Beedle Seethwright. Seethwright, after a Lewis Carroll-style discussion on the realness of reality, agrees to send Carmody on to a Where and a When Earth, but he is not able to solve the Which Earth problem; Carmody must do that himself. But with reality being what it is, any Which world might seem like the right world to Carmody, since he will fit into each and not realize that it is not his Which. The only clue will come from the Carmody eater. As long as the predator is still after him, Carmody will know he is on the wrong Which Earth. But the only way he may find out for sure that he is on the wrong Which Earth is if the predator eats him, in which case the knowledge is of little use. Carmody is faced with a problem of no small dimensions.

Seethwright sends Carmody next to an Earth with a City that is perfectly willing to look after him for the rest of his life, but with certain restrictions. Carmody must do what the City asks of him, because all the City's requests are for his own good. The City is Big Brother, or Big Momma, with a vengeance. This is not Carmody's idea of life, nor is it a suitable world for him, and he exits quickly.

The next Which Earth seems to be New York City, but the fact that Carmody's predator almost manages to eat him by disguising itself as an IRT subway is proof enough that this is not Carmody's Earth. The next Earth, where advertising is a way of life, almost convinces Carmody, until the appearance of a second Carmody, whose Earth it really is, sends our hero out again on his quest.

The next Earth was the Earth of Carmody's childhood — or rather, of the childhood he wished he had had — a world where Lana Turner was a school chum, and Burt Lancaster was the friendly village policeman. It was a world of dreams found only in the back row of a movie theater with a box of popcorn and some jujubes. Carmody leaves this world only when he realizes that it contains background music to each scene, and thus cannot be real. Reality does have the flaw of lacking dramatic music to set off its high points.

Finally, Carmody locates his real home, the Earth we know and live in, an Earth with soot-browned trees, carbon monoxide air, PCP, muggers, and more waste than we know what to do with. But Carmody, safely home at last, free of his predator, decides he does not wish to live here; he throws himself back onto the probability wheel and goes in search of other Earths. He may not find a Utopia, and his predator is now back on his trail, but at least he is alive in a Universe full of possibilities.

Carmody, like all of us on Spaceship Earth, may only have moments to live, or a lifetime, but he will make each minute count. That, perhaps, is Robert Sheckley's message: in a world of possible realities, we must make each minute count. We alone can make reality real.

Criticism:

The Encyclopedia of Science Fiction and Fantasy. Compiled by Donald H. Tuck. Chicago: Advent Publishers, Inc., 1978, p. 386. This article gives a brief summary of Sheckley's career.

DOWNWARD TO THE EARTH

Author: Robert Silverberg (1936-   )
First book publication: 1970
Type of work: Novel
Time: The twenty-third century (2248)
Locale: The planet Belzagor (formerly called Holman's World by Earthmen)

Edmund Gundersen seeks rebirth and redemption through the intermediary of the nildoror native life forms of the planet Belzagor

> *Principal characters:*
> EDMUND GUNDERSEN, a man concerned with sin and redemption
> JEFF KURTZ, the Earthman symbolic of the degradation of Belzagor's natives
> VAN BENEKER, Gundersen's former clerk, now an alcoholic, who provides much of the necessary expository information
> SRIN'GAHAR AND NA'SINISUL, the two chief nildoror with whom Gundersen journeys to the Mist Country and exchanges ideas

By the time Robert Silverberg published *Downward to the Earth* (first serialized in *Galaxy* from December, 1969, through March, 1970), he had found those basic themes and techniques which have characterized his most mature work to date: the human encounter with alien intelligence, immortality, and redemption. He had passed through that dark period which produced such painful portrayals of isolation and alienation as *Thorns* (1967), "Passengers" (1967), and *The Man in the Maze* (1969); he had achieved the ambiguity of what probably remains his finest short story, "Sundance" (1969); but he had not yet reached the sometimes erratic lyricism of *Son of Man* (1971) or the final reconciliation — to this date — of *Shadrach in the Furnace* (1975), after which he stopped writing science fiction for at least three full years.

One should notice, first, the relatively brief span of time during which all of these stories and novels — including the complex and controversial *Tower of Glass* (1970) and the highly regarded "Born with the Dead" (1973) — were created. More importantly, one should notice that in all of these works Silverberg sought to expand the established parameters of science fiction in order to give symbolic insight into modern, twentieth century man. That is to say, he attempted to use science fiction to gain the same ends as so-called "mainstream" fiction. His success, cumulatively and individually, may be debated; however, in one instance at least, he achieved his aim: *Downward to the Earth*.

During the last generation, many literary critics have insisted that the reader must consider a work without regard for the author. This method undoubtedly has some merit, especially in that it makes the reader look for patterns within the individual work as well as throughout the numerous works by a single author. Yet it ignores the individuality with which any writer treats his own perception and experience as well as the literary form(s) with which he works.

To cite an example within science fiction: one must go beyond the narrative to a knowledge of Ray Bradbury, Robert Heinlein, Isaac Asimov, and Larry Niven in order to gain a full appreciation of the fiction of those writers. Thus, in like manner, one cannot ignore Silverberg's repeated statement that during the late 1960's his own work was governed by his growing cosmic consciousness, and that *Downward to the Earth*, specifically, had been inspired in part at least by a trip to Africa.

Two major points dominate *Downward to the Earth*. First, Silverberg so completely abandoned that reliance upon external plot action which had characterized his earlier fiction that *Downward to the Earth* becomes essentially a study of the consciousness and sensibility of its protagonist, Edmund Gundersen. Second, as Silverberg has acknowledged a number of times, the novel becomes his adaptation (*not* imitation) of Joseph Conrad's *Heart of Darkness*. Soon after its appearance, a number of reviewers spoke of it as being a story concerned with "inner space" as much as "outer space." They might also have said that, as in the case of Conrad's narrative, it parallels Marlow's journey into the interior. One might also note that Silverberg explores man's encounter with alien intelligence much in the manner that Conrad explored the European encounter with the jungle (the primitive world).

After an absence of eight years, Gundersen returns to Belzagor, where he had spent a decade as a top colonial administrator. He had left not by choice but as part of the deliberate action of Earth to end a long period of imperialism and surrender the occupied worlds of the galaxy to their intelligent species — their people — in this instance the elephantine nildoror and the seemingly secondary sulidoror, baboonlike creatures who have an unexplained but intimate relationship with the nildoror. Gundersen returns to this pastoral world because of a general feeling of guilt; he has a sense of sin and a desire for redemption. He realizes that the nildoror have been treated as beasts of burden, as slaves. Specifically, he is most troubled by an incident when, faced by a crisis after a dam broke, he forced seven of the beings into conscriptive labor, thereby preventing them from continuing their way into the Mist Country to participate in the religious ceremony of rebirth. The need to undertake that journey is a matter of mystic compulsion to the nildoror; they have no control over its occurrence, and if they fail to obey the "summons," they do not know when (or if) it will occur again. (Yet the most respected among them are referred to as "the many-born.") Gundersen threatened to kill the seven if they did not work for him; indeed, to save face before them and other men, he burned one slightly with a fusion torch — the one who had said that he pitied Gundersen. By now the concept of rebirth (Gundersen has somehow come to think of it in terms of redemption) fascinates the Earthman.

Early in the narrative Gundersen commits that blunder so common to many of Silverberg's protagonists of the period: while a nildor carries him to the one remaining automated spaceport and while he converses with one of the few

Earthmen who remained on Belzagor after the general evacuation, he explicitly refers to the nildoror as beasts /animals instead of intelligent *people* who merely differ in appearance from men. Despite this inadvertent and seemingly ingrained human sense of uniqueness and superiority, he is permitted to join a small group of nildoror who venture northward to the Mist Country to undergo rebirth. Thus begins the journey to the interior.

Once again one is reminded of Conrad. As he so often showed the conflict between the primitive and the civilized, with a resultant degeneration of the European, so, too, does Silverberg show how Earthmen have been captured by Belzagor. There is, however, an essential difference. In *Heart of Darkness*, Marlow and the reader end up amid terror and, at best, ambiguity; in *Downward to the Earth*, Gundersen and the reader achieve enlightenment and transcendence.

So far as plot action is concerned, *Downward to the Earth* either presents fragments of Gundersen's memories of his career or, more often, focuses upon his present encounters with Earthmen who have succumbed to Belzagor. At the spaceport he converses with Van Beneker, once his clerk, who reminds him that Gundersen always despised the nildoror, that he himself believes they hate mankind and his remnants, and that no man should become involved in the ceremony of rebirth. Van Beneker, an alcoholic, is content to serve as guide to the tourists who come to these far reaches of the galaxy only to complain about the waste of potential profit, denounce those who ended Earth's imperialism, and otherwise think of Belzagor only in terms of the scenes which have bored them on innumerable other planets. The presence of a party of them in the novel serves to underscore typical human reaction, especially to a primitive world

As he travels toward the Mist Country, Gundersen finds a couple who have become hosts to a parasitic growth. At Shangri-la Falls he meets a former lover, Seena, whose belly and loins are embraced by a gelatinous amoeba which conveniently moves when she wishes it to. Were all other parallels absent, Conrad would be called up by the magic name of her husband: Kurtz (first mentioned at the spaceport). She is married to Jeff Kurtz, who long ago milked serpents of their venom and fed that venom to nildoror, himself, and even Gundersen. Significantly, even in its weakest form, as Kurtz procured it, it had hallucinogenic effects; in a much stronger form it is used as part of the rebirth ceremony. Thus Kurtz profaned the most important rite of the nildoror religion, treating it as sport and entertainment. Much later, when he attempted to go through the process of rebirth, he emerged in monstrous form.

Faced by the corruption of Kurtz and told by Seena that he will lose his humanity, Gundersen still chooses rebirth. He finds transcendence, for he gains a unity with the nildoror, sulidoror, and even those men who have undergone the process before him. In this unity there is peace. In terms of Belzagor, rebirth explains the relationship between the nildoror and sulidoror, for periodically they are transformed from one to the other. In a sense they (and all who are reborn) become immortal, for the cosmos becomes an unending cycle and each individual retains the wisdom from all previous existences. One must underscore this idea of breaking down the isolation between intelligent creatures; by very different means Silverberg had achieved such a transcendent unity in his little-known novel *Across a Billion Years*, also published in 1969. The two themes — immortality and transcendence — haunt all of his fiction from the 1960's on.

For some readers, the lack of physical action and the philosophical exchanges, particularly between Gundersen and the nildoror, will weaken their interest in *Downward to the Earth*. Others will find that the ideas, instead of traditional gimmicks, strengthen it. Certainly the novel lies outside the expected parameters of science fiction. Two judgments seem inescapable. By concentrating the narrative upon the consciousness of Gundersen, Silverberg has produced one of the notable studies of character in the genre. Second, and perhaps more important for Silverberg, *Downward to the Earth* achieves the simplest and most affirmative statement of the unity of all intelligent beings that Silverberg has given voice to.

THE DRAGON MASTERS

Author: Jack Vance (1920-   )
First book publication: 1963
Type of work: Novella
Time: The distant future
Locale: The planet Aerlith in a distant star cluster

A combination of adventure tale and parable concerning the conflict between men and aliens, both of whom use members of the other species as slaves and selectively bred domesticated animals

> *Principal characters:*
> JOAZ BANBECK, leader of Banbeck Vale, a human settlement
> ERVIS CARCOLO, ruler of Happy Valley, a rival settlement
> THE DEMIE, priest-chieftain of the sacerdotes, descendants of earlier human immigrants
> BASICS (GREPHS), reptilelike non-humans, dominant life-form of the cluster
> DRAGONS, descendants of captured Basics, bred by men of Werlith into specialized forms to serve as fighters

The setting of *The Dragon Masters* is typically Vancean in its complexity and richness. Aerlith is, as its name implies, a planet of wind and stone, its surface scoured by daily dawn and evening storms. Men live in valleys and crevasses where the wind has deposited enough soil to support vegetation and thus settlements. The valley-dwellers' society is semi-feudal, controlled by hereditary leaders whose chief pursuit is the domination of rival settlements. The Sacerdotes' way of life is a mystery, their organization apparently a theocracy (as their name — "priests" — suggests); they carry on some trade with the valley-dwellers, but otherwise hold themselves aloof. The stability of this arrangement was disturbed about 250 years before the story's present action by the first raid by the Basics. First, the twenty-three Basics captured by Joaz's ancestor, Kergan Banbeck, provided the beginnings of a new military technology — specially bred dragons analogous to the Basics' own domesticated humans. Second, all human society on Aerlith is now threatened by the roundups the Basics conduct to improve their breeding stock.

All this takes place in a future so remote from our own time that the original world of men is remembered — or half-remembered — as "Eden" or the "Arch-World." Successive waves of colonization have washed through the stars; the valley-dwellers, refugees from the War of Ten Stars, have been on Aerlith for at least hundreds of years, the Sacerdotes for much longer. Man has passed away as the dominant species, at least in this cluster; the grephs rule and view humans as intelligent animals. In this distant time, things are at once alien and familiar — the domestication of intelligent beings and feudal rivalry, the Rationale of the Sacerdotes and Ervis Carcolo's ambition. Star travel, energy weapons, and other products of advanced technology (Joaz Banbeck's "armamentarium," for example, which must be a subminiaturized astronomical computer of considerable sophistication) can be taken for granted, even though they cannot be reproduced or sometimes even operated by the men of Aerlith. Technology thus approximates magic (to paraphrase Arthur C. Clarke), and the atmosphere approaches that of fantasy rather than hard science fiction. Vance is not the only science fiction writer to employ setting to this end — Robert Silverberg in *Nightwings* and Frank Herbert in *Dune* come to mind — but more than most he has made it his trademark.

The style of Vance's work, here and elsewhere, also contributes to the tension between familiar and alien. Where the mainstream of science fiction depends on the description of ideas, objects, and actions in neutral, transparent prose to establish the science fictional feeling of futurity (Robert Heinlein is the master of this technique), Vance establishes the otherness of his settings partly by means of verbal surface itself. His generally acknowledged mastery of visual imagery is present throughout in descriptions of sunrises, dragons in their armor, the costumes and trappings of free and domesticated men, or the decorations of Joaz Banbeck's apartments. In addition, his diction is studded with archaisms (*brach, armamentarium*), coinages (greph), and oddities (fugleman). This is the wordmaking and borrowing not of the modern scientist but of the renaissance scholar, and it invokes not the future but the past — appropriately so, for Aerlith is an old world and its people are dominated by tradition rather than the search for novelty (note Joaz Banbeck's pain on seeing the destruction of his family's reliquarium). To the reader, however, this ancient future is all new, whatever its associations with our past, thus the unfamiliar familiarity of the language. The tension is increased by vivid descriptions that work against the alienating effect of the exotic vocabulary: language creates a world that is at once richly present to the senses and distanced from the understanding.

From a literary-historical point of view, however, much of *The Dragon Masters* seems all too familiar. A cold description of some of its features makes it sound like any number of pulp space operas: dragons and swordbearing warriors in battle with each other and with reptilian aliens who arrive by spaceship; a race of mysterious, cave-dwelling magicians; feudal rivalries; minstrel-maidens. The combination of science fiction and fantasy atmospheres is by itself enough to prejudice many purists who esteem "science fantasy" or "sword-and-spaceship" stories even less than space opera. The roots of *The Dragon Masters* are indeed to be found in space opera and planetary romance, specifically in the adventure fiction of the pulps of the late 1940's and early 1950's in which Vance published his early work (particularly *Thrilling Wonder Stories* and *Startling Stories*). In the purist view, what Vance has produced is a highly decorated and charmingly written example of a subgenre that has no value beyond that of light entertainment and deserves no attention beyond surprise at the weight of ornament such a slight object can be made to bear. While it is probably not possible to establish absolute literary value without a few generations' hindsight, it should be possible to suggest some of the ways that *The Dragon Masters* escapes the trivializing label of space opera.

There are two narrative structures that interpenetrate to produce the plot of *The Dragon Masters*. The more fundamental of the two is the story of the conflicts between Banbeck and Carcolo and men and grephs; it is excessive attention to this part of the whole that leads to the misapprehension that the story is no more than the usual sword-and-spaceship recitation of intrigues, chases, and battles. This kind of action certainly does provide much of the narrative thrust, but there is another "plot" that can be characterized as parabolic — that of the conflicts among differing world views and ways of acting in the world. This plot resides in the competing values and behaviors of the major characters and groups — Joaz Banbeck, Carcolo, the Sacerdotes, and the Basics — and is revealed partly in debates and confrontations and partly in the adventure plot which serves as a testing ground for these views.

While the story is not an allegory but something looser and less mechanical, it is clear that two of the forces involved, Sacerdotes and Basics, act out of philosophical beliefs and are to be understood not as individuals but types. Ervis Carcolo, while he has no explicit ideology or philosophy, is so dominated by pride, greed, and wrath that he becomes almost a caricature. Joaz Banbeck is at the focus of these forces, and it is he, as protagonist, whose actions provide the connections between the action and parable plots. It is Joaz (except in one case where his ancestor, Kergan, serves as a substitute) who engages in exchanges with all three antagonists and thus serves as mediator as well as normative figure.

Carcolo is the closest to an individual antagonist Joaz faces; he is also closest to being a conventional melodrama villain, and his participation in that convention correspondingly robs him of individual character. Carcolo is so dominated by his heritage — the feud with the Banbecks — that humbling his enemies becomes more important then securing the survival of his own Happy Valley. His energy is devoted to breeding better dragons rather than improving his domain, and he will not credit Joaz's warnings about the return of the Basics. While he possesses strength, courage, and cunning, his obsession with the destruction of his enemy prevents him from applying his talents to matters outside the feud; as a result, the Basics take Happy Valley by surprise while Carcolo tries to take Banbeck Vale. The extent of Carcolo's inflexibility and vainglory is apparent when, having lost his people and exhausted his ability to make war on his rival, he persists in behaving as if his will alone were sufficient to dominate Banbeck. Exasperated, Joaz has him executed.

The Sacerdotes are not so conventional in their beliefs, though they are nearly as inflexible. What we see of them suggests that they are a rigid theocracy, a community dedicated to a single set of values and acting with unity of purpose. The Rationale by which they live demands "absolute passivity and absolute candor," and, more than that, noninterference in the lives of those they call the "Utter men." The center of Sacerdote belief is the *tand*, an object that symbolizes "Final Sentience" and upon which each Sacerdote models a *tand* of his own. Any whose *tand* — and thereby whose character — is judged unacceptable is ejected from the group, to live on the surface. The totalitarian overtones of such a belief system are apparent, and the Demie's revelation to Joaz of Sacerdotal intentions make them explicit: the Sacerdotes await the extinction of the Utter men, the "under-folk," so that they, the "ultimate men," may "renew the cosmos" by resettling the depopulated worlds. For all their extrasensory powers and all their communal wisdom and experience, the Sacerdotes are only another version of the Man of Faith, and Joaz's shrewd maneuvering of them into using their half-built space-drive as a weapon demonstrates that they do not possess the omniscience they claim.

The Basics resemble the Sacerdotes in their certainty of the correctness of their views, although they are anything but passive noninterventionists. They are the dominant life form in this cluster, and they seek to include the men of Aerlith under their Rule or destroy them; as a Weaponeer, speaking for his masters, tells Joaz before the climactic battle: "All residual pockets of disorganized life are to be expunged, though it would be preferable that the men surrender themselves and the valuable 'content of [their] genes.' " This is not mere slave talk, for even though the domesticated men cannot imagine freedom ("To whom would we look for law, control, direction, order"?), the Basics themselves seem to surrender to a deterministic view of reality. The Weaponeer calls his message "an integration of the instantaneous vectors of destiny. An interpretation of the future." Apparently the resultant integration of such "vectors" cannot be changes. The Weaponeer who parleyed with Kergan Banbeck twelve generations earlier characterized the fate of the human captives as "parceled, quantum-type, ordained. Established." Existence is the "steady succession" of "units of certainty, quanta of necessity and order"; all else is "absurdity." When Kergan resists the Basics successfully, the tame men go mad and destroy the ship. The twenty-three captured Basics surrender to their fate: "The texture of Destiny was inevitable. . . . The twenty-three, hence, were something other than the Revered: a different order of creature entirely." And different they indeed become — dragons.

Joaz Banbeck is clearly at the center of all this, and his success indicates some resolution of the various dialectics implicit in the action. By outmaneuvering Carcolo, forcing the hand of the Sacerdotes, and anticipating the raid by the Basics, he demonstrates an intelligence unhampered by egotism and free of ideology. His own aims are simple: survival for his people, the neutralization of threats; he possesses curiosities rather than metaphysical certainties. He is, to put it oversimply, a pragmatist, a voluntarist, an individualist, and thus differs from the theoretical, determinist, collectivist tendencies of Sacerdotes and Basics as well as from the ego-driven passions of Carcolo.

At the risk of pushing the story into allegory, it can be argued that Joaz

Banbeck possesses the balance, flexibility, and freedom of the authentic human, while his opponents are all in some way enslaved or dominated by emotional or philosophical systems that prevent them from responding adequately to the challenges posed by a universe of infinite variety. The closed systems of the Basics and Sacerdotes provide an order that places them at the pinnacle of the universe — but these systems prove inadequate when faced with Joaz Banbeck's refusal to take his place within them. Joaz is free of their crippling rigidity in the same way that he is free of Carcolo's obsessive pride and wrath. His world-picture may not be so orderly as theirs, and he may know doubts and uncertainties, but he is free to survive and even prevail.

The parable of *The Dragon Masters* is rather more delicate than this, in keeping with Vance's characteristic irony and his unexpected use of adventure-story conventions. There is, for example, something elegant and fascinating in the philosophies of the Sacerdotes and Basics, as there is something admirable in Carcolo's singlemindedness and energy. Certainly Joaz Banbeck himself would be doubtful of the allegorizing in the previous paragraph. Nevertheless, a fascination with slavery, both physical and mental, with the question of authentic humanity and the variety of shapes it can take, and with the depiction of the alien have been present in Vance's work since the 1940's; *The Dragon Masters* presents that fascination in a distilled and essential form.

THE EMBEDDING

Author: Ian Watson (1943-   )
First book publication: 1973
Type of work: Novel
Time: The present
Locale: Haddon, England; the Amazon Valley; Nevada; outer space

A nightmarish picture of the late twentieth century where highly complex techno-logical experiments with communications systems to achieve mind control are employed by three disparate groups, two human and one alien, with unforeseen disas-trous consequences

> *Principal characters:*
> CHRIS SOLE, A British linguist
> PIERRE DARRIAND, a French social anthropologist
> VIDYA, a three-year-old Indo-Pakistani orphan
> BRUXO, a Xemahoa tribal shaman
> KAYAPI, his bastard son
> PH'THERI, an alien being from Sp'thra

In *The Embedding*, Ian Watson has seen the enemy and it is "us." The action is divided among three discrete groups representing increasingly com-plex stages of evolution: primitive Indians in Brazil; sophisticated scientists at Haddon, England, and in the United States; and pure automatons from outer space. The critical problem that unites the three groups is, what will they do with the technology they have acquired.

All three groups are experimenting with language as a key to absolute real-ity, but in their utter callousness and ruthless pursuit of knowledge, they become clockwork figures and create monsters who are devoid of human feel-ings. The experiments prove the insufficiency of a scientific approach to lan-guage — indeed the horrible chaos that results when beings evolve beyond their natural capacities.

The novel proceeds chronologically through the twelve days from Christmas to Epiphany, but the time sequence is the only constant. The scenes shift back and forth from one locale to another in a stream-of-consciousness manner, with shifts in thoughts and perceptions reflecting the various embedding experiments and the various levels of reality being probed.

The narrative begins at Haddon, a hospital ostensibly designed to treat brain-damaged children, but in reality, containing in its underground chambers three hidden units where United States financed experiments are being con-ducted using three- and four-year-old Indo-Pakistani children as subjects. The experimenters — Chris Sole in the embedding world, Dorothy Summers in the logic world, and Richard Jannis in the alien world — are attempting to free these subjects from the natural constraints of language, sensation, and percep-tion through an artificially contrived computer-run laboratory using giant video-screens, sleepteaching, and a drug called PSF to speed up the learning process.

Chris Sole, a linguist, is testing Noam Chomsky's theories about language. According to Chomsky, human beings have a natural set of rules built into their genes which enable them to generate surface structures (sentences) from embedded structures (or deep structures) in the brain. For communication between human beings to take place, language must have an orderly and systematic framework. Such an organization is limiting, but necessary — indeed, the only way language will work. Consequently, the embedding process in language is the natural control mechanism by which human beings fit into their existence by having their capacities limited. Reversing the natural process and embedding artificial languages in the children's minds, Chris Sole hopes to find a key to a new reality which has been bracketed out of existence by natural language. He wants the naked children to break free, at right angles to "this-reality."

As a scientist, Sole thinks he has risen above human feelings such as guilt from his shocking manipulation of Innocents as laboratory rats and jealousy of Pierre, his friend, who has been his wife's lover and whom he suspects of fathering his child. A letter from Pierre, which almost penetrates his armor and arouses human feelings, carries the plot forward and reinforces the theme at critical points.

In the letter, Pierre, a French social antrhopologist and Marxist, announces his discovery of a rare and unique creature among a primitive Amazon valley Indian tribe, the Xemahoas. He is the tribal shaman, Bruxo, who has managed to reverse the natural language process by the use of a fungus (dubbed embedol by Pierre), which has freed him and his people from the restrictions of their language. This drugged dance and speech, referred to experimentally as Xemahoa B, frees their myths as living realities and enables the people to fight "this reality," the advancing floodwaters from a United States financed dam which is embedding them in a huge lake. The Xemahoa B speech minimizes the reality of the flood; the result is a reversal of real and unreal. Ordinarily, in this culture only men take the drug. However, to avert the disaster of the impending flood, Bruxo impregnates a woman with his seed and the fungus, hoping to bring forth a Deliverer. The villagers deify the Madonnalike figure and her unborn child, a "Christ-thing," in a very unholy mockery of the Advent. Pierre, too, takes the drug and under its influence escapes both the boundaries of time and space and the ordinary restraints on semantic features of a language to such a degree that he is able to understand clearly the puzzling surrealistic Roussel poem that has been his elusive intellectual mistress.

The third strand of the snarled and tangled plot surfaces when an alien spacecraft lands. Dr. Sole, because of his language expertise, is summoned to Nevada to join the secret U.S.-U.S.S.R. welcoming party. The alien visitor, a giant nine-foot spaceman, Ph'theri, speaks for the group to whom he is attached *via* scarlet wires attached to a box on his chest. Because the Sp'thra are language traders, listening and speaking have accentuated the evolution of highly sensitive ears and a large, flickering butterfly tongue, their two predominant features. Dr. Sole notices Ph'theri's flat nose, membranous eyes, and lack of incisors; apparently violence is not an inherent part of their nature. However, their evolution seems quite different from Darwin's theory of evolution. A type, a representative of the Sp'thra, Ph'theri has no distinguishing personality, no sense of a living, vibrant being.

Highly sophisticated technologically, the Sp'thra have come to Earth from their twin worlds 1,103 light years away by riding the energy tides of the galaxies, a technique acquired from the Wave Readers who have this knowledge instinctively embedded in their genes (not very Darwinian, either). The alien signal traders offer a roadmap to the nearest habitable planet together with the technology to get there in exchange for representative samples of human language generated from living brains. If they can penetrate the depths (recesses) of the human mind, they will be able to penetrate the depths of the universe.

Ph'theri explains their motive, their sense or urgency and their impatience. He says that thirteen thousand years ago the Change Speakers, who had embedded the Sp'thra, broke free and left them "by modulating their embedding in reality." Their absence has left the Sp'thra with something missing in their existence, what they call "The Bereft Love" for the Change Speakers. Only when they have acquired all the languages of the universe and superimposed them on their Language Moon, will they be able to grasp the "Other-Reality" and escape their embedding in "This-Reality." Then, they will be free to locate the Change Speakers, but they are unable to predict what they will do when they find their love, (just as Sole is unsure what will happen when his brain-children grasp another reality, and as Bruxo is unsure what will happen when his progeny senses another reality).

As the first step in the bargaining process, the scientists bring six sedated human bodies — Japanese, Eskimo, Russian, English, Vietnamese, Persian — representing all the basic language types on Earth (agglutinative, monosyllabic, inflective, incorporative) with instruction tapes. Experts at trading, the Sp'thra want more trade units. When Chris Sole shows them Pierre's letter describing Bruxo's self-embedded brain and the freedom from "This-Reality" it has attained, they risk missing the energy tides home to wait for Bruxo to be brought to them. With his self-embedded brain, their inventory will be complete, and they will be free of "that vibration in . . . [their] minds, imprinted so many centuries ago" by the Change Speakers.

It is a supreme irony that a ticket to the stars hinges now on a primordial Indian in a primitive, savage jungle in South America. But the U.S.-U.S.S.R. politico-scientific team risks the use of nuclear weapons to blow up their enormously expensive dam, killing thousands of people in order to preserve the symbiotic environment of Bruxo and the fungus. When the three-man delegation arrives to kidnap Bruxo, they witness the birth of the unnatural drug child — actually a grotesque freak with no eyes and a brain protruding from three hernias. By tampering with the natural and imposing the artificial, Bruxo has produced a monster, the culmination of the Indians' primitive technology. The plan has backfired, as will the other two plans.

Political intrigue complicates the plot. When the Chinese Communists detect the nuclear explosive with a spy satellite and expose the incident, the Russians and Americans unite to quash a Latin American revolution by revealing the visit of the Sp'thra and blaming them for the incident.

With Bruxo dying, his bastard son, Kayapi, after three days of thinking and planning, eats the living freak's turgid brains, then buries the baby, telling the Indians that their dreams have now entered him. Here, the novel reaches its climax. Sole vomits with revulsion. Disillusioned and saddened, Pierre recognizes Kayapi as a slick *arriviste*, who has no profound understanding of man's essential nature. He is not a teacher, but a "village Hitler." Looking around at the "natural" — the teeming village life, the making of fish nets (artistic creations), the games the children are playing — Sole realizes his own utter hypocrisy, how in his mad pursuit of science he has missed the brilliance and beauty of life and the uniqueness of each specific individual. When these human feelings begin to assert themselves, Sole decides to rescue his brain-child Vidya from the hidden, subterranean galleries of Haddon, but in so doing he opens a Pandora's Box.

Vidya now reflects the negative image of what the hospital projects: rehabilitation. Actually he represents the nucleus of humanity — primitive, sensual, beautiful — but the scientists have managed through their experiments to destroy every viable and organic quality which makes him human. Rejecting the artificially embedded speech, Vidya, now violent, his brain overloaded, begins transmitting to other brains by a process of "projective empathy." When Sole rescues the child, who is now insane, Vidya imprints (embeds) Sole, enabling him to apprehend reality by direct sensory perception. Without the boundaries of time and space and the aid of symbols and distancing by words and abstract thoughts, Sole's mind cracks as well.

In the concluding chapters, Sole's madness is counterpointed by Dr. Pip's plundering of the spoils of the spaceship trying to save the collected brains of the universe so they can be rescued by cyrogenics for research purposes. The parallel from *Moby Dick* suggests that he, too, is demented.

The Sp'thra and their extraterrestrial world are now lost to man. But their very nature serves as a warning because they represent the essence of the weakness of modern science. They have blinders on and have bracketed all that man perceives as human out of their existence. It is in the questions that they do not ask, really their failure to communicate the most important things in man's life (the architectonics of a bird song, what it is like to fall in love, what strikes a person as funny) that they reveal their lack of understanding of human beings and human values. Conversely, the scientists cannot comprehend the Sp'thra's nature: their sense of time, their trade-assessing, their concept of Bereft Love.

At the end, Pierre sadly realizes that human beings may never achieve that perfection which will allow them to live in complete harmony, in spite of Karl Marx. Moreover, when any agent programs or indoctrinates an individual to rid that person of undesirable traits or change his basic nature, it may destroy the most worthwhile and valuable impulses as well.

The structure of the novel takes the reader forward into the future and backward into the primitive past, glimpsing the various stages of evolution. Throughout, there is a sense of impending and enveloping disaster, really the "negative pay-off" from exploring frontiers that carry too great a risk, from learning about humanity through inhuman means.

THE FIRST MEN IN THE MOON

Author: H. G. Wells (1866-1946)
First book publication: 1901
Type of work: Novel
Time: The early twentieth century
Locale: Lympne, England; the moon

Two men reach the moon in a Cavorite sphere, and when the Selenites attack them, one escapes and gets back to Earth, while the other later radios his account of lunar civilization

Principal characters:
BEDFORD, the narrator
CAVOR, the scientist who invents Cavorite

The First Men in the Moon, the last of the early "scientific romances" that made Wells's reputation, is the one he himself called the best. Even though astronauts and cosmonauts have found no life on the moon, the book is still a gripping adventure story as well as a historic milestone in modern science fiction.

Bedford, the teller of the tale, is an engaging antihero, self-centered and generally incompetent but amiably candid about his faults. Cavor, the somewhat comic absentminded scientist, seeks pure knowledge as avidly as Bedford does gold. Bankrupt when they meet, Bedford scents possible millions in Cavor's invention of a gravity screen; he ingratiates himself with Cavor to help build the sphere. Taking off from the mudflats of Kent, they reach the moon together.

A purist might call their story more fantasy than hard science fiction, because Wells was following the classic pattern of the cosmic voyage, a literary genre older than the telescope. His lunar plants, for example, come not from any observations by modern astronomers, but rather from Johannes Kepler's dream-narrative, *Somnium*. In shape and equipment, his moon-ship resembles the hollow cannonball Jules Verne had designed decades before for his own moon story, though Verne protested in bewilderment that Cavorite was pure invention, with no basis in physics.

Fantasy or not, the novel is a brilliant demonstration of Wells's own method for creating such imaginative fiction. He limits each story to a single new or fantastic proposition, made believable by keeping everything else as familiar and logical as possible. Here, he interests us first in the characters: Bedford, hiding from his creditors and living on the trust of neighborhood merchants while he dreams of getting rich by writing a play; Cavor, a ridiculous little man in odd attire who gesticulates and buzzes like something electric when he walks. We listen to his plausible explanation of the gravity screen and witness an accidental windstorm caused by it before we hear of any trip to the moon. Once that trip begins, every detail is vividly convincing. The lunar plants may have come from Kepler, but Wells re-creates them with a fine imagination and the insight of a trained biologist.

The lunar day is two weeks of Earth-time. At sunrise, the frozen air thaws and evaporates; the lunar seeds soon sprout; the plants grow explosively into fantastic jungles that mature and die as the deadly night returns. Lost in this strange and ever-changing moonscape, the two explorers are captured by Selenites pasturing their mooncalves. They are carried down into the moon, which is porous, with vast systems of caves. The lunar craters, they learn, are simply the circular mounds of debris from huge shafts the Selenites have dug down through their caverns to the central sea, hundreds of miles below.

These moon-beings may well have been suggested by the writings of Wells's great teacher, T. H. Huxley, who speculated that the evolution of more complex societies means an inevitable loss of individual freedom; he even compared the social evolution of men to that of insects, commenting that each bee has its duty and none has any rights.

Wells's Selenites have evolved their own highly complex and insectlike social order, with a place for everyone and each exactly fitted to his place. Long-limbed, leather-skinned Selenites herd mooncalves; big-brained Selenites replace libraries; siren-voiced Selenites screech news and orders. Though this is all designed to make a satiric comment on our present world and present a grim prediction of our probable future, Wells never lets his message get in the way of his story. Bedford and Cavor are neatly opposed symbolic types: Bedford is the unspecialized individualist resisting the law of the hive, while Cavor is the intellectual specialist dependent upon it. In their conflicts with the Selenites and with each other, they translate the theme into dramatic action.

The suspense is always strong. The fast-growing jungles help create an atmosphere of wonder and menace. We hear the booming of unseen underground machines, see the opening of the lid above the bottomless shaft, meet the grotesque herdsmen and their monstrous cattle. Captured, we follow a river of cold blue fire down into the mysterious depths of the moon.

Bedford, lacking special adaptations, is ready for anything but good for nothing except the primitive animal violence he displays in his battles with the Selenites. He gets lost on the moon, gets drunk on lunar mushrooms, gets himself and Cavor captured. He is too egotistical to admire the rational complexity of the moon civilization as Cavor does. All he cares about is his own survival — and the gold which is more common than iron on the moon.

In the lesser gravity, the moon-beings are flimsy, and Bedford finds himself a relative superman. He can bend gold bars and snap gold chains. His primitive body can smash a Selenite like "a sweetmeat with liquid in it." He and Cavor battle their way back to the surface and separate there to search for the sphere. Bedford locates it. After some delay, he goes back to look for Cavor and finds a torn note telling him that his companion has been recaptured.

Winning a desperate race with the air-freezing lunar night, Bedford gets back to the sphere and returns to Earth alone, landing on an English beach.

Incompetent as ever, he leaves the sphere unguarded, and an inquisitive small boy climbs inside and takes it on a last accidental flight. Left with only a fortune in lunar gold and a strange tale to tell, Bedford is serializing the story under the byline "Wells" when Cavor begins to radio his own narrative from inside the moon.

Cavor's captors are intelligent Selenites with enlarged brain-cases. They have taken him down to their more important centers, deep in the moon, have learned English and begun explaining their highly specialized society, which Cavor feels is far superior to man's. Each Selenite is carefully shaped, by birth and training and surgery, to be a "perfect unit in a world machine." Some of the less fortunate, destined only to mind simple machines, are grown in bottles to stop the development of everything except one projecting hand — a more humane procedure, Cavor feels, than our Earthly method of letting children grow into human beings and then making them into machines.

The Grand Lunar, who at last receives Cavor, is an enormous brain, many yards in diameter, with the merest vestige of a body. Their meeting may well have been patterned after the adventures of Gulliver — Wells admired Jonathan Swift. This ruling Selenite seems as purely rational as Swift's Houyhnhnms. Like those superior horses, he finds mankind far short of meeting his rational norms. Yet neither Wells nor Swift intends to praise pure reason. Both are satiric. The Grand Lunar cannot move his own body. Sitting in solitary splendor with attendants spraying his throbbing brain to keep it cool, he is both pitiable and absurd.

Here we find the science and the serious purpose beneath Wells's fascinating fantasy. Equipped with a biologist's understanding of the then rather new science of evolution, he had seen the past advances of humanity as a process of ever-further division of labor and ever-greater specialization, a ceaseless surrender of individual freedom to the needs of the group. In one novel, he extrapolates this process to a painfully logical ultimate. The result is both merciless satire and disturbing prediction.

Wells himself was certainly disturbed — this story shows a striking shift of attitude from *The Invisible Man*, written only a few years earlier. Griffin, his transparent man, is pure self and pure evil, a tragic hero destroyed by the folly of his war on society. Bedford is less symbolic and more human. In unselfish moments, he regrets his own faults. Wells lets us like him. Yet, in contrast to Cavor, he remains the elemental individual, bent on self-preservation and selfish gain. He intends, until the sphere is lost, to go back with guns for more lunar gold.

Cavor is his polar opposite, the social man. With too little self-regard to seem really human, he has comic traits that remind the reader of a machine. His movements are jerky, and he hums to himself mechanically. Yet he, too, has another dimension. Sometimes he shows a flash of human liking for Bedford; he feels moments of horror at the ruthless efficiency of the Selenite society and apparently revolts against it before he dies. As Gulliver does, Cavor tells his hosts too much about mankind. When the Grand Lunar hears about the arts of war and learns that Cavor is about to transmit the secret of the gravity screen back to Earth, the radio signals are abruptly cut off.

In *The First Men in the Moon*, Wells is examining specialization — particularly intellectual specialization — as the way to future progress. Taking the evolutionary history of the social insects as a model, he projects future human evolution to infinity. As a scientist, he can see possible adaptations that will make the race more efficient, avoiding many sorts of loss, avoiding all the hazards of conflict and change.

As a human being, however, the author is appalled by what he foresees. Cavor is betrayed and destroyed by his own inquiring intellect; Bedford is saved and enriched by his unregenerate individualism. Their opposition no doubt reflects a parallel conflict in Wells's own nature, and his shift in attitude since *The Invisible Man* seems to show him working toward a solution of it. Allowing Bedford to call himself "Wells," he appears to be settling the conflict by accepting his own self-identity.

Wells's later career seems to offer evidence of such a resolution, as if that old internal conflict had supplied an emotional power to the early fiction which has now disappeared. There are intriguing ideas and vivid writing in *The Food of the Gods* (1904) and *In the Days of the Comet* (1906), but he has begun to allow his social comment and his pleas for social reform to overwhelm story interest. Though he went on producing books for another forty years, many of them patterned as "scientific romances," none has the dramatic intensity of *The First Men in the Moon*.

The last of Wells's really great science fiction novels, *The First Men in the Moon* was a major addition to the current of anti-Utopian pessimism that we can trace from Jonathan Swift, down through Wells's early work, to such popular present-day writers as Frederik Pohl and Harlan Ellison. Aldous Huxley's *Brave New World*, for example, owes a heavy debt to Wells. Picking up that haunting vision of the young Selenites grown in bottles to shape them for their social roles, Huxley brings the nightmare down to Earth with his human babies grown in bottles, some nourished to become ruling Alphas, others starved and poisoned and carefully conditioned to make them into happy Gammas.

History, in the world of reality, began long ago to realize Wells's darkly prophetic forebodings. The socialistic states have become as efficient as the Selenites in shaping youth to fit their ideologic requirements and equally efficient in liquidating the individuals who oppose them.

Criticism:

Bailey, J. O. "Is Science Fiction Art? A Look at H. G. Wells," in *Extrapolation*. II (December, 1960), pp. 17-19. Bailey emphasizes that Wells's writings be looked at as allegories.

Wallheim, Donald A. *The Universe Makers: Science Fiction Today*. New York: Harper & Row, 1971. This book establishes Wells as one of two traditions in science fiction and insists that the essential view held by the genre is optimistic.

Zamyatin, Yevgeny. "H. G. Wells," in his *A Soviety Heretic: Essays by Yevgeny Zamyatin*. Chicago: University of Chicago Press, 1971, pp. 259-290. Zamyatin considers the range of Wells's work but concentrates on the scientific romances.

FIRST ON MARS

Author: Rex Gordon (Stanley Bennett Hough, 1917-   )
First book publication: 1956
Type of work: Novel
Time: The present
Locale: Mars

The first man to land on Mars overcomes all obstacles through his resourcefulness and ingenuity, then meets the Martians, who convince him that all striving for knowledge and power is useless

> Principal character:
> GORDON HOLDER, first man on Mars

A person at odds with his environment may resolve that conflict in one of two ways: either the person changes the environment or the person changes himself. When it rains, one either builds a shelter or gets used to being wet. A good case could be made that the choice of these two solutions defines the difference between Western and Eastern culture, but that larger philosophical issue is not now in question. It is sufficient to say that science fiction is full of environment-changers.

The nature of the genre almost dictates that this should be so. Human beings cannot "get used to" not breathing, so for a trip to the moon or the stars, they build spaceships. If the phrase "environment-changer" calls to mind some hairy-chested, two-fisted warrior such as John Carter in the novels by Edgar Rice Burroughs, the picture is misleading, because not just the Conan-like ones, but almost every character in science fiction is an environment-changer. For all of *Dune*'s ecological awareness, Muad'Dib and the Fremen of Frank Herbert's novel do not change themselves, they change their surroundings. The still-suits, the rendering of water from the dead, and all the rest of their skills are bent toward the active fulfillment of their objectives, even if that goal is only survival.

The environment-changer is not just a creation of male authors: Ursula Le Guin's Genly Ai in *The Left Hand of Darkness* has desires, plans, and goals toward which he works, even if he does bring himself to the planet Gethen to be changed rather than to change, to understand rather than to be understood. And a feminist critic who rightly or wrongly complains that much of science fiction is unfair to women is more likely to be calling for stories with active women than for ones with passive men.

Finally, the environment-changer is not a product of the American pulps, regardless of the scientific movers and shakers of Hugo Gernsback and his spiritual descendants. In the British science fiction of Aldous Huxley, George Orwell, and C. S. Lewis, to name only three, we see characters who without exception either have changed or tried to change their environments to suit their natures, whether their purpose be as banal as Mustafa Mond's, the

World-Controller of Aldous Huxley's *Brave New World*, as politically revolutionary as Winston Smith's in George Orwell's *Nineteen Eighty-Four*, or as spiritual as Elwin Ransom's in Lewis' Perelandra trilogy.

If we seek an illustration of the other alternative, of the way of passivity and self-change, we should look perhaps to characters such as Malachi Constant in Kurt Vonnegut's *The Sirens of Titan*. We should not observe Constant at the beginning of the book as the richest man in the United States, nor Constant the drugged and brainwashed soldier in the Martian invasion army, nor even Constant stuck in the caves of Mercury and yearning to return to earth. Rather we should seek characters like the Constant in exile on Titan, who has learned, in the spirit of Ecclesiastes, that all is vanity, the Constant who accepts everything and desires nothing. Characters like this are rare indeed in science fiction. The field champions action, mental if not physical; those parts of it that do not welcome change at least tolerate it; and literally dozens of science fiction writers and critics have heaped praise on the genre for its ability to help its readers to adapt to change. All this is why Rex Gordon's *First on Mars* is a very unusual book.

Rex Gordon is the pseudonym of Stanley Bennett Hough, an English writer whose best-known science fiction novel, *First on Mars*, was published in Great Britain in 1956 under the title *No Man Friday*. The British title is far more meaningful, since it emphasizes a comparison that Gordon stresses again and again between his story and Daniel Defoe's picture of the quintessential environment-changer, Robinson Crusoe. Perhaps what stays with us longest in Defoe's peculiar work is not its rather pedestrian prose, but the illustrations: whether done in a nineteenth century line engraving or in a Howard Pyle color wash, Crusoe striding along with his goatskin umbrella overhead and his rifle on his shoulder practically defines the man who will change the world to his liking, even if it means converting Friday to provide himself with some Christian company.

Thoughts of Crusoe frequently occur to Gordon Holder, the sole survivor of a clandestine first voyage to Mars. Like Defoe's castaway, he picks from his wreck those treasures that will aid his survival in a harsher climate than ever faced Crusoe.

And the climate is fierce. *First on Mars* is hard science fiction; it incorporated the most up-to-date information then available, even if that information has been subsequently found to be erroneous by the Viking landings. In his novel, Gordon presumed that Mars had an atmosphere with a pressure of one hundred millibars, mostly carbon dioxide, with about one percent oxygen. Since human beings need only about sixty millibars of pressure to fill their lungs, all that Gordon Holder has to do to breathe normally is wear an oxygen mask. Gordon's picture of Mars is that of an arid, cold planet, a picture that was in many respects confirmed by the Viking missions. While his hero does not face as severe a set of conditions as would a real traveler, he still faces a great many major problems, and he sets to work at a task familiar to us — trying to change his environment.

That struggle is unquestionably heroic. Gordon Holder is a resourceful and imaginative man; perhaps more important, he is dauntless in the best sense of that overused word, without being arrogant. His periods of fear and doubt are as frequent as his triumphs of confidence, but he decides more than once that if he should die, and he knows there is a very strong probability of that fate, it will not be for lack of resolution and energy on his part. By his efforts he hopes to justify the deaths of his companions and to show that their lives were spent striving for a worthwhile goal.

As an example of his ingenuity, consider how he solves his first problems, the scarcity of water and oxygen. He sets to work on a still to capture the dew that falls each night. When he succeeds, he turns his attention to the problem of oxygen. The sun provides him with an inexhaustible power source. He uses it to heat oil placed in a closed system of pipes, causing it to vaporize and expand through pumps salvaged from the wreck and placed in the system. The pumps turn the electric motors that once powered them, and a few simple changes convert the motors to generators. With power in the usable form of electricity, he charges batteries and drives smaller pumps that push the Martian atmosphere through constricting valves and into expansion chambers converted from tanks salvaged from the wreck. As the pressurized gas quickly expands, it cools; running the same gas through the system over and over eventually chills it, in a well-known process used industrially, until it reaches the temperature at which oxygen liquifies and falls to the bottom of the tank. He can then tap the liquid oxygen and fill cylinders with it. Despite the scarcity of the gas in the atmosphere, he now has an unlimited supply of the life-sustaining element.

He eventually surmounts the problem of food with similar ingenuity. Mars has a marginal growth of vegetation which bears a fruit he experiments with. It is edible if not palatable, and while he does not know its nutritional value, the likelihood of disease from vitamin deficiency is a longterm, not a shortterm problem. Holder recognizes that seasonal variations will make it necessary for him to follow the crops as they ripen to maintain his food supply. So he sets to work once more and builds portable models of his still and his air-separation plant, mounts them on a homemade halftrack, and drives away from the wreck into the unknown parts of Mars.

At this point, the reader must surely feel high admiration for Holder. In the face of every difficulty, despite every obstacle, he has changed his environment, wrenching an existence from a planet hostile to his kind. His efforts lend him the luster of the explorer or the pioneer. But then he experiences something that completely changes his own regard for himself, and the new outlook that he comes to accept is violently in opposition to that which the reader holds. He encounters Martians.

Holder has met animal life already, beings that are shaped like humans, but as witless as insects. When the reader first hears of the humanoids, he thinks that the Crusoe analogy will now be completed — that Friday has been found. When these creatures turn out to be no more intelligent than a snail, that expectation is frustrated. But on his trek, Holder does meet the intelligent Martians, huge creatures as large and long as railroad trains, covered with flashing lights by means of which they communicate. Holder turns to the technology that has served him well and attempts communication by means of remote-controlled lights and colored cloths. But the Martians discover and capture him, and the anticipated situation is neatly reversed: the character we had thought of as Robinson Crusoe turns out to be Friday.

When Holder has learned enough of their language to speak with the young alien who is keeping him more or less as a pet, he discovers that he has encountered beings more passive than Hindu hermits. Like Archibald MacLeish's idea of a poem, they do not mean — they are. Nor do they seek for meaning to their existence: they are born, eat, sleep, beget, and die. Yet they hint that they know levels of existence and command powers beyond the dreams of Holder.

When Holder tries to bargain with them, offering his mechanical knowledge (they have no artifacts whatsoever), they ask what his machines are for. He replies, to keep him alive. When they ask him in return why he has come to a place where he cannot live unaided, his standard mountain-climber's response — because it is there — seems hollow to them, and Holder begins to question it himself. When they discover that he has no way to return to earth, they suggest that, to their way of thinking, he should simply die. They counter his arguments and reduce him to a state of nervous exhaustion not through malice, but simply by destroying his belief in the value of his own struggle. If Holder had been a devil-take-the-hindmost human imperialist like the explorers of Venus in Olaf Stapledon's *Last and First Men*, his torment might be called retributive justice, but Holder is a decent and likable individual.

His stay with the Martians lasts fifteen years, and the chapters of his apprenticeship are interspersed with the account of the American crew that, much to their surprise, finds him there. He approaches the American ship as an ambassador, bearing the Martians' wish (and his own profound hope, by now) that the earthmen will leave and never return to Mars. As Holder had suspected, the Americans refuse to make an agreement on their own initiative which would be binding on all of humanity. Although disconsolate at the loss of his chance to return to earth, Holder feels bound to return to the Martians as hostage and confess his failure. The Martians then extend their power and bend space itself, preventing him from leaving the vicinity of the ship.

Holder returns to earth with the Americans, feeling that a conflict is coming. There can be no meeting-ground between environment-changers and self-changers, and Holder (and the reader) is left with a frightening loss of faith in the value of meaningful united action. The Martians, far from being primitive, have gone beyond desire; they are not savages to be converted. Yet he believes the humans will eventually win their battle and discover that through the victory they have missed a chance at something of more value than all their triumphs.

THE FOREVER WAR

Author: Joe Haldeman (1943-   )
First book publication: 1974
Type of work: Novel or story cycle
Time: 1997 to 3143
Locale: The Earth and various points within our galaxy and the Greater Magellanic Cloud

A draftee, born 1975, hangs onto his life and much of his sanity throughout a pointless war which drags on over astronomical expanses of space and time

> Principal characters:
> WILLIAM MANDELLA, a draftee who rises from the rank of private to that of major in an army he hates
> MARYGAY POTTER, his lover and eventually his only link with the twentieth century

The Forever War is an outgrowth of the Vietnam war experience — the experience of the American nation in general and in particular of Joe Haldeman, who served in combat in Vietnam in 1968. (The name "William Mandella" seems to derive from the author's middle name plus an anagram of "[H]aldeman.") The cynicism and relative pessimism of *The Forever War* ally this science fiction war story to Harry Harrison's farcical *Bill, the Galactic Hero* published early during the period of American involvement in Vietnam (1965), but distinguish it from Heinlein's *Starship Troopers*, written before American entry into the conflict (1959), and from the motion picture *Star Wars*, produced after disengagement from the war (1977).

Like many works of science fiction, *The Forever War* sits somewhere on the dividing line between the novel and the story cycle. The volume consists of four divisions, each of which originally appeared in 1972-1974 as an independent story in *Analog*. Mandella and Potter are the only characters from the first story to survive through to the last one, and Mandella himself (who is also the narrator) is the one character to appear in each division. While this episodical structure is probably responsible for certain minor confusions and inconsistencies, it does parallel Mandella's own experience: he is sent out on various missions and then, because of relativistic time dilation, must adjust to changed conditions at the "rear."

The author has stated in interview that he was more interested in setting up his story than in portraying a probable future — he actually believes that interstellar war is logistically impossible. Indeed, Haldeman has posited a number of extremely unlikely events to fill in the quarter-century between the publication of the first story of the series in 1972 and its opening in 1997. During this twenty-five years, the world; achieves unity and disarmament under the United Nations; invents an essentially unlimited power source having something to do with tachyons; and uses the "tachyon drive" to travel at near light speed to a newly discovered, conveniently placed black hole ("Stargate"), through which spaceships can travel instantaneously to other black holes (the "collapsar jump"). On consideration, the implausibility of these sudden developments becomes clear, but Haldeman is careful to give the reader no time for such reflection. Instead, the reader's eyes, with Mandella's, are fixed in horrible fascination upon the war and its corollary, the United Nations Exploratory Force.

When the first story opens, Mandella is in basic training, drafted out of graduate school by the Elite Conscription Act of 1996 and preparing to fight a mysterious extraterrestrial opponent. As far as Mandella knows at the time, the war began when, after several unexplained losses of colonization ships, an escort drone returned with the report of the destruction of a ship by an alien vessel. By the last story, Mandella learns that the facts in support of this interpretation were "laughably thin," just as doubt was eventually cast on the supposed torpedo-boat attack on U.S. craft which led to the Gulf of Tonkin resolution. But Earth's former military leaders, who have been shunted off into space exploration since disarmament, are still spoiling for a fight, and political and economic factors make war attractive to other world figures. The result is a surge of war fever, leading to the strengthening of space forces ("navy," as Mandella says) and the establishment of a tactical assault force which can take and hold planets orbiting the collapsar gateways. By function, this force should be nicknamed the marines, but instead Mandella and the other draftees call it the army. This misnomer, like the "army's" powered fighting suits, would seem to be borrowed from Heinlein's *Starship Troopers*.

Haldeman's attitude toward the military, however, differs considerably from that expressed by Heinlein. The tone is set by the opening scene in the first story, in which the draftees are shown a videotape on "eight silent ways to kill a man." The "actors" in the tape are convicts who actually die. The rationale for this brutal realism is that no one under middle age on Earth has seen actual combat; but the reasoning is not sound — at this point no one has so much as seen a Tauran (the extraterrestrial enemy), but it is certain that their weak spots are not the same as humans'.

With similar half-logic the draftees are given cold-weather training on Earth in "preparation" for the totally dissimilar cryogenic environment — only a degree or two above absolute zero — in which they will be expected to fight. Such, at least, is the original plan, but after taking forty percent casualties — mostly deaths — in further training on Charon (a posited tenth planet even darker and colder than Pluto), Mandella's unit is sent on a mission to a planet of an ordinary star, in alien "grass" lands where the temperature is only a little below the boiling point. The whole aim of this mission is to catch a live Tauran for study, but the army is so dedicated to the principle of no quarter that it has hypnoconditioned the soldiers to make sure their ruthlessness does not flag. This plan results in the mission's failure — after their one Tauran prisoner commits suicide, there are no others left alive at the enemy base.

But Haldeman is not ranting mindlessly against the military. Mandella, Potter, and their fellow draftees are trained and led by middle-aged Vietnam-veteran career types who within their sphere are brave, intelligent, resourceful, and sometimes even sympathetic. Mandella himself, for all of his philosophical superiority, is forced by events to behave much like his instructors when he is given command responsibilities. The blame for the situation falls in part on everyone, in part on no one, and in part on political leaders whom we never see on stage. Haldeman is more concerned to depict than to judge.

Also marked by strong verisimilitude is Haldeman's treatment of technological and social developments. The UNEF fighting suit may be two hundred years ahead of its time, but the reader knows exactly what it feels like to wear one. The "tachydon drive" may be sheer magic, but once granted this source of unlimited energy, Haldeman deduces spaceship maneuvers, shipboard conditions, and military tactics with scrupulous logic. Similarly, Haldeman's sexually integrated army, complete with bunkmate rotas in basic training, seems one plausible response to the stated social and military situation, and it is depicted vividly. The remainder of the book is spent chiefly in elaborating upon the background and themes already stated or implicit in the first section, and if only for that reason it seems a little weaker.

The second division consists of two fairly independent episodes. In the first, Marygay Potter is injured in a malfunctioning acceleration shell and almost dies, but is saved with some help from Mandella. The Potter-Mandella relation had been quite tentative in the first story, but by this one she has become Mandella's steady — though not exclusive — lover. "Mary Gay Potter," with a difference only in spelling, was the maiden name of Haldeman's wife, so it seems likely that a deepening Potter-Mandella relation had been intended from the beginning, but perhaps the transition as depicted is a trifle too abrupt.

The latter part of this section examines what the leaders of Earth who sent Mandella off to war have been doing back home during the twenty-six years he has been gone. (Subjectively less than two years have passed, thanks to time dilation.) The world government seems to have weathered the crises brought on by modernization, automation, increasing population, exhaustion of natural resources, and the like, but it has done so only through a total restructuring of society and through liberal application of conditioning techniques similar to those used on Mandella. To have more than a bare minimum of housing has become something shameful, and homosexuality is encouraged as a population-control measure. Most people live off government allowances sufficient for necessities but for few luxuries. To most individuals the war effort is no more than a pinprick — the mechanics of the collapsar jump make it possible to conceal the locations of both Earth and the Tauran home planet — but UNEF is not yet ready to give up on Mandella and the other survivors of his unit. It is now 2024, and the Vietnam and Middle Eastern veterans who instructed the first UNEF inductees are dead or too old to fight. Mandella and his companions are the first people to return to Earth with ground combat experience. Still, for that very reason they are also useful propaganda symbols, and hence UNEF hesitates to do anything so bald as unilaterally extending their term of enlistment. Instead, every pressure is brought upon the veterans to re-enlist: they are blacklisted from employment or further education, their accumulated back pay is taxed away, and so on. Even so, Mandella and Potter are determined to stick it out on the dole. However, they change their minds after they witness how Mandella's aged mother is callously allowed to die without medical care: on her seventieth birthday it had been determined that she was of no further use to society. But Potter and Mandella re-enlist only after they have been guaranteed assignments to training positions on the Moon. Mandella has a brother there, and conditions on the Moon are better than on Earth. Then, on the very day of their arrival at their guaranteed assignment, they are "reassigned" to combat study.

The third section of the book is the shortest, but also the most poignant, particularly in its original magazine appearance, where the remaining half-volume was not present to remind the reader that this episode could not be the last. Both Mandella and Potter are wounded in the same action. Thanks to a system for preserving internal pressure in a damaged fighting suit, each loses a limb. They believe that this will get them invalided out of the army, and they even receive a sermon from their shipboard doctor on the likely course of love put to the test of an amputated arm and an amputated leg. But soon after their arrival at the military hospital-and-resort planet of Heaven, they learn that medical science can now regenerate missing limbs. (Thanks to time dilation, the year is now 2389.) Potter and Mandella are not out of the army after all, and their chance of surviving the three subjective years each has left to serve is effectively zero. They have a desperately good time for six months of rest-and-recreation at Heaven's resorts (the inflated prices here being UNEF's way for recouping disbursements for back pay; salaries are based on *objective* time, which makes every soldier a billionaire). They use the period as a sort of honeymoon: each is the other's only link to the lost twentieth century. At the end of leave they learn they have been assigned to separate missions. This means parting forever, since, even if by some miracle both of them lived out their enlistments, differing periods of time dilation would put their discharges centuries apart. Again we see the stupid, heartless bureaucracy: most of the members-to-be of Mandella's new unit have not even been born yet — they will grow up while he travels under time dilation — so there is no valid reason why Marygay could not accompany him. But rules are rules. Mandella considers suicide, but decides it would be a victory for UNEF, and forbears.

The conventions of storytelling require that things should look blackest for a hero just before the resolution, and Haldeman follows this advice in *The Forever War*. Already stricken by separation from Potter, Mandella is given a job he cannot handle. UNEF has decided to make a major out of him, largely for the bureaucratic reason of his seniority: few other inductees from the beginning of the war remain alive. Despite the fact that Mandella's psychological profile shows him unsuited to military command, he is given a cram course in small-unit leadership and put in command of a strike force numbering 119. The other 118 men and women are homosexuals — the leaders of human society have decided that the best way to handle the complicated problems of population control and genetics is to centralize childbirth and give the masses a more harmless outlet. Moreover, under a veneer of military standardization, Mandella's subordinates differ radically from him in language and culture. Mandella's personal style wins over a couple of his officers, but he has no success at all with the enlisted personnel, whom he cannot approach in the same way. Tension and alienation finally reach the point where a large part of the force refuses to heed a warning from Mandella, thinking it a trick, and are killed as a consequence. But at this nadir, for his first and only military success of the book, Mandella figures out a scheme (involving a "stasis field" and a "nova bomb") to destroy the attacking Taurans. Their own base destroyed, Mandella and the few other survivors limp back to Stargate.

Mandella expects to be court-martialed for losing his command, but at last his luck has changed. It develops that human genetic management has undergone another change in policy, and now practically all of humanity is composed of male and female clones of one ideal genotype. For some reason (which Mandella is told is beyond his comprehension) this results in a single group mind, which proves able to communicate with the similar group mind of the Taurans and to stop the war, which has been over for 221 years by the time Mandella gets back to Stargate. Just in case this genetic policy turns out to have unforeseen defects, the clone entity Man maintain planets on which babies are produced in the natural fashion. Many veterans are being resettled on such worlds. What is more, Mandella finds in his file a 250-year-old note from Potter. She had been discharged at a time when the war was winding down, and (for once allowed to keep one of those huge accumulations of back pay) she has banded together with other veterans to buy a surplus cruiser which they are using strictly for time dilation, as a "time machine." She is alive, still young, and waiting for Mandella.

From a final appended clipping from a folksy-sounding newspaper, we deduce that Potter and Mandella have settled down together to a determinedly humdrum existence on a backwater planet, and are engaged in living happily ever after.

Mandella has not triumphed, but he has survived. His sardonic sense of humor, along with his ability to distance himself from what is happening to him, has kept him sane. Even much of his idealism has come through — UNEF has found it simpler to get around his scruples, through conditioning or simply by lying about the facts, than to try to subvert them. As with any war, there has been a large element of luck in Mandella's survival, but his fierce instinct for self-preservation has impelled him to take advantage of whatever luck comes his way. Similarly, Potter has had both the initiative to instigate the relativistic shuttle and the devotion to spend over two subjective years there on the mere hope that Mandella may come back from his mission alive.

Potter and Mandella are appealing characters caught in an unappealing situation. As such they represent a transition between the total gloom of much science fiction in the late 1960's and early 1970's, and the current (late 1970's) reality, in which some people are so distanced from fact that even war might be accepted again. But transitional or not, in the mind of all but the youngest contemporary reader *The Forever War* is indissolubly linked with another war that seemed as if it would drag on forever. Whether the novel will re-create the feeling of the years of American involvement in Vietnam for future generations, whether they will find it incomprehensible, or whether historical perspective will bring other of its aspects into center view is something only the years will tell.

THE GODS THEMSELVES

Author: Isaac Asimov (1920-   )
First book publication: 1972
Type of work: Novel
Time: 2100
Locale: The Earth and its Moon; the para-Universe

The tense stories of the struggles of three beings, two human and one alien, against the stupid exploitation of a scientific discovery which could destroy the Universe in which the humans live

> *Principal characters:*
> FREDERICK HALLAM, a famous but intellectually limited scientist
> PETER LAMONT, a disaffected young physicist in Hallam's employ
> BENJAMIN DENISON, Hallam's contemporary and enemy, now fled to the Moon
> DUA, the Emotional in a Triad of Soft Ones in the para-Universe
> ODEEN, her Rational partner
> TRITT, their Paternal partner
> SELENE LINDSTROM, a female Lunarite spying on, then helping, Denison
> BARRON NEVILLE, her sometime Lover and Denison's opposition
> KONRAD GOTTSTEIN, Lunar Commissioner

Since Isaac Asimov's best-known "novel" is really not a novel at all, no reader should be surprised that his Nebula award "novel" actually is not one, either. Like the *Foundation* books, *The Gods Themselves* consists of independent stories, separated in setting, time frame, and protagonists from one another. As in the earlier works, however, Asimov provides thematic unity to such an extent that the work seems reasonably whole to the reader, despite a few annoying loose ends. The thematic unity works so well, in fact, that Asimov is able to indulge in some quite uncharacteristic technical experiments with point of view and chronology in the course of the book. *The Gods Themselves* thus becomes the most complex, most careful, and ultimately most rewarding Asimov fiction in years.

The basic structure of the book is a set of variations on a theme. The proposition, which Asimov hands the reader as the titles of the three related but distinct stories which make up the work, is a quotation from the German dramatist Friedrich Schiller. "Against stupidity," Schiller wrote in 1801, "the gods themselves contend in vain." What Asimov gives us are three major sorts of stupidity and a wide range of responses to stupidity, all centering on a scientific discovery of great possible value but equally great catastrophic potential. His enormous cast — human and nonhuman, scientist and nonscientist — struggle with the issues to the very brink of catastrophe before resolving them, for a time at least. The reader's interest is thus divided between the abstractions which Asimov presents for consideration and the slickly contrived embodiment of those points of conflict between various chambers. Asimov's avocation as a popularizer of ideas has never been put to fuller use in a work of fiction.

The first and shortest tale, "Against Stupidity," establishes the setting, the central conflict of the plot, and, of course, the theme. It is a neat, deft piece of traditional science fiction that would not have been out of place in *Astounding Science Fiction* thirty years before its actual publication. The time is the early twenty-second century, the place our Earth. Human society, as the result of a marvelous stroke of serendipity forty years before, has an apparently inexhaustible supply of energy, provided by the Inter-Universe Electron Pump, which transfers electrons to another universe (called the para-Universe, for parallel universe, in the book) by swapping pieces of ordinary tungsten for the bizarre element plutonium-186. This substance has the same atomic number as the tungsten but, because of the unusual distribution of protons and neutrons in its nucleus, is highly (and increasingly) radioactive. Hence, it can serve as an energy source, and the tungsten transferred to the para-Universe can serve as an energy source there, seemingly without interference from the laws of thermodynamics which apply to more normal energy sources. The Electron Pump (always written and spoken of in caps) has, at the opening of the book, brought about unprecedented human prosperity; it is seen as an unmitigated boon, and its proposer, the radiochemist Frederick Hallam, on whose desk the first interuniverse transfer had occurred, has become famous and powerful.

That particular situation is the source of the plot of "Against Stupidity." The problem with the Pump's success — and Hallam's attendant success — is that opposing and questioning voices are rapidly stilled. The protagonist of this story, Peter Lamont, is one such voice. He had begun work on a history of the Pump Project, working from his privileged position as a scientist in the organization. Unfortunately, he offends Hallam by suggesting that the para-men are more intelligent than the human Project engineers — after all, they initiated the transfers; all Hallam and his co-workers did was to ascertain how to continue, and make use of, the exchanges. The angry Hallam cuts the young man off from meaningful work, forcing Lamont into an effort to disprove Hallam's assumption that the Pump has no real consequences. What Lamont discovers is that the actual natural laws of the two Universes are being mixed by the Pump's actions, and that a very real chance exists of the sun's exploding as a result of an increased rate of hydrogen fusion. His alarm is increased by the messages sent from the para-Universe on pieces of iron foil; one reads F-E-E-R, interpreted by Lamont as "fear." (The other messages are in para-symbols which, despite the efforts of the linguist Myron Bronowski, are undecipherable.) But no one — political leader, revolutionary, or Pump scientist — will listen to Lamont, who has been blacklisted and slandered by Hallam. Mankind is headed for extinction as a result of "sheer thickheaded stupidity," as reputation, security, and intellectual inertia combine to prevent Lamont from getting any modification in Pumping activities. The outlook at the end of the story is quite grim.

"Against Stupidity" is not a particularly good work of fiction. Its characters are dreadfully stereotyped: there is the malcontented boy genius; the stupid, famous old man; the wise, cynical humanist; and the selfish public figures. The open ending undermines the effectiveness of the story's plot, though of course it assists the overall shape of the book. The style is pedestrian, even boring, as Asimov resorts too frequently to lecture and to a question-and-answer routine in his attempt to explain the principles behind the Pump. An attempt to liven up the tale by fracturing chronology — the fictional present of the book begins with the sixth section of this story, a section divided into four parts and interleaved with the first five, so that the book actually begins with a section numbered "Six" — seems more clever than functional, especially since Asimov provides a note claiming subtlety for the device. But the theme has been introduced and the groundwork laid for the remainder of the book.

"The Gods Themselves," the middle section in both size and placement, is also the center conceptually and aesthetically. Here, Asimov gives us his para-men, creatures utterly unlike anything in our universe; yet he presents them with such detail and care that they become the most real characters in the work. They are beings which exist in two principal states, Hard and Soft, the latter being the immature, procreative phase of the former. Hard Ones have bodies like those in our Universe, permanent in shape until death but sexless. Soft Ones occur in three types different from each other and radically different from the Hard Ones: Lefts (or Rationals), Mids (or Emotionals), and Rights (or Parentals) all have exceptionally tenuous physical beings — they can melt into rock and do, in fact, melt into each other during sexual congress. During these periods of melting a Triad, the Hard One whom they will eventually become materializes and acts, while the Soft Ones' personalities are suspended in sexually blissful unconsciousness. A Triad becomes mature after producing a new Soft One of each kind; then, at a time chosen by the Rational member, the three melt into one another for a final time and become a single permanent Hard One. This complex race is, unfortunately, a dying one. Once there had been thousands of Hard Ones and millions of Soft, but now the numbers have dwindled to fewer than three hundred and ten thousand, respectively; for their sun is also dying. The energy transfer which they have arranged is their attempt to keep the population from declining still further.

The protagonists of "The Gods Themselves" are the three members of an important Triad, contrived and designed by genetic engineering to produce a scientist of the highest order, one who can solve the problems of a dying sun. This Hard One, Estwald, designs the Pump during the periods of his Soft Ones' melting; but this fact is revealed only at the end of the novella, when the final melt occurs. Before this, we are alternately placed in the consciousness of Odeen, the (male) Rational who comes to comprehend the actual nature of the Triad and at that point directs the final melt; Tritt, the (male) Parental who rears the young and directs normal melting; and Dua, the (female) Emotional whose activities carry the theme of the work. For it is Dua, an unusual Emotional with Rational characteristics, who responds passionately to the discovery that the Pump will destroy the human Universe, who sends the messages to Lamont begging him to shut down the Pump, and who delays the Triad's final melting (and, hence, the permanent incarnation of Estwald) because she does not wish to lose her own hardwon individuality. Her struggles, first for consciousness and then against what she sees as injustice and death, are presented in a series of eighteen sharply written sections, alternating among the persons in the Triad until the final stepping forth of Estwald, the only character in the very short last section.

While such an alternating point of view is hardly a new literary device, Asimov rarely attempts to embody his story and his theme in an unorthodox technique. Here, it works splendidly, since Asimov not only keeps the characters distinct but modulates his prose style to suit each of them. Asimov may never have been a better literary craftsman than in this novella; at least one reader has exclaimed over the moving sensuality of the passages describing the Soft Ones' melting, and Asimov may never have been better at rendering a character's emotions than he is with Dua's. Her struggles against the stupidities she perceives in the Hard Ones, in her mates, and in the other Soft Ones (who generally shun her) are fully convincing, in sharp contrast to the conventional maneuverings and frustrations of Peter Lamont. Like Lamont, she loses, finally melting into Estwald, father of the infamous Pump; but the context strongly suggests that a permanent Estwald, one-third of whom is Dua, will solve the problem and save the human Universe.

In fact, the solution unexpectedly comes not from Estwald but through Benjamin Denison, Hallam's colleague whose gibes many years before had provoked Hallam and set in motion the chain of events which produced the Pump. Hounded out of the scientific community, Denison has worked so successfully for a cosmetics manufacturer that he can now emigrate to the Moon and try to take up a new life in science. In "Contend in Vain," the last and longest story in the book, Denison employs the scientific establishment of the Moon, where Hallam has not permitted the establishment of a Pump Station, to investigate his theories about the dangers of the whole Pump process. His hunch is similar to the theory of the discredited Lamont; his desire is to use the Lunar proton synchrotron in a series of experiments to verify the hunch. The Lunarites, however, distrust him, not least because their principal energy scientist, Barron Neville, is a leader in a Lunarite independence movement. Neville sends his girlfriend, Selene Lindstrom, a tour-guide with strong intuitions, to keep an eye on Denison, who is attracted to her. Neville fails to take the woman's honesty into account, however, and Selene comes to realize the truth in Denison's position and the indefensibility of Barron's. Denison and Selene, working together, achieve the solution to the danger which Hallam's people refuse to admit; they devise a source of both energy for the Moon and counter-force to the Pump, the tapping of an anti-para-Universe with opposite charac-teristics to the one which works through the Pump.

The Lunar Commissioner, who administers the colony of ten thousand, is per-suaded that Denison is right and throws his weight behind the new Cosmeg Pump; Lamont (who does not actually appear here) and Denison are vindicated; Hallam is set out to pasture. A major crisis in human history has been solved. However, the reader may not be wholly satisfied with this most formulaic of the three stories in the work. There are disturbing loose ends — most notably, the relationship between human and para-Universes now that Estwald has matured, and the lack of any resolution of the human-alien relationship. Fur-thermore, much of the novella is taken up with either textbook explanations of the scientific principles involved (probably necessarily), or items of adolescent titilation, such as the growing sexual involvement between Ben and Selene (probably unnecessarily).

The Gods Themselves is, then, an uneven but significant work. In its center section, Asimov achieves his best depiction of an alien environment and physiology and the psychology appropriate to them. In the other sections, in which he casts his central idea in human terms, he produces sound, well-crafted formula stories in which a problem is defined, investigated scientifi-cally, and solved by a plausible combination of insight and persistence. The work never comes together as a whole, partly because the shifts in setting and protagonists are demanded by the development of the idea rather than by any literary imperatives. (For instance, Lamont could function easily enough as the protagonist of the third section; and the tightly described Lunar community and impressionistically rendered world of the para-Universe, while memorable examples of the best sorts of extrapolation, pull in aesthetically opposite direc-tions.)

The various examples of stupidity are, however, finely crafted; and the didactic structure and tone of the work and its parts demonstrate well the claim of some writers and critics that science fiction is dominantly a literature of ideas. Like his humans, Asimov's para-men — gods themselves, superior to the human "we ourselves" — are paralyzed by their own selfish stupidity, as Schiller had said they would be. In showing *how*, Asimov has produced a complex work not without flaws, but nevertheless possessing several excel-lences of the kinds only science fiction can provide.

Criticism:

Watt, Daniel. "A Galaxy Full of People: Characterization in Asimov's Major Fiction," in *Isaac Asimov*. Edited by Joseph D. Olander and Martin Harry Greenberg. New York: Taplinger, 1977, pp. 154-157. Watt's evaluation praises *The Gods Themselves* as being a remarkable book, although he realizes some strong weaknesses in the work. He compares his character development with that of Ursula Le Guin.

HARD TO BE A GOD
(TZUNDO BIT' BOGOM)

Authors: Arkady Strugatsky (1925-   ) and Boris Strugatsky (1933-   )
First book publication: 1964
English translation: 1973
Type of work: Novel
Time: Several centuries in the future
Locale: The Earth, and the distant planet Arkanar

A novel about a complex, tragic, and heroic mission of a group of the Earth's representatives carried out on a backward and gloomy planet still passing through a historical stage reminiscent of Earth's Middle Ages

> *Principal characters:*
> ANTON (DON RUMATA OF ESTORIA), a member of the Experimental History Institute
> PASHKA (DON HUG), a member of the same Institute
> KYRA, an Arkanarian girl, Anton's sweetheart
> DON PAMPA, an Arkanarian baron, Don Rumata's friend
> DON REBA, the Minister of Internal Security at the King of the Arkanar, an illegal conspirator
> ARATA THE FAIR, an insurgent, the leader of the peasant army

Hard to Be a God is probably the most popular book written by the Strugatsky brothers. It has been translated into nearly every European language and published in the United States. In both structure and conception it is one of the most refined and satisfying books by the Strugatskys.

The fact that *Hard to Be a God* was first published with *Far Rainbow* is not a mere coincidence nor the fancy of the publishing house. After having raised the moral and logical problems about the Man-Nature interrelations (*Far Rainbow*), the Strugatskys made a logical step forward by including social problems into this sphere as well. The theme of interference in the history of an alien planet is common to Western science fiction readers. The unusual thing is how the Strugatskys solve this problem.

Strictly speaking the novel is not a hard-core science fiction work. It is actually a moral parable about human gods capable but not willing to interfere in the historical evolution of an alien planet. Because of their humane nature these men-gods cannot indifferently view bloodshed, suffering, mediocrity, or the downfall of civilization. Such events offer concrete associations with our own earthly past.

The Strugatskys have deliberately parallelled the quasihistorical background of their novel with our own earthly conditions while slightly displacing some of the well-known elements and changing numerous details known to the reader. We can easily relate to the Arkanarian Middle Ages, and in the heavy stamping of the Arkanarian Sturmovics (stormtroopers) we clearly hear echoes of Munich and Nuremberg. Such familiar things on an alien planet are not weaknesses, but rather strong points in the Strugatskys' imagination. They do not want to lead us out of familiar historical surroundings into an imaginary country; on the contrary, they strive to return to the facts of our own well-known history. Thus, this novel deals with the people of the Earth and their deeds, presented from behind a distant galactic curtain.

The spirit of the beginning of *Hard to Be a God* is similar to that of *Far Rainbow*. There is the same feeling of a vague threat which disturbs the serene existence of the main characters. These characters are Anton, Pashka, and Anka, who look like the pupils of a boarding school in other Strugatsky novels: *Noon: Twenty-second Century* and *Far Rainbow*.

Like all children, they have escaped to the forest to play games of pirates and noble dons, or to imitate other popular characters from the books they have read. But all their games do not seem to come from books. Their imagination is full of a bloodchilling reality and historical details, and the repertoire of their games is well thought out. These things are further supplemented by some unusual trifles, such as "a hoarse, shrill voice, quite unhuman." (Where and when could they have heard such a voice? Scarcely in the warm, bright, and absolutely human future.)

This prologue to the novel is openly symbolic. In a game Anton, expressing mature judgment, refuses to play William Tell because the children have real crossbows, and a real apple on Pashka's real head. In another scene, when the children come across a deserted road with an old traffic sign that reads "Do Not Enter," we realize that these events set a keynote for the whole plot of the book.

Two simple truths are suggested by these incidents: the first, no one can use weapons against a human being; the second, history is an "anisotropic one-way road." Without this prologue the moral chord of the novel, running through the book up to its epilogue, might have been lost. By presenting the main characters on the Earth, in their natural surroundings, the prologue and the epilogue substantiate the actions of these persons in quite different surroundings on Arkanar.

As the novel proper begins, we find ourselves in a gloomy atmosphere on an alien planet. The workers of the Experimental History Institute are carrying on their uneasy "intelligent watch." Suddenly we recognize Anton in Don Rumata of Estoria, a dashing cavalier, dueller, and man about town; Pashka is Don Hug. The game is over; ahead of them lies the hard road of the explorers, with a possibly fatal outcome. Society on Arkanar is undergoing a difficult period. Events are occurring which cannot be explained by existing theoretical schemes. These developments alarm Anton and his friends. The events also evoke unpleasant associations for the reader. Memories of historical injustices are triggered. While persecution was common in the Middle Ages, there was not a well-organized Grey Militia, consisting of small retailers, narrow-minded people, and massacrers. There were stupid and narrow-minded monarchs and cruel favorites, but the sinister image of Don Reba reminds us of more recent historical events. The Minister of Internal Security is neither an adventurer nor a politician. He is simply a personified symbol of stupidity, narrow-mindedness, and triviality.

The anxiety of the observers mounts, but they can interfere only marginally to save a few outstanding individuals such as doctors, scientists, and poets. Even Arata the Fair, the leader of the local "Jacquerie," is deprived by the "Gods" of such intervention. Why is it so?

In *Hard to Be a God* the Strugatskys have made their first mature attempt to formulate an attitude towards the problem of interference in the process of historical evolution. The problem is ambiguous. To interfere means to deprive a nation of its history; as the main character of "The Escape Attempt" has put it: "History is the backbone of humanity, and by destroying history one breaks the back of humanity." But noninterference holds the danger of killing the personal feelings of human brotherhood and generating a hatred of everything unhuman. But at the same time the Strugatskys clearly and with journalistic enthusiasm express their own point of view: a person has neither the possibility nor the right to escape from the necessity of solving these problems by hiding behind an elevated godlike façade.

The Strugatskys carry on a subtle polemic against the mass of science fiction books in which advanced earthly civilization imposes justice and order on the Cosmos by using fire and sword as was done by our predecessors on Earth. Why have the Strugatskys chosen to present their case in a science fiction novel? What is there so fantastic in it? The stormtroopers on the absolutely earthly narrow streets of a medieval town as well as the adventures of our up-to-date characters traveling by "time-machine" into the stormy and romantic past are typically earthly. Was it not possible to avoid such science fiction props as spaceships, orbital satellites, and minitransmitters disguised as jewelry? Was it not possible to drop the purely fabricated situation on Arkanar and have the main character safely travel to Munich of 1933 by such an unscientific method as time displacement or a somnambulistic sleep such as Mark Twain's Connecticut Yankee?

Had this been done, we would have been deprived of a bright, picturesque, and unique world. Despite analogies with our well-known past, this fictional world is unearthly, interesting, and petrifying. In addition, the main characters would have had no trouble in making their moral choice, because the developments on the Earth after 1933 are known. And finally, it would have been impossible to carry out an extremely valuable sociological experiment, which can be realized only in science fiction — to show the spiritual alliance between the Middle Ages and Fascism. The authors have managed to single out the common elements in these two dark periods of our history: obscurantism, ignorance, and an animalistic hatred of everything intelligent.

But let us not allow these philosophical concepts, sociological modeling, and moral principles to obscure the fact that this is a first-rate story. This novel could have been entitled "Three Musketeers in Space," and it was first conceived exactly in such a key. Consider the wonderful gallery of characters. Rumata, likable Don Pampa, Reba, Doctor Budach, the peasant leader Arata, and Rumata's sweetheart Kyra all stay in one's memory for a longtime. They are flesh and blood characters, not mere personified ideas. The proper names are rich and the dialogue is lively. For example, the slang conversation between Don Reba and Waga Koleso (Waga the Wheel), the leader of "the night vagabond army," is a brilliant and perhaps untranslatable example of an artificial, but animated acceptable language. Unfortunately this scene, as well as a number of others, has been rather simplified in the translation by Wendayne Ackerman so that some nuances have been lost.

Impressive as they are, the backgrounds are not the main things in the book. The intellectual and emotional climax of the novel lies in Rumata's conflict with himself, while the description of his image and the fixation on his mental suffering contribute to the development of the plot. This conflict is between a "god" who does not kill even in fights, and a man, whose race has experienced its own "Don Rebas" and "Grey Sturmoviks" in its own past. The Strugatskys are interested in the individual moral choice of Rumata and not in his sociological conception of interference. *Hard to Be a God* remains a moral parable, not a sketchy science fiction novel. That is why the Strugatskys have chosen for the novel's epigraphs words by Ernest Hemingway and Pierre Abelard (omitted in the English edition), authors who preferred human personal moral feelings to abstract sociology.

Hard to Be a God is not a static and moralizing monologue; by the end of the novel the action has become even more dynamic. A tragedy takes place on Arkanar: one unhuman state system has been replaced by another more unhuman power — Don Reba leads a revolt and seizes power. The gloomy atmosphere on Arkanar turns into a dark and starless night. Now even the visitors from Earth have no time for their historical discussions; they must save the remnants of the planet's culture and its few very rare bright spots of humanity. Rumata finally has to draw his sword, but he does so only after his limits of suffering have been surpassed: his only intimate friend and sweetheart Kyra has been killed.

A comparison with the works of Ursula K. Le Guin suggests itself: like Genly Ai, Shevek, and her other characters, Anton-Rumata makes a peculiar round trip and returns to his initial point as a quite different person. Even the duality of his character, which results from his role of an explorer, reminds one of the immortal wisdom of Taoism, so brilliantly expressed by Ursula K. Le Guin: "Light is the Left Hand of Darkness, and Darkness is the Right Hand of Light."

And what about the problem of interference in the process of history? It is hard to find a definite answer in the novel itself, but the book provides much food for thought. The absence of a definite conduct prescription is justified by the fact that such a prescription does not exist in real life either.

Had Rumata deeply interfered in Arkanarian affairs, and helped the Arata insurgents, the aftereffects could have been even more tragic. The dialogue between Rumata and Arata is one of the most remarkable scenes in the novel; in it the Strugatskys subtly dispute the proponents of the "revolution export" theory. Rumata declines to render any help, because his earthly past is a reliable guide in his deliberations. This past reminds him of the ultimate effects of the accessibility of modern weapons for a people whose intelligence and social consciousness are ages behind the proposed technical possibilities.

The same problem, although on a different intellectual level, is raised in the dispute with Budach, an outstanding Arkanarian doctor, and again the Strugatskys are consistent: the "gods" cannot help Arata because they know what price will be paid by the Arkanarians when such superfantastic weapons fall into the hands of Don Reba and his supporters (and sooner or later this must happen). Neither can the visitors from Earth help Budach, a representative of the first Arkanarian intellectuals. To give a powerful and abrupt push forward to the planet's progress is to deprive its inhabitants of their own history.

It is possible to make a delicate distinction between the position of Arthur C. Clarke's Overlords in *Childhood's End* and other "good strange gods" of Western science fiction and the point of view of the "gods" in the Strugatskys' novel, and this distinction unavoidably affects the final decision. In books by Clarke, Clifford Simak, and others, the interfering forces are absolutely sure of the necessity to interfere: in the above books humanity on the Earth has reached the critical stage of a looming thermonuclear war that endangers more than human culture and its best representatives. It threatens the very existence of human civilization. At all times and in all societies it has been considered moral for a doctor to fight for the life of all patients, even those who have attempted suicide. Such an analogy justifies extraterrestial interference in human affairs as well.

The tragedy of Rumata is of a quite different nature. Despite the dark and unhuman night on Arkanar, the population of the planet must fix this night in its memory too. Rumata is a historian and he well knows the stages of his own history: the philosophical conception of humanism itself did not arise at random but during the early stages of the Middle Ages. After a stormy night one appreciates a bright and fresh morning even more. The dark night over Arkanar is not a finale, it is only a turning point. In a distant future "the still unborn boys and girls, who will be sitting before the dictascopes of the schools in the Communist Republic of Arkanar" will use their past to study the ABC's of humanism. An immediate interference by Rumata at a point when the Arkanar population is far behind the proper stage of humanity might deprive them of ever experiencing that stage.

Such are the complicated schemes and sophisticated sociology, which explain the ages of history and the destinies of various nations. But Rumata is only human; he is not a "history demon" observing the slow flow of history from above. Therefore, he cannot help interfering. Therein lies the duality and tragic dialectics of people for whom it is "hard to be a god." But is that really so? The Strugatskys state that it is very simple to be a god, but it is extremely difficult (though necessary) to remain human. It is a simple conclusion, but after reading this novel the reader should arrive at the same conclusion, accepting it not as a bookish morality, but as the essence of our existence.

THE HIGH CRUSADE

Author: Poul Anderson (1926-   )
First book publication: 1960
Type of work: Novel
Time: 1345
Locale: The Earth and the Galactic Empire

When unsuspecting aliens, bent on invasion by intimidation, land in a medieval English village, the local gentry and peasantry subdue them, take over their ship, and begin to conquer the galaxy for England

Principal characters:
> BROTHER PARVUS, the Chronicler, a Franciscan
> SIR ROGER, BARON DE TOURNEVILLE, a vassal of Edward III, leader of the people of Ansby
> LADY CATHERINE, his wife
> SIR OWAIN MONTBELLE, the handsome younger son of a petty baron

A chief theoretical problem in the genre of imaginative fiction is the relationship of science fiction to the outright fantasies, disparagingly called "sword and sorcery" fiction. Yet, as the popularity of such writers as Edgar Rice Burroughs, Fritz Leiber, and Leigh Brackett demonstrates, many readers find a quasi-medieval world as satisfying mentally as a remote planet, with a sword or battleaxe holding more romance than a laser or disintegrator ray, and a barded horse being a better vehicle for their imaginations than a spaceship.

Poul Anderson's *The High Crusade* is a thoroughly successful *tour de force*, combining the best of both worlds. The inhabitants of an English village during the Middle Ages are pitted against a star-trekking race of alien conquerors, and emerge on top. There is both sufficient action to satisfy the lover of sword and sorcery, and sufficient scientific accuracy to satisfy John W. Campbell, Jr., in whose *Astounding Science Fiction* it was first published in serial form in 1960.

Anderson's task is large — as large as the successful attempt of Isaac Asimov to combine science fiction and the detective story in his *Caves of Steel*. The blending of two disparate genres always presents a greater challenge and carries a greater risk, because it demands competence in both fields. Anderson has produced a convincingly standard alien superpower in science fiction setting, within which he has moved characters that are true to their medieval, spiritual, and cultural background. Yet Anderson, who has been praised for the accuracy of his settings, past, present, and future, is equal to the task.

He opens the story with a framing device characteristic of medieval literature. Chaucer used the Canterbury pilgrimage as the medium for his collection of stories, and Boccaccio has refugees from the plague tell one another the tales of *The Decameron* at his villa near Florence. Anderson's frame is also a masterpiece of economy, relating the situation to the reader in less than a page. The captain of a spaceship lands on an alien planet, and is confronted by the translation of an ancient manuscript that presents astonishing evidence. Although the original of the translation has been written more than a thousand years before the time when the story opens, the captain dreads its impact on his present society. As he begins to read, the story begins.

The manuscript itself is written as a medieval chronicle. It tells how its author, a poorly educated, rural Franciscan monk named Brother Parvus, eye-witnessed the events of May 1, 1345, during the reign of King Edward III. An alien spaceship on a mission of conquest, filled with a crew of soldiers of the race called Wersgorix, lands in a pasture near the town of Ansby in Lincoln-shire. Their procedure is to seek out less advanced cultures, make a show of scientific and military strength, and use their superior technology to awe the natives into submission.

Rather than a village full of farmers, they find a town full of armed veterans in which Roger de Tourneville is gathering an army for a campaign in France. Four aliens emerge to overawe the crowd; then one of them fires a laser. He and the others are killed with a swarm of arrows, and the assembled army storms the spaceship's gangplank, floods through the airlock, and takes the rest of the crew.

Sir Roger decides that the spaceship is heaven-sent, and that with its aid, he could win the war in France, retake the Holy Land, and be home in time for harvest. Setting a surviving Wersgor named Branithar to navigate the ship, he loads the entire village of Ansby — people, cattle, pigs, chickens, and all aboard, and prepares to depart. Instead, Branithar sets the autopilot for a flight to the nearest planet in the Wersgorix galaxy. The English see earth recede beneath them as they unwittingly begin the high crusade.

Anderson throughout stresses the single theme of English adaptability — and exemplifies the theme in a series of confrontations between old and new technologies. By the time the ship appears over one of the three fortified cities on the planet Tharixan, the knights have already learned how to use the ship's armament. The sophistication of advanced weapon technology has simplified the job of the human agent; the English find a target much easier to hit with a self-guided missile or a laser that locks onto its target than with a bow and arrow. The theme's corollary is that much of value has become obsolete and therefore forgotten in the scientific advance of the Wersgorix. Brother Parvus observes that the Wersgorix are not adept at hand-to-hand combat, and although they have force-fields to counter laser beams, they city falls because they do not take the simple precautions of medieval warfare. Having bombarded the city from the air, the English land to do close combat. The Wersgorix's attempts to get airborne in a small craft are foiled by jousting knights in full armor who simply knock it over.

The English succeed, because of their adaptability and their military train-ing and experience, against seemingly more capable foes. However, the Wers-gorix have indulged in ease for so long they have become overly dependent on their machinery; when their machines fail, they are helpless. Thus, while vehicles similar to tanks fall into the camouflaged pits the English have prepared, archers and mounted knights scatter the supporting infantry.

The English success depends on more than might. It depends equally on the faith that the Lord of Hosts is with them, or an unshakable confidence in their prowess, and sometimes on a mixture of craftiness and Christian charity. And the conflict among all these elements and the modern technology of the Wersgorix is a constant source of humor. During a conference with Huruga, the supreme Wersgor commander on Tharixan, the English pause for prayer. The Wersgorix are unfamiliar with the concept, and their lack of knowledge of the language leaves them wondering whether "God" is a mighty computer with which the English are in contact telepathically. (Some hypothesize that prayers are mental exercises through which the English temporarily increase their physical powers.) Throughout the contacts between the two races, Sir Roger's continuous bluffing leaves the Wersgorix hamstrung with indecision: they can see that the English wear armor and carry weapons that the Wersgorix have not used for centuries, but they can never be certain whether these knights, yeomen, and peasants are savages or the representatives of a culture so superior that it needs only a handful of warriors to counter the Wersgorix Empire.

At one point, Huruga and his armed force barricade themselves in their last stronghold on the planet — a fort impregnable even to the nuclear bombs being dropped from the highly automated aircraft the English have learned how to operate. With plenty of provisions for a seige, Huruga is prepared to wait in the fort during the few weeks it will take to summon help from a military base on a planet circling a neighboring star. Being experienced at seiges, Sir Roger scours the countryside and rounds up a horde of Wersgorix civilians — women, children, and old men and sends them to the fort. Faced with the thought of feeding them, Huruga surrenders.

Anderson continues his theme that technological advancement does not necessarily assure victory. Sir Roger is aware that a relief force from the military base will soon end his conquests, and that his enemies will have little use for diplomacy. Thus, leaving a force to hold Tharixan, he sets off to meet the representatives of three races subject to the Wersgorix and unites the subjugated peoples in a revolt. With medieval foresight, he has bribed key members of the other diplomatic parties into making each of the ambassadors think that the other two were also ready to move.

Since the English can outthink as well as outfight the Wersgorix, the outcome would not be much in doubt in the final third of the novel, were it not for still another characteristically medieval touch — an adulterous love affair. Like Tristram and Isolde, like Lancelot and Guinevere, Sir Roger's wife, Lady Catherine, and Sir Owain Montbelle see more of each other than either does of Sir Roger, whose attention is fully occupied, though not overtaxed, by leading an interstellar war. Although Catherine resists Owain's pleas to consummate their love, Sir Roger's trust of his wife is strained and Owain's loyalties become doubtful.

Anderson's final scenes blend remarkably the two cultures he has skillfully developed to a climax. The feudal system with all its chivalric trappings has proven so effective an instrument to overthrow a tyrannical society, that a spacesuit with plume and crest no longer seems ludicrous. The resolution of the lovers' triangle is dramatically satisfying and winds down in good time.

The English win in more ways than one. Although their way back to England is lost, even centuries later they have not lost their desire for home; they hope that humanity will develop space flight on its own and eventually find them. During the interim, they have set about building new Englands throughout the galaxy under the benign and businesslike rule of the descendants of Sir Roger de Tourneville, aided in the job by the Wersgorix, who enjoy their new freedom.

IF THE STARS ARE GODS

Authors: Gregory Benford (1941-   ) and Gordon Eklund
First book publication: 1977
Type of work: Thematically related short stories
Time: 1992, 2017, 2052, 2060, 2061
Locale: Mars, Earth (especially Africa), the Moon, Jupiter, Titan (a satellite of Saturn)

Bradley Reynolds encounters various alien life forms as he explores the nature of man and the possibilities of gods

Principal characters:
BRADLEY REYNOLDS, an astronomer
JONATHAN, the captain of an alien starship
MARA, an extremely beautiful and intelligent product of genetic manipulation
COREY, a brilliant but horribly mutated product of genetic manipulation

In *If the Stars Are Gods*, the authors, through three short stories, present a delightful trip through Dr. Bradley Reynolds' long, productive, provocative life. The three episodes are woven around themes which may be dissected into subthemes. The major thread is the god-alien theme. This fine, thoughtful work deserves more than a cursory reading to discover the intertwining themes revealed through the character of Reynolds.

The first episode of the three-part story line is set in 1992 on Mars. Bradley Reynolds is a young, self-motivated, highly political astronomer assigned to a manned exploration of Mars; life has been discovered there, and Earth must investigate. Reynolds observes that the density and complexity of life forms increase as the exploration party moves toward a calculated point on the surface of Mars. The hypothesis is that this point is the origin of life on Mars — a "Garden of Eden." However, accidents or mishaps kill the other members of the landing party, leaving Reynolds alone, clinging to the surface of Mars. Left alone to determine the true meaning of life on Mars, Reynolds' answer is a bitter one; life on Mars is apparently the result of contamination from an early Earth probe. Reynolds reacts to his understanding of the nature of research and pursuit of knowledge in Earth societies and makes a unilateral, godlike decision to withhold the facts for the good of further exploration. He returns to Earth apparently having failed to answer the questions about life on Mars. The venture can only be considered a failure, yet Reynolds is proclaimed a hero.

The second episode moves in time to 2017 and in space to the Moon. Once again, Reynolds alone is thrust to the edge of human knowledge and experience when he is selected as envoy to an alien spaceship orbiting the Moon. This is the first of several examples of the authors' ability to take the improbable and make it, if not probable, at least lovely and thoughtfully enjoyable. The aliens are beautifully described intelligent "giraffes." They are in the midst of a long journey, the purpose of which is to meet and talk with stars. Reynolds has been chosen as envoy because he knows more about our sun than any other human.

One of the most interesting aspects of this, the second section of the novel, is the author's use of elements derived from Jonathan Swift's *Gulliver's Travels* to enrich the writing. The specific voyage which Benford utilizes is the one to the Houyhnhnms. We recall the great ironic reversal with which Swift is concerned: horses are godlike; men are Yahoos, veritable animals. Benford gives us, instead of horses, the "nice, kind, friendly, pleasant, smiling, silent giraffes," whose leader is named, significantly Jonathan. The aliens are both familiar and unfamiliar. They have no science as such, but they do, like Swift's prototypes, have a science of the mind, and perhaps even a science of the spirit; they consider astronomy and astrophysics as religious or theological arts. The stars *are* gods, and they worship with a religion totally foreign, indeed almost unacceptable, to the minds of men. They have no contempt, at least on the surface, for humanity, and they do respect Reynolds. While the parallels to Swift are not completely explicit, they are sufficiently indicated to provide the reader with another dimension in his understanding.

An interestingly warm, albeit suspicious, relationship develops between Reynolds and Jonathan — the Earthly name assumed by the captain of the alien ship. Through this relationship, Jonathan is revealed to be an acceptable though faulted being. He is a chronic and inept liar; whenever he lies, he blinks his eyes madly.

Reynolds is charged with discovering as much from the aliens about their planet and technology as possible. He does not have to do this; neither is he successful in this task. Reynolds, however, does attempt (perhaps successfully) to talk to our sun. The experience so moves him that he becomes retrospective and feels he has experienced a measure of fulfillment only twice in his life, once here with the aliens and once on Mars. In a well-written scene, Reynolds renounces his world and man with it, and he requests to go with the aliens on their journey. They refuse him and leave him with a confused concept of the nature of stars. Are they beings? Even gods? Once again, although his mission has "failed," Reynolds comes out a hero.

The final episode moves from a short but informative interlude in Africa in 2052, to Jupiter in 2060, and finally to Saturn's satellite Titan in 2061. Bradley (he has renounced his other names along with the world) has withdrawn to the sanctuary of a religious commune. But at the age of ninety-five, he is called back to the world he left after the encounter with Jonathan and the star. This time his task is to decipher a message received from an intelligent life form somewhere in the universe. Once again he is at the edge, directing the four hundred or more people who work and live on the laboratory orbiting Jupiter. The have come to Jupiter because of information gathered from the part of the message which is understandable.

At this point the authors introduce the reader to Mara and Corey. These two inhabitants of the Orb, central characters in the book, are "Nips" — the result of genetic manipulation intended to produce superbeings with superintellects. This potentially hackneyed idea is treated with freshness and insight. There are, of course, the "Christers" who view these experiments and their products as evil and deserving of destruction. On the other hand, there are those who view these beings as perfect, almost godlike. We see the two extremes in Mara and Corey. Here is another opportunity for the authors to develop the personality of an improbable being — Corey is so badly mutated that to sustain its (is it male or female?) life, to move it, even to communicate with it, it must be kept inside a steel box. As with Jonathan, Corey's personality comes complete with a variety of human frailities.

Mara, on the other hand, is physically beautiful with a superintellect, the epitome of what man can create. Of course, she too is flawed, but her personality grows and a warm compelling relationship develops between her and Bradley. Mara is on the Orb (as is Corey) because of her intelligence. She and Corey are the ones, if anyone can, who will crack the code and interpret the message. Although Bradley's authoritative position is weakened by his refusal to destroy the two "Nips" as was ordered after an earthly religious revival, his tenure as commander of the Orb is continued by Earth when Mara deciphers the message and solves the puzzle.

The scene in which the key to the message is found at the cost of Corey's life is probably the best in the book for cleverness, emotion, and description. The decoding of the message introduces some very imaginative concepts. Corey had studied the language of dolphins and whales and found their language significantly different in form and complexity from that of humans. Dolphins move in a three-dimensional environment, while man moves in a two-dimensional environment. Dolphins, therefore, conceive words in three space, humans in two space. Once the assumption that the message-senders also thought in a higher-dimensional space is made, the key to the code becomes the correct topological transformation. The ensuing mathematical discussion, which possesses just the right balance of accuracy and interest, produces a comfortable sense of authenticity. The message, appropriately, is primarily concerned with mathematical truths unknown on Earth, which lead directly to further exploration.

Bradley apparently dies the next year while exploring a new life form on Titan. He has made the unauthorized trip to Titan to see, investigate, and hopefully communicate with yet another life form. But because the trip is unauthorized, he is removed from command and ordered home. Now that his mission is finally successful, he is considered a failure on Earth for the first time.

The god theme is intricately woven throughout the novel. Reynolds worships the reality, the "true meaning," of exploration and being on the edge of contribution. His childhood heroes were "the first men who conquered Mount Everest . . . mountaineers clinging to the edge of that white god." To worship is to be on the "cutting edge of discovery." As he explains to Jonathan, "anything a man does that no man has done before — whether it is good or evil or neither one or both — is considered . . . a great accomplishment." The edge, the void, and exploration are methods of being godly or of worshiping a god. Intelligence, alien or terrestrial, is treated as a divine entity. Bradley speaks of the sun as a "greater, vaster being, more powerful and knowing [than Earth]." Mara holds a similar reverence toward Jupiter. The authors achieve something comparable to a marriage of Zen and C. S. Lewis in presenting all objects as possessing a godly visage. Each planet seems a power and a force — even Mars seems to strike down intruders on her surface as a dog might dispose of fleas on its back.

The god-intelligence-theme is diminished near the end of the book. Bradley declares that, with a clearer vision because of old age, he realized that intelligence is not all people believe it to be. On Earth, a religious revival insists that "Nips," the ultimate in intelligence, are in fact blasphemous. Perhaps stars are the only gods after all.

The god theme is, however, only one of several attractive themes Benford and Eklund introduce. Bradley himself catalyzes them all. He is old for most of the story — an old hero, a champion for the ever-growing number of us growing ever older. He is endearing and fallible. The careful reader will discover that Bradley gives misinformation about his age on at least two different occasions, and on those occasions he says he is older than he in fact is. He observes that he will be the first of a line of ancient leaders and heroes.

If the Stars Are Gods does not overpower one with messages. The writing style is easy and enjoyable to the point of allowing the reader to browse. This is entertainment with enough interesting scientific and science fiction ideas to hold the reader's imagination.

IMPERIAL EARTH

Author: Arthur C. Clarke (1917-   )
First book publication: 1976
Type of work: Novel
Time: The Quincentennial Year, 2276
Locale: Titan and the Earth (Washington, D.C., New York, the Caribbean, and Saudi
   Arabia)

*Duncan Makenzie officially visits Earth from Titan and offers the world a great new
enterprise for developing the technique of contacting alien intelligence*

> *Principal characters:*
> DUNCAN MAKENZIE, Titan's representative to Earth for the Quincen-
>   tennial celebration of the American Revolution
> KARL HELMER, his estranged friend and a communications scientist
>   of genius
> CATHERINE LINDEN ELLERMAN, ("CALINDY"), an Earthwoman for
>   whose favors Duncan and Karl are rivals
> GENERAL GEORGE WASHINGTON, the Quincentennial master of cere-
>   monies in Washington
> IVOR MANDEL'STAHM, a gem dealer and confidant of Duncan
> AMBASSADOR BOB FARREL, an Earthman representing Titan's inter-
>   ests
> SIR MORTIMER KEYNES, the world's leading genetic surgeon

Imperial Earth is a speculative science fiction novel written as Arthur C.
Clarke's contribution to the American Bicentennial celebration. It is a novel
bristling with ideas and insights of the "politics of time and space," the title
of one of the early chapters. The tradition in which this novel takes its place is
more that of Isaac Asimov's *Foundation* and *The Gods Themselves*, Robert A.
Heinlein's *Stranger in a Strange Land* and *The Moon Is a Harsh Mistress*, and
Ursula K. Le Guin's *The Dispossessed* than the galactic empires of Frank Herbert's *Dune* or Larry Niven and Jerry Pournelle's *The Mote in God's Eye*. This
novel is also one that draws rather heavily on earlier work, particularly *Prelude to Space*, *The City and the Stars*, and *The Deep Range*, as well as some
short stories and essays. It combines three of Clarke's favorite interests: space
travel and communication with alien intelligence, political and social evolution
driven by technological development, and the world beneath the sea. Added to
these interests is a new emphasis on interpersonal relations, the psychology of
such relations, and a more fully developed symbolism than Clarke had employed in any of the earlier novels, even *Childhood's End* and *2001: A Space
Odyssey*.

   Imperial Earth is narrated from the perspective of an envisioned divergence
in the ethnologies of the Terran motherworld and Titan, a colony world of
special importance because of its virtually limitless hydrogen reserves. In
Clarke's imagined future it turns out that Titan, a moon of Saturn, is the most
hospitable of extraterrestrial worlds in the solar system, because it possesses

both adequate gravity and an atmosphere. The gravity is only one fifth that of Earth, a difference which makes adjustment to Earth difficult and even perilous for a Titan resident. However, the two worlds are separated by more than a billion kilometers and variant gravities. From the beginning Titan has been a hard working and productive world in which the human race has had to struggle with alien elements and an environment that will support life only with the intervention of an advanced technology. Life on the surface of Titan is impossible because of the cold, an ammonia atmosphere, and catastrophic winds that occasionally blow across the land. Life is lived mostly below ground in what is called a "corridor society." Moreover, the population is small and interdependent to a degree that is completely foreign to human society on Earth. Each world has reached a historic crossroads as the story opens. Titan's hydrogen based economy is threatened by a new power source developed for space travel called the Asymptotic Drive. The new drive makes possible much faster space travel and does not require hydrogen for fuel. Long term implications for the Titan colony are therefore serious. Earth has also reached a turning point in its development. Its people have become increasingly prosperous and self-interested. Their idealism has also become identified more and more with a nostalgic interest in the past and its charms. The Quincentennial Year becomes the focal point for the cult of the past, which is one of the indicators of a developing decadence in the generation that is beginning to grow up at the time.

Clarke sets the stage of his future history world with the careful attention to detail of the mature writer, sure of his powers and experienced in his craft. The corridor world of Titan recalls similar lunar colonies in Asimov's *The Gods Themselves* and Heinlein's *The Moon Is a Harsh Mistress*. Rather than giving the reader the kind of spectacular action effects characteristic of those writers, Clarke focuses on the history of Titan as a frontier world and on the Makenzie family as its architects and principal clan. Clarke also has to account for three hundred years of future history. The story begins on Titan, where the Makenzie family has just received an invitation to the Quincentennial celebration. The family consists of Malcolm, the patriarch, a vigorous man more than 120 years old. We learn quickly that life expectancy, while not indefinite, has been extended to perhaps triple the current averages. Colin Makenzie is Malcolm's clone, separated by one generation in time and trained to develop complementary powers of administration to go with Malcolm's engineering skills. Although Malcolm had succeeded in setting up the first colony on Titan, and the Makenzie family has controlled the political and economic life of Titan, they live a rather Spartan life because there is little room or inclination for luxury. Clearly, they are supposed to recall the honest, hard working families of the Roman republic and of colonial America whose inner strength of character, frugal habits, and idealism made them the backbone of new cultures and the foundation of new dynasties.

Malcolm's only natural child was born with a genetic deficiency which claimed her life early. Her death led to the estrangement of Malcolm and his wife Ellen. Hence, the Makenzie dynasty was preserved by cloning, first, Colin and then, another generation later, Duncan. When the invitation from Earth arrives, Duncan is thirty-one years old and is the logical candidate to represent the family interests and those of Titan at the Quincentennial. It is time for Duncan to have a clone made, and the trip to Earth will offer the perfect opportunity to insure the perpetuation of the Makenzie dynasty. The cloning of offspring is necessary because Duncan carries the same damaged gene as Colin and Malcolm, effectively prohibiting the fathering of natural children. Duncan is married to a woman with children of her own, who are reared as Duncan's and as members of the clan, but without the expectations that they will eventually run the family business or occupy the political leadership of Titan.

The Makenzies are not without rivals on Titan, and the most serious challenge comes from the Helmer family, which prides itself on its more recent earth origins and ties. The great hope of the family is Karl, Earth born, a young man of extraordinary personal attractiveness, and a genius. Karl is erratic, however, and has suffered from a mysterious breakdown, the cause of which we learn near the end of the story; but he is also gifted with exceptional powers of reasoning and intuition that distinguish him from Duncan, with his talents for organization and applications. Clarke sets up the classic rivalry and contrast between Shem and Sean which is to dominate the psychology of the entire novel.

During their childhood Duncan and Karl were best friends. Karl was older by several years and was more mature in almost all phases of life. The family rivalry was soon compounded by a rivalry for the affections of a visitor of extraordinary beauty and sex appeal from Earth. Calindy was the prize that inevitably went to the older, handsome, self-confident, and brilliant Karl. Perhaps as a result, Calindy remained for Duncan a dream woman, an ideal. We learn soon enough that the sexual mores of the twenty-third century are considerably more permissive than they are at present or ever have been. The simplest term in which they may be described is bisexual free love. This sort of sexual utopia is one of the least convincing of the science fiction conventions Clarke relies on in setting up the narrative references of his story. Karl and Duncan had been lovers before Calindy arrived on the scene. The break between the two friends occurred after the rivalry over Calindy's affections and following Kark's mysterious breakdown. Much later we learn that Karl's collapse had been the result of Karl's experimental use of the "joy machine," a device for enhancing sensation and experiences, during a sexual encounter with Calindy. The result of Karl's forbidden use of the machine was a kind of permanent imprinting of Calindy as an orgasmic and romantic ideal which not even she could hope to satisfy. Karl has become emotionally arrested and fixated on Calindy as she was when they first met. Not only can no other woman ever satisfy Karl, but also Calindy herself proves unequal to the task. While she has changed, her imprinted image never does, nor can her natural self hope to compete with her electronically enhanced ideal.

When Duncan leaves for an Earth that is under a rather loosely and benignly administered "Pax Americana," the Calindy episode has faded into a somewhat distant if poignant memory. Duncan and Karl are estranged, and Karl is presumed to be working on a new and mysterious research project on the outermost of Titan's moons, Memnosyne. As he leaves Titan for the first time, Duncan and the reader are aware that his visit to Earth will change his life, perhaps in ways that no one can anticipate.

The journey to Earth features three exceptional momen.·. The first comes as Duncan sees Earth, the home planet of the human race, for tɪɛ first time with his own eyes. It is such a moment that Clarke may well have imagined for himself as he was writing *2001: A Space Odyssey* and filed away for future use. Whatever the case, it is a stirring and even symbolic moment in which the reader imagines Duncan aboard the *Sirius* between the great gas giant Saturn and the remote but luminous Earth. The second moment is another visual encounter, this time with the heart of the Asymptotic Drive. Duncan contrives to sneak a glimpse of the mysterious and secret power plant with the help of a sympathetic crew officer. What he sees on the viewscreen seems to have promising symbolic potential: a small dot slowly moving along a grid of lines. Strangely, the moment is soon over, and much of the impact is lost and then forgotten in the narrative movement. It is the last time the Asymptotic Drive is mentioned, and the reader is left to puzzle over that one glimpse. Was it perhaps a quantum black hole or some artificially produced neutrino molecule? We do not know and are never to learn.

But the third moment is quickly upon us, and it is one that more than makes up for any disappointment we may feel about the A-Drive. It is a scene out of *2001: A Space Odyssey*, but it is more effectively realized than anything Clarke wrote in the earlier novel. Perhaps, he was thinking of Stanley Kubrick's stunning visual effects when he describes the vista of Earth from the orbiting Port Van Allen Space Station. There are two other scenes in the novel that have similiar visual impact, but none has the grandeur and the power of stimulating awe and wonder to match Duncan's first close encounter with the beautiful and fabled planet of his dreams. For those who remember the scene in the film version of *2001: A Space Odyssey*, Clarke mentions the "Last Chance Toilet" aboard the space port, an allusion that brings a smile of recognition to the reader's face. It is also one of the many details that create a verisimilitude in the novel that is one of its strongest features — a quality that science fiction readers have come to expect from Clarke, and in which they will not be disappointed.

If we are to be disappointed in this novel, it is with Clarke's failure to do more with his characters and their psychology. The purely secular moral values to which the characters casually adhere is a diluting agent that makes it difficult to grasp the conflict and tension that Clarke tries to build through Duncan's yearlong visit to Earth. The reader's slightly bemused discovery that Duncan Makenzie is black, points up another weakness in the design of the story. Clarke wants to establish some basic differences between Bicentennial and Quincentennial America, and one way he does this is to indicate that both the racial question and religion have become specters of the past. Clarke has some fun with these ideas by making General George Washington black and having black university professors acting at footmen and butlers for the Quincentennial jubilee. Roman Catholicism is dimly recalled as a religion associated with a ritual called "Bingo." But the humor does not really disguise the fact that there are no plausible standards of conduct left to guide human behavior except a naïve humanism which never could have produced the kind of demi-Utopia Clarke describes.

Perhaps the difficulties Clarke has in making his characters personally interesting are compounded by the logic of the narrative. Once Duncan arrives on Earth as a human-alien who is accustomed to gravity at only one fifth Earth force, Clarke is committed to having Duncan discover Earth and its culture. Of the several roads that Clarke could have taken, he seems to have chosen the least effective approach. Duncan is simply not an interesting enough character through which to reintroduce the reader to the Earth he knows and make him experience everyday realities as though they were wonders.

In the midst of this strain for poetic effect and bathos, Clarke dazzles us with a genuine wonder. A group of humans who can afford it and who have an adventurous nature are treated to experiences guaranteed to be both unorthodox and satisfying as part of a future mystery tour. Duncan and the reader are taken to the New York waterfront to visit the raised and restored *Titanic*. It is another of those moments in the novel that the reader is not likely to forget. It is almost matched by Clarke's truly inspired description of Duncan's snorkel visit to a coral reef and his encounter with the long-spined sea urchin. The urchin's spiney, starburst configuration is woven subtly into the fabric of the novel's symbolism from this point on, connecting both the origins of terrestrial life and its eventual destiny beyond the solar system.

The chief argument of the novel concerns this very linkage, which is worked out deliberately, indirectly, and slowly; but when Karl Helmer finally makes his appearance on Earth, the various motifs are gathered together to give us the vision of Karl, Duncan, and Clarke himself that will give new purpose and direction to human history. Karl has been secretly staying with Calindy while he develops the final phases of his dream for setting up a cosmic antenna system. It would be constructed beyond the orbit of Saturn in order to pick up longwave radiation that would be a more certain sign of advanced technology than the shortwave radio signals humans have been using to scan the heavens. Karl's rationale is that a highly advanced culture will have outgrown the kind of radio and television signal twentieth century civilization had become accustomed to when interstellar listening stations were first built. When Duncan and Karl finally meet in a mood of mutual suspicion and fear, it is at the site of *Cyclops*, an antenna farm of hundred-meter dishes covering a circular area of five kilometers. Produced by the "brief but brilliant Muslim Renaissance," the spectacular antenna collectors were assembled in the "Empty Quarter" of Saudi Arabia. The great successes of *Cyclops* were things of the receding past by the time the two rivals from Titan meet high upon an observation tower on one of the antennas.

At this point, Clarke opts for the simplest way of cutting through the complications of the plot. Karl dies in an accident, leaving behind in his notebook and recorder the information needed for Duncan to unravel the mysterious project on which Karl had been working. The code name "Argus" held the key to Karl's design of a great antenna system that would be able to search the heavens for the kind of long wave signals a really advanced civilization would be emitting. Duncan and Karl had indeed once recorded a mysterious signal when they were adolescents, but could make nothing of it except that it seemed important. The reader, therefore, understands the importance of the project and its probable success. Duncan makes Karl's plan the center of his Independence Day address, and it creates a sensation. Moreover, the opening of such a great new frontier of scientific investigation will solve Titan's dependence on a one element economy. In the future, Titan is bound be become a great base of scientific study and eventually the base of departure to the stars.

Duncan and Calindy console one another before Duncan's return to Titan, but each realizes that their future destinies are to be very different. Duncan returns to Titan not with his own clone but with a clone of his dead friend Karl. It is more than a gesture in memory of his lost friendship. It answers the need articulated by Sir Mortimer Keynes to bring a new strain into the Makenzie bloodline. It solves the problem of the damaged gene and insures that the Makenzies will be able to reproduce naturally in the future. It makes the peace between the leading rival factions of Titan and preserves Karl's genius unimpaired by the destructive effects of the "joy machine" experiment.

The contrivances and the increasingly sentimental revelations of the concluding chapters are disappointing. They necessarily distort and soften the final impact of the novel, working to undo the effect that the architecture of ideas, symbols, and mythic allusiveness may otherwise have produced. If the novel is disappointing, it is because Clarke fails to realize the potentials of his own vision and the materials he developed. Although *Imperial Earth* fails to meet the standard of Clarke's best work, it will occupy a place of importance among the second rank of science fiction novels. Moreover, no reader of Clarke will want to ignore the outstanding success with which the author manages his special effects and the skill with which he again brings together scientific symbols and mythic patterns to give expression to his vision of both a possible and hopeful future. For the general reader, *Imperial Earth* will be remembered as a novel which achieved some supreme moments of science fiction mythmaking and one which symbolizes the affirmative potentials of science for the future. In the history of the genre, *Imperial Earth* may well come to occupy a curious place as a Bicentennial future history story which is both a product of its times while it articulates visions and intuitions that readers at the Tricentennial may return to with wonder and reverence.

If Clarke is right about longwave radiation and in some of the other guesses he offers, *Imperial Earth* may survive its own artistic weaknesses. Yet how quickly science changes our basic vision of things! When Duncan set out for Earth, there was but one planet in our solar system with rings, and that was in 2276. Now there are three. Perhaps future readers will smile as readily at this statement as we now do at Duncan's reflections of Saturn, *the* ringed planet.

Criticism:

Brigg, Peter. "Three Styles of Arthur C. Clarke: The Projector, the Wit, and the Mystic," in *Arthur C. Clarke*. Edited by Joseph D. Olander and Martin H. Greenberg. New York: Taplinger, 1977, pp. 15-51. Clarke combines his detailed scientific knowledge with mystical elements, according to Brigg.

Plank, Robert. "Sons and Fathers in A.D. 2001," in *Arthur C. Clarke*. Edited by Joseph D. Olander and Martin H. Greenberg. New York: Taplinger, 1977, pp. 121-148. An analysis of *Imperial Earth* is given here with emphasis on Clarke's use of the number four.

IN THE OCEAN OF NIGHT

Author: Gregory Benford (1941-   )
First book publication: 1977
Type of work: Novel
Time: 1999-2018
Locale: The Earth, the Moon, and points in space within the solar system

A haunting evocation of technological man's first contact with aliens, and the growth of one man's consciousness to assimilate the experience without becoming totally cut off from his own roots

> Principal characters:
> NIGEL WALMSLEY, an astronaut and space scientist
> ALEXANDRIA ASCENCIO, an airline executive, Nigel's lover
> SHIRLEY, lover of both, convert to the New Sons religious cult
> NIKKA AMAJHI, a pilot, technician, Nigel's lover after Alexandria
> MR. ICHINO, a computer technician, Nigel's friend and confidant
> THE "SNARK," a touring representative of ancient machine civilization
> BIGFOOT, a large, manlike creature
> PETER GRAVES, a hunter, threat to Bigfoot

In a number of stories and novels, Gregory Benford has tried to sum up the centrality for him, and probably for science fiction, of the theme of confrontation with alien life. The alien may be the future, our own selves seen at a distance, or an intelligent being of extraterrestrial origin, but the effect of the alien, and of the search for him, permeates Benford's fiction, from the paranoid fantasies of "Deeper than the Darkness" (*The Magazine of Fantasy and Science Fiction*, April 1969; novelized 1970; rewritten as *The Stars in Shroud*, 1977) and "White Creatures" (*New Dimensions 5*, ed. Robert Silverberg, 1975) to the exploration stories of *Jupiter Project* (*Amazing Science Fiction*, September-November 1972; rewritten for book publication 1975) and *If the Stars Are Gods* (coauthored with Gordon Eklund, 1977).

Like *If the Stars Are Gods*, *In the Ocean of Night* concerns an astronaut, somewhat alienated from his own race, who seeks the alien for what it or he can teach us, either about how the universe works, or about who or what we are. Like the collaboration, *In the Ocean of Night* is the result of years of thinking and reshaping (the earliest version of its conclusion was published in *Amazing Science Fiction*, November 1969, two years before work had begun on the other novel), and most of it had appeared in fragmentary form before the final assemblage. Unlike the collaboration, however, which remains five sometimes brilliant separate episodes, *In the Ocean of Night* is, if not a seamless web, an organic whole which amounts to more than the sum of its parts.

In this book, Benford has made a largely successful attempt to turn the traditional "first contact" romance into a novel of social interaction and character. The focus is not on Man, but on a particular man who, as an astronaut, encapsulates Man's probes into space, but who, as an individual, is rooted firmly in the world from which those probes are launched. Himself an alien, an Englishman in an American space program, Nigel has a critical eye for NASA and American behavior patterns and a longing to transcend his flaws and frailties as well as those of his Earthbound fellow human beings.

He sees the enemy, if there is one, not as the alien, but rather as the rigid, paranoid bureaucracy of the American government. Threatened by economic rivals from abroad (Brazil is prominent) and increasingly under pressure from irrational religious elements internally, the United States, as a corporate structure, can respond to the alien challenge only as a threat to its hegemony. But Nigel the alienated individual, sees in the alien a possible source of help for his and for mankind's problems.

The alien in this story is a representative of a machine civilization in relation to which we are one of those rare and transitory organic life forms that sometimes threaten the stability of things before they give way to machines or wink out of existence. The "Snark," as Nigel names it, emphasizing its unknowability through the allusion to Lewis Carroll's poem, "The Hunting of the Snark," interacts with human beings in several ways, primarily with individuals, and most often with Nigel. First to identify it, he circumvents NASA security by linking its communications directly to himself. Through his unwitting agency, the Snark takes over a human body, that of his lover, Alexandria, at the moment of her death. Later it uses Nigel's own senses to further explore the terrestrial environment and viewpoint. Nigel's friend, Mr. Ichino, programs messages to the Snark, chief among which are cultural artifacts that help it to understand humanity and serve to enrich its lonely journey. Finally, the Snark confronts Nigel in space in a NASA interceptor, and educates him in the realities of "the ocean of night."

This confrontation might have been the climax of a lesser novel, but here it is only the second of Nigel's three meetings with alien vessels. The first, based on the novelette, "Icarus Descending" (*The Magazine of Fantasy and Science Fiction*, April 1973), concerned a body misidentified for years as the asteroid Icarus, whose probable collision with Earth Nigel was sent to disrupt. Discovering the ship's true nature, Nigel delayed its destruction to explore its interior, risking the wrath of a panicky planet. His conviction then that man had much to learn from the aliens was not vindicated by the puzzling artifacts he extracted, but his motivation and first encounter with alienness are convincingly represented.

The erupting of that ship, resulting in an escape of atmosphere that propelled it toward Earth, was coincident with the sending of a distress signal summoning the Snark from its intended course. Nigel, meanwhile, still holds his position with Pasadena's Jet Propulsion Laboratory, a testament to his tenacity in bureaucratic infighting and his stature as a public figure earned from press conferences, talk shows, and so on. Having maintained his astronaut's rating, he is a logical if resisted choice, not only to pilot the interceptor, but also to work on the lunar project in which Earth scientists pry information from still a third alien ship, reactivated by the Snark in passing.

In this section, the fragmented Nigel of earlier narratives approaches wholeness in his human affairs, as well as in his grasp of human-alien relationships. His *ménage a trois* with Alexandria and their mutual lover, Shirley, was wrecked first when Alexandria contracted lupus, a pollution-linked disease, and then when both women defected to the charismatic religious cult, the New Sons of God. Alexandria's death and her transfiguration by the Snark won fame for the faith, but Nigel was plunged into a "dark night of the soul" from which he emerged, partly because of his own interaction with the alien, able to love in a less self-centered way. Nigel shows this ability not only in his sexual liaison with Nikka, an Oriental girl he meets in the lunar project, but also in his asexual relationship with Mr. Ichino, an older, more ascetic version of what Nigel could become. In this second triangle, Nigel is involved in a merging of East and West, in a bipolar connection with male and female, youth and age, in love relationships held together by shared interests and outlooks.

Nigel and Nikka extract secrets from the alien hulk, interact with each other in analyzing them, and manage to make much of their information public, despite attempts by the project's bureaucracy, infiltrated by the New Sons, to block transmission of material that might upset mankind's mythological self-portrait. Meanwhile, in the Pacific Northwest, Mr. Ichino independently confirms the ancient alien contact with the legendary "Bigfoot," though he destroys the evidence gathered by the white hunter, Graves, who would exploit the creatures rather than respect their privacy. These plot threads are tied together in the epilogue, which takes place at Mr. Ichino's cabin, and reveals the distance Benford has come from the melodramatic adventure story.

Nigel has come to know the alien far better than anyone, including Nikka and Mr. Ichino, because he absorbed a charge of alien information in the "library" of the alien craft, which built on his previous contacts and radically reorganized his world view. His transcendental insights are rendered in a stream-of-consciousness internal monolog as he chops wood outside, while indoors Mr. Ichino explains to Nikka the peace of mind required to understand a Japanese motorcycle. This oblique explanation of internal transcendence is punctuated by the blows of the axe and given visual point by the sight of Nigel outside, framed by the window (much as he has framed the alien before), with the vast expanse of the woods and the limitless background of the sky behind him.

Set in this context, the return of Graves is anticlimatic, melodramatic, and essentially trivial. Nigel dispatches him with inaudible words of wisdom, then sees the man's helicopter shot out of the sky by a distant humanoid shape, presumably using a weapon Mr. Ichino has returned to the Bigfoot tribe, who revered it for millennia before being disturbed by Graves. "Everyone learns from experience," intones Mr. Ichino, and his words fit not only Bigfoot, but also Nigel, his companions, and, one hopes, the human race.

Nigel's last series of revelations parallels the concluding statements of potential given the protagonists in Arthur C. Clarke's *2001: A Space Odyssey* and Robert Heinlein's *Stranger in a Strange Land*, without the metaphysics those authors felt compelled to use. Nigel's situation is always explicable in naturalistic terms; the beauty of his vision of a Universe alien to Man lies in its existential reality, rooted in the nature of Man rather than in the transcendental value of alien powers. It is not evident how Nigel will use his newfound perceptions — his peaceful solution to the Graves problem is countered by the Bigfoot answer — but his insights are accessible to others, both in the book and in the audience.

Though Nigel's quest is not for the mythological, it is nonetheless religious in a profound sense. His opposition to the New Sons is so vehement that it is apparent they must exert an attraction on him. He sees a reasonable parallel between the arrested development of Bigfoot, too enamored of alien "toys" to improve upon its "given" nature, and the regressiveness of the New Sons, who want only to retreat to mindless rituals, dances, and chants. But Nigel resists seeing his own commitment to progress or to assimilation of the alien as a complementary religious drive, although it is no more justifiable in logical terms than the actions of his opponents.

In a sense, Nigel's longing for space and its potential, and his victories over the forces of darkness, are appropriate to the formula demands of the romance, adapted to the space frontier. But his dependence on technology, on society, even on family, as "life support systems," contrasts starkly with the rejection of all three by the knight-errant or the lone gunslinger riding into town out of the desert. Where the space opera hero may fly by the seat of his pants, Nigel is disciplined, both as a scientist and as a social animal. Though his mind may be an "outlaw" yearning for the impossible, he knows he can never merge with the "other." But as a scientist, he must learn what he can, he must approximate in his terms and ours, what he senses that is beyond him. As a child progressively internalizes the world outside, Nigel encompasses the alien, formulating a paradigm which unites even organic and machine civilization against the awesome backdrop of the emptiness between civilizations.

Our own civilization, the thin veneer of culture which continually threatens to break down under economic, religious, and technological assaults, may not be adequate to the paradigm, but it is the only civilization we have. Nigel clearly lives in and is a product of an advanced, even decaying, technological society which Benford plausibly extrapolates from the contemporary situation of Western man, from shortages of raw materials (including water as well as gasoline) to changing evaluations of art and history (Bob Dylan and the Beatles are musical "classics," and Berkeley's Telegraph Avenue is a culturally frozen tableau of the 1960's.)

Nigel, certainly, has both feet planted firmly on solid, realistic circumstances. He eats and eliminates, drinks and fights, thinks and makes love, living a life which is not limited to the great adventure to which he is committed. Alexandria and Shirley, Nikka and Mr. Ichino, too, have lives of their own, even though we see them primarily in relationship to Nigel. Even minor characters, like Nigel's NASA and JPL coworkers and the administrators in Washington and on the moon, seem rooted in the society of their time. If some of the villains are too melodramatically menacing, too drawn to type, the obstacles that they pose are serious and plausible. The reality of life near the turn of the century is well-grounded and contrasts well against the potential transcendence of the alien, keeping in check the tendency of the theme to dwarf the participants.

Contrast, balance, distance are key concepts for the expression of the narrative as well. It fairly bristles with differing points from which to view the events, changing point-of-view characters so as to juxtapose and counterpoint not only lines of action but also image patterns and modes of thought. Whatever there is of the transcendent that is not domesticated by realistic detail is restrained by artistic form.

The tension between this control and the ostensibly uncontrollable nature of the theme is summed up nicely in the confrontation of Nigel and the Snark beyond the moon. Unknown to Nigel, he does not have control over his interceptor's missiles; his overtures of peace are belied by his ship, yet the Snark believes him. The Snark destroys the weapons with an effortlessness that hints at unused powers capable of destroying planets and stars; but the Snark is only interested in doing its job. Within the limits built into it, the Snark has marvelous self-control, which Nigel envies. The Snark also has consciousness beyond the intent of its builders. This allows it to imagine what it can never have or feel or originate, like man's culture, and allies it to Nigel, for whom the subjective world also goes far beyond what social rules and natural law permit.

Thus the object of contemplation, which suggests religious awe or mythological wonder, is not the alien itself, but the backdrop against which both man and alien are puny — the Universe, the "ocean of night" in the title. But the focus is always on the man for whom these thoughts are possible and assimilable, which argues for the classification of this book not as just another "first contact" romance, but as one of science fiction's few successful attempts at a serious novel of character, incorporating the theme of the alien.

LAST AND FIRST MEN

Author: Olaf Stapledon (1886-1950)
First book publication: 1930
Type of work: Novel
Time: From the 1930's to two billion years in the future
Locale: The Earth, Venus, Neptune

A history of mankind from the 1930's to two billion years in the future

When analyzing the first fiction work of Olaf Stapledon, *Last and First Men*, care must be taken to evaluate the book in the terms the author intended. Stapledon wrote in his preface to the novel that "it is an essay in myth creation," and it must therefore be accepted as such. It is not an attempt at prophecy, and any analysis based on such an assumption would be misleading and misguided. Stapledon used the concept of a future history to embody his own philosophic understanding of the human condition.

Last and First Men is a history of humanity from the 1930's to two billion years in the future. The historical events immediately following World War I are recounted in great detail, and the manner in which the world comes to be dominated by America and China is outlined. The fall of this civilization and the rise of a new culture in Patagonia follows. The Patagonian culture destroys itself in an atomic conflagration, leaving only a handful of survivors. This pitiful remnant succeeds in keeping the human species alive, but by the time the Earth again becomes generally habitable, the survivors have split into two distinct human races, the admirable Second Men and a contemptible subhuman species which is subjugated by a mutated race of monkeys. Conflicts arise, and after the ensuing struggles the Second Men gain dominance of the planet.

Earth is then invaded by Martian cloudlets whose modes of perception and philosophical outlook prevent them from being able to recognize the Second Men as intelligent creatures. Tens of thousands of years of conflict between the two species follow until mankind succeeds in destroying the invaders, but at the cost of almost destroying itself. Another Dark Age occurs and the Third Men arise from the diseased survivors of the second human species.

The civilizations of this species flourish until genetic engineering creates a race of giant brains, the Fourth Men. The Fourth Men virtually exterminate their creators and embark upon a program of mental exploration of the world. Concluding that pure mentality is insufficient for an understanding or appreciation of existence, the giant brains design the Fifth Men. This race achieves a culture which surpasses that of all previous species. They undertake the physical exploration of space and the mental exploration of the past. However, before they have more than begun to understand fully their world they are forced by an astronomical catastrophe to flee the Earth and terraform Venus.

On Venus man once again transforms himself. The Seventh Men, a winged race, comes to dominate the planet. This race is succeeded by a pedestrian species, and man is once again forced by an astronomical calamity to abandon his home; the race moves to Neptune. On this giant planet mankind undergoes many transformations which ultimately result in the rise of the Eighteenth Men, who are the culmination of human evolution.

After millennia of cultural achievement, the Eighteenth Men discover that a third astronomical catastrophe will destroy the Solar System. They attempt to seed space with molecules which have the potentiality for evolution into "human life" under favorable circumstances; and they undertake the mental exploration of the past so that they and the races which they have succeeded can fully understand and appreciate the human achievement.

It is to one of these "mental explorers" that we owe the chronicle which is called *Last and First Men*. Stapledon uses the fictional device of having one of the Eighteenth Men communicate the history of humanity to one of the last men. He seeks to understand fully his present world by exploring the common human experience. To him, we, the First Men, are the original ancestors to which all succeeding Men, in a sense, pay homage. By trying to return to his origins and to trace their influence, the narrator gains an understanding of what it means to be human, in the same way that contemporary man returns to his ancestors in ceremonies and festivals celebrating origins and rebirths.

Stapledon has used his knowledge of the myth of the past to create a myth of the future. Many of the themes which he explores are familiar to us from the myths which belong to our classical past. The woman who rises from the sea and becomes an instrument of conciliation to the opposing forces of East and West reminds us of the birth of Venus, the goddess of love. The Patagonian prophet who destroys the idol of the temple and who is killed for his attempt to bring understanding to his people reminds us of figures in legend and myth who are killed, but who are then resurrected to become gods. Stapledon also dramatizes one idea which appears again and again in myths: that of immortality or extreme longevity. He uses his portrayal of a culturally advanced species whose members live for thousands of years to explore the consequences such an extended existence might produce.

Many of the races portrayed in *Last and First Men* serve as mirrors to reflect past civilizations, including our own. Stapledon was aware of the scientific revolutions, in both the physical and biological sciences, which had been taking place in Western civilization; and he focused on certain aspects of these revolutions to explore the human condition.

Industrialism for its own sake seemed a fruitless pursuit to Stapledon, and we, the First Men, are portrayed as carrying a fascination with industrialism and the material fruits of scientific research to its ultimate end — the creation of a religion which worships energy and destroys itself by exhausting the resources of the planet. Many future races in the novel are also shown in pursuit of the chimera of industrialism at certain immature stages of their development, but the societies which overcome this fixation are able to achieve an equilibrium between the physical and the mental aspects of humanity.

To emphasize either the physical or the mental to the exclusion of the other is, in Stapledon's view, a certain cause for failure. The giant brains, the Fifth Men, represent pure mentality, and they themselves come to realize that they cannot be fully human because they have relinquished the physical aspects of the race. The Seventh Men, the flying men of Venus, on the other hand, represent pure physicality. They interact successfully with their environment, but they have sacrificed all pursuit of mental activity to the physical delights of flight (a pursuit to which the First Men are also portrayed as being addicted). Ultimately the flying men are replaced by a pedestrian race.

Stapledon views the human drama as a conflict among various aspects of man's own psyche and between man and nature. We, the First Men, are portrayed as being too individualistic and unable to resolve the demands of the individual and society without recourse to dogma and the worship of energy or wealth. The Second Men achieve a precarious balance between these two demands, until an outside force, the Martians, leads to their downfall. The Third Men are consumed by the ambition to alter nature, both animal and human. They succeed with their plans and bring about their own destruction by producing the giant brains, the Fifth Men. These creatures in turn realize their inability to be fully human, and therefore engineer more well-rounded successors. The Sixth Men are confronted by natural forces which they cannot conquer, and flee to Venus.

A cursory reading of *Last and First Men* might lead one to believe that Stapledon was a cultural relativist, but this opinion would be ill-founded. Instead, the concept of "Community" is central to the author's view of the human condition. Stapledon defined community as a group in which all individuals consciously cooperate in a common life approved by all. Each member must respect the personalities of the other members, and recognize their value as individuals. The people who best illustrate this concept in the novel are the Eighteenth Men, who differ from one another radically in both physical and mental qualities but who cooperate with one another fully. Another central concept is that of "Spirit"; this concept, the author believed, lent purpose to human existence. Only by attempting to understand and work towards the "Spirit" could an individual or a community fulfill its destiny.

In *Last and First Men*, Stapledon attempted to write an "essay in myth creation," and the reactions of several generations of science fiction readers testify to his success. He was to attempt on other occasions to create myths for our age: *Star Maker* represents his grand synthesis of metaphysics, science, and history, while *Odd John* and *Sirius* are concrete depictions of mythic elements in our present society. On his own terms, Stapledon is unequaled, and he certainly has been one of the major influences on contemporary science fiction.

Criticism:

Glicksohn, Susan. "A City of Which the Stars Are Suburbs," in *SF: The Other Side of Realism*. Edited by Thomas D. Clareson. Bowling Green, Ohio: Bowling Green University Popular Press, 1971, pp. 334-347. Glicksohn examines *Last and First Men* to show how it approaches the limits of the imagination.

Smith, Curtis C. "Olaf Stapledon: Saint and Revolutionary," in *Extrapolation* XIII (December, 1971), pp. 5-15. Smith examines Stapledon's mythmaking in *Last and First Men*.

THE LAST CASTLE

Author: Jack Vance (1916-   )
First book publication: 1966
Type of work: Novel
Time: The distant future
Locale: The Earth

The aristocratic "lords" of Earth face a rebellion from the Meks, a servant class determined to kill their human masters

> Principal characters:
> O. C. CHARLE, the "first gentleman" of the castle and presiding officer of the governing council
> O. Z. GARR, an outspoken gentile dandy
> CLAGHORN, an elder of the Claghorn family, a student of Meks
> XANTEN, an elder of the Xanten family
> MEKS, the manlike aliens with rust-brown skin imported as slaves
> GLYS MEADOWSWEET, a young lady being reared outside the castle

Jack Vance received both a Hugo and a Nebula award for this short novel that shows many of the strengths of the author at his best. The plotting is adroit, building inexorably to a climax followed by an effective *dénouement*. A carefully selected sequence of events clearly delineates the thematic problems. Vance's succinct approach invites comparison with H. G. Wells's *The Time Machine* and *The Island of Dr. Moreau*, with their great impact within a limited scope.

Like Wells, Vance depicts social and intellectual conflicts of the present projected into the future. The "gentlefolk" of Vance's book represent the worldwide succession of dominant upperclass aristocracies — the brilliant, "civilized," idle rich, whose refinement oozes from every sentence of their inconsequential conversation, and for whom individuality or even eccentricity is the approved ideal.

The Meks are sentient creatures robbed of their natural identity and forced into slavery. They are made to perform *mech*anically; their abbreviated name suggests the *mech*anized force of a technology that applies human labor to the formation of an efficient but dehumanizing system. Vance describes them as reduced to the level of insects, employing an image that Franz Kafka also found descriptive of modern man's condition: "Working in the mass, by the teeming thousands, he seemed less admirable, less competent: a hybrid of sub-man and cockroach." Their lack of individuality is understandable as a collective reaction to their common lot, but it is also a rationalization by the nobles in whose interest it is to believe that they are subhuman.

Vance's skill in plotting, his clear, economical style, and his concern for the survival of humanity, make this a piece of classic science fiction in both form and substance. The conditions and prospects of society are revealed in action. Characterization is kept to a minimum; events, rather than characters

— and *types* of human behavior rather than specific individuals with flaws, tragic or otherwise — determine the course of the story. The very form and style of the book suggest that the future is determined not by individuals but by collective human tendencies and their inevitable conflicts. (In the light of this orientation, criticism of Meks for lacking individuality is very ironic.) The conditions leading to the sweep of events have their roots in the present, and this brings us to see both the original depopulation of Earth and Earth's re-structuring into the Castle society, as reflections of current behavior. It is a futuristic parable with action as the metaphor.

For the most part, Vance's style stresses the denotative rather than the connotative aspects of language. He is highly effective in limiting his description to factual matters; and once we accept his statements as fact, we are the more ready to believe in his future reality. Metaphoric or symbolic language occurs primarily in the names Vance gives his characters and places, as in the case of the Meks. It is interesting to observe that the most "poetic" passage is an inventory of castle names delivered as an ominous death chant in the brief second section of Chapter Five. The Birds, raucous creatures used by the "gentlemen" for conveyance through the air, report what destruction they have seen in their aerial scouting, and they sound like a Greek chorus:

> Sea Island is deserted. Marble columns are tumbled along the beach. Pearl Dome is col-lapsed. Corpses float in the Water Garden . . . Delora: *a ros ros ros*! A dismal scene. . . . Alume is desolate. The great wooden door is smashed. The Green Flame is extinguished.

The names of the castles and artifacts suggest rare achievements and ir-reparable loss, and as these enclaves fall one by one, the last castle becomes supremely important. The title focuses action on this stronghold, Hagedorn, and while the "castle" is a literal one, the word, indeed the very concept of this type of residence, carries overtones of *caste*, suggesting a rigidly classed society that the gentlefolk have chosen to perpetuate on Earth. In Hagedorn, Vance has devised a richly metaphoric name for the edifice that will be the final outpost in the class struggle. A "Hag" in ordinary parlance is an ugly woman often believed to be a witch. This implication that the castle life has a feminine rather than a masculine orientation is broadly ironic, especially in light of the treatment of the wives and Phanes, the latter being gossamer female spirits proudly collected by the "gentlemen." "Hag" may also be a verb, to "chop or hew," suggesting the current use of such a word as "hag-gle." "Dor" is a "trick or deception." The splendor of Hagedorn is thus a deception, nothing but trickery. These associations constitute a jarring note when set longside the more genuine *"hagios"* (meaning "sacred") and the sacred texts *haggada*, which teach the law by parables rather than by the mere listing of prescriptive rules for conduct. Hagedorn's pretenses and trickery fi-nally give way to a parable whose meaning we may take as the central theme of Vance's story.

The balance of power in Hagedorn has been recently tested in the election of a new "first gentleman" of the castle. The most likely contenders for the post, Garr and Claghorn, held strongly opposing points of view and ultimately canceled each other out, leaving the position to the ineffectual O. C. Charle. Garr, a staunch defender of the ruling class (we are told that he "exemplified the traditional virtues of Castle Hagedorn") is effete and overly fond of Phanes. His name stems from the root of "garrulous" — descriptive of one who talks too much, and often about trifles. Claghorn, as "horn" implies, is a strident trumpet warning the complacent rulers. "Clag" is a "clot or clog," a bar to action, yet capable of keeping a wounded man from bleeding to death.

Vance depicts a situation in which the two aristocrats have nullified each other — garrulous, complacent conservatism negating abrasive, liberal sooth-saying. Charle, "a gentleman of no remarkable presence," represents the out-come of the clash. The author perhaps suggests a parallel with leadership in contemporary society. Charle has the indecisive, lukewarm personality of the worst sort of politician, closer in sympathy to Garr than to Claghorn, since it is safer to do nothing than to act to change the *status quo*. The other intermediary between these conflicting views, a character more sympathetic to Claghorn, is Xanten, whose very name begins with a nullifying "X" mark, a person willing to forsake the habits of the past to fight for future survival. He ultimately breaks the deadlock of battle in the Meks's seige of Hagedorn, arriving by Bird to announce simply, "We are fighting." He has summoned his courage as in the heroic resistance of Xanthus in ancient Lycia, and in this case, though the castle culture is destroyed, the human spirit survives.

Xanten is the first man of action in the story. He crosses the lines of stag-nant impasse reached by the Council by moving to reconnoiter the Space Depot and discover whether the Meks have sabotaged the only means of es-cape, the spaceships that could take the humans back to their Home Worlds. Borne aloft by six swift Birds, Xanten is given a strange preview early in the book: "[An] astonishing vision, so simple and yet so grand that he looked around, in all directions, with new eyes. The vision was Earth re-populated with men, the land cultivated, Nomads driven back into the wilderness." Hav-ing begun to act, he is allowed to see a possible alternative outcome for his actions. He is physically and metaphysically relieved to have left the Castle behind and to be *doing* something, and his feelings are described in terms that rebuff Garr as representative of a life "as artificial, extravagant and intricate as life could be." Xanten projects his feelings onto the Birds: "To Xanten's re-lief, their *garr*ulity lessened; silently they flew south. . . ."

At the Space Depot, Xanten finds Meks destroying the equipment, and he orders them to stop and go back to work. Instead of obeying, they attack him, but he coolly fights them off by employing tactics forshadowing those to be applied later to the entire invading Mek force. He traps them inside a building where he is able to overpower them. Xanten's initial actions thus foreshadow the only viable human way out of a doomed system, and he alone of the characters in the castle seems capable of such action. He concludes his investigation by capturing a Mek and discovers that the creature has returned to its natural state. It has no syrup sac and is therefore free from the nutrient system implanted by the humans to control the Mek population.

On his way back to the castle, Xanten continues to explore conditions and alternatives, and the reader is given greater understanding of the situation on Earth. He meets a party of Nomads, wandering survivors of old Earth days, and addresses their Hetman to ask that a party of their men be trained at the castle to fight off the Mek rebellion. The Hetman refuses, with a ferocious grin, and expresses satisfaction that "your beasts have finally risen up to rend you." He considers the castle dwellers to be aliens and invaders, and advises Xanten that if they want to save themselves they should desert the castles and become Nomads.

Next he encounters a semireligious band, the Expiationists, and speaks with a former gentleman among them, Philidor. When Philidor hears that Xanten wants them to form themselves into an army, he rejects the idea as incompatible with his chosen life: "The Meks are here, likewise Peasants and Birds and Phanes, all altered, transported and enslaved for human pleasure. Indeed, it is this fact that occasions our guilt, and for which we must expiate, and now you want us to compound this guilt!" Philidor expresses his moral concerns clearly, just as the Nomads expressed their sense of physical justice. He tells Xanten that he has "chosen a morality which at least allows me calm. I kill — nothing. I destroy — nothing." Xanten and the reader must slowly begin to realize that neither the physical toughness of the surviving Nomads nor the moral commitment of the Expiationists can be rallied to the castle's defense.

Yet, both physically and morally the gentlefolk are inert. Claghorn, who has long urged them to stop depending on outside labor and to return the Meks to their native planet, has always previously been ignored, nor is his advice followed once the rebellion erupts. In complete frustration, Claghorn leaves the castle to join the simpler village life outside. Xanten is the only sensible man left in the castle, and he proceeds to question his captured Mek as the other nobles turn to their vain amusements.

The only event in the novel competing for interest with the Mek attack, and the sole activity that has full approval of the nobility (except for Claghorn and Xanten, who keep no Phanes), is a ceremony called "The Viewing of Antique Tabards." Despite the title, the intricately woven cloaks made by the Phanes are far less noticeable than the Phanes themselves. The occasion is a kind of beauty contest in which each man can parade his prize possession: his Phane. Vance explains that

Possibly half the gentlemen, but less than a quarter of the ladies, kept Phanes. These were creatures native to the caverns of Albireo Seven's moon: a docile race, both playful

and affectionate, which after several thousand years of selective breeding had become
sylphs of piquant beauty. Clad in a delicate gauze which issued from pores behind their
ears, along their upper arms and down their backs, they were the most inoffensive of
creatures, anxious to please, innocently vain.

From the outset we are aware of a feminine rivalry centered on these delicate
creatures, for "rumors sometimes told of ladies drenching an especially hated
Phane in tincture of ammonia, which matted her pelt and destroyed her gauze
forever."

The useless pageant, "never overtly a competition," is an opportunity for
male ego gratification, since "all watching made up their minds as to which
was the most entrancing and graceful of the Phanes, and the repute of the
owner was thereby exalted." It is like Nero fiddling while Rome burns. More
specifically, in this situation it is another example of purposeless degradation
of the individual into a mere possession. It reveals the Hagedorn society as
being clearly dominated by men with male chauvinist values. If a "hag" is a
woman believed to be in league with the devil, Hagedorn itself may be looked
upon as a male establishment that forces its women into the image of its own
vanity — and this is perhaps one appropriate definition of the devil at work,
from Eden to the present day. If these women are in league with the devil, it is
because their men *are* that evil force. Female characters in the book merely
reflect the personalities of their husbands or owners; in this sense they are like
the Meks, but they are Vance's most conspicuous symbol of an intrinsic attitudinal problem within the society.

Claghorn, who kept no Phanes, was also the one who had urged that the
Meks be sent back to Etamin Nine. Since the Meks's slavelike duties and
rust-brown skin might suggest comparison with black minorities, the proposal
to send them home might sound like an argument for shipping the blacks back
to Africa. Vance, by showing the same exploitation in the case of Phanes and
women, broadens the case to reveal a fundamental error of perception. The
ruling class lacks any self-sufficiency whatsoever; it depends for its status, as
well as its food, on the exploitation of other creatures.

The pitiful impotence of the rulers is clearly seen in their penchant for
Phanes. Vance explains that "a gentleman besotted by a Phane was considered
a figure of fun. The Phane, though so carefully bred as to seem a delicate girl,
if used sexually became crumbled and *haggard*, with gauzes drooping and
discolored, and everyone would know that such and such a gentleman had
misused his Phane." The use of "haggard" — echoing the "hag" element in
Hagedorn — is significant. The Phanes epitomize the life of Hagedorn, a
selective refinement beyond purpose. The sexual attraction a man might feel
for a woman is only mockery in the case of Phanes, who become haggard
whenever a natural impulse is followed. They are the very embodiment of a
rarefied, transparent, and useless social fabric. The human women have in the
process been reduced to a single role as well; since they can only be consid-

ered as sexual objects, they respond "by conducting themselves with such extravagant provocation that the Phanes in contrast seemed the most ingenuous and fragile of nature sprites." They have made their women into sexual servants, and once the males are no longer charmed by the beauty of their Phanes, the worn-out sylphs encase themselves in gray gauze and perform menial household chores, serving again as slaves.

The single exception to this bleak feminine helplessness is Glys Meadowsweet, nearly victimized by Garr but fortunately set free. She maintains a relatively independent existence outside the castle, in the village where Claghorn has taken up residence. When Xanten visits Claghorn for advice, he meets the girl. He has been frustrated during his conversation with Claghorn, and complains to Glys that he has not been able to discover the secret of survival under the Mek siege. Her response is surprising: "Glys Meadowsweet laughed — an easy, merry sound, like nothing Xanten had ever heard at Castle Hagedorn. 'Secret? When even I know it?'" She whispers the advice to him, and he replies without recognition of her simple wisdom: "No secret there. Only what the prehistoric Scythians termed *bathos*. Dishonor to the gentlemen"!

Only after Castle Janiel has fallen does Xanten recognize the truth in what Glys has whispered — a truth earlier taught in different ways by the Nomads and Expiationists. He offers the council his understanding: "Now is our last opportunity to escape the great cage that Castle Hagedorn is to become." Indeed, it has long been a cage for many. Vance's point is clearly that in enslaving others one eventually enslaves himself. Xanten has at last come to see this, but the others ignore his advice. He leaves the castle with those who will follow him, but he does not abandon his fellow men. The castle is besieged and about to fall when Xanten returns by Bird to announce that he leads a coalition of men from the castle, Epiationists, and Nomads, and that they have begun attacking the Meks with great success. Joined by some of the last of the castle crowd, including Charle, they entrap the remaining Meks in the castle and eventually force their surrender.

Vance is optimistic about human intelligence and action. Xanten succeeds in crushing the rebellion, and sends the Mek survivors back to their home planet. He marries Glys Meadowsweet and lives in the country near a river, and has two children. In the final pages of the book he and his family return to visit the castle, which has become a museum with Charle as its curator. They find that the elected leader of the gentlemen has aged, and that his face has become thin, "almost waxen," as though he too is a museum piece. He tends the ghosts of the idle past, while the vigorous Xanten asserts, "We are men now, on our own world, as we never were before."

Vance's parable attacks all those who derive their identity and purpose from the labor or virtual slavery of others. He asks us to look honestly at whether we can call our lives our own. To what extent has our dependence upon imported labor, imported goods, and mechanical production with borrowed energy caused us to live lives less than fully human? To what extent are women in our society defined by men whose highest concept of beauty is close to the adorable unreality of the Phanes or the sexual exhibitionism that the nobility have forced upon their women? When he had first heard the "secret" of avoiding death in the last castle, Xanten was prompted to speak of the chores involved in saving his life as a gentleman's descent into *bathos*. This surely is the term that ought to be applied to the so-called "civilization" that the castle society represents, and perhaps also to the social and political posturings of our day. In straining after the sublime, the "gentlemen" have overshot the mark and sunk into the ridiculous. To what extent, Vance asks, has the "civilized" behavior of our time made all our lives *bathetic*, causing us to aspire only to ridiculous mediocrity unredeemed by pity or fear?

THE LENSMAN SERIES

Author: Edward E. Smith (1890-1965)
First book publications: Triplanetary (1950); *First Lensman* (1950); *Galactic Patrol* (1950); *Gray Lensman* (1951); *Second-Stage Lensman* (1953); *Children of the Lens* (1954)
Type of work: Novels
Time: Approximately one thousand years in the future
Locale: Many worlds in the First and Second galaxies

The story of the war between the Galactic Patrol, whose senior members are equipped with "lenses" which give them special powers, and a great conspiracy of the enemies of Civilization

> Principal characters:
> KIMBALL KINNISON, a Lensman and officer in the Galactic Patrol
> CLARRISSA MACDOUGALL, a nurse, later his wife
> VIRGIL SAMMS, the first Lensman
> NELS BERGENHOLM, an eccentric scientist
> WORSEL, a Lensman from Velantia III
> TREGONSEE, a Lensman from Rigel IV
> NADRECK, a Lensman from Palain VII
> MENTOR OF ARISIA, the molder of Civilization
> GHARLANE OF EDDORE, the archenemy of Civilization
> CHRISTOPHER,
> KAREN,
> KATHRYN,
> CAMILLA, and
> CONSTANCE, the children of Kimball and Clarrissa Kinnison

The Lensman series initially consisted of a series of four magazine serials written for *Astounding Stories* (later *Astounding Science Fiction*): *Galactic Patrol* (1937-1938), *Gray Lensman* (1939-1940), *Second-Stage Lensman* (1941-1942), and *Children of the Lens* (1947-1948). When the series was prepared for book publication, however, it was extended "backwards," new material being added to an earlier novel, *Triplanetary* (serialized in *Amazing Stories* in 1934), to build it into the series, and an entirely new novel, *First Lensman*, being written to fill in the gap. *Triplanetary*, *First Lensman*, and *Galactic Patrol* were all first issued in book form in 1950; *Gray Lensman* followed in 1951, *Second-Stage Lensman* in 1953, and *Children of the Lens* in 1954. A series of stories set in the same universe, with several Lensmen as characters, was published in the minor pulps *Comet* and *Astonishing* in 1941-1942 and combined into the book *The Vortex Blaster* (later retitled *Masters of the Vortex*) in 1960. Though not part of the extended series, it has been marketed as such by paperback publishers for commercial reasons related to the spectacular renaissance of interest in Smith's work during the last decade.

Together with the earlier *Skylark* series, the *Lensman* series provides the paradigm for the subspecies of science fiction usually known as "space opera." It is exemplary of a literary strategy which exploits the illusion of plausibility conferred by the use of scientific and pseudoscientific jargon to turn the cosmos into a colossal playground where assorted heroes can do battle on a spectacular scale with entire races of loathsome aliens. Space opera is basically costume-drama of a very simple and elementary kind, but its essential simplicity and repetitiveness are cloaked by a continual escalation of magical superscience. Smith was the first writer to realize and exploit to the full the fact that the pretence of fidelity to known science and future possibility maintained by science fiction was not an imaginative constraint at all, but permitted absolutely anything to happen at the whim and convenience of the author, provided that a suitable jargon of apology was included. This fact, he discovered, made science fiction a much more permissive medium than any species of traditional fantasy (despite its protests to the contrary), and therefore made it the perfect medium for the development of wish-fulfillment fantasies, especially power fantasies.

Smith was an inelegant writer and an unimaginative one, but neither of these failings proved to be the least handicap to him, for the nature of his endeavors made them irrelevant. The raw audacity of his adventure stories gave them the capacity to exercise an almost mesmeric effect over many readers, pandering to one of the most elementary of human needs: the need for compensatory fantasies in which to express impulses that have to be restrained in everyday social intercourse. This aspect of his work gives it a childlike quality, but the appeal of his novels (like the appeal of all effective fantasies) is not so much to the childishness of children but to the child which hides within the adolescent or adult. Real children have no need of the jargon of apology which disguises the true nature of space opera and its kindred subspecies of genre fiction, but it is essential to the strategy of preparing naïve wish-fulfillment fantasies for an older audience.

The story told by the original tetralogy is mainly that of Kimball Kinnison, a young graduate of the Tellurian Academy of the Galactic Patrol. As a member of the Patrol's elite he becomes the proud possessor of a Lens: a crystal which exhibits some of the properties of life and which confers upon its wearer telepathic and other powers (thus acting, among other functions, as a translation device facilitating communication between alien races). Kinnison finds himself thrown into a struggle between the Patrol and the pirates of "Boskone," who have emerged as a serious threat to the emerging galactic civilization. Together with an assortment of alien allies, Kinnison embarks upon a great crusade against Boskone. In *Galactic Patrol*, he penetrates the Grand Base maintained by Boskone's "Director of Operations," Helmuth, and manages to destroy it. In the process he is twice elevated in rank, first becoming a free agent acting under his own initiative rather than under orders from above — a "Gray Lensman" — and later traveling to the world of Arisia, from which the mysterious Lenses come, for special training and advancement to the higher status of Second-Stage Lensman.

All four novels in the tetralogy have the same plot. In each of the last three, Kinnison discovers that the base which he destroyed at the end of the preceding book was merely one stage in a vast hierarchical conspiracy, subject to a higher authority which has to be taken on afresh. In *Gray Lensman* he has to destroy the disgusting alien Eich of the Second Galaxy. In *Second-Stage Lensman* he is pitted against the Thrale-Onlonian Empire. In *Children of the Lens* he and his children go forth to battle the Ploorians; the children then finally penetrate to the *real* heart of the conspiracy, the Eddorians, led by the All-Highest and his minion Gharlane (who, in a variety of guises, has been interfering with human history for a very long time). Eddore is scoured clean of life in the climax of *Children of the Lens*, so that both the First and Second Galaxies can become a suitable home for the Civilization which the Arisians planned millions of years in the past and which the Boskonian conspiracy has tried so desperately to destroy.

In the four magazine serials, this gradual pattern of discovery is shared by Kinnison and the readers, but in the book versions, the new prologue of *Triplanetary* reveals from the very beginning that what is really going on is the culmination of a conflict between Arisia and Eddore that dates back to the days when a temporary merging of the First and Second Galaxies "precipitated" millions of solar systems ready for the evolution of life on a grand scale. Arisia itself existed before this "Coalescence," but Eddore was an invader from another space-time continuum, alien to the entire cosmos. In the same prologue we learn of a longterm program in eugenics established by the Arisians to produce, ultimately, the "children of the lens," who are destined to defeat the diabolical Eddorians and bring about the salvation of Civilization.

Extra scenes written into the later novels in their book versions make sure that this context remains visible to the reader throughout, informing him that what is involved in the various skirmishes between the Galactic Patrol and the pirates of Boskone is no mere game of cops and robbers or petty political dispute, but part of the great war between ultimate Good and ultimate Evil. The series thus becomes a secular myth-system, fully comprehensive in its account of the origins and purpose of man and his universe. The Arisian Mentor who confronts the Lensman demigods at various stages in the drama is an individual containing four separate persons, and the entire world of Arisia undergoes a kind of apotheosis at the end of *Children of the Lens*, leaving the children themselves to be the Guardians of Civilization. This final novel ends with an appeal addressed by Christopher Kinnison to "The Entity Able To Obtain and Read It," in which the series becomes a purposive revelation:

> You have already learned that in ancient time Civilization after Civilization fell before it could rise much above the level of barbarism. You know that we and the previous race of Guardians saw to it that this, OUR Civilization, has not yet fallen. Know, now that the task of your race, so soon to replace us, will be to see to it that it does not fall.

The nature of Smith's basic psychological appeal to his readers is much more clearly revealed by the Lensman series than by the *Skylark* novels, for it was here that he perfected his strategy. The relationship of the children of the Lens (which, in a metaphorical sense, includes all the heroes) to the Arisians is that of child to parent and creation to creator. The Arisians are all-wise, perfectly good, and very powerful, and the heroes are desperate to please them and live up to their expectations. Mentor of Arisia is a father-figure in every sense of the word, and in relation to "him," Kimball Kinnison and his allies are hyper-archetypal children, living in a protected universe whose natural order is a framework of unlimited opportunity and whose moral order is magnificently simple. Its politics are breathtakingly simple: the good guys accept the (literally) paternalistic power structure without question, and the bad guys are annihilated to the last molecule of organic matter. However, as the above account makes clear, there is a sense in which the politics of the galactic civilization in its war against subversion are not politics in the usual sense at all — to treat them as such would be as foolishly absurd as to regard the series as a religious allegory.

The primary function of this kind of fantasy is to provide an escape from reality, and it would be naïve and unreasonable to expect to discover within such a fantasy a mirror-image of the real world or principles of action which might be carried back to the real world. Actually, the violent arena of this kind of fantasy-world probably allows the harmless exorcism of brutal impulses and the safe indulgence of antisocial sentiments. Its distorted world view is supportive rather than subversive.

The *Lensman* series has a special appeal to adolescents embarked upon the long and arduous journey into adulthood because it allows relaxation from the strain of change without its infantile qualities being obvious. In serving this end the series is extremely effective and has genuine merits. Many writers copied, or attempted to copy, Smith, but virtually all of them reproduced the superstructure of his work without the base. John W. Campbell, Jr., Edmond Hamilton, and Jack Williamson all worked within the same area at the same time, but though they had merits of their own, they could not reproduce the essence of Smith's success. Smith's real intellectual heirs are those who forsook the actual props that he used but retained the basic structure of the fantasy — most notably Isaac Asimov in the *Foundation* series and Roger Zelazny in the *Amber* series. Both of these writers were much better prose-mongers than Smith, and both, in their different ways, were far cleverer in designing the apparatus of their fantasy worlds; they have, therefore, appealed to a wider audience. Each of them, however, requires of his readers a level of intellectual sophistication that excludes some potential users of the fantasy who can still be captivated by Doc Smith and Kimball Kinnison.

Criticism:

Ellik, Ron and Bill Evans. *The Universe of E. E. Smith*. Chicago: Advent,
1968. Ellik and Evans give a complete discussion of all of the Lensman and
Skylark novels.

THE LISTENERS

Author: James E. Gunn (1923-   )
First book publication: 1972
Type of work: Novel
Time: 2025-2118
Locale: Puerto Rico

A study of communication between humans and aliens, husbands and wives, fathers and sons, writers and readers, and individuals and themselves

> *Principal characters:*
> ROBERT MACDONALD, the director of The Project
> MARIA MACDONALD, his wife
> ROBERT MACDONALD, JR., their son
> GEORGE THOMAS, writer and public relations chief for The Project
> WILLIAM MITCHELL, a staff member of the public-relations sections
> ANDREW WHITE, President of the United States
> JOHN WHITE, his son
> THE COMPUTER

Within the last few decades there has been a vast amount of speculation as to whether man will ever be able to prove the existence of alien races with civilizations equal to or greater than human civilization. James E. Gunn's *The Listeners* is a fictional history of a project dedicated to finding such evidence. In six chapters, *The Listeners* presents The Project from just before a message is received from Capella, a planet of double stars, to the final message from that same planet ninety-three years later. In tracing the history of the project, the author explores a wide variety of attitudes toward the possibility of communication with aliens, and how that possibility affects communication between the human participants.

In the first chapter, "Robert MacDonald — 2025," the characters' reactions range from the patient confidence of Robert MacDonald, director of The Project, to the panicked fear of scientist Bob Adams, who believes that man may be alone in the Universe and considers such cosmic loneliness as the most frightening possibility of all.

In the fourth chapter, "Andrew White — 2028," the political implications of communicating with the aliens are explored as White, the black President of the United States, fears public reaction to the message that man is not alone. In particular, he fears that a superior alien race might turn communication with Earth to their own advantage.

Finally, in Chapter Six, "The Computer — 2118," the alien view is presented. For a brief moment the people of Capella, now long dead, are allowed to speak to the people of Earth to explain their own need for communication — a need which perhaps aeons from now man himself will have to acknowledge. What the listeners finally learn is that the message is the Capellans' last legacy: when their system could no longer support life, the Capellans themselves were doomed, but their message preserved their history, science, culture, technology, and philosophy.

The protagonist of the novel is Robert MacDonald, who holds The Project together by his genuine ability to listen to others. When the other characters speak to him, he understands the hopes, fears, triumphs, and defeats hidden beneath their statements, as well as the overt meaning of the words. It is this ability that enables MacDonald to hold The Project together during the early years when no message is received, to attract to The Project the right personnel for its future to be assured, and to handle each opponent of The Project.

It is, moreover, his ability to listen that makes Robert MacDonald such a sympathetic character, and makes the reader accept his point of view. If the reader triumphs in the reception of a message from Capella, it is because Robert MacDonald triumphs; if the reader defends the project from the political manipulation of Andrew White, it is because MacDonald does. And, if the reader sees along with Robert MacDonald, Jr., the shade of his father overlooking The Project in 2058, it is because MacDonald, Sr., deserves to know of the fruit of his labor. Gunn has created in MacDonald the perfect listener and the perfect guide. Certainly the Capellans could not have asked for more.

However, there is one situation in which MacDonald does not listen at all well. In the first chapter, he is faced with the growing frustration of his scientists and engineers as they face the fact that during its fifty-year existence, The Project has received no hint of a message, no evidence that the scientists are even on the right track. Thus, MacDonald is first presented in the role he performs best: listening to the problems of his fellow scientists and soothing their frustrations. Yet he fails to see the frustrations building in his wife, Maria, or at least he fails to see how significant they are.

Maria is torn between demanding more attention from MacDonald and keeping her needs bottled up so that he can continue to devote his time and energy to The Project. When she does ask for attention and goes so far as to take too many sleeping pills, MacDonald still does not accept the seriousness of her message and ignores her call for help. Thus, when Maria's frustrations and fears overcome her and she slashes her wrists, MacDonald is consumed with guilt. In the one situation where he has failed to listen, he almost loses the most important person in his life, the person he most needs to keep his own mental balance as he empathizes with all the other workers on The Project. While Maria does not die, the scars that remain on her wrists, which are referred to throughout the balance of the novel, graphically illustrate that even the best listener can fail.

Failure to communicate marks the theme of the second through fifth chapters as well. In each case the outcome is never as serious as in the first chapter, but the problem is evident. In the second and third chapters, "George Thomas — 2027" and "William Mitchell — 2028," the issue is one of communication between men who should be specialists in communicating with their audiences. George Thomas is a successful translator and novelist who is bitter over what he sees as the basic blindness of the human race. His bitterness has turned into a cynicism which prevents him from writing novels, since he distrusts words and sees them only as tools for self-advancement. A public relations specialist, Mitchell ironically has no tolerance for other points of view, and cannot even speak with the father of the girl he loves because the father's beliefs are beyond his patience.

In the fourth and fifth chapters, "Andrew White — 2028" and "Robert MacDonald — 2058," the issue is communication between a parent and child. Andrew White, a former black radical who has become President of the United States, wants his son, John, to understand the past history of the black movement and to distrust the present because of that past. John, on the other hand, wishes to ignore the past and accept the present in its own right. Communication between the two is blocked because neither will accept the other's point of reference. In the fifth chapter, moreover, Robert MacDonald, Jr., has the same sort of problem. Returning to Puerto Rico after the death of his father, he must finally come to terms with his own love and hate for his famous father; blaming him for his mother's loneliness and death, Robert has not communicated with his father for fifteen years.

In each character's life, the message from Capella plays an important role. George Thomas is awed by the urgent need that the Capellans must have felt to devise a system to communicate in the first place. William Mitchell learns that, as significant as the Capellan message is, it can have different meanings for different people. Andrew and John White learn that the significance of communication lies in the future understanding it might make possible, regardless of the different personalities and backgrounds of the individuals involved. And, finally, Robert MacDonald, Jr., learns what a legacy of love his father has left him and what an act of love that legacy is. Robert can come to terms with himself because he ultimately realizes how much his father loved him and how that love is expressed through The Project.

Chapter Six contemplates the idea of communication between humans and aliens. While the humans will receive much from the Capellans, continued communication with them is impossible since Capellan civilization was destroyed long ago. In spite of the final sentence of *The Listeners*, in which the reader is told that the next alien message will come from the Crab Nebula, believed to have been formed by a supernova explosion in the year A.D. 1054, the author's message seems to be that man's most important communication must be with himself.

LITTLE FUZZY

Author: H. Beam Piper (1904-1967)
First book publication: 1962
Type of work: Novel
Time: The future
Locale: Zarathustra Planet

The discovery of a lovable, cuddly creature on a resource-rich planet initiates an understanding both of sapience and humanity

> *Principal characters:*
> JACK HOLLOWAY (PAPPY JACK), a sunstone prospector
> VICTOR GREGO, director of the Zarathustra Company
> LITTLE FUZZY, a native Zarathustran
> MAMMA FUZZY AND BABY FUZZY, Little Fuzzy's immediate family
> BEN RAINSFORD, a Naturalist
> GERD VAN RIEBEEK, a Xeno-naturalist
> RUTH ORTHERIS, a Xeno-psychologist
> LEONARD KELLOGG, Chief of the Division of Scientific Study and Research, Zarathustra Company
> ERNEST MALLIN, a Xeno-psychologist
> GUS BRANNHARD, an Attorney
> LESLIE COOMBS, an Attorney, Zarathustra Company
> FREDERIC PENDARVIS, Chief Justice

When a reader meets a native of the planet Zarathustra, the experience is much like having a teddy bear walk into the living room. No wonder the corporation governing the planet in H. Beam Piper's *Little Fuzzy*, 1962, has such trouble taking the Fuzzies seriously. But Piper's main character, Jack Holloway, takes the Fuzzies very seriously, and his struggle to prove that they are sapient beings becomes the main plot of the novel. Fuzzies prove to be charming creatures, so charming that Piper continued their adventures with Holloway through a second novel, *The Other Human Race* (1964).

The setting and time of *Little Fuzzy* are both somewhat nebulous. Obviously, the time is far in the future because humans have colonized areas beyond our solar system and have met various types of sapient beings in the process. Zarathustra, however, is supposedly a planet without sapient natives, and so a corporation has been granted rights to the raw materials. As part of the novel, Piper shows his views of the American industrial complex extended through time into space, harvesting new planets for the profit of Earth. In his scenes describing the way in which the company has ruthlessly disrupted the planet's natural environment, Piper gives a short but eloquent comment on an industry's attitude toward an ecological balance. The only concern of the Zarathustra Company is profit, a profit derived from the efficient acquisition of natural resources.

One of the major resources of Zarathustra is a gemstone, the sunstone, which glows when warmed by a human body. The novel's hero, Jack Holloway, is a rugged, mature sunstone prospector. In Holloway, Piper has created a character who could be played by the older John Wayne: a loner known for his independence, his maverick ways, his quick draw, and his accurate aim. Though the machinery that Holloway uses in his mining is that of typical science fiction antigravity technology, the guns with which he protects his loved ones are a pistol and a 6 mm. rifle. A seasoned prospector, he puts in a hard day working his own stake and then comes home to his pipe and his evening drink, or two, or three. But he is also a man who appreciates nature, especially the beauty of the sunstones and the harmony of the environment, and he has a high regard for life itself.

To balance Holloway, the natural man, Piper develops the industrial executive Victor Grego, the director of the Zarathustra Company. Though Grego is not exactly a "bad" character, he is presented initially as an antagonistic force: the efficient executive bent on making a profit for both his company and himself. He wants expedient action but prefers to have other people responsible for any "dirty" work which might be involved. While Holloway lives by himself, simply, in a natural setting, Grego lives in an urban world of offices, technology, and cocktail parties. Holloway enjoys having money but only enough to supply his immediate pleasures, which are few, and to assure himself of some future security. Grego, on the other hand, is a character who wants money for the sake of power, as exemplified by the globe of Zarathustra he plays with in his office.

Around these two men Piper groups what will be the opposing forces in a power struggle over control of the planet. The charter held by the Zarathustra Company is valid only if the planet is uninhabited by a native population. When Holloway meets the Fuzzies, he quickly determines that the little furry, golden creatures with big, loving eyes are, indeed, sapient. Their sapience would void the Zarathustra Company's charter automatically, dissolving the company and eliminating Grego's power. The power of various corrupt political characters is also in danger because they are all company men. Thus the antagonistic forces which Holloway and his friends face are political as well as corporate. So the pro-Fuzzy people set out to document proof of the Fuzzies' sapience while the anti-Fuzzy people bring in their own experts to prove that Fuzzies are merely fur-bearing animals, perhaps even a future source of income through the sale of their pelts. The pro-Fuzzy scientists and sympathizers are ethical, careful people, but the anti-Fuzzy scientists are, once again, company controlled people whose ethics are determined by the needs of their employers rather than by a search for truth. Piper uses this group of negative authority figures to exemplify scientists who carry on experiments which will supply supporting evidence for predetermined conclusions. In the process of the two groups' searches for evidence, violence occurs in the form of two murders. The majority of the novel evolves from each group's effort to build its case for the impending murder trials.

The Fuzzies, who are the source of everyone's problems, are carefully introduced by Piper. When Holloway returns home from a hard day at his sunstone mine, he is greeted by a "yeeeek" from his shower stall. Out comes Little Fuzzy, a living teddy bear whose hands have opposing thumbs. Holloway, delighted by his visitor, names him, plays with him, and then discovers that the creatures loves Extee Three (Terran Federation Space Forces Emergency Ration, Extraterrestrial Type) which seems to be the future equivalent of K-rations. Holloway becomes "Pappy Jack" to Little Fuzzy and, eventually, to all of the Fuzzies in Little Fuzzy's family. Holloway first treats his visitor like an intelligent pet, but he quickly discovers that Little Fuzzy is more like a very intelligent human child. To gain some type of authoritative confirmation of the Fuzzies' probable sapience, Holloway calls on his friend Ben Rainsford, a naturalist. Though they can see evidence of intelligent, thoughtful action in the Fuzzies' behavior, they must be able to prove sapience within the standard definition of the Terran courts; the men must show that Fuzzies have a language and can build fires. The Fuzzies are obviously tool-users and conceptual innovators, but they appear to have no language system and seem to have no need for fires.

As the various characters try to work out definitions of sapience useful to their causes, Piper develops several interesting theories. He seems to be exploring not just what it is to be sapient but also what it is to be human. Throughout the novel the various characters exhibit egotistical attitudes toward sapience. One primary intellectual hindrance seems to be appearance (if it doesn't look like me, it can't be sapient), shown by characters who make derogatory references to sapient creatures of nonhumanoid form. The Fuzzies are slightly humanoid with faces which resemble people's faces, but they are diminutive and cuddly, making them hard to accept as potential intellectual equals. Even Holloway has difficulty giving them credit for independent action, but this attitude stems primarily from his paternal concern for them. Piper gives the Fuzzies innocence, if sapience, by crediting them with the intelligence level of an average, inexperienced twelve-year-old child. Little Fuzzy, Mama Fuzzy, Goldilocks, and the rest are all characterized as loving, precocious, childlike beings who are trusting but clever. Sapience appears to be acceptable in nonhumanoid creatures if those creatures have positive characteristics. By the end of the novel, there are more people who want to adopt Fuzzies than there are Fuzzies to satisfy the applicants. Through Holloway's viewpoint, Piper shows the Fuzzies as models of humanity who can remind people of the positive forces in life, the forces of innocence and love. Fuzzies are not aggressive, will not fight, act only out of self-defense, and tend to group in monogamous but extended family relationships. They offer an interesting parallel to Holloway, who is also basically peaceful and loving, but when threatened, he can abandon his innocence and kill in self-defense. Piper's message is a Romantic one, calling for a return to innocence in a rational, peaceloving world.

Piper also shows that one must be sensitive to individual attitudes toward life to understand human beings. By controlling the point of view of his novel, Piper compares and contrasts his characters' attitudes toward life. Rather than use an omniscient unknown narrator and rather than develop the novel exclusively through Holloway's point of view, Piper uses multiple, limited third person points of view. The reader enters the novel in Holloway's world, understanding Zarathustra from the hero's point of view, but then the viewpoint shifts to Grego and to his understanding of the planet. The reader immediately becomes aware of conflicting attitudes, and though Grego is used as a major antagonist in this novel, Piper develops this character quite thoroughly within the passages given in his point of view. Thus Piper has created a character with positive as well as negative attributes so that Grego can become an acceptable protagonistic force in the second novel. Piper develops both protagonists and the antagonists in this manner, affording the reader a complete understanding of both their motivations and their actions. He thus gives many of the characters a depth which eliminates the "black hat/white hat" stereotyping which easily could have resulted within the plot of this novel.

The major portion of the story is told from Holloway's point of view, but Piper also develops the viewpoints of the opposing attorney, the opposing scientists, the trial judge, and the murderer both before and after he acknowledges the sapience of his victim. Even Little Fuzzy provides two passages from his point of view, though Piper postpones these passages until late in the novel. The reader may have accepted the sapience of Fuzzies throughout the majority of the novel, and these passages give proof of their humanness as well. The novel concludes in Little Fuzzy's viewpoint, thus emphasizing the positive attributes of the Fuzzies; they will accept the benevolence of people and in return will give the people love and make them happy.

To facilitate the plot, Piper keeps several characters' viewpoints hidden and, thus, supplies surprises for the reader. He also adds a subplot of a male-female love relationship which suffers several reversals. Though the novel resolves the primary thematic problem by establishing a legally acceptable sapient identity for the Fuzzies, Piper leaves some problems unresolved. The Fuzzies may be sapient, but they have difficulty bearing infants who can survive to maturity. The problems of propagation of the Fuzzy species and establishing a functioning, humane political system on Zarathustra remain for Piper to solve in the second Fuzzy novel.

Little Fuzzy is a novel of action, intrigue, and suspense, but it is also a novel of character. The theme of the Romantic, innocent savage who must be saved from the corruption of a sophisticated civilization is developed within an entertaining story line. Holloway could be a hero out of the American western novel or movie while Grego is definitely an extension of the businessman character from the mid-twentieth century American urban novel. For Piper the possession of conceptual intelligence is not enough to establish humanity in a creature. A human being must also accept the basic values of truth, beauty, and love. When a Fuzzy community plays with shape and colors, its goal is to produce intricate patterns which give aesthetic fulfillment. They do not seek knowledge as a means to a profitable end. They form relationships which are mutually supportive and beneficial rather than seeking manipulative, self-aggrandizing, power-producing associations. As Holloway says when speaking of the wisdom of Fuzzies, "They stick to the important things."

THE LOVERS

Author: Philip José Farmer (1918-   )
First book publication: 1961
Type of work: Novel
Time: 3050
Locale: The Earth and the planet Ozagen

In a future theocratic dictatorship, love for a nonhuman female leads an ordinary man out of his pathological, repressive conditioning and into emotional, intellectual, and sensual freedom

> *Principal characters:*
> HAL YARROW, a linguistics joat (jack-of-all-trades), a misfit, trapped in an unhappy marriage
> MARY YARROW, his wife, tangled in a neurotic love-hate relationship with him
> KEOKI AMIEL PORNSEN, Hal's gapt (Guardian Angel Pro-Tempore — spiritual adviser and watchdog)
> JEANNETTE RASTIGNAC, Hal's Ozagenian lover, a *lalitha*, an intelligent mimetic insect who appears to be a beautiful woman
> FOBO, a wogglebug (Ozagen's dominant species), an empathist, and Hal's friend
> UZZITES, URIELITES, AND LAMECHANS, respectively, the Sturch's police, priesthood, and elite; lamechans wear a gold Hebrew letter L, the *lamech*

The Lovers appeared as a magazine novelette in 1952 and was revised and expanded for book publication in 1961. It was Philip José Farmer's first published science fiction work, and was received enthusiastically by readers; on the basis of this story and perhaps his next two or three ("Sail On! Sail On!," "The Biological Revolt," "Mother"), Farmer won a 1953 Hugo Award for Best New Author. The story was more than an auspicious beginning for Farmer's career; in the folklore of science fiction, it is cited as the story that broke the sex taboo for the genre. To be accurate, this is true only for the magazine-science fiction ghetto, which in 1952 still lived by the boys' fiction standards of the pulps; two notable works of science fiction outside that ghetto, *Brave New World* and *Nineteen Eighty-Four* had already dealt with sex as an integral part of their fictional worlds. In any case, whatever historical significance *The Lovers* possesses, its place as a work of enduring interest in the science fiction field depends not on whether it was the first to treat its themes, but whether that treatment is interesting in itself.

Hal Yarrow lives under the rule of a familiar type of dystopian government, the theocratic Struch (state-church). Organized by Isaac Sigmen out of the chaos following the Apocalyptic War, it is a syncretic religion whose scriptures include a *Pre-Torah*, the *Western Talmud*, the *Revised Scriptures*, Dunne's theories of time, and Sigmen's own accounts of his travel through time. Backing up his farrago of pseudoscience and invented theology is an advanced technology that includes truth drugs, the "Elohimeter" (E-meter), and all the machinery necessary to a police state. In addition to the usual techniques of dictatorship, the Sturch keeps its members under control by means of a pair of complementary pathologies — the repression of normal sexuality and the entertainment of paranoid fantasies. The latter spring from the purported ability of Sigmen, the Forerunner, to travel in time and space in order to secure the "real" future for his followers. (In a sequel, *Timestop!*, it is revealed that the culmination of the Forerunner's work will be a millennial situation in which each of the faithful is given a personal universe to rule as a god.) The Forerunner is opposed by his evil brother, Jude Changer (the Backrunner), and Anna Changer (the Scarlet Woman). The job of the faithful is to avoid "unreality" and to resist the Backrunner's temptations to realize pseudofutures, those not ordained by Sigmen's prophecies.

Being "real" or "shib" (from *shibboleth*) requires increasing degrees of asceticism as one advances in the Struch; for example, Hal is expected to have transcended smoking and other minor unrealities on attaining the status of lamechan. For all members of the Sturch, however, the appetites are curbed. Alcohol is forbidden, eating is done in private, and, most important of all, sexual activity is rigidly controlled. Frequency and even specific details of intercourse are prescribed by the Sturch and the *Western Talmud*; dogma asserts that sexuality is "beastly," something man will evolve beyond. In the meantime, intercourse serves as a means of procreation, nothing more. All this has what must be the intended effect on Hal: with his wife, Mary, he is potent but anesthetized; sex brings anxiety rather than pleasure; he is unfulfilled, restless, and fearful.

Jeannette Rastignac instinctively understands that in turning sexuality inward, the Sturch turns libido into aggression, love into hate. It is not surprising that men and women thus cut from their own gentler emotions should accept the fear- and anger-dominated world view of the Sturch — that all nonbelievers must be enemies, that wogglebugs (neatly shortened to "wogs") or any other nonhuman species can be destroyed to make room for man. It is not only believer against unbeliever or man against wog, but believer against believer. The Sturch is a perfect Orwellian paranoid inferno in which a wife may report the unrealities of her husband (as Mary does) or a supervisor may threaten to let a subordinate go because of a low Morality Rating (M.R.). The institution of the Guardian Angel Pro-Tempore and the pyramidal organization of these informer-advisers is the backbone of the system; no one can escape the attention of the guardians of orthodoxy — except the elite, the lamechans, who are theoretically above suspicion thanks to screening with truth drugs and E-meter processing.

The book is unevenly divided into sections with contrasting settings. The Sturch-run Haijac Union (for Hawaii, Australia, Iceland, Japan, America, and Caucasia) of the first four chapters is not only a fear-saturated dictatorship, it is also overpopulated. North America is almost completely urbanized, its population in the billions. The Yarrows share a tiny apartment with another couple on a schedule of twelve-hour shifts. In this claustrophobic environment, the Sturch still conditions its followers to stricter than Victorian standards of modesty, including even eating masks for those situations where one must eat in the presence of others. By contrast, Ozagen's wogglebugs have attained only an early twentieth century level of technology and population density; their cities are open, with widely spaced buildings; there is still wilderness with dangerous fauna. Wogglebug society encourages the release of tensions in argument, drinking, and even fistfights and has partially institutionalized this attitude in Fobo's profession of empathist. Here are also the *lalitha*, nonhuman but apparently perfect females, suited by evolution for the task of attracting and holding a human mate — the perfect temptation for a repressed Haijac citizen.

The central action of the book can be seen as Hal's movement from Earth to Ozagen, from the tutelage of Pornsen to that of Fobo, and, most important, from his destructive marriage to Mary to his liberating affair with Jeannette. In agreeing to go on the Ozagen expedition, Hal consciously wishes to escape the intolerably crowded and paranoid Haijac Union, the miseries of his marriage, and the unwanted attentions of his lifelong gapt. This in itself, as Pornsen recognizes, is already unshib, unreal behavior, but it is also only a reaction to pressure rather than a positive rebellion. In the less intense atmosphere of Ozagen, Hal moves closer to overt rebellion when he finds himself able to contradict and confound Pornsen in an argument — a small matter. But it is Jeannette who inspires him not only to risk an affair (a crime of lust), but also to outwit the Uzzites and the E-meter in order to gain the status of lamechan (a crime much more serious). The fact that he attains the *lamech* in order to make the affair possible makes the moving force behind his behavior clear.

Once he is committed to Jeannette, Hal's transgressions increase in number if not always in severity: he procures and even drinks alcohol, he abandons the eating mask, he refuses to grow the beard appropriate to a lamechan, and he commits fornication, all for Jeannette. These are, the distorted views of the Sturch notwithstanding, minor matters. Hal still passively cooperates with the expedition's main objective, Project Ozagenocide, a plan to depopulate Ozagen by means of a mutated virus in order to make room for human colonists from the Haijac Union. He tells Jeannette of the scheme and tentatively plans for them to escape the general destruction and live out their lives in the eighty-year period before the Sturch's forces can return with the first colonists. Despite his affection for Fobo, however, he does not tell him of the project, nor does he in any way commit an act of what we would recognize as treason. Instead, he explores and expands his new personal world of heart, body, and mind with Jeannette.

The central event of Hal's personal adventure is the physical consummation of his affair with Jeannette; it signals the breakdown of his Sturch conditioning and the birth of a new self. The bane of his life on Earth was the conflict between conditioned compulsions and repressions (which the Sturch would characterize as "real") and an understandable urge to escape from these restraints and give expression to the drives and appetites of the body (drives that Hal thinks of as his "dark self"). Jeannette senses this division — the Sturch, she says, has made him a half-man — and intuitively understands the political uses of displaced libido — "timid lovers" make for "fierce warriors." Their union will make him whole: "Become a baby again," she tells him. "And I will raise you so you forget your hate and know only love. And become a man." In performing his Sturch-appointed duty with Mary, Hal had felt physically divided — "A zone of unfeeling, a nerve-chilling area, a steel plate cut through him. He felt nothing but the jerkings of his body. . . ." With Jeannette, his sensations are restored to him, and he is at least a whole man in body.

Hal and Jeannette are not the only lovers in the book. Hal's Earth marriage represents a kind of pathological love in which resentment and compulsiveness masquerade as affection. Even more curious is Hal's relationship with Pornsen. Pornsen claims to love Hal, and is required by this love to keep him from unreal behavior — thus the whippings, the lectures, the unfavorable M.R. Love is the exercise of power over another: Pornsen tells Hal, ". . . you have felt my love often . . . ," and Hal glances at the "lover" in question, a seven-lashed whip, its handle ironically in the shape of a *crux ansanta*, the Egyptian symbol of eternal life. This whip sums up the Sturch's idea of love: authority, power, the threat or actuality of pain and humiliation. Nonetheless, Pornsen is not a hypocrite; he believes he loves Hal (as did Mary) and is unaware of the complexity of his own emotions and motives. When in terror and pain, blinded by nightlifer venom, it is in the name of love rather than authority that he appeals to Hal for help.

Fobo never claims to love Hal, but he does unofficially take Pornsen's place as adviser and guide, and he shows a warmth and tolerance that the gapt never could. In the course of their debates over Sturch dogma and policy, Fobo helps to make Hal intellectually whole, as Jeannette helps him to become emotionally and sensually whole. Hal finds that "though he hated Fobo for what he said, he derived a strange satisfaction from the relationship. He could not cut himself off from this being whose tongue flayed him far more painfully than Pornsen's whip ever had." Fobo, of course, is in some sense a professional lover, just as Jeannette is an instinctive lover; as an empathist, it is his function to understand his patients from the inside. This sharing of subjectivities is conspicuously absent in Hal's Sturch-approved relationships with Mary and Pornsen.

The story's unhappy ending, in defiance of most of the conventional wisdom of pulp fiction, is perhaps one of the reasons it was perceived as a taboo-breaker on its first publication. The misunderstandings and well-meaning deceptions that trigger Jeannette's death do give the story an atmosphere of romantic tragedy unusual in science fiction of the period, but, more than that, they confirm the implications about the nature of love that constitute the book's theme. There is an ironic bite in this fantastic *Romeo and Juliet*, pointed up by Hal's exit line: "Jeannette! Jeannette! If you had only loved me enough to tell me. . . ." His love, he seems to say, could have withstood the shock of discovering her true biological nature, if her fear had not exceeded her trust in him. It is Hal, however, who gives her the alcohol substitute — for her own good, he thinks — that robs her of her protection from pregnancy and thus guarantees her death. While he feels himself to be acting out of love, Hal is behaving much as Mary did when she reported him for minor unrealities, or even as Pornsen did when he supressed Hal's petition for divorce. In manipulating and deceiving Jeannette in order to do her the favor of matching his own system of values, Hal repeats in small that perversion of love practiced by the Sturch — the refusal to let the loved one be what it is.

THE MARTIAN CHRONICLES

Author: Ray Bradbury (1920-　)
First book publication: 1950
Type of work: Thematically related short stories
Time: 1999-2026
Locale: The United States, Mars

Twenty-six ironic and yet lyrical "chronicles" dealing with Earth's exploration and colonization of Mars

In *The Martian Chronicles* there is no consistency in characterization or unity of plot. The work is a collection of short stories which is held together by the author's unrelenting ironic tone and his virtual obsession with the interplay between past and future, illusion and reality. The premise upon which the book is built is that Earth's destruction by nuclear war is imminent and that Mars will afford certain lucky colonists a chance to begin anew. Once they begin arriving, however, the Earthmen soon discover that the past and the future are not so easily distinguishable, and that if one is not careful, a second chance can kill.

This is precisely what happens to the members of Captain Black's Third Expedition, who, after having traveled through space on a perilous and exhausting journey, discover a setting that appears to be more Earthlike than Earth. What greets them is a small, early twentieth century Midwestern village, just the kind that Black (and Bradbury) had known as a boy, filled with quaint Victorian houses, colorful geraniums, chestnut trees, even a band playing "Beautiful Ohio." Needless to say, the Captain and his crew are thoroughly bewildered. Expecting to discover some exotic, alien land, they find instead only pieces of their own pasts, pasts made irresistible by the reappearance of members of their own families. After an initial period of skepticism, they succumb to the seductive charms of being allowed another chance at reliving their childhoods. But in doing so they have doomed themselves, for the Martians have tricked them by using their highly developed telepathic imaginations to construct a deadly counterfeit reality. As each of them is securely and snugly locked within his own boyhood home, he is coldly and remorselessly murdered by his own Martian "family."

It is Mars as Earth, as the past, that kills them. This theme, that patterns of behavior learned on Earth are highly destructive when transplanted to Mars, is extended throughout the book. Hauling Oregon lumber through space, for example, as the colonists did in order to build houses for themselves, surpasses mere folly and takes on the character of mass psychosis. By treating the Martians as if they were some ignorant and primitive tribe, the colonists imitate behavior patterns of the Europeans who subjugated Earth in earlier centuries, and thus they destroy an entire civilization. It is here that Bradbury seems to be the most bitter, as he describes the manner in which a gentle and intelligent culture is exploited and then finally obliterated by people like Biggs and Sam Parkhill.

The fact that the colonists from Earth were not able to throw off their most destructive, dysfunctional Earthbound patterns of behavior is seen most clearly in the September, 2005, entry, "The Martian." The protagonist of this story is a young man who has the uncanny ability to take on the characteristics of deceased Earth people. As a Martian he is able to become whoever the colonists want him to be, and as such he is soon transformed into a fragile complex of ever-changing roles by which he is able to fulfill the needs of those around him. Again, then, the visitors from Earth are presented with a second chance on Mars as the young boy becomes several *personae* at once, all of them dead friends and relatives of the colonists.

One such *persona* is "Tom," the son of Mr. and Mrs. LaFarge. The LaFarges are perceptive enough to know that they would be better off if they could let go of the past. " 'We should try and forget him,' " Mrs. LaFarge tells her husband, " 'and everything on Earth.' " This, of course, is just the dilemma that has faced the colonists from the beginning: forget the past or be continually tortured by it. Yet, typically, the LaFarges cannot forget. They treat the Martian as if he *were* Tom, despite the fact that all he really wants is to be accepted as he himself is — a unique "Martian" who in his own way is as much in need of love as they are. But the LaFarges and their fellow colonists, in their inability to rise above a necrophilic attachment to their own pasts, tear him apart, along with any hopes they might have held for a future of peace and happiness. Thus Tom is destroyed for the same reasons that all of Martian culture was destroyed, because of the greed and shortsightedness of those who received a second chance for life and growth.

In time Mars becomes a veritable "tomb planet" populated only by such odd solipsists as Walter Gripp and Hathaway, a dying remnant from the Fourth Expedition, who lives in his stone hut with the robots who attend him as the perfect replicas of his family on Earth. Here at last is a second chance that seems to work, albeit in a morbid, melancholic fashion. But Bradbury does not end the book on this note of bitterness and despair. There is, in the final chronicle, a hope for an integration of the old Earth with the new Mars. The Thomas family, soon to be joined by a handful of like-minded people, has arrived on Mars just before Earth reaches its final destruction. As former Governor Thomas burns some official state papers in a purifying bonfire, he speaks for this final group of colonists. " 'Life on Earth,' " he says, " 'never settled down to doing anything very good. Science ran too far ahead of us too quickly, and the people got lost in a mechanical wilderness, like children making over pretty things, gadgets, helicopters, rockets; emphasizing machines instead of how to run the machines.' " Clearly, this is the author speaking. This is the voice of the Bradbury of *Fahrenheit 451* and "Rocket Man" and "The Veldt," the Bradbury who often decried the blind mechanization and totalitarianization of modern life, and who, even in his calmer, less fretful moments, still felt a great ambivalence about the road postwar America seemed to be taking towards technological complexity and away from the freedom and sanctity of the individual.

A second, closely related theme that serves to unify the various stories in the book is the relationship between illusion (or fantasy, or insanity) and reality. Bradbury begins to develop this theme with the coming of the First Expedition in February, 1999. After having left Earth in a blast from a rocket that temporarily turned an Ohio winter into spring, Captain York and the members of his crew arrived upon Mars only to be killed as innocent, unknowing recipients of a husband's jealousy. In a dream York had come to Ylla, an obscure Martian woman. He had flirted with her, told her that she was beautiful, and then asked her to come away with him. As soon as he and his men land, they are done away with, not only because they are seen as dangerous invaders from another planet, but also because Ylla's husband is not able to control his feelings of jealousy. The First Expedition therefore comes to its ignoble end in an ironic and, from the Earthmen's point of view, wholly denigrating air of unreality.

The members of the Second Expedition also find themselves caught in a perplexing web of fantasy and madness. Again, Bradbury's use of irony is immensely effective. Expecting a heroes' welcome, Captain Williams and his crew are instead immediately discounted by the Martians as being nothing more than paranoid projections. Rather than being treated as warriors and explorers from another planet, they are hustled off to an insane asylum where they are locked up with Martians who demonstrate their insanity by telepathically projecting their fantasies outward until they take the form of objective reality. As a consequence, what is real to the Earthmen (the fact that they are actually from Earth) is treated as if it were illusionary madness by the Martians. This, of course, is the exact reverse of the situation in which the Third Expedition will find itself, for there the Martians will be the ones in touch with reality, and it will be they who self-consciously manufacture illusions as a means of defending themselves against the encroachments of a culture that is, as far as technological development is concerned, more highly advanced.

As the book progresses, Bradbury drops the more deadly aspects of this theme and concentrates instead on its subtler, more melancholic dimensions. Perhaps its fullest development is achieved in the section called "August 2002: Night Meeting." Here, an obtuse Earthman by the name of Tomás Gomez happens to meet Muhe Ca, a Martian who, despite having melted gold for eyes, sees no better than he does. In the dark Martian night, deep within the barren Martian desert, illusion and reality meet once again. This time, however, it is a standoff. Neither Tomás nor the Martian can accept the existence of the other. First one, then the other, accuses his opposite of being an insubstantial figment of his own imagination, a mere hallucination. Again there is no coexistence, as each claims that the other is a phantasmagoric relic from the past, a ghost having no substance and no significance. It is a fruitless and frustrating study in solipsism, for neither of them is able to reach out to acknowledge the dual realities of Earth and Mars. As Tomás puts it, " 'If *I* am real, then *you* must be dead.' "

Certainly, this is Bradbury at his most bitter; again and again he gives his characters another chance, and yet again and again they fail to take advantage of it, slipping back repeatedly into hopelessness and despair. They remain this way not simply because they are stupid and small, but because they are selfish. Nowhere is this made more apparent than in the December, 2005 entry, "The Silent Towns." After an eternity of believing that he is the last man on Mars, Walter Gripp gets a phone call from a woman named Genevieve Selsor. But when, after much difficulty, they finally get together, and Genevieve does not meet his preconceived fantasies of what a woman should look like, Walter unceremoniously dumps her, preferring to spend his remaining years alone rather than accepting her as she is, in all her human imperfection. It is an ironic twist on the familiar last man motif. Here is a last man who chooses to remain within his own lonely and illusion-ridden solipsism rather than reach out to embrace a present reality that might make demands upon him to change and to accept another existence besides his own.

Like this last story, Bradbury's *The Martian Chronicles* as a whole is a bleak and despairing book, filled with stories of absurd death, of genocide, and of self-serving and self-defeating narcissism. However, one may look to the book's final entry for some glimmer of hope. For even though the Thomas family can find only their own reflections staring back at them from the canal as they look about them for signs of life on Mars, at least they, of all the book's characters, must realize that Earth, and the past that it represents, has died, and that they, finally, are the Martians.

Criticism:

Forrester, Kent. "The Dangers of Being Earnest: Ray Bradbury and *The Martian Chronicles*," in *Journal of General Education*. XXVIII (1976), pp. 50-54. Forrester gives a concise analysis of Bradbury's *The Martian Chronicles*. He finds, however, that Bradbury is vulnerable as a science fiction writer.

Scholes, Robert and Eric S. Rabkin. *Science Fiction*. New York: Oxford University Press, 1977, pp. 65 and 118-119. Scholes discusses *The Martian Chronicles* in depth, comparing Bradbury's prose to Sturgeon's.

Stupple, James. "The Past, The Future and Ray Bradbury," in *Voices for the Future*. Edited by Thomas D. Clareson. Bowling Green, Ohio: Bowling

Green University Popular Press, 1976, pp. 175-178. Stupple offers a discussion of Bradbury's use of the theme of the past and future in his novels.

MARTIAN TIME SLIP

Author: Philip K. Dick (1928-   )
First book publication: 1964
Type of work: Novel
Time: 1994
Locale: Mars

An autistic ten-year-old boy who can see and travel through time becomes the focus of land speculation on an Australialike colonial Mars

> *Principal characters:*
> JACK BOHLEN, a repairman and borderline schizophrenic
> SILVIA BOHLEN, his wife
> LEO BOHLEN, Jack's father, a land speculator from Earth
> ARNIE KOTT, the head of the Water Worker's Local, Fourth Planet Branch
> MANFRED STEINER, an autistic, time binding ten-year-old
> NORBERT STEINER, his father, a neighbor of the Bohlens, and a black marketeer
> OTTO ZITTE, his employee and pretender and heir to his black market business
> HELIOGABALUS, Arnie's tame Bleekman
> DOREEN ANDERTON, the Union treasurer, Arnie's mistress, and Jack's lover

By 1994 Mars, explored and colonized from Earth in the 1970's and early 1980's, is a neglected frontier. Because of difficult conditions and lack of material and moral support from home, immigration has been virtually non-existent for a decade, leaving the population thinly scattered in towns and suburbs across the web of the partially operative old canal system. Mars has too much sand and not enough water; the only settlement that really prospers is New Israel, but Mars is more like Australia than Palestine, supporting (after a fashion) a race of neoaboriginal Bleekmen and a species of kangaroo-sized boxing bugs resembling the praying mantis. But schizophrenia, not the problems of frontier life on another planet, is the thematic focus of the novel from the very first sentence. The disease is endemic in the 1990's, reflecting, as the story makes clear, society's inability to prepare its members to cope with the realities of their existence. To put it another way, "the reality which the schizophrenic fell away from — or never incorporated in the first place — was the reality of interpersonal living, of life in a given culture with given values." The "given culture" in this case is one not unlike ours. There and then, as here and now, sex and death, greed and human kindness, are the substance of social life. The main plot focuses on land speculation, minor ones on competition in the black market and the bedroom.

In a sense all the characters in the book, with the exception of the Bleekmen and (perhaps) the teaching robots, are affected by the schizophrenic process. The first character to break down is Norbert Steiner, a black marketeer, who, after visiting his autistic son Manfred in the camp for anomalous children, runs deliberately into the path of a tractor bus. It is particularly appropriate, in light of the symbolic function of machines in this story, that Steiner, a self-confessed mechanical incompetent, should choose a machine as the vehicle of his death.

Norbert's son Manfred is the consummate schizophrenic in the book. At ten years of age he is totally incapable of social intercourse. His madness is apparently either the cause or the result of his ability to see the future, to see himself in old age, kept alive in a decaying nursing home (which at the time the story takes place has yet to be built), an object not a person, with most of his organs replaced by machines. Manfred's combined personal and public entropic vision casts mere social existence, including language, into an impossible perspective until he meets Bleekmen.

But Manfred's madness, involving both precognition and the ability to travel in and otherwise manipulate time itself, is more symbolic than realistic. He is not exactly Everyman, but his eventual acquisition of speech is symbolic of the compromise we all make, consciously or unconsciously, with the knowledge that we shall die some day.

If Manfred sees his own future as a machine however, the "second-best" schizophrenic in the book, the repairman Jack Bohlen, has visions of *others* as machines, mechanically lifeless. His first "episode" had occurred on Earth before he emigrated in (approximately) 1984. For fourteen months he had tried to get an apartment in a huge new co-op building, a kind of condominium enormous enough to support its own shopping center, but when he did it was a disaster for him. He began to feel that his life no longer had a purpose, that the future had ceased to exist. However trivial, the apartment had given him a socially acceptable direction; without it he wandered about aimlessly, lost track of time, forgot to cash his paychecks, and, when called into the office where he worked, he had a vision of the personnel manager as a lifeless thing, a robot whose organs had been replaced by plastic and stainless steel.

This same sequence of material success followed by a vision of a human machine is repeated later. After Jack gets on Arnie Kott's payroll (a step up for him), he sees the psychiatrist Dr. Glaub "under the aspect of eternity." The "truth" of Jack's vision is to suggest the mechanical nature of life lived according to the materialistic values of this (our) culture. This point becomes symbolically clear when Jack visits "the great self-winding entity of their lives, the unique artificial organism that was their public school" (run by the United Nations) and encounters his son's teachers, robots with the names and "personalities" of various human types (Kindly Dad, Angry Janitor) and historical figures (Thomas Edison, Jack's favorite, and Caligula) and whose function is, of course, to reproduce the culture that has been programed into them.

Jack is the most sympathetic character in the story, the one about whose fate we care the most; but he is not the center of the plot. After all, he survives. It is his counterpart among the politically powerful, Arnie Kott, who is most completely destroyed by the direct and indirect effects of the schizophrenic process. As the story opens, Arnie has recently inveigled his way into leadership of the Water Workers' Local, Fourth Planet Branch, clearly an important position in a water based economy. Exactly as Jack after getting an apartment in the co-op, Arnie needs new worlds to conquer. His major schemes involve an attempt to replace Norbert Steiner in the black market food business and an attempt to find out what is going on in the F.D.R. Range in time to profit by it. In the first project his motivation is primarily personal — he has been one of Steiner's best customers, and depends on amenities from home to entertain his mistresses. He sets up his own business, but then discovers that he has a competitor (Steiner's repairman, Otto Zitte who, as part of the inbreeding of personal relationships on Mars, seduces Jack's wife Silvia). When Arnie destroys Otto's landing field with a small nuclear bomb, he provokes, as it happens, his own murder, leading Jack (who knows the man if not the facts) to say that Arnie "at last, had brought about his own death; he engineered it somewhere along the pathway of his life."

Though the black market scheme (like Steiner's tractor bus) kills him, Arnie's main efforts have been directed elsewhere, in a direction more significant for Mars and, had he lived, for himself as well. The United Nations and the co-op movement are about to build AM-WEB in the F.D.R. Range, a huge new project that will revitalize colonization and utterly change the (human) face of Mars. AM-WEB will not prosper — in its ruins Manfred will lie in a nursing home — but meanwhile it will have an enormous effect on property values. Although he does not know it, this project will change the balance of power on Mars so utterly that Arnie will be once again unimportant, which is one explanation for Jack's perception that Arnie "has brought about his own death," after failing to get a piece of the AM-WEB action. Meanwhile, in his attempts to do just that, Arnie takes the curious route of employing Jack to build a machine (of all things) to make possible communication with Manfred in case he does actually see the future. The machine does not work; Jack's father Leo, a land speculator from Earth with an inside tip, lays claim to the appropriate land; and Arnie, through the mediation of his "tame" Bleekman, Heliogabalus, to whom Manfred's thoughts are "as clear as plastic," tries an even more desperate maneuver. He takes Manfred to the Bleekie holy place in the F.D.R. Range, Dirty Knobby, where they both go into a trance designed to send Arnie back into the past to beat Leo to the claims office. Although it at least appears to Arnie that he does enter the past, all he experiences are symptoms of schizophrenia and an inability to do what he wants.

In these operations Arnie is a bit like Faust. Though Leo has inside information, he at least operates within the acceptable rules of the game (which Jack condemns). Arnie's attempt to pass through schizophrenia, even someone else's, places him outside himself in a way which suggests magic in Manfred's powers, the use of Dirty Knobby, and the drunken Bleekie priest (who, ironically, demands payment). We can see Arnie's Faustianism in two ways: first, as a desperate attempt to maintain his position in society; and second, as a sign of schizophrenic withdrawal, a loss of contact with reality engendered by his recent successful rise to the head of the Water Workers' Local. In any case, he returns from (his schizophrenic vision of) the past and believes that he is still in a trance when Otto shoots him. He dies believing he is still alive.

Commodity culture and schizophrenia blur the distinction between life and death, the first by externalizing human purpose in materialistic goals — an apartment, land, power, a mistress — the second by cutting the subject off from the outside world and "the warmhearted people there." Commodity culture is schizophrenogenic, giving its subjects materialistic goals and then either preventing their achievement or disappointing them with success. In commodity culture success and failure are equally fatal. The truth of this in Dick's universe is seen in the counter example of the Bleekmen. On the one hand, they are a Stone Age culture, living off the land, "owning" nothing but the absolute essentials: bows and arrows, paka shells for carrying water, pounding blocks for grinding meat or grain, an animal skin each for clothing. This is a life they have in some way chosen, for, as Jack reminds us, their ancestors built the great canal system, but they have forgotten even how to throw pots. They have no purpose as we know it, and as a result, perhaps no sense of time.

In any case, they can see ahead like Manfred, and read thoughts, but it does not terrify them. Theirs is a kind of Zen-consciousness. As Helio says,

> Purpose of life is unknown. . . . Who can say if perhaps the schizophrenics are not correct? Mister, they take a brave journey. They turn away from mere things, which one may handle and turn to practical use; they turn inward to *meaning*.

Manfred's happy ending is to join the Bleekmen, a culture that does not bind him to materialistic goals and to time.

It is in the light of the Bleekie solution that we can understand the ending of the book. Jack and Silva cannot, of course, follow the Bleekmen into the desert — if they did they would be no examples for us — but Jack can readjust his goals to make his life somewhat livable. He has a final schizophrenic attack when he cannot reconcile his ambition — to remain in Arnie's employ — and stay with the mistress he has acquired from Arnie — with his familial ties. The crisis arises when he discovers his father Leo's interest to be the same as Arnie's; the effect of his breakdown is to keep the knowledge of AM-WEB and its location from Arnie until after Leo has filed his claim. After Arnie's death, which is an indirect consequence of Jack's crisis, Jack and Doreen, his mistress, separate, and Jack goes home to Silvia with two truths: that the difference between Manfred's world and everyone else's is mainly a matter of degree, and that "A person can always find two places to choose from. Home, and the rest of the world with all the other people in it." In the final scene, Jack and Leo set out with flashlights to hunt for Erna Steiner (who has been frightened by the reappearance of her son Manfred, returned from the future with his mechanical body) and see if she is all right. Here is a kind of goal that depends, not on things, but on human feeling — to take care of one another.

The message of the book seems to be to stay small, to help one's neighbors if one can while maintaining a low profile in the world at large. Arnie, Otto, and Jack all suffer from being too ambitious and, according to Manfred's vision, so does the United Nations in its abortive AM-WEB project. There is neither fundamental despair here, nor the escapism of a "separate peace," but a return to the local social group as a way of remaining human — to escape becoming either a machine or a schizophrenic. In this way the family operates to mediate between the absolutely personal, schizophrenia, and the absolutely social, the vision of citizens as machines.

Criticism:

Aldiss, Brian W. "Dick's Maledictory Web: About and Around *Martian Time Slip*," in *Science-Fiction Studies*. II (1975), pp. 42-47. Aldiss reveals the inner workings of the plot.

Gillespie, Bruce. *Philip K. Dick: Electric Shepherd*. Melbourne, Australia: Nostrilla, 1975, Gillespie reviews the events in *Martian Time Slip*.

MARTIANS, GO HOME

Author: Fredric Brown (1906-1972)
First book publication: 1955
Type of work: Novel
Time: 1964
Locale: The Earth, mostly Southern California

A satiric fantasy of humanity beseiged by insubstantial but foul-mouthed Martians who allow no one a moment of privacy or a shred of secrecy

> *Principal characters:*
> LUKE DEVEREAUX, a thirty-seven-year-old science fiction writer
> MARGIE DEVEREAUX, his estranged wife, a psychiatric nurse
> CARTER BENSON, his friend, another writer
> DR. ELLICOTT H. SNYDER, a psychiatrist
> YATO ISHURTI, Secretary-General of the United Nations
> HIRAM PEDRO OBERDORFFER, an inventor
> BUGASSI, the witch doctor of an African tribe

Luke Devereaux, a science fiction writer going through a writer's block, borrows his friend Carter Benson's cabin in the desert outside Los Angeles to help him get started on a novel. The night the Martians come, he is working on his third drink and beginning to get an idea for a new science fiction novel: what if the Martians. . . . He is interrupted by a little green man who claims to be a Martian and spews forth a stream of abusive, rather Runyonesque English, addressing Luke as "Mack." The Martian taunts and insults the disbelieving Luke until, after downing another three or four drinks in rapid succession, the writer passes out on his bed.

When he awakens the next day, the Martian is gone from the cabin, but Luke discovers it sitting on the radiator of his car, abusive as ever. Hallucination or not, Luke cannot see through the creature, so he drives to the diner down the highway with his head sticking out the window to see around the Martian, who refuses to get off the hood. The Martian follows Luke into the diner. The counterman groans. "Oh, God, another one of 'em."

Luke's Martian is one of a billion rude, sharp-tongued little creatures that have appeared all over the Earth at exactly the same time. They are about two and a half feet tall, with large spherical hairless heads and spindly arms and legs and emerald green skin. They are bent on antagonizing every human being with whom they come in contact. Since there is one Martian for every three people on earth, they contact almost everybody; and since they can see in the dark and see through solid objects, read letters and papers in closed boxes and locked safes, they have plenty of material to be insulting about.

All privacy or secrecy ends. The Martians are interested in everything, they love to tell secrets. There are no longer any military secrets, top or otherwise. On a much smaller scale, the arrival of the Martians makes poker impossible: one cannot have a poker game if everyone knows everyone else's hand and if there is a Martian present calling out the cards before they are dealt. Even the world's most popular indoor sport is no longer a game for the sensitive to play. Most couples start using ear plugs and keeping their bedrooms and other places of assignation dark, so that even though the Martians can see *them*, they do not have to see the Martians, or hear their ribald commentary.

No one knows very much about the Martians — their sex or lack of it, what they eat, where they sleep, or whether they are physically present on earth or simply projecting a mental picture. No one is even sure they are Martians. The Martians do not volunteer much information; they claim they "kwimmed" to Earth from Mars, and that they are much more intelligent than human beings. They can be photographed and their voices recorded on tape, but they do not show up on radar. Their bodies are insubstantial but opaque. A large number of accidental injuries and deaths are caused by people trying to attack Martians physicially — at first, because people did not know that Martians are invulnerable, and later, because they are too frustrated to care.

The economic effect of the Martians' arrival is enormous and depressing. A drastic cut in defense spending leads to increased unemployment. The stock market falls, and the bottom drops out of the entertainment business, because Martians interfere with actors and announcers, baiting and mocking them on the air. Crime, especially planned crime, occurs less frequently because the Martians tell tales. (Not that they are opposed to crime — they just love to make trouble.) The emotional stress that the Martians cause, however, leads to increased crimes of passion and violence.

In Long Beach, unable to find any kind of writing job, Luke Devereaux is running out of cash. For seven weeks, he has been trying to get a job. He has wanted desperately to call Margie, his ex-wife (or almost ex-wife: he wasn't quite sure), but his pride prevents him as long as she has a job and he does not. Down to his last six dollars, Luke runs into Carter Benson, who has a check for Luke from his publisher, an advance on the reissue of a Western novel that Luke wrote twelve or fifteen years earlier. The publisher says that mysteries and Westerns are in great demand, and sends Luke a thousand-dollar advance on another Western.

Luke's writing block is dispelled; he dashes home to his typewriter, ideas coming thick and fast. He has half a sentence on paper when a Martian appears astride his typewriter carriage, yelling "Whoopie! Faster, Mack, faster!" Luke screams and tries to throw himself out the window, but he lands on the fire escape. His landlady calls a doctor, who contacts Margie. Wary of Luke, but obviously still in love, Margie arranges for him to be sent to a private sanitarium.

When Luke recovers consciousness, he can no longer see the Martians, and regards them as having been a temporary hallucination. Deaf and blind to Martians, he works eight to ten hours a day on his Western novel. This places his psychiatrist, Dr. Synder, and Margie in a quandary. Should they try to cure him, thus rendering him susceptible to harassment by the Martians, or should they leave him insane but productive?

Luke finishes the book, which promises to be a best seller. He resumes married life with Margie in the sanitarium, and she calls off the divorce suit. He accepts the fact that other people still see Martians — or that they think they see them. Dr. Snyder recommends keeping Luke in the sanitarium, in case he should come to disbelieve not only in Martians, but also in other human beings. Since Luke thinks that the Martians were a figment of his imagination, he might come to believe that he has invented the rest of the world, too.

Once Luke finishes his novel, he suddenly has time to think about the Martians. He is certain that he is sane and that Martians are nonexistent. Does this mean that everyone else in the world is crazy? What if he did invent the Martians? He had been working on a plot about Martians the night they arrived. What if he only imagines his entire universe? And what if, while inventing a science fiction plot, a small fiction within his larger fictional universe, he has accidentally crossed wires and made the Martians part of the large universe?

Luke decides that the solution is to relay the message that Martians do not exist to his unconscious mind; then they will vanish for everyone else, too. He decides he will have to go back to the shack in the desert, and he escapes from the sanitarium immediately.

The same day, Yato Ishurti, the Secretary General of the United Nations, delivers a radio speech to the world and to the Martians in which he proposes a plan. Ishurti reasons that the Martians are on Earth either to unite men in a common cause or to prevent humans from landing on Mars. He asks that all people on Earth pledge no longer to fight among themselves and to promise that they will never send a spaceship to Mars. A deafening roar of agreement breaks forth from the people of Earth. The Martians, however, do not leave, and Ishurti commits ritual suicide.

Several weeks later, on August 19, other programs to rid the world of Martians come to a head. In Chicago, a janitor and amateur inventor named Hiram Pedro Oberdorffer is completing a contraption he calls an antiextraterrestrial subatomic supervibrator. He waits for it to build up potential. It is 11:05 P.M., Chicago time. That afternoon, Margie Devereaux, who has been looking for Luke for two weeks, figures out that he must be at Carter Benson's shack, and leaves for the desert.

At about the same time, an African witch doctor named Bugassi prepares a juju against the Martians, who have spoiled his tribe's hunting and left them on the verge of starvation. It is a juju to end all jujus; he finishes just before dawn. When the sun strikes the juju, says Bugassi, the Martians will leave. At that exact moment, Hiram Pedro Oberdorffer sits sipping beer and waiting for his subatomic supervibrator to build up potential.

Less than an hour before, in a shack in the desert, Luke had made his third drink. It was the fourteenth evening he had spent at the shack trying to get the upper hand on his subconscious. The problem, he thinks, is that he lacks faith in himself. Maybe if he imagined something completely different and brought that into existence, then his subconscious could not deny that he had invented the universe. So he imagines Margie driving through the desert. Pretty soon he hears her car. When she gets out, he concentrates on the thought, *There aren't any Martians*. It is approximately 9:05 P.M., Pacific Time. Meanwhile, in Chicago, Mr. Oberdorffer sips beer and waits for his supervibrator to build up potential, and in Africa, Bugassi waits for the sun's first rays to strike the greatest juju ever made.

Four minutes later, the Martians disappear simultaneously from everywhere on earth. To this day, no one knows why they left, but a great many people have strong opinions on the subject. Millions still believe that they were devils and went back to hell. Even more millions believe that they were Martians who went back to Mars because of Yato Ishurti's speech. No standing armies have been built up, and no country is planning to send rockets to Mars, just in case. An African tribe knows that Bugassi's juju made the Martians leave. A janitor in Chicago knows that he did it himself with his subatomic supervibrator. And, of course, Luke knows he did it.

Luke is now a very successful writer with a happy marriage and twin sons; he is satisfied with the universe as he imagines it now. On one point, at least, everyone agrees: nobody misses the Martians at all.

In a postscript, Fredric Brown addresses the problem of who is right: who really made the Martians leave? Brown explains that "Luke is right, the universe and all therein exists only in his imagination. . . . But then, I invented Luke. So where does that leave him *or* the Martians? Or any of the rest of you?"

This light fantasy satirizes the classic science fiction cliché of the hostile alien invasion. It presents the stereotypal little-green-men Martians as hostile visitors, but it makes their hostility purely verbal — the Martians do not attack people physically. Since most hostility in the world actually is verbal, and physical violence is usually a last resort, the concept provides a solid satiric base for viewing human beings and their foibles.

MEMOIRS FOUND IN A BATHTUB
(PAMIETNIK ZNALEZIONY W WANNIE)

Author: Stanislaw Lem (1921-   )
First book publication: 1961
English translation: 1973
Type of work: Novel
Time: The fourth millennium A.D., with flashbacks to the near future
Locale: The Rocky Mountains, the United States

A satire applicable to several targets, caricaturing blind devotees of nonfunctional social systems, surveillance-happy militarists, and fumbling bureaucrats

Principal characters:
> THE NARRATOR
> GENERAL KASHENBLADE, the Commander in Chief
> UNDEREAVESDROPPER BLASSENKASH
> MAJOR ERMS, a Third Pentagon functionary
> CAPTAIN PRANDTL, Department of Codes
> ANTHEUS KAPPRIL, Custodian Ninth Degree
> "THE ADMIRAL," active in Degradation proceedings
> PROFESSOR DOLT, an authority on blackmail and treason
> PROFESSOR DELUGE, cabalist and collaborationist
> FATHER ORFINI, co-conspirator with The Narrator

The preface to this narrative tells how, in the fourth millennium A.D., archaeologists excavated the "Third Pentagon," last of the redoubts of American capitalism. This had been a huge underground headquarters, well-camouflaged and supplied with such great reserves of food, water, and compressed air that it could be cut off completely and prolongedly from the outside world. Faced with a massive defection or revolution of the American people, the masters of the Pentagon did isolate the "Building," as it is usually called in the narrative. After seventy-two years of this isolation, molten lava filled the Building and preserved its contents for the future archaeologists. Meanwhile, on the Earth's surface, a mysterious catalyst from Uranus had destroyed all paper, a substance which Lem describes wryly as regulating all human activities and determining the fates of individuals. The loss of all paper, books, and documents disorganized civilization severely for some time and deprived mankind of most of its historical records. Thus the discovery of a journal preserved by the lava in a bathroom of the Third Pentagon provided a precious, though often puzzling, acquisition for the future historians.

The skeletons of the Narrator and of Father Orfini, a denizen of the Building in whom he undertook to confide, were found with the journal, and in this document we read of the misadventures suffered during the Building's period of isolation, when the Narrator somehow entered it. His itinerary through its myriad offices becomes a saga of confusion, absurdity, and despair, a tour of a bureaucratic Inferno reminiscent of Dante's *Divine Comedy*.

The besetting sins and suffering of the Building's people derive from their persistence in carrying on the routines of military planning, intelligence gathering, and surveillance, even though their isolation makes it all vain and artificial. Deprived of external targets for their operations, the people of the Building have internalized their espionage. This internalization resembles the historical phenomenon of imperialist nations which, when they are no longer achieving imperialism abroad, turn it against their own citizens in the form of authoritarian government. The situation in the Building also reflects the readiness of most bureaucracies to invent functions, to continue activity when their original, valid functions have ceased to exist.

A thriving bureaucracy needs an adversary, so that dangers or emergencies may stimulate its work. Accordingly, the Building has invented the *Antibuilding*, the supposed headquarters of its enemies, and from it the Building is allegedly infiltrated by hostile agents. Some people say that the Antibuilding is completely infiltrated and controlled by the Building's operatives, and there is also the horrid suspicion that the agents of the Antibuilding have taken control in the Building itself.

The denizens of the Third Pentagon have learned to eavesdrop on one another. They produce double agents, triple agents, codes of all sorts, intricate systems of security and counter-espionage. Their surveillance devices include polygraph mittens, which check the truthfulness of the wearers, and microphones in pillows, to catch the words of persons who talk in their sleep. All drainpipes are monitored and all sewage is filtered. Uncertainty reigns: Who works for whom? There are many alternate codes and plans, and nobody knows which of these, if any, are valid.

The characters of this book, as may be gathered from their names and titles, serve to describe the organizational flavor and bureaucratic morass which characterizes the story. The characters are not developed as individuals; they have no depth. Even the Narrator himself is nameless, and we know him only as a pitiable human being who is caught in the maze of the Third Pentagon. He tries to make sense of that organization, but there is no sense to be found. He is assigned a mission by General Kashenblade but cannot clarify it. His movements are watched, and meticulous reports thereof are prepared and duly filed. *Agents provocateurs* seem to be drawing him out, and various tests of his loyalty are devised. He wishes to distinguish reality from absurdity but cannot. Many escorts or guides present themselves to him, but upon none of them can he rely. Father Orfini, the last and most promising of these, has become a suicide at the story's end, and the Narrator has followed him into voluntary death.

Lem appears to apply his bitter satire to all the militarists, bureaucrats, surveillance artists, and secret police oppressors of our world, whether they emanate from Washington, Moscow, Warsaw, or any other center of power. To demonstrate the need for interpreting Lem very flexibly, it is necessary to consider his life and the background of genuine authoritarian hazards in which he had to live. Born in 1921 in Poland, he began his medical studies, but the Nazi invasion and occupation intervened. He had to work as a mechanic during those years — a fortunate job, perhaps, as his interest in engines and electricity was keen. However, he was thoroughly exposed to the clumsiness and brutality of armies and authoritarian regimes. At one point the Germans came close to executing him.

It is evident from his writings that Lem's education included a large dose of philosophy — the traditional scholastic approach as well as the often obscure or uncertain meanderings of modern thought. From these sources and from his enormous general fund of words, concepts, and knowledge, he developed an ability to play with ideas most dextrously, and an inclination to toy with the reader, leaving him uncertain as to which of several meanings might be derived from his stories.

After World War II, Lem became an increasingly successful writer of science fiction, extremely popular in Poland, the Soviet Union, and Germany, and well known elsewhere. He was a pioneer in cybernetics and produced works of philosophy. Wishing to flourish as a writer in avowedly Communist Poland, he had to be mindful of the strictures of censorship and surveillance there. Not only did Poland have its own standards of Marxism and expectation of socialist realism incumbent on writers, but also Warsaw had to live in the shadow of Moscow.

Until Stalin died in 1953, the Polish subservience as a satellite of the U.S.S.R. was complete. Since then there have been discernible trends of relaxation or liberalization, but with occasional retightening of the screws on writers. Protected somewhat by his considerable fame, Lem has had to be careful even so, as he desires to continue to be published in the Communist nations, where the publishing houses are controlled by the governments. What better way, then, to attack secret police, bureaucrats, and militarists than to assail them ostensibly as Americans, as he does in this book?

We should consider particularly the state of Eastern Europe and the Cold War psychology which pervaded the world in the years preceding the publication of *Memoirs Found in a Bathtub*. In 1956 there were riots in Poland and East Germany, while in Hungary there was brief warfare. This unrest engendered greater secret police activity and crackdowns throughout the Eastern Bloc of countries. Stalinism was denounced, and the power of the neo-Stalinists was much reduced by 1957, but the crises between East and West continued to occur. This was the era of Secretary of State John Foster Dulles and his policy of "brinkmanship," with threats and counterthreats of "massive retaliation." In 1960 came the U-2 Affair and an acrimonious meeting between Khrushchev and Eisenhower. The same year witnessed John Kennedy's campaign for the Presidency, keynoted by his allegations of a "missile gap" which could expose the United States to a devastating attack.

The idea would occur readily enough to many of Lem's readers in either

Eastern Europe or the Western nations that the "Third Pentagon" bore a certain resemblance to Moscow's Ministry of Defense and KGB centers. The "Seminars on Applied Agony" held in the Building suggest this, as do the references to taking people to the Cellar Section for a little slapping around, a boot in the face, and the loss of some teeth, to induce confessions.

Nevertheless, the Building of this novel is specifically located in the Rocky Mountains, at the foot of Mount Harvard in the Collegiate Range. Also, the genuineness of the Rocky Mountain location is enhanced by the fact that the actual underground headquarters for the air defense of the United States and Canada, the North American Air Defense Command, is indeed located near Colorado Springs, deep under Cheyenne Mountain. Comparable headquarters have been visualized in other science fiction literature too, notably in Robert Heinlein's stories. Furthermore, in this book and elsewhere in his writings, Lem evinces a clear dislike of capitalism and is often quite critical of the culture and institutions of the West.

This novel offers clues to Lem's approach, observing that a way out of all monstrous absurdities may be found through *mystery*. Another key point is the dependence of the Building on the concept of the Antibuilding. In real life the builders of power in Moscow or Washington depend on allegations of external menace to ratify their positions and to secure approval of the desired budgets for "defensive" programs.

The translators of Lem's works deserve more notice and credit than do most persons who render literature from one language to another. Lem's playfulness, his double and triple entendres, his ambiguities, and his use of proper names to convey atmosphere or to hint at situations, all make the translator's task most challenging. How is he to convey material from the Polish original, and in some cases from an intermediary German or French version, into English, while preserving the puns and multiple meanings of the original? Fortunately, many of the words on which the meanings turn are of Latin or Greek origin, and can be reintroduced into the English text in modified form. At any rate, not only is Lem's own work quite a marvel of literary expertise and dexterity, but also we should recognize that his translators have mustered comparable qualities.

THE MIDWICH CUCKOOS

Author: John Wyndham (John Beynon Harris, 1903-1969)
First book publication: 1957
Type of work: Novel
Time: The present
Locale: Midwich, a rural English village

A literate and thoughtful treatment of the theme of superman as gestalt, and of the reaction of civilized humans to a challenge to their evolutionary supremacy

Principal characters:
 RICHARD GAYFORD, a writer
 JANET GAYFORD, his wife
 GORDON ZELLABY, a philosopher, teacher, and author
 ANTHEA ZELLABY, his wife
 FERRELYN ZELLABY, his daughter
 BERNARD WESTCOTT, a Colonel in Military Intelligence
 CHARLES WILLERS, the village doctor
 REVEREND HUBERT LEEBODY, the village vicar
 THE CHILDREN, a group mind with strange powers

Cuckoos, it is well known, lay their eggs in the nests of other birds and thus trick the hens of other species into raising and nourishing their young. Similarly, postulates John Wyndham, a superior alien race might well choose to "seed" the Earth by implanting its own young in the wombs of human women; this theme is essentially the plot of *The Midwich Cuckoos*, one of Wyndham's finest and most controlled novels. In his other works Wyndham has a tendency to introduce too many science fiction elements and thus strain the reader's credulity. Here he confines himself to exploring a single concept in detail and with great intelligence. The concept — children being reared by parents not really theirs and who are found to possess strange powers — is one already familiar to us through fairy tales of changelings and the psychologists' foster child fantasy. But the potential of this theme as science fiction had not been fully exploited until Wyndham's treatment of it.

The ideas inherent in such a theme are certainly provocative: xenogeny, or impregnation through an external source; the social and cultural pressures on women to accept the role of mother even over children that are not their own; the conflict between what we value as civilized behavior and our own need to survive as a species; the attitudes of humans toward those who are "different" or not fully understood. To these, Wyndham adds a theme of his own: the notion of a gestalt consciousness or "contesserate mind," in which any member of the group learns what a single individual is taught, and which develops not only remarkable intellectual powers, but powers of mind control as well. Wyndham's superchildren are themselves neither good nor evil — they are presented merely as an embattled new species struggling to survive in an overwhelmingly hostile environment. But because of what they are, and what they represent to humanity, they become the focus of a drama that is essentially a highly sophisticated Darwinian struggle for survival of the fittest. It is worth remembering that in an earlier novel, *Re-Birth* (1955), Wyndham had treated a similar group of evolutionary mutations as his heroes, and told the story from their point of view.

In this novel, however, mankind is the focus, and specifically "civilized man" as represented by the obscure, sleepy English village of Midwich. The setting seems a deliberate *hommage* to H. G. Wells's *The War of the Worlds*: that novel is alluded to at several points in the narrative, and it also concerns an alien invasion set in the complacent English countryside. Midwich is isolated, making it a convenient setting for reasons of plot (the horror is contained, but absolute within the limits of its power); but it is also an archetypal image of stability and security. Nothing much has happened there, we are told, in over a thousand years; but the mere fact that Midwich has survived that long suggests the extent to which man has become firmly entrenched as master of his environment. What threatens the stability of Midwich, it would seem, threatens the stability of human civilization itself — and this, it turns out, is indeed the case.

Among the residents of Midwich is Gordon Zellaby, lord of Kyle Manor and an embodiment of many of the values that Midwich represents. A man of letters of the old school, Zellaby has published a philosophical work, entitled with prophetic irony *While We Last*, and sees himself as an enlightened rationalist who recognizes that humor, compassion, and morality are the luxuries of a dominant race, comparatively recent inventions in the course of evolution. Such luxuries, he feels, are affordable only as long as the basic necessities of survival are assured. But such theorizing remains comfortably abstract for Zellaby. He becomes one of the first teachers in a special school created for the superchildren, and soon finds his theories being echoed in terms of a harsh reality: the children realize that they are a threat to the ascendancy of the human race, and thus also a threat to the values and behavioral standards that make us human.

When it is discovered that colonies of superchildren other than Midwich had been scattered in various locales around the globe, it soon becomes apparent that the more "uncivilized" the culture, the more effectively it is able to deal with the threat. A remote village in Mongolia destroyed the children — along with their mothers, who were suspected of lying with devils — before the infants matured enough to develop their psychic powers. An Eskimo settlement exposed the strange children to the cold — suggesting that physically, at least, the children are as susceptible to the natural environment as are humans. And a Soviet village was remotely destroyed by an "atomic cannon" shortly after the threat represented by the children became apparent. Of the known colonies of children, the only one to gain power unchallenged is that in Midwich, and Wyndham strongly implies that this is due to the democratic humanism of a culture that values the rights and security of the individual over the good of the whole.

But it would be misleading to view *The Midwich Cuckoos* as a plea for totalitarianism, or worse, barbarism. Wyndham is more concerned with reminding us of the tenuous threads by which our civilization is knit together. When Zellaby succeeds in destroying the children, it is by exploiting one of the most cherished elements of civilized behavior — their trust in him as a teacher — and the cost is the sacrifice of his own life, which has become the symbol of all that is decent in English humanistic culture. The survival of a society that values honesty and trust is secured only through deception and betrayal. Mankind, apparently, remains dominant, but has received a reminder that it is after all only one species among many struggling for dominance and survival in a competitive universe.

Wyndham unfolds this narrative through the eyes of a writer named Richard Gayford. Though initially a resident of Midwich, Gayford has been living there for only the past year, having moved to Canada during the crucial eight years while the children are growing up. His actual involvement in the struggle is minimal; and his perspective serves to distance the reader from the events being described in order to give it something of a quality of an epic struggle for survival. Even his wife is spared the terrifying "host" pregnancy that is visited upon every other fertile woman in Midwich, because they happened to be out of town celebrating Richard's birthday.

The limited-omniscient viewpoint — Gayford intersperses narratives of his own experiences in Midwich with reconstructions of events at which he was not present (and at one point even apologizes for "the suggestion of disquieting omniscience" that results) — also enables Wyndham to unify a narrative that naturally breaks into two parts: the events surrounding the birth of the children (the mysterious sleep that overcomes every living thing in Midwich, the sighting of a UFO in the vicinity, the later discovery of the pregnancies and birth of the children); and the final confrontation with the startlingly matured children (who have physically attained the appearance of older teenagers) eight years later. By removing Gayford to Canada during this crucial eight-year period, Wyndham obviates the necessity of detailing the growth and maturation of the children, and is able to present it to us in summary when Gayford returns to the village for a visit shortly before the final confrontation.

Despite its naturalistic style and believable attention to detail (somehow, one never questions the reality of the children's psychic powers, even though this is characteristically a difficult concept to dramatize in science fiction), *The Midwich Cuckoos* has much of the quality of myth about it. Even C. G. Jung, the leading psychoanalytical theorist of myth and magic, read and commented on the novel. The children, after all, are apparently of celestial origin, and their golden, shining eyes associate them with the sun. Their corporate mentality suggests a long-standing dream of overcoming the problem of human isolation, and their psychic powers hint at omnipotence. They are, in this sense, a dream of what humans might someday become. In this perspective they hold out the promise of the final realization of total communication and empathy for which the "humanistic" values they so threaten strive. Yet their repeatedly demonstrated cruelty, their excessive overreaction to any threat, real, implied, or even accidental, is not fully explained. Perhaps Wyndham intends to remind us that they are after all children, and not morally superior to the humans they threaten to replace. But perhaps he is suggesting that we cannot intensify those human qualities we most value without also intensifying those qualities of selfishness and cruelty that we value less.

Much in the book remains unexplained. Why is the group mind sexually differentiated (the boys apparently constitute one consciousness, the girls another)? Why are the children portrayed as virtually without emotions? Are emotional attachments to be regarded as a sign of evolutionary primitivism? How do the children plan to reproduce? Will each child born of the group automatically become part of the group mind, or will the group have to produce a whole new batch at once, to create a new gestalt? To what extent are the children really the same, and does this sameness really represent a higher form of intelligence, or is it merely a parody of an ideal Marxist state? And what might the motives of the aliens be in "implanting" these children on Earth? Certainly, not all of these questions need be answered to make the narrative rewarding and exciting, but they are logical outgrowths of issues that Wyndham raises quite consciously.

One might answer that Wyndham does not purport to be a philosopher but a storyteller, or that it is sufficient merely to raise such questions. But *The Midwich Cuckoos* is authentically that which much science fiction claims to be — a novel of ideas — and it is something of a disappointment to find that not all the ideas are fully worked out. Superior in plotting, style, and characterization, *The Midwich Cuckoos* is only slightly short of being a science fiction masterpiece.

MINDBRIDGE

Author: Joe Haldeman (1943-   )
First book publication: 1976
Type of work: Novel
Time: 2034-2281, centering on 2051-2054
Locale: Colorado Springs, New York State, and other locations on Earth; the second planet of the star Groombridge 1618; unspecified planets of 61 Cygnus B and Archenar; Hell, a planet of Tau Ceti; outer space near Sirius; and other locations offplanet

Jacque LeFavre brings his murderous temper under control, and in so doing accomplishes a psychological alteration which not only qualifies him for the "Tamers," a paramilitary organization for interstellar exploration and development, but also eventually makes him the one person psychologically capable of communication with a superior alien race

> *Principal characters:*
> JACQUE LEFAVRE, a Tamer and the first surviving human to be given telepathic abilities *via* a Groomsbridge bridge
> CAROL WACHAL, a Tamer whose first mission coincides with LeFavre's, later his lover
> TANIA JEEVES, a more experienced Tamer, mentor to LeFavre and Wachal

Mindbridge deals with telepathy, teleportation, first contact, and the future of the human race. Much of the action takes place in a paramilitary organization. All of these are quite conventional science fiction subjects, but they are dealt with in an unconventional way. The novel consists of two stories, but what is crucial to the actual plot is Jacque LeFavre's character, which is revealed to us at the very beginning of the novel. What may at first sight look like the plot, contained in the long stretch of connected action taking place between the years 2041 and 2044, is in reality a largely independent and subordinate subplot involving the same characters, but with a climax and resolution of its own.

Conventional wisdom tells us that in a traditionally structured story, the resolution must either come about because of a change in the protagonist's character, or at least it must illuminate that character. (In its purer form, such an illumination deals with the personality as formed, but at least as common is a mixed approach which starts with a formed character but looks back to the previous changes which have shaped it.) Most fiction deals with the first of these options, character in change, probably because it is easier to dramatize. Hamlet finally summons the resolution to act against his mother and uncle; Speaker-to-Animals (in Larry Niven's *Ringworld*) comes to realize that he must look to the long-term advantage of his species and withhold knowledge of the "second quantum hyperdrive" from them. When an author does want to study a finished character, he often supplies other characters whose outlooks are changed by what they learn about the more static personality — the reporters in *Citizen Kane*, Eric Wace and Sandra Tamarin in Poul Anderson's *The Man Who Counts / War of the Wing-Men*. *Mindbridge* rejects this particular tactic, but the novel still must cope with the problem of keeping things moving fast enough to satisfy the none-too-patient science fiction reader.

Accordingly, *Mindbridge* employs a number of devices to increase reader interest in Jacque LeFavre. On the grandest scale, the novel has LeFavre save the world just by being who he is. Misunderstanding prevails when humankind first comes in contact with the powerful L'vrai race, and humanity almost launches a war which would lead to its own destruction. The L'vrai have more than half a mind to destroy the human race anyhow, as a preventative measure. The telepathy-inducing "mindbridge" animal might prove a means of opening communication with the aliens, but from the L'vrai point of view, humans are too-quickly-evolved, dangerously unstable creatures with whom telepathic rapport is impossible. Fortunately, LeFavre proves to be an exception. As a L'vrai spokesman who takes over LeFavre's mind explains, "This one is different from most of you. He has brought the animal part of his nature into harmony with the . . . angel part. He does not attempt to separate them. Because of this, he and I can talk. . . . You keep your animals and angels separate: you would have the angel prevail. It never can."

Since this incident does not occur until the end of the book (though a few anticipatory hints are dropped earlier) the need remains for other devices to keep up interest. Chief among these is the subplot concerning LeFavre's experiences in the Tamers. The subplot does depict a change, a maturation, in LeFavre's character. During the years that the subplot overlaps with the main plot, the change is a mere rounding-out, but it is sufficient to hold the reader's attention and to provide the basis for a linear narrative of LeFavre's first years as a Tamer, from his graduation from the academy of the Agency for Extraterrestrial Development in 2051 to his encounter with the L'vrai in 2054, before jumping ahead to a climax in 2149. The 2051-2054 narrative is presented in those segments called "chapters," and it serves to orient the reader between the chronological jumps embodied in many of the remaining segments.

The subplot is the story of twenty-five-year-old Jacque LeFavre, a man with considerable capacity, but most of it still unrealized. At last he graduates from the AED Academy and goes on active duty with the Tamers. One after another he encounters the trials of maturity, and for many years emerges from all of them victorious. He has professional success in the Tamers — his very first mission, to the second planet of Groombridge 1618, discovers the "mindbridge" animal that serves as a telepathic link between two organisms touching it simultaneously, and his later success in using the mindbridge to communicate with the L'vrai makes him a legend in his own time. He emerges from adolescent rebellion and comes to terms with the memory of his father, with whom he had not spoken for eight years before the father's death. Most satisfyingly of all, LeFavre enters into a permanent love relationship with Carol

Wachal, another Tamer. It is not made clear whether LeFavre and Wachal ever get married, but they start a family and their relationship lasts for decades. Then LeFavre's luck turns. Wachal dies, in 2112. LeFavre carries on for another thirty-seven years, but mostly out of a sense of duty to humanity. He is still the best (though no longer the only) liaison with the L'vrai. When his own time has finally come, he welcomes and hastens his demise. But LeFavre knows a victory even over death, again more because of who he is than what he does. His telepathic sensitivity enables him to discover on his deathbed that (just as the L'vrai have hinted) there is an afterlife, and that Wachal is there waiting for him.

Haldeman gets through this ticklish deathbed scene rather deftly by presenting it as the report of LeFavre's great-granddaughter Tania, perhaps twelve years old, who had been in telepathic rapport with LeFavre at his death. Tania fully expects the adult world to assume she made up the whole thing, so of course we believe her instead. This scene is one example of the utility of a shifted viewpoint. Changing the perspective also serves to infuse a feeling of movement into an inherently rather static character study. *Mindbridge* is structured to take maximum advantage of the freedom of perspective shift without confusing or disorienting the reader. The 2051-2054 flow of narrative continues until some incident serves as the occasion for a flashback or an explanation, and then is interrupted by illuminary material of various sorts. Most of this comes in the form of written documents — LeFavre's diaries, AED reports from various hands, letters, popular science articles, and even one very convincing script for a holovision commercial. But there are also narrative sections from the viewpoints of various characters and omniscient-author segments reaching far into the future.

Much of this material hints at — though it does not fully explain — how Jacque LeFavre got to be what he has become by 2051. Piecing together flashbacks, diary entries, and other material, we learn that LeFavre was born in Switzerland in 2025 and subjected thereafter to a series of wrenching traumas and uprootings. At about the age of five he is taken to New York City, where his father, a prominent physicist, has accepted a position. Jacque is maladjusted in school, promoted beyond his age group but still smarter than his older classmates. In 2034 LeFavre's father, who is of a strangely conservative cast of mind for a prominent physicist, undergoes professional disgrace when his brilliant theoretical refutation of the "Levant-Meyer Translation" is itself refuted by experiment. The "LMT" becomes the basis for an extensive program of interstellar colonization by means of teleportation. The elder LeFavre cannot spring back from the blow, and instead moves upstate to a junior college.

Probably in reaction to this move, and to the strains on his parents' marriage, Jacque is involved in some sort of animal-torturing incident. By 2035 he is seeing a child psychiatrist. In the same year Jacque's mother leaves the family, and in 2037 his older sister Maria dies. Jacque mentions Maria only once in the novel, and then only when knowledge of her is forced out by the mindbridge. This would seem to be a result either of shame at the incestuous feelings twelve-year-old Jacque was developing toward her, or of profound grief at her death. LeFavre's maladjustment in school continues through the years. In 2042 he is attacked and almost killed by a gang of street thugs for no reason in particular, and he and his father move back to Switzerland mere months after he officially dropped the s from his first name so that Americans would pronounce it right. By now he is so Americanized as to be a foreigner in the land of his birth, and conflicts with his father go on. In 2045 he is accepted by the AED Academy (which apparently has taken over the facilities of the U.S. Air Force Academy with the coming of world government) and moves back to the United States. At the Academy the stresses placed on him continue, and indeed increase as a result of deliberate psychological provocation, but the Academy is willing (for its own institutional reasons, not out of any special concern for LeFavre) to invest considerable resources into helping him get his head straight. Since he has already been subjected to enough trauma for several lifetimes, LeFavre's and the Academy's triumph over this psychological imprinting amounts to the creation of a psychic superman.

Haldeman manages to work several bits of scientific background into the biographical flashbacks. A scene in a science class not only indicates Jacque's maladjustment in school but tells us something about cosmology; the disgrace of Jacque's father gives us information on the LMT, which is the basis for interstellar colonization. Several popular science articles and similar reports also elaborate on this latter important piece of background. In what is becoming a characteristic move for him, Haldeman starts with an inherently implausible idea and then describes it in such detail, and works out its ramifications so thoroughly, that the reader soon forgets on what a weak foundation this structure of ideas rests. In this particular case the difficulty is not so much in the interstellar teleportation — a science fiction device of venerable age which received its classical treatment in Robert A. Heinlein's *Tunnel in the Sky*, and which now seems to be getting some slight support from theoretical physics — but in the seemingly arbitrary "slingshot effect" which causes teleported items to return after a time to their starting point. An even greater stumbling block is the assertion that the slingshot effect does not apply to children born on alien planets, even though their every molecule may be of Terrestrial origin. But anyone whose suspicions about the slingshot effect have not been eased by the Westinghouse International holovision commercial or the scene depicting the LMT chamber with its harried tight scheduling and ulcer-ridden controllers will surely be won over by the solid-looking equations, tables, and graphs of the "Numbers and Dollars" segment. It is somewhat less likely that even the tale of Primus Kovaly will reconcile the reader to the exemption by right of birth from the slingshot, but it should be noted that this loophole in natural law not only makes possible the colonization depicted in the novel, but, by marking out human beings as something special in the scheme of things, breaks the ground for the novel's further excursions into near-mysticism.

The material outside the narrative flow also sheds some light on the society of the twenty-first century, illumination that is of particular interest since most of the 2051-2054 narrative involves members of the AED, a governmental organization and almost a military one. The makeup of such organizations changes less quickly over the decades than does the structure of society in general. Except for further advanced sexual integration (indeed, female pre-dominance, thanks to the breeding program for colonization) and a casualness about the value of human life beyond contemporary Western peacetime stan-dards, AED functions much like analagous groups of today. In the outer world, the entire population has been brought up to a reasonably high standard of living through the application of large quantities of power from solar-energy satellites. But the technological and ecological balance is regarded as some-what precarious, and indeed one of the public justifications for the coloniza-tion program is that it will ensure the continued existence of the human race in the event of collapse on Earth.

Institutionalized altruism is always dubious, and more likely causes for the continuance of the program are the utility of such a dollar sink for economic planning, the bureaucratic imperialism inherent in any governmental agency such as AED, and the interest of many of the multinational corporations. For example, Westinghouse sells AED both power and equipment, and the world-wide physics research organization the Institut Fermi depends on AED for some scientific facilities. But whatever the motivation, the outcome seems rea-sonably satisfactory. Indeed, it is the multinationals and other nongovern-mental social groups who run the world, and they are doing a fairly good job of it. Nations remain only as cultural entities, and even in culture the whole world is becoming Americanized. Much science fiction views with alarm such a supposed power shift toward the multinationals — a perceived trend which does not really seem very convincing in an era when throughout the world an ever increasing proportion of GNP is being channeled through governmental budgets — but few ill effects are apparent in *Mindbridge*. Indeed, the division of power among a large number of international groupings, while scarcely ushering in utopia, seems to have reduced the threat both of tyranny and of war.

Finally, *Mindbridge* includes in the nonnarrative segments some omniscient-author discourses which tie up loose ends. With a characteristic burst of sardonicism, Haldeman tells us that the mindbridge animal is really nothing more than a bioengineered telepathic scorekeeper in a game played by a race of near-gods. In a burst of eschatology recalling the clone-entity Man in *The Forever War*, Haldeman tells us that in a thousand years humankind will resemble the L'vrai, with a group mind and the knowledge that individual consciousness is an illusion. So far these little doses of the meaning of it all play much the same role in Haldeman's work as does the soupçon of mysticism in early and middle Heinlein. It will be interesting to see whether over time they increase to the significance that such philosophizing has in the work of, say, Gordon Dickson.

But any such possibility is still a long way from realization in *Mindbridge*. If anything, the novel tends toward excess in the other direction, toward excessive frivolity. Haldeman has solved a difficult technical problem in making a novel of character read as quickly and excitingly as an adventure story. But perhaps *Mindbridge* goes a little too far in its efforts to keep the groundlings supplied with the titillation of violence and sex. We are given no sufficient explanation either for AED's own callousness or for the fifty-percent mortality rate among Tamers. Even granting the preposterous exemption-by-right-of-birth from the slingshot effect, AED's every purpose could be better served by artificial insemination than by the natural servicing depicted in the novel — except, of course, the affording of an excuse for a sex scene. The frivolity of *The Forever War* was a counterbalance to the background of disorientation and death. In *Mindbridge* it is out of place, or at least out of proportion, and it makes the novel a little less than what it might have been.

MINDSWAP

Author: Robert Sheckley
First book publication: 1966
Type of work: Novel
Time: Several centuries in the future
Locale: The Earth, Mars and points west

A satirical novel about a young man's bizarre adventures as he travels around the universe inhabiting body after body with his mind, searching for his own body that was stolen from him

> Principal characters:
> MARVIN FLYNN, the adolescent hero whose body is stolen
> ZE KRAGGASH, the Martian who steals Marvin's body
> URF URDORF, the Martian detective who helps Marvin
> CATHY, the love of Marvin's life
> VALDEZ, a trusted friend of Marvin

As is typical in Robert Sheckley novels, the plot of *Mindswap* concerns the odyssey of an innocent as he progresses from a seemingly simple situation through a series of increasingly surrealistic encounters. Nothing is ever quite what it seems, and even when its true nature is unmasked, the reader is still left wondering whether there might be further surprises in store. With Sheckley, there usually are.

Marvin Flynn is the archetypal Sheckley hero, the quiet, restrained Everyman who would like the Universe to be a simpler place than it is. He is from a quiet town, Stanhope, New York, where nothing much ever happens. At thirty-one he is still considered an adolescent and, though he has had the standard twelve years of school and four years of college, he is unprepared for the larger universe he is about to face. Sheckley wastes little time dropping his hero into trouble. To satisfy his burning desire to travel, Marvin and a Martian named Ze Kraggash mindswap: that is, the two exchange bodies, and Marvin ends up on Mars. However, the unscrupulous Kraggash has pulled a major swindle, and Marvin finds himself in an illegal body with an order to vacate it in six hours. Marvin then sets out on his unlikely odyssey in an effort, literally, to find himself. The plot is important only insofar as it forces Marvin into strange circumstances and meetings with even stranger people. Everyone Marvin meets is better equipped to cope with the Universe than he is, and everyone generously gives advice. The advice may suit their own circumstances, but it never seems to work for Marvin.

In *Mindswap*, everyone is a philosopher. Each character has developed a system to cope with the random insanity Sheckley throws his way. Sheckley delights in finding logical fallacies and screwball theories, blowing them up to their logical extremes, and then demolishing them.

Urf Urdorf, the detective to whom Marvin applies for aid, believes strongly in the philosophical approach to catching criminals. By delving thoroughly into Kraggash's personality and motivations, Urdorf feels certain he can catch the culprit. It matters little to him low long it takes or whether Marvin is alive at the end of the search. Urdorf is also a firm believer in the laws of probability, which are overwhelmingly in his favor. After having failed in 158 straight cases the sheer weight of statistics favors his solving this one, if Marvin can stay alive that long.

The less-than-legitimate Mindswappers who help Marvin along his path have their own views of life. A streetwise cynic named McHonnery believes that the whole point of human intelligence is to put itself out of work, but fortunately, humans are too stupid to do so. Another man, known only as the Hermit, will speak nothing but verse when he's outside his own house. This is a safeguard against getting killed, he informs Marvin; he's seen plenty of men get killed while speaking prose, but not a single one killed while speaking in verse.

The sharpest, and most useful, philosophical parody within the book is the Theory of Searches, as elaborated upon by Valdez, Marvin's trusty companion. Marvin meets and falls in love with Cathy, the love of his life who leaves him less than an hour after she meets him. In proposing to find her, Valdez explains the Theory of Searches, which is brutal in its irony and its simplicity. He claims he can find Cathy without knowing anything about her, simply by utilizing the Theory. Although Marvin points out that it would be easy to find Cathy if the reverse were true — that is, if they knew everything about her and nothing about the Theory of Searches — he agrees that the opposite method also stands a chance.

The Theory of Searches accepts the axiom that when a seeker finds the person he is looking for, that person finds the seeker at the same time. Therefore, the person being sought is also conducting the search, however unaware of that activity he might be. Since there is a great chance the two people will miss each other if they are both in motion, one of them should remain stationary. Since Marvin and Valdez have no control over Cathy's actions, they must assume that she will go on "searching" regardless of what they do. Therefore, Marvin, the seeker, must stay in one place and let Cathy find him. The Theory works to perfection, which should not surprise anyone at this point in the story. In a Sheckley universe, skewed logic is the best logic.

Parallels may be drawn, in fact, between *Mindswap* and Lewis Carroll's books about Alice's travels through equally strange worlds. They, too, are stories of an innocent's wanderings through a place where seemingly anything can happen, and where logical arguments may be twisted and perverted to suit the arguer's end. Carroll, of course, was a mathematician and was quite familiar with the manipulation of postulates and premises in the byplay of formal debate. Sheckley, too, shows evidence of a mathematical background; much of the doubletalk his characters employ comes straight from the jargon of the theoreticians, and particularly from the field of statistical analysis.

Statistical analysis may indeed be the key to *Mindswap*. Sheckley is very casual about the probability (or improbability) of events, while at the same time having his characters argue in terms of likelihood. He thinks nothing of introducing enormous coincidences into the action of his story, and the *deus ex machina* is a common device whenever he wants a change of pace. In a lesser writer this could be interpreted as sloppy craftsmanship, a simple lack of foresight in plotting the work, or an unwillingness to go back and do the necessary rewriting to foreshadow correctly the later developments. This is not the case with Sheckley. Upon closer examination, the reader will notice that the author has planted all these devices early in the novel. Whether they happen to occur at an opportune or an inopportune time is of little importance. There is no doubt a theory somewhere that would make such a coincidence not only acceptable, but even inevitable. As Sheckley himself puts it, "Anything that *is*, is improbable, since everything is extraneous, unnecessary, and a threat to the reason."

It is the very randomness of the Universe that is at the heart of this book. Sheckley's characters, for all their posing and philosophizing, are essentially creatures of order struggling to cope with the disorder of life around them. Each devises his own cockeyed theories to impose a system of values upon a universe that cannot be understood. Stability is shown to be, at best, a temporary state that, once lost, can never be regained. Marvin Flynn leaves Stanhope, New York, the epitome of solid changelessness, in search of exotic adventure. He finds that adventure, but only at the cost of losing his security forever. In mathematical terms, Stanhope was situated at an unstable equilibrium point. Everything was fine as long as Marvin stayed there, but the very act of movement brought Marvin's world out of equilibrium and destroyed the balance. In the end, Marvin ends up as far from equilibrium as it is possible to go — in the Twisted World, a place where even skewed logic and insane probability no longer work.

However, Sheckley's characters do not merely accept the randomness of the Universe in which they find themselves; they fight against it, each in his own way. Some, like Valdez, try to codify it, as though the very act of defining what the Universe can and cannot do is putting limits on its cruelty. Others, like Detective Urdorf, attempt to tame the Universe and bend it to their wills; the detective's high failure rate may show how futile that endeavor is, but Urdorf keeps on trying rather than surrender. Still others, like McHonnery and the Hermit, look for the loopholes in life and make their own cozy niches therein; they use the randomness of the Universe to their own advantage by flowing with it and coaxing it in the proper direction.

Of the supporting players, only Ze Kraggash does not attempt to order the billowing chaos. Instead, he gives himself over totally to the randomness, becoming an active agent of disorder. He personifies the haphazard cruelty of the Universe, and his decision at the end to flee into the Twisted World to avoid Urdorf's trap demonstrates his dedication to those principles. By acting on behalf of chaos, by accepting it into himself, he has made his own accommodation with the Universe.

Marvin Flynn deliberately fights against the randomness and perversity of the cosmos, as every good hero should. While everyone around him finds his own niche and comes to terms with the existing Universe, Marvin stubbornly fights to reestablish the Universe as it should be. Stanhope, New York, is his ideal, and he will not settle for less. By following Kraggash into the Twisted World, he is defying the Universe to do its worst, issuing the ultimate challenge in his search for perfection.

The Universe wins — it always does. Yet, in its own bizarre way, it does make concessions to Marvin's dream. Perhaps it is out of respect for Marvin's courage; perhaps it is because Marvin's perseverence might have paid off eventually. More than likely, however, it is but the latest in the Universe's long string of practical jokes.

In addition to the parody of logic, Sheckley indulges in some brilliant literary parody as well. The most outstanding example is the lengthy segment near the end of the book that spoofs the swashbuckling swordsman epics. There is the obligatory barroom fight wherein the dandy, Marvin, outfights the ruffian; the plots and counterplots, and the shifting of friends to enemies; the incipient revolution against the established order; and the mind-curdling recitation of the age's political history. All these elements are woven with typical Sheckley brilliance into a wonderfully funny tapestry.

It would be possible to criticize the book as having an uneven pace or unconvincing characters, except that a Sheckley book is like a soap bubble: it exists for its own beauty, and any serious attempt to dissect it destroys the beauty with a sudden pop. Instead, the reader should sit back, relax, and enjoy the shimmering effects.

A MIRROR FOR OBSERVERS

Author: Edgar Pangborn (1909-1976)
First book publication: 1954
Type of work: Novel
Time: 1963 (10,963 Martian time) and 1972 (10,972 Martian time)
Locale: Latimer, Massachusetts, and New York City, with a brief scene in Northern
City, a Martian underground city in the Canadian Northwest

A Martian Observer is sent to watch an unusual human child and protect him
against the corrupting influence of a Martian who has renounced his culture's princi-
ples and seems to have plans to use the child in his design to annihilate humanity

> Principal characters:
> DROZMA, the Martian Director of Missions and Counselor of North-
> ern City
> ELMIS, a Martian Observer sent to observe Angelo Pontevecchio
> NAMIR, a Martian Abdicator who hates humanity
> BILLY KELL/BILL KELLER, his son in human disguises
> ANGELO PONTEVECCHIO, a child prodigy with latent powers, when
> grown becomes "Abraham Brown"
> ROSA, his mother and owner of a Latimer boardinghouse
> JACOB FEUERMANN, a retired railroadman and one of her boarders
> SHARON BRAND, a talented ten-year-old, in love with Angelo
> JOSEPH MAX, a neo-Nazi bent on world domination, and organizer
> of the Organic Unity Party

A skillfully told story of the role played by Martians at a critical moment in
Earth's history, Edgar Pangborn's *A Mirror for Observers* is also a commentary on the nature of man himself. In addition to the standard science fiction
devices, Pangborn also depends on effective literary devices to mold his
observation. Humanity reveals itself as the human characters move, oblivious
of any determining force, within an imperceptible alternative condition: the
unknown presence of Martians on Earth. The perception of mankind that
results is deepened through the archetypal structuring of the novel around the
struggle between good and evil, the development of the potentially powerful
child, and the transformation from death to rebirth. While admitting the
impossibility of eradicating evil from human nature, Pangborn offers the hope
that man, once he understands empirical truth, can "reach the stars": achieve a
high level of ethical maturity with the insight to rely on love to establish justice and peace.

The "Prelude" that introduces the two-part novel serves to explain the Martian presence on Earth. Namir, who has rejected the culture and ethics of the
established Martians, returns from traveling around the world for 134 years in
one disguise or another. While he visits with Drozma, we learn that the Martians, forced to flee a slowly dying Mars, sent an expedition to Earth 30,963
years ago. Few Martians (and only one animal, the ork) survived the rigors of
the journey or the ordeals of adaptation to their new planet. Rather than take'

over the planet, the Martians, through a personality quirk that views the destruction of or interference with different species as inherently evil, concentrated on survival (even now there are only about two thousand Martians in the underground cities, plus a few dozen Abdicators) and limited their contact with humans to observation.

Qualified Martians, gifted with a five to six hundred year life span and made presentably human by face and hand surgery (Martians have only four fingers on each hand), have been sent regularly on missions throughout the world since the dawn of human history. Through their social, political, philosophical, and anthropological studies, the Martians have made themselves masters of human culture; they have examined our art, learned our music, read our literature, and experienced our history. At the same time, however, they have developed their own subculture. More technically advanced and astute than humans, they not only invented the telephone years before Bell "reinvented the wretched thing" in 1876, but also, for their own protection, a scent-destroyer to mask the distinctive Martian scent, undetectable by humans but maddening to animals, especially horses. Their goal is union with human beings, an ideal merger that can be possible only if man experiences a genuine ethical revolution.

Although Namir, the Abdicator, is contemptuous of mankind and doubts that "human beings can ever amount to anything," Drozma lives in the hope that humans can progress spiritually, and he looks forward to a Martian association with Earthmen in about five hundred years. As soon as Namir leaves, Drozma commissions the Observer Elmis to go to Latimer, a small town in Massachusetts, to "observe" an extraordinary human child about twelve years old who has caught the attention of Namir during his travels. Believing the child, Angelo Pontevecchio, may be potentially important in human affairs, Drozma is anxious to protect him from the corruption of Namir, who frankly admits his hatred of the human race and his interest in its destruction.

In spite of their noble intentions not to interfere in human affairs, the Martians do, albeit undiscernibly. Although the humans in the novel are unaware of the Martians, they are still affected by them. The Martians are added to the world like a subtle spice: undetectable, they nevertheless alter events — as Elmis does once he becomes involved with the fortunes of Angelo — in significant and irrevocable ways. This interference is justified by an even nobler precept than the policy of noninterference: they "hope to promote human good and diminish human evil," so far as they themselves can know good and evil.

Based on Elmis' observation, the novel takes form as the official "report of Elmis" to Director Drozma; as such, its style — crisp, graphic, and witty — reflects the lively personality of Elmis, a delightful chap who "admires human creatures a little too much." Once in Latimer, Elmis (in the human guise of Benedict Miles, a retired schoolteacher writing a book) applies for a room at Rosa Pontevecchio's boardinghouse and immediately confirms Drozma's suspicion: Angelo is indeed a child prodigy. His name, Angelo (Angel), suggests the miraculous element in the child archetype; although the child may be of lowly birth, he is endowed with superior powers: he is "divine." Elmis (Ben) has no sooner settled into the "first-floor back" than the boardinghouse is burglarized. Elmis knows that the culprit is Namir but is unable to foresee how he intends to continue his campaign for the destruction of the human race. One step obviously will be to convert Angelo, whom Namir sees as a potentially powerful tool, to his nihilistic philosophy.

In his attempts to protect Angelo's soul by recommending a broadly humanistic reading program and by urging Angelo toward ethical behavior, Elmis finds an ally in Sharon Brand, a talented ten-year-old just beginning a promising musical career as a pianist. A charming girl addicted to fantasy and inflated diction but careless of her pronunciation, Sharon assures Elmis that she loves Angelo "beyond comprehemption" and joins him in warning Angelo against Billy Kell, a fourteen-year-old tough who has been trying to persuade Angelo to join the Mudhawks, a street gang he has organized and leads. And their apprehensions about Billy prove to be only too well justified. Elmis, quite disturbed by Billy's hostility toward Sharon, follows him to his home and gathers enough evidence during his shadowing (Billy abruptly and deliberately crosses a street to avoid passing a horse, for example) to make him suspect that Billy is not only a Martian but also the son of Namir.

Hard on the heels of this calamity, comes another. Elmis becomes puzzled by the striking change in the usually warm and friendly attitude of Jacob Feuermann, another lodger in the Pontevecchio boardinghouse who is also a supporter of Angelo, and at first suspects that Namir has poisoned Feuermann's mind against him. However, when he hears "Feuermann" giving Angelo some decidedly un-Feuermannlike advice, he learns the appalling truth: that Namir has murdered Feuermann and assumed his identity to have access to the boy. Although loath to kill, but bound by the law of 27,140 that calls for the elimination of any Martian who harms his own people or humanity, Elmis realizes he must execute Namir once he has positive proof of Feuermann's death. Since the marked change in Feuermann had first occurred upon his return from a visit to his wife's grave, Elmis begins his search at the cemetery; he is interrupted, however, by Namir who freely confesses his crime. Unfortunately, Elmis' attempt to kill Namir fails, but he does learn from Namir before he escapes that the Mudhawks (whom Angelo has joined) are at that very moment engaged in battle with the Diggers, a rival gang. Fearful for Angelo's safety, Elmis hurries to rescue the boy, whom he has learned to love as a son.

Angelo escapes serious physical injury, but is irreparably (one may say "mortally") wounded when his mother, a victim of heart disease, collapses and dies upon learning of his role in the ugly street brawl. Blaming himself for his mother's death, Angelo flees, never to return. Though saddened that he must leave Sharon whom he now regards as a daughter, but happy that he has provided for her education as a pianist with an excellent teacher, the blind Sophia Wilkanowska, Elmis prepares to continue his mission. He alters his appearance and sets out on his quest, determined not to return to Northern City until he finds Angelo. The fruitless search continues for more than nine years.

In 1972, Elmis (now Will Meisel) is attracted to New York City by a newspaper photograph of a man who resembles Billy Kell. Once there, Elmis succeeds in contacting both his "children": Sharon, now a pianist of great stature, at her brilliant New York debut and Angelo, now Abraham Brown, at Bill Keller's (formerly Billy Kell) apartment where Namir, disguised as Keller's Uncle Nicholas, also resides. The photograph which led Elmis to Keller identified him as a high-ranking member of the Organic Unity Party founded by the infamous Joseph Max, a racist and latter-day Hitler, who gains adherents through the emotional gimmicks of racial "purity" and American domination of the world. Devoted to rule by the elite (meaning himself) and endowed with "the paranoid intensity of Hitler" and "plenty of naked power hunger," Max (actually schooled by Nicholas) has financed the development of a virus capable of destroying much, if not all, of the human race. Armed with such a deadly weapon, Max and Keller plan to seize control first of the Americas and then the world.

Once convinced that "Will" is his beloved "Ben," Angelo/Abraham tells Elmis about his six years in a Kansas City reform school — the "abandonment" of the child archetype and Angelo's symbolic "death." Again his name, Abraham, is significant: father of a new and chosen people and leader of his race. Although "physically" reborn, Abraham does not experience spiritual rebirth until he repudiates Keller and leaves, or rather escapes from, Keller's apartment where he has been entombed and stagnating. Significantly, Abraham had never, despite Keller's urgings, joined the Organic Unity Party; this resistance is a contrast to his succumbing (largely motivated by Billy Kell's lies) to the Mudhawks. Abraham is stronger than Angelo and more mature, a quality Elmis believes is essential in Abraham's progress toward his full potential.

Once Abraham and Sharon are reunited, they discover that their childhood love never died; it has, in fact, deepened over the years. Their rekindled rapture is overshadowed, however, by an imminent disaster: Daniel Walker, a disgruntled Party worker, has stolen a vial of the lethal airborne virus and has tossed it from the roof garden of Max's thirtieth-story penthouse moments before he plunges to his death. Although a necessary climactic action of the plot, Walker's sudden defection over a reprimand for a minor infraction of Party rules is inadequately motivated and is without question the structural weak point of the novel. This negligence is much more obvious than the omitted explanation for Billy Kell's presence in Latimer *prior* to Namir's discovery of Angelo.

In scenes reminiscent of those in Albert Camus' *The Plague*, Pangborn generally and specifically describes the virus-triggered pandemic in frighteningly graphic terms: cold but shocking statistics of the numbers afflicted and dead alternate with close-ups of old men and animals dying in the streets. Abraham, with a courageous disregard of contagion, labors untiringly at a hospital tending the sick and dying. When the plague finally subsides, after raging nearly three months, it leaves forty-two million (out of two hundred million) dead in the United States alone, among them Max and Sophia. Stricken with the disease, Sharon recovers but is totally and, for a pianist, tragically deaf.

As for Nicholas, Elmis accepts his terrible duty to eradicate the evil Namir by regarding the execution as "an act of mercy": Namir is finally free from his corroding and "very human sickness of hate." Bill Keller, however, escapes with a new face to the Northwest. Thus, evil remains: hampered or sidetracked though it may be, evil abides. Just as Thornton Wilder must have Henry (Cain), "strong unreconciled evil," hovering in the wings in the final scene of *The Skin of Our Teeth*, so must Pangborn preserve Keller; being an essential part of human nature, evil in the human scheme of things cannot be destroyed. While Abraham and Sharon withdraw to the quiet of a small village in Vermont to restructure their lives, Elmis takes a slow boat to Manila for a few months' vacation before returning permanently to Northern City.

Even though he has momentarily retired to gather his strength, Abraham remains the hope of the human world; his growth in the novel gives us auspicious testimony. Once aroused by Elmis from the apathy he suffered in Keller's apartment, Abraham gains power as he resists compelling pressures to return. And he continues to grow "in wisdom and in strength." The patients at the hospital — the conscious and even the almost unconscious — react to the messianic quality in Abraham; somehow he achieves "communication" with them. He endures not only Sharon's illness, but also the final ordeal of her life-devastating deafness, and rescues both Sharon and Elmis from despair. Elmis confesses that Abraham "upheld all three of us, forcing us to understand what richness of life remained in spite of everything." Elmis, of course, is the one whose faith endowed Abraham with "potentially great insight" and the ability to "train that insight . . . on the more dangerous and urgent of human troubles." Thus, in Jungian terms, the "child" has distinguished himself "by deeds which point to the conquest of the dark."

However, while Abraham may be the "hero" of the novel, Elmis is its delight; a strongly fairy-godfather figure, with a wry sense of humor, he charms us with his innate kindness and love for, as well as faith in, humanity. Although bemused by the contradictions and foibles of humankind, he believes that man has "the essentials of maturity" and never abandons his conviction that "Union may be possible" toward the close of his son's life. If all Martians (excluding the Abdicators, of course) are like Elmis, one cannot help wishing union could be accomplished five hundred years sooner than the target date.

Elmis' worthy qualities inevitably cast him as a symbol of good in opposition to the evil of Namir. Although there is a weak attempt during the execution scene to justify Namir's malevolent view of mankind, Elmis points out the fallacy of his insistence that human beings have "no truth in them." While acknowledging the evil in man, Elmis faults Namir for wanting to throw out the baby with the bath water and contends that Namir's is a one-sided appraisal based on the very essence of Namir himself: he has invariably demonstrated "no truth." Earlier Elmis had insisted on the need of seeing both good and evil in humanity and of keeping them in perspective:

> Men trick themselves with the illusion that good and evil are neat opposites. . . . Good is a far wider and more inclusive aspect of life. I see its relation to evil as little more than the relation of coexistence. . . . Good is the drink, evil only a poison that is sometimes in the dregs; in the course of living we are likely to shake the glass — no fault of the wine.

Since Namir never really offers a motive for his unrelenting persecution of humanity, we can only conclude that he acts out of a deeply rooted, inexplicable evil in his nature. Thus, acting with a commitment to evil so absolute as to defy rational explanation, Namir becomes another embodiment of "motiveless malignity": evil incarnate. Not that this limited focus of Namir is a flaw in Pangborn's technique; it is more an intensity of characterization than a narrowness. Namir has, in spite of — or perhaps because of — his singularity, a certain Satanic grandeur and arouses the fascination evil holds for us.

When defining his less important characters, Pangborn has an eye for the telling detail: Feuermann cherishing his horse-head meerschaum, Rosa preparing tempting Italian specialties and exuding Latin hospitality, Mac placing his toilet articles with meticulous precision. Even a character as minor as Mac comes alive with sure, deft strokes. Elmis has no sooner told him about the burglary, than Mac is into his pants and "barking about the old ladies." Approving of his speed, Elmis remarks: "Nice boy. Plain-spoken. He'd have the house steaming in three minutes." Once all are aroused, Elmis is impressed by Mac's heraclean efforts to calm the panic: "Having touched off the eruption, he was shoving the lava back, barehanded," and comments tersely, "I liked Mac." So does the reader.

Thematic use of metaphor is another of Pangborn's strong points. The "mirror" of the title — which refers to the novel itself as a surveillance of the human scene — becomes a three-way mirror. It is the mirror wherein the Martian Observers learn much, not only about men, but also about themselves; Elmis returns to Northern City a wiser Martian than the one who departed. It is the mirror that reflects for the readers the truths of human nature as Pangborn sees them. And it is the mirror the men of the novel (who are in truth reflections of ourselves) need for self-awareness, but ironically are unable to use. For some reason, men will not or cannot take a good hard look at themselves.

The bronze Minoan mirror Drozma gives Elmis for Angelo is the symbol of truth, the complete self-awareness that is undoubtedly beyond the grasp of most men but not Abraham. Shaken when he first looks into the mirror as a child, Angelo/Abraham is finally able, after gaining maturity from his ordeal, to confront the mirror and accept what it shows him: that he is "human" after all, with all that that implies. This knowledge leads Abraham to insist that the cause of the plague be universally known. Realizing that men, if given half a chance, will avoid looking at themselves, Abraham wants the entire world to know that the tragedy was *man-made*. Abraham can then accept the Minoan mirror as a gift because he has learned how to look in the mirror and has seen the final truth: man himself is the source of his own evil. Abraham also sees himself "as a human being with possibilities that are not to be thrown away or lost or stultified"; and as such, the novel ends with the hope that Abraham with his potential power, his messianic qualities, will be able to lead men not only to the understanding of ethical necessities but also to the willingness to let them rule their actions.

MISSION OF GRAVITY

Author: Hal Clement (Harry Clement Stubbs, 1922-   )
First book publication: 1954
Type of work: Novel
Time: The future
Locale: Mesklin, a distant and unusual planet

A quintessential example of "hard" science fiction, in which caterpillarlike aliens help Earthmen recover a damaged spaceship on a planet with variable high gravity

Principal characters:
BARLENNAN, commander of the Mesklin ship *Bree*
DONDRAGMER, his first officer
CHARLES LACKLAND, the principal human who guides the Mesklinites

Hal Clement has been a science teacher in a private Massachusetts school for many years. He is probably the best known proponent of "hard" science fiction — that is, fiction based on and derived directly from contemporary knowledge of the so-called "hard" sciences of chemistry, astronomy, physics, and biology, as distinguished from the "softer" social sciences, whose results do not readily permit controlled experimentation and the formulation of precise laws. All of Clement's works, from his first novel, *Needle* (1950), to *Star Light* (1971), a partial sequel to *Mission of Gravity*, exhibit his careful craftsmanship. *Mission of Gravity*, his best known and most popular work, is the one on which he has stated he is content to let his reputation rest. If Jules Verne has a contemporary descendant, it is Hal Clement.

When the story opens, an unmanned terrestrial research ship has been disabled near the south pole of Mesklin, a planet whose unusual characteristics shape much of the novel's action. Charles Lackland, the Earthman through whose eyes we view much of the story, has landed near the equator and made contact with an intelligent life form. These caterpillarlike creatures, about fifteen inches long and two inches in diameter, are covered with tough, chitinous skins or exoskeletons and have very strong pincers for hands. A Mesklenite named Barlennan commands the *Bree*, which sails the planet's liquid methane seas, trading for products which are later sold for profit. He has learned English from Lackland as the story begins, although how this was accomplished is never explained. Barlennan agrees to travel to the disabled ship in return for products and knowledge which the humans can provide. This journey is a major undertaking for such creatures, whose sailing experience has been extensive but limited to familiar "waters."

Mesklin is an enormous and unusual planet. Its polar diameter is twenty thousand miles, but its equatorial diameter is forty-eight thousand miles, giving it the appearance of a fried egg. Its extremely high rotational velocity results in a gravity three times that of Earth at the equator, but seven hundred times that of Earth at the poles. A "day" is eighteen minutes long, and the planet follows a long ellipse around its sun. The fall and winter seasons are two Earth months in length, but spring and summer are each twenty-eight months long.

Because the Mesklinites normally live near the pole, their bodies are well-designed to bear the extreme gravity in polar regions, where a six inch fall would usually mean immediate death, much as falling from a tall building would for us. Their psychology has therefore been shaped by their environment. Heights and objects above them, which could fall and crush them, are both feared. The entire concept of flying or even throwing an object is unknown to them. Clement thus suggests that our own physical environment heavily shapes our perceptions. For example, the world would look far different if human vision extended into the ultraviolet or infrared, and our language would reflect this difference. The Mesklinites' perceptions must be presented in English for fictional purposes, and this sometimes results in a bit of verbal humor. Barlennan, for example, remarks at one point: ". . . there's something about them that bothers me, though I can't exactly put a nipper on it."

Our perceptions of our environment shape our understanding as well. A flat earth was assumed until recently in human history. As our knowledge grew, aided by the development of what we now call science, our perceptions changed. Similarly, the Mesklinites view their world as a concave bowl, and their geographical knowledge is shaped accordingly. A slow transformation of this world view occurs as the novel progresses. The conclusion suggests that the pragmatic "how" of the Mesklinites will be enriched and ultimately transcended by the "why" contained in the scientific knowledge provided by the humans.

The novel is a careful blend of the familiar and the strange. The unusual features of Mesklin are progressively revealed during the journey through action, dialogue, and unobtrusive explanation. Dramatic tension develops as obstacles are met and overcome. Clement is a skilled writer and is extremely knowledgeable in several sciences. He avoids a major flaw which undercut the fictional integrity of innumerable stories of the pre-1940 period, where scientific explanations interrupted the narrative while the story leaked away. In many such stories the Great Scientist deigned to explain his clever invention or idea to a listener, all too often a brainless female whose only function was to serve as an admiring companion. This clumsy narrative device was common in Jules Verne's work, and was often employed by Hugo Gernsback, the founding editor of *Amazing Stories*, who encouraged contributors to include some sugar-coated science in their stories, thus giving them redeeming social importance. This tradition fortunately died out several decades ago, and most science fiction writers have developed various techniques to provide background information without interrupting the story. Clement is generally successful in *Mission of Gravity*, but is much less so in the sequel, *Star Light*, which has far too much technical exposition.

Clement has discussed in detail the creation of imaginary but plausible societies on several occasions. At the time the three-part serialization of *Mission of Gravity* was running in *Astounding Science Fiction*, he published a companion article, "Whirligig World," in which he provided a detailed scientific explanation of how he created Mesklin and derived much of the plot from its physical characteristics. Although creating from notes is not unusual for fiction writers, Clement often works out the technical details first and develops a story around them. Thus, the externals and the ideas are dominant and the inner lives of the characters are rarely explored — an approach characteristic of *Astounding Science Fiction* (now *Analog*) under the long-time editorship of John W. Campbell, Jr. As Brian Aldiss comments in his perceptive history of science fiction, *Billion Year Spree* (1973): "There were times when *Astounding* smelt so much of the research lab that it should have been printed on filter paper."

Such rigor is probably of interest to a relatively small minority of science fiction readers. H. G. Wells felt that a plausible bit of "scientific patter" was often sufficient to achieve verisimilitude. The pseudoscientific explanations of the Time Traveller are incidental in *The Time Machine*. Some writers dispense altogether with any attempt to achieve scientific credibility. In what is probably the most popular post-World War II work of science fiction, Ray Bradbury's *The Martian Chronicles* (1950), the Mars depicted is that of the poet, not the barren, lifeless world of the scientist. Yet the vignettes which comprise the novel are not weakened by the lack of scientific accuracy. The *mise en scene* for Bradbury is shaped by dramatic, not scientific considerations, an attitude at sharp variance with Clement's. Readers who feel that the psychological exploration of character should be the central concern of any novelist may dismiss the "hard" science fiction of Clement and similar writers as simply pornography for engineers.

Clement's work far transcends the Gernsbackian school of hardware and fictionalized science by fusing action, character, and, above all, setting in an enjoyable and often fascinating blend. His Mesklinite creatures are odd but likable and admirable, and are far more interesting than the humans. Although Clement remarks that Lackland gained very little insight into Mesklinite psychology, Barlennan and his crew are far from alien except perhaps in appearance. While a truly alien form of life can be described (Olaf Stapledon was fairly successful in this area), it rarely can be anything other than an intellectual curiosity to a human. The Mesklinite behavior is all too human, exhibiting intense curiosity, loyalty, resourcefulness, and a considerable amount of intelligent self-interest. Barlennan resembles nothing so much as a shrewd Yankee trader, as befits a maritime nation. Clement occasionally uses these similarities for satiric purposes. For example, when a violent storm forces the voyagers to seek shelter on an island, where they encounter a similar species which has achieved flight in gliders, the spokesman for this species is somewhat disdainful of Barlennan and his crew, referring to them as barbarians. But this other species' superiority is shortlived. Barlennan outwits them, just as he later bargains on his terms with the humans. The analogy with colonists and natives is not forced, but an attentive reader cannot help but be aware of it.

Similarly, the attentive reader might well note that Clement, although by profession a teacher of science, not literature, has cleverly utilized many of the major devices of the epic form throughout the book. If we define the epic as an extended narrative by means of which we learn of the better aspects of an entire civilization or culture through the character of a single hero, then *Mission of Gravity* is almost a science fiction exemplar.

Barlennan is the hero, of course, and it is his struggles and eventual triumph over almost incredible obstacles that form the core of the novel. While Barlennan is singularly inhuman in appearance, nonetheless his Yankee canniness or Odyssean wiliness enables him to assume many so-called human characteristics. He is sage, cowardly, brave, adventurous, boastful, and inventive by turns. Each of these qualities serve him well on his monumental journey across Mesklin. This journey certainly qualifies to be called "epic" even in terms of Mesklinite tradition. Barlennan and the crew of the *Bree* are driven by the overpowering urge for profits and adventure. This crass motivation always remains, of course, but it is supplemented as time passes by an even more powerful incentive, the acquisition of knowledge.

Knowledge can assume many forms, of course, and among the various aspects of Mesklin which impel Barlennan are knowledge of the planet itself — the lure of distant shores. Scientific knowledge is one of Barlennan's hidden objectives, just as it was Odysseus' in several of his exploits. At the end of the novel, when Barlennan has found the object of the epic search, the substance of priceless value in mythic terms (a grounded research rocket near the seven-hundred-gravity south pole of Mesklin), Barlennan insists that he and his people be taught everything: why fire burns, how a ship floats, and all the elementary scientific facts necessary for Barlennan's people to move into the age of science. An even more subtle aspect of the knowledge sought is psychological. Here, and in many places throughout the novel, Clement projects Earth standards or customs onto the Mesklinites, but gradually, almost inperceptibly, Barlennan, Dondragmar, and the other members of the crew of the *Bree* overcome their instinctive overwhelming fear of heights or of falling. The word or the concept of "throw," for example, does not exist in either the Mesklinite vocabularly or psyche. To by struck by any object falling under the power of five hundred gravities would mean instant death, and horizontal motion of an object through the atmosphere is literally inconceivable. Yet carefully, subtly, through a series of logical incidents in the episodic, epic nature of the book, Barlennan and the crew gradually and almost unconsciously overcome this primal fear.

Other epic characteristics abound. The story begins *in medias res*: prior to the opening of the novel, Lackland has already contacted Barlennan, who has begun to learn English. Lackland's continuing help, first when he is physically present on the lower gravity centers of Mesklin, and later by radio from an orbiting space ship, can easily be construed as intervention of the gods, a science fiction *deus ex machina*. Monsters are met and overcome, giants are defeated, and the hero learns from his mistakes.

If this novel is a mission of gravity, as the title indicates, the hero of that mission is Barlennan. He grows, develops, and emerges into wholeness as a result of what he has learned. What he will be after he acquires the further scientific background may be a matter of conjecture, but the reader comes to appreciate not only Barlennan, but the Mesklinite culture and civilization which produced him. We have, therefore, come to understand aspects of an entire culture through the deeds of a single hero.

But what is finally most important about the novel is that our sympathies with Barlennan's efforts to overcome his racial acrophobia are strongly engaged. We have become empathetically involved with this struggle, and on the final pages, when the *Bree*, now modified into a kind of hot air balloon, lifts off the surface, we cheer Barlennan's efforts. Barlennan's final mission of gravity, in other words, is to overcome gravity and to learn, as mankind did, to fly, to soar the nets which held him to the surface of his world.

From one point of view, *Mission of Gravity* is a curiously two-dimensional book, in the same sense that Abbot's *Flatland* attempts to re-create a two-dimensional reality. Gradually Barlennan and his people are introduced to "depth" or "height"; and if they can overcome their primal fear of gravity, they will become citizens of a multidimensional universe. Clement may have been aiming at allegory here, for the novel was written years before the space age began. He may have been suggesting that if mankind can overcome the gravity problem and begin to explore space, then his future is assured. Such a vision is surely epic in scope.

THE MOTE IN GOD'S EYE

Authors: Larry Niven (1938-   ) and Jerry Pournelle
First book publicaiton: 1974
Type of work: Novel
Time: 3017, the one hundred and fourteenth year of the Second Empire of Man
Locale: The Trans-Coalsack Sector

An exploration of the problems arising from the first contact with intelligent aliens, told from both human and alien points of view

Principal characters:
RODERICK HAROLD, Lord Blaine, the commander of battlecruiser
    MacArthur
KEVIN RENNER, Sailing Master of the *MacArthur*
SANDRA FOWLER, an anthropologist engaged to Lord Blaine
HORACE BURY, a trader and traitor
DR. ANTHONY HORVATH, Minister of Science for Trans-Coalsack
    Sector
DAVID HARDY, Chaplain, Imperial Space Navy
SENATOR BENJAMIN FOWLER, Chair of the Imperial Commission on
    Aliens
THE MOTIES, the aliens

The Mote in God's Eye is ambitious in purpose and convincingly executed; despite some literary weaknesses the novel works, providing quality science fiction entertainment.

Although *The Mote in God's Eye* shares many characteristics of a space opera, it does not suffer from many of the historical weaknesses of that subgenre. Typically in a space opera, the emphasis is on vicariously thrilling but frequently intellectually stultifying physical action; this novel has enough fast-paced action and suspense to satisfy an adventure story enthusiast. However, in addition to its space battles, the story includes an interesting intellectual puzzle; it is also a detective story in which two widely divergent cultures — human and Moties — must attempt to understand one another in order to satisfy their self-serving purposes. Also, each species must try to conceal its less favorable cultural characteristics which, if revealed, might make future contact undesirable and intergalactic war inevitable long before it is prepared to defend itself and/or annihilate the enemy.

In presenting and developing the mystery of the unknown alien, the authors also avoid another historical weakness of the space opera, which is to portray aliens one-dimensionally. Typically, these aliens lack specific and logically developed cultural, biological, and technological characteristics, and tend to personify some human vice such as greed, lust, or ruthlessness. The role of these physically grotesque, one-dimensional threats to humanity is to provide cannonfodder for the disintegrator ray guns wielded by larger-than-life humans. The Moties, however, are a unique species. Their culture is complex, reflecting and originating in their biological, historical, sociological, and technological evolution, and significantly, their culture is basically nonhuman.

Instead, in this case the characters lacking significant development are the human ones, who resemble the stereotypes of historical romances. The hero, Lord Blaine, for example, is a latter-day Horatio Hornblower, ruggedly handsome and decisive in action, although the victim of self-doubt. Lord Blaine's heroine is Sally Fowler, who is beautiful and wealthy, trivial and fatuous, a member in good standing of the Imperial Aristocracy and a doctoral candidate at the Imperial University of Sparta. Determined to make a name for herself as an anthropologist before settling down, her professional goals are nevertheless secondary to her primary purpose of "settling down"; she misses "what she thought of as girl talk. Marriage and babies and house-keeping and scandals: they were a part of civilized life." For an anthropologist, she is incredibly prudish; for example, while discussing the use of birth control devices by unmarried women, "her distaste was impossible to disguise." The representative military type is Vice Admiral Kutuzov, who is fiercely loyal to the Empire, and enjoys pretending to be a nineteenth century White Russian. On his ship, the *Lenin*, he burns candles before religious icons; in addition to drinking an inordinate amount of tea, he spends most of his time issuing abrupt, no-nonsense orders such as, "Da. Shoot." Then, there is Jock (Sandy) Sinclair. He is from the colony of New Scotland and, therefore, is a Chief Engineer, He has lines such as "Mon, we will nae show dirty pictures aboard this ship — and what with a chaplain aboard! Not to mention the lady."

These and countless other stereotypes are forgivable, perhaps, because they free the reader from character analysis, allowing him to concentrate, along with the Moties, on the densely detailed, although not particularly unique, history of mankind up to and including the time of the Second Empire of Man. This background is necessary to place in context the problems of a first contact between cultures from different worlds, and to indicate parallels between the two civilizations and their different evolutions. Human history is presented as cyclical; civilizations rise and fall, the collapses followed by Dark Ages. This pattern continues even after the invention of the Alderson Drive — a faster-than-the-speed-of-light form of transportation which enables mankind to escape from his crowded solar system and begin colonizing the planets of other stars. On the other hand, the Moties are bottled up in their overpopulated solar system. Among other effects, the Alderson Drive has given mankind an optimistic outlook, since it allows the belief that all problems have attainable solutions — a viewpoint not shared by the basically fatalistic Moties.

According to the facts of the authors' fictional history, during the colonization of the stars, the First Empire of Man was formed only to collapse as a result of the Secession Wars. To overthrow the First Empire many of the colonies, essentially feudal estates with typical divisions of labor and responsibilities, went to great lengths to extend their powers. One colony, the Sauron colony, attempted to breed a class of supermen warriors through genetic engineering. Following the Secession Wars, mankind returned to barbarism.

Eventually, the Second Empire of Man was founded by Leonidas IV of Sparta. The Second Empire, still technologically inferior to the First but slowly catching up, is a shaky coalition of colonies obviously modeled after the British Empire. It is ruled by the Imperial Aristocracy, membership in which is hereditary. The decision-making process is aided by a parliament made up of representatives of the colonies, and by such special interest groups as the Interstellar Trade Association and a Humanity League. The interests of the established Church are considered, also, but all final decisions are made in the interest of preserving and strengthening the Empire. Decisions are enforced by the Imperial Space Navy, which is capable of and quite willing to annihilate totally a colony and its planet in order to preserve the Empire. Admiral Kutuzov is called the Tzar because he once reduced a populated planet to molten lava.

Despite the Empire's military power, revolts still occur, and it is shortly after the revolt on New Chicago has been put down that a Motie probe is discovered entering the Empire from a previously unexplored region of the galaxy. Immediately, Lord Blaine, Commander of the *MacArthur*, is sent out to make contact with the vessel, which is powered by a light sail. Blaine is forced to attack the light sail when it fires on the *MacArthur*. The alien crew is killed.

The Empire then sends out a counterprobe to the unknown space of the Mote, a G-2 yellow dwarf thirty-five light years away. The Empire's probe is composed of two ships — the *Lenin*, is to avoid all contact with the aliens and to insure that the military secrets aboard the *MacArthur*, the contact-ship, are not learned by the Moties. The *Lenin* is under orders to destroy the *MacArthur* and its personnel if necessary to preserve the secrets of the Alderson Drive and the Langston Field, a shielding device. In addition to a full crew of brave and dedicated military personnel, the *MacArthur* houses the probe's scientific team, a collection of well-meaning fools in search of knowledge who are hopelessly convinced that the Moties pose no threat to the Empire. The *MacArthur* also carries two characters who are aboard only to advance the plot. Sally Fowler, whose presence is only thinly justified by her profession, is the only woman aboard, and is included to provide romantic interest; additionally, she functions as a spokesman for the Moties' interests. Horace Bury, called the Empire's trade representative despite the fact that the navy is collecting indisputable proof that he is a traitor, is the instigator of the New Chicago revolt. At first, Bury hopes to capitalize on the Moties but later wants only to help destroy them.

Eventually, the representatives of the two cultures meet, first aboard a Motie ship and then on Motie Prime, the aliens' home planet. To the scientists, it is soon apparent that the aliens are intellectually superior to humans. Their civilization is very old; technologically, they are more advanced than the

First Empire of Man, despite the fact that they have not yet discovered the Alderson Drive. In their metal-scarce solar system, devices are designed to serve multiple yet seemingly dissimilar functions, and when a specific device is no longer needed, it is miraculously reengineered to meet a new need. The complex Motie culture is based on a system of "industrial feudalism," in which cultural developments are the direct and logical result of the rigid demands of Motie biology. Each Motie fits into a caste system in accordance with his predetermined physical and psychological makeup. Similar to ants, Moties are born Masters, Mediators, Engineers, and so on. Only the Mediators are permitted contact with humans, since they are capable of empathizing so completely that they learn to think like humans while still maintaining their individual outlooks. However, on occasion, some Mediators become so confused by the multiple roles played by humans that they go mad. There is also a subspecies in the culture called mini-Moties, who are not intelligent, but who instinctively know how to construct and improve almost any machine or tool.

While the scientists are deeply involved in their investigations, an emergency occurs aboard the *MacArthur*, prematurely terminating the probe. Here the time sequence in the novel becomes complicated. When the expedition begins its return trip to the Empire, three crewmen, presumed dead after attempting a forced reentry into Motie Prime's atmosphere, are left behind. During the time the human probe travels through normal space to the nearest Alderson Jump Point and before three Motie ambassadors can join the returning probe, the story of the stranded crewmen is told. In these six chapters, which comprise a suspenseful and thematically significant portion of the novel, secret aspects of the Motie character are dramatized. As a consequence, the reader knows in advance those secrets which the expeditionary probe members must discover for themselves once they return home. A sense of urgency is created because the secrets of the alien mystery must be revealed if mankind is to survive.

Back on New Scotland, an Imperial Commission is established to determine the Empire's self-serving policy toward the Moties. The formulation of the policy includes considerable old fashioned politicking by pressure groups as the Commission constructs an interpretation of the nature of the Moties. The interpretation is made by attempting to pull together the information collected by the probe's military intelligence agents and the scientists: the anthropologists, astrophysicists, biologists, linguists, veterinarians, and xenologists. This list suggests how exactly the authors invented and presented the Motie culture. Simultaneously with the deliberations of the Imperial Commission, the Motie ambassadors are attempting to solve their alien mystery in order to determine the best approach for convincing the Empire to help them establish colonies outside their solar system. Furthermore, the Moties must discover in time to attempt to prevent its disclosure how close the Commission is to uncovering their terrible secret — that once they are allowed to enter the

Empire they biologically cannot help but threaten mankind's existence.

Once the species solve their respective mysteries and once official policies, attitudes, and positions are established, accompanied by appropriate actions, the novel closes in the best tradition of the historical romance. Marriages are made, promotions granted, and punishments dealt, leaving the reader to speculate comfortably about the manner in which the First Contact will ultimately influence the cultural evolutions of each species.

THE NAKED SUN

Author: Isaac Asimov (1920-   )
First book publication: 1957
Type of work: Novel
Time: An unspecified but distant future
Locale: The Earth and Solaria

A continuation of the exploration of the man-machine relationship begun in The Caves of Steel, *here broadened to examine opposing varieties of human frailty exposed in an interstellar murder investigation*

Principal characters:
ELIJAH BALEY, a New York City detective
R. DANEEL OLIVAW, a robot and representative of the planet Aurora
GLADIA DELMARRE, the wife of the murder victim
JOTHAN LEEBIG, a Solarian roboticist

In *The Naked Sun*, Isaac Asimov offers, as in his earlier work, *The Caves of Steel*, a convincingly crafted blend of two separate genres, science fiction and the traditional murder mystery, combined with a careful exploration of the relationship between man and machine. Here, however, Asimov takes his exploration a step further, lending the murder and its investigation an ironic balance of opposing human weaknesses, the first contributing to the mystery and the second to its resolution.

Asimov brings to the combination a notable reputation in each of the genres, and it is not surprising that he should succeed in blending the two forms. As with *The Caves of Steel*, the particular success of the work actually lies in the interdependence of the two parts, each requiring the other for its very existence. The murder of an eminent Solarian scientist is a baffling matter for the Solarians, since the low population and peculiar living conditions of Solaria have heretofore precluded any crime, much less murder. Therefore, it is the Earth detective Elijah Baley who is called to resolve the case. It is Asimov's skillful blending of the elements of two genres, at this point, that provides the complexity of the case.

At odds in resolving the mystery are the three traditional requirements for murder drawn from the mystery genre (motive, means, and opportunity) and the celebrated Three Laws of Robotics (taken from science fiction and in particular Asimov's own seminal works with the robot theme). Of the humans involved, Gladia Delmarre, the victim's wife, appears to be the only human who had the opportunity and motive to commit the murder, but not the means. Conversely, though a number of robots had the opportunity and were physically capable of committing the murder, the Three Laws of Robotics emphatically deny their committing or even allowing the act. Here, then, is presented the problem of willingness without capability on the one side, and capability without willingness on the other.

Further complicating the problem, and adding a certain pressure to the difficulties of the detective's job, are the political nuances involved. Earth is overpopulated, underproductive, militarily weak, and, therefore, both isolationist and isolated. It is embarrassingly subject to its children, the fifty Spacer planets, which all have low populations and high resources. They treat Earth and Earthmen with arrogant condescension. That the Solarians called in Baley, an Earthman, is a victory in itself. His task, however, made clear to him by the officials of his own government, is not only to solve the murder, but to show the level of competence on Earth and at the same time gather information to better his planet's position.

Baley is an adequate detective, more dogged than brilliant, more analytic and plodding than given to inspiration. The complexity of his task is magnified first by the political pressures, second by his total ignorance of Solarian society, and third by a particular frailty endemic to the people of Earth and a distinct handicap in this new society. Baley is subject to incapacitating agoraphobia; this fear of open spaces, sunlight and sky, distance and depth is a neurosis developed in the cities of Earth — crowded, sheltered, controlled places now the habitation of almost all men. This phobia, developed and manipulated in *The Caves of Steel* as a device affecting the course of the story, touches all Earthmen in varying, but always intense, degrees and limits their horizons as effectively as chains. For Baley, the prospect of venturing into space to Solaria is terrifying, and once there, his motion and mobility are strictly limited, a problem made more intense by the nature of Solarian society. At first, Baley spends the majority of his time learning to cope with his own terror, struggling to make progress in the murder case from the confines of his own prepared and sheltered quarters, and developing slowly his ability to tread tentatively and finally with growing assurance beyond the accustomed security of walls and ceiling, light switches and air conditioning.

Contrasting with Baley's physical weakness is the poised and polished perfection of the robot R. Daneel Olivaw, the partner assigned to him in the case. Olivaw is sent into the case by the world of his creators, Aurora, the oldest and strongest of the Spacer worlds. His task is to identify the Solarian problem and determine if it might affect Aurora. Possessed of all the physical capability and calm certitude that Baley lacks, a perfect imitation of a man — or perhaps an imitation of a perfect man — Olivaw has the potential to dominate the situation. He possesses a vast store of factual knowledge and the perfectly logical mind for assimilating data and drawing conclusions. During the first stages of the work, he is always far ahead of Baley, informed, competent, quietly decisive, and physically dominating. Yet for all his skill, he is only a robot, and if he knows the data and records the most minute detail of every event, he still does not know men and mankind. He first serves, as in *The Caves of Steel*, as an irritant to Baley, then as an associate, and finally as an assistant. Never in his remorseless robot logic is he able to make the intuitive leaps of which Baley is ultimately capable; never in his static physical perfection does he reach beyond the limits of his nature, as Baley ultimately does.

The only suspect in the murder is the victim's wife, Gladia Delmarre. Given the circumstances of Solarian life, it seems almost impossible, both to the Solarians and to Olivaw, that anyone else could have committed the crime, even though other circumstances — the absence of a weapon and the certainty that she could not have carried it away — deny this assumption. Gladia exhibits the conditioned response of all Solarians, an extreme abhorrence for the personal, physical presence of any other person, a neurosis as incapacitating in its way as the agoraphobia of Earthmen. This response is a product of the calculated isolation of Solarian life — a population of only twenty thousand is spread over the face of a world — and of the impersonal, genetically calculated birth and rearing of children beginning with fetal "farms" and steadily increased isolation from human contact. The Solarian phobia produces an incapacitating physical repugnance at the prospect of another's presence or the hint of a touch. This in itself, then, leads to general suspicion of Gladia, for spouses alone, and even then under the most strained conditions, are occasionally in each others presence. That another Solarian could have ventured within murdering reach of the victim is an unlikelihood too outrageous for the Solarians to consider.

This trait is most strongly demonstrated in the roboticist Jothan Leebig, a man to whom Baley's suggestion of actual presence rather than the common "viewing" is infuriatingly offensive. A conservative even by the standards of the Solarians, Leebig hides his fear of other people behind anger and arrogance, responding unwillingly and condescendingly to Baley's inquiry at first, then crumbling to shaken acquiescence in the face of Baley's threatening persistence.

These contradictory frailties, Baley's agoraphobia and the Solarian isolationism, provide continued complexity to the problem until at last Baley manages to escape the influence of his robot partner and his own fear. Having become confident and more competent himself, he is able, through the clues provided by his own weakness, to transcend the known facts and come to the possibilities: to combine the frailties of Earthman, the neuroses of Solarian, the limitations of machine, and thus finally to identify the single course through which murder could have occurred.

In its conclusion, the novel becomes grimly cautionary, evoking shadows of NASA's lunar retreat twenty years before the actual event. Baley achieves his success by overcoming his own weakness and manipulating the weaknesses of the Spacers, providing the victory and demonstration of competence demanded by his government. Beyond his victory, Baley realizes the characteristic weakness of Earth's inhabitants, an insight that requires him to lead others out of the safe womb of the Cities and into the open space he once feared.

Criticism:

Pierce, Hazel. "Elementary My Dear," in *Isaac Asimov*. Edited by Joseph D. Olander and Martin Harry Greenberg. New York: Taplinger, 1977, pp. 44-46. The merits of *Naked Sun* are discussed as a sequel to *The Caves of Steel*.

NEEDLE

Author: Hal Clement (Harry C. Stubbs, 1922-   )
First book publication: 1949
Type of work: Novel
Time: The present
Locale: Massachusetts and a small atoll in the Society Islands

In this benchmark portrayal of intelligent alien life, an alien detective chases a fleeing criminal to Earth, adapts to his new environment, enlists the aid of a human, and succeeds in his task

> *Principal characters:*
> THE HUNTER, an alien detective
> THE QUARRY, an alien criminal fleeing the Hunter
> ROBERT KINNAIRD, a high-school student, friend of the Hunter
> MR. KINNAIRD, Robert's father
> CHARLIE TEROA,
> NORMAN HAY,
> HUGH COLBY,
> SHORTY MALMSTROM, and
> KEN RICE, friends of Robert

Since the 1940's Hal Clement, the pseudonym of Harry C. Stubbs, a high-school science teacher by profession, has written short stories and novels that are definitively "hard" science fiction. In the growing critical terminology of the genre, hard science fiction is that which rigorously adheres to the framework of present-day scientific knowledge and confines its speculations about future developments to that framework. It typically eschews the postulation of new discoveries that upset or reverse what we now consider scientific laws. For example, a story set in a universe in which nothing moves faster than light is "harder" than one which utilizes space-warps, fourth dimension drives, or other sleights of hand to evade the Einsteinian restriction.

Yet, even the writer of the hardest science fiction will allow himself to extrapolate from what is now known. Otherwise all science fiction would concern itself with the known characteristics of human beings living on earth in the present. As Isaac Asimov, Poul Anderson, Larry Niven, and others have done, Hal Clement has used interstellar settings, has presumed the existence of faster-than-light drives, and has challenged contemporary science-fiction thinking when necessary, but without endangering his reputation as a writer of logical, carefully worked-out, scientifically defensible stories.

Prior to its first book publication in 1953, *Needle* was serialized in 1949 in the pages of *Astounding Science Fiction,* the standard-bearer of the harder side of the field. It appeared ten years after the publication of an important nonfiction article in the same magazine, L. Sprague de Camp's "Design for Life" (*Astounding Science Fiction,* May-June, 1939). De Camp argued that the human form was the near-optimum shape and size for an intelligent creature, and that any intelligent being in the universe would probably not depart much from the humanoid form. As a key point in his reasoning, de Camp estimated that the size of an intelligent being would fall somewhere between that of a small dog and a large bear. The lower limit is determined by the minimum number of brain cells required by a thinking creature. The upper limit is determined by the size of the body such a brain could control without the specialization seen in marine mammals: a dolphin's brain is larger than a human's, as is its body, simply because the exigencies of living in water require that a disproportionately large amount of the dolphin's brain tissue be devoted simply to the three dimensional movement of its correspondingly large bulk.

With de Camp's size restrictions in mind, Clement created an intelligent being smaller than the lower limit, one of the most memorable aliens in science fiction — the Hunter. Agreeing with de Camp that a thinking creature would be multicelled, and agreeing on the minimum number of cells such a creature would require, Clement evaded the size limit by presuming the individual body cells of the Hunter to be much smaller than those of human beings. Although the Hunter weighs only four pounds, he has thousands of times as many separate cells as a man. Whereas multicellular terrestrial life evolved from the protozoan, the Hunter's kind evolved from the much smaller viruses.

The Hunter differs from a human in another respect. Except for those cells used for memory storage, his equivalent of a brain, the Hunter's cells are not specialized or differentiated one from another; consequently, he does not have a specific shape. Like an amoeba, he moves by extending pseudopods, which, because of his smaller cells, can be slender enough to move with ease through a pore in the human skin. However, he is not reduced to an aimless mass; he has something akin to conscious muscular control, and can shape his body as the occasion demands. For example, if he needs to see, he simply forms part of himself into an eye, complete with lens, optical chamber, and retina.

In spite of his advantages, however, the Hunter is weak and unprotected in comparison to even a squid or a jellyfish, since he lacks a skin. On his native planet, therefore, the Hunter's species has adapted to a symbiotic life with intelligent creatures more familiar to us, ones with rigid skeletons and specialized organs. Members of the Hunter's race live literally inside their companions, the "host"-"guest" relationship being entirely normal and desirable to both parties. The host provides the guest with protection, greater mobility, food, and oxygen. Although most of the Hunter's matter lies in the abdominal cavity of his host, the Hunter takes nourishment and oxygen from the host's bloodstream and disposes of his wastes through the host's excretory organs. As compensation, the guest keeps the host free from external and internal parasites. The host is thereby safe from disease and distress, except accidents and the natural aging of the body. The Hunter's species is able to speed the healing of cuts and scratches for their hosts; in the novel, Robert Kinnaird receives a gash eight inches long and a half-inch deep, which the Hunter immediately closes and holds together with his own tissue. Finally, the host and guest provide each other with mutual affection and companionship, forming close and longlasting (usually lifelong) relationships.

Although these creatures have no personal names, they do have identities, personalities, and even professions. On his home planet, the Hunter is a police officer, the companion of a person who holds a position similar to that of an Assistant Police Chief. Individuals of the Hunter's species are by and large extremely law-abiding and benevolent creatures. The reasons for this are, first, that much of their success in finding an intelligent host depends on their good behavior as a group, since they clearly cannot overpower and enter a host. Second, since a host is entirely at the mercy of his guest, he would obviously not accept one were there any risk involved. The host realizes that if a guest operating from within closed a major blood vessel or paralyzed an important nerve, he would die in a matter of minutes, and after the guest vacated his body, the murder would be undetectable as such.

Though crime is extremely rare among the Hunter's kind, it does occur, and from this fact springs the plot of *Needle*. Guests are not dependent on their hosts for travel, either earthly or interstellar. They can also employ the bodies of small, nonintelligent animals such as monkeys when it is necessary for such jobs as manipulating the controls of small spaceships. As the novel opens, a criminal, identified only as the Quarry, is fleeing punishment for some heinous crime, using an animal host to pilot his spaceship. The pursuing Hunter knows that if the Quarry lands on a planet, he will be almost impossible to find. In the desperate chase which follows, both Hunter and Quarry are forced to crash-land on Earth. The Hunter's animal host is killed in the wreck, and he loses contact with the Quarry; thus begins the search for a "needle in a haystack" which gives the novel its title. Fortune favors the Hunter at first, since both the Quarry and the Hunter have crashed close to the shore of a small Pacific island near Tahiti, effectively restricting the Quarry to a relatively small area.

The Hunter's first move is to try to find an intelligent host, and in this task he is less fortunate. He chooses one of a small group of teen-aged boys who are playing on the beach, and enters his body while the boy naps. The boy is Robert Kinnaird, a tenth-grade high school student, the son of an engineer in the island's only industry, the production of petroleum products through bacterial action. Since the Hunter has no way of knowing that his choice of host is not an adult member of the species, he can hardly be blamed for his selection; since he also has no way of communicating with his new host, he is essentially helpless. Furthermore, to his chagrin Robert boards a ship, travels to another island, gets on a plane, and flies to what the reader (but not the Hunter) realizes is a boarding school in Massachusetts (much like the one at which the author teaches). It soon becomes clear to the Hunter that, even after he succeeds in communicating with the boy, he will not be able to provide independence of movement because of his age.

But Robert's youth has advantages, too. His enrollment in English classes speeds the Hunter's learning of the language. Eventually the Hunter achieves communication with Robert; by lightly pressing on selected nerves in the boy's retinas, he can cause words to appear against a blank background. He can now enlist Robert's active and very useful help. A second instance of good fortune occurs at this point, almost offsetting the Hunter's bad luck in his choice of a host. The discovery that an alien creature is living inside him has, to put it mildly, been a shock for Robert, producing a noticeable change in his behavior. The school doctor misdiagnoses its cause as homesickness and prescribes as a treatment that Robert return to the island. After months, the Hunter can now resume the chase.

From this point on, the reader's attention is centered on Robert, with the Hunter playing a large but subsidiary role. It becomes clear that Robert and the Hunter form a complementary team. The Hunter's role becomes advisory, while the boy exercises his ingenuity; the Hunter knows how the Quarry would think and act, while Robert is familiar with the island and its inhabitants.

Two factors narrow the pursuer's task. First, they assume that the Quarry would choose an intelligent host (rather than a fish or an animal) to gain maximum freedom of action. Fortunately, the island is populated solely by the small number of workers at the petroleum facility and their families, and nobody has left the island during the interim between Robert's departure for school and his return. The story thus becomes a classic tale of the sleuth and his assistant as the pair searches for clues, follows false leads, eliminates suspects one by one, and eventually locates and destroys the criminal.

Needle is a very fine detective story. One can imagine fans of Agatha Christie or John Dickson Carr finding a great deal of enjoyment in it. But the novel offers more. In its portrait of the Hunter, we have a convincing alien, astonishingly different in unexpected ways, yet completely believable. Like many other fine science fiction novels, *Needle* was inspired by the writer's determination to provide a counterexample to a presumed general rule; and through his portrait of the Hunter, Clement succeeds entirely. The competent and likable little alien whom we get to know only as "the Hunter" has few peers in the genre.

NIGHTWINGS

Author: Robert Silverberg (1936-   )
First book publication: 1969
Type of work: Novel
Time: The far future
Locale: Roum, Perris, and Jorslem

A *chronicle about the "redemption" of Earth both from outside invaders and from its own progressive deterioration*

> Principal characters:
>   WUELLIG (TOMIS), initially a Watcher, subsequently a Rememberer, then a Pilgrim
>   AVLUELA, a Flier
>   GORMON, an alien masquerading as a Changeling
>   THE PRINCE OF ROUM, a Dominator
>   OLMAYNE, a Rememberer

The first part of *Nightwings* was originally published as a novella bearing the same title in 1968 and won a Hugo award. The two remaining sections, expanding the story to novel length, also saw separate publication before the book appeared.

The story is set in a distant future referred to as the Third Cycle; the First Cycle was the period of man's rise from savagery to civilization and the Second the period of his technological magnificence. The Earth of the Third Cycle is decadent; the human race has been humbled by a self-inflicted catastrophe and the period of confusion which followed it, though the relics of the technology of the Second Cycle are still used for various purposes. Society is divided into a series of occupational guilds, which define for each man a place within the scheme of things and regulate both his behavior and his opportunities. One such guild, the Fliers, consists of individuals equipped with insectlike wings — a product of Second Cycle genetic engineering. The process by which these wings permit flight is mysterious and quasi-magical, but is subject to the restriction that the wings are only operative by night when the pressure of the sun's radiation is absent; thus the novel acquires its title. Other products of Second Cycle experiments in genetic engineering and teratogenesis are the guildless Changelings, monstrous creatures generally regarded as subhuman. The Changelings were once guilded, but lost that status following an abortive rebellion in which they temporarily seized the most important of human shrines, the city of Jorslem.

The protagonist of the novel is, during the first section, a member of the guild of Watchers, whose function it is to "tune in" periodically to a kind of psionic scanning device which allows them to sense the approach of invaders from outside the solar system. An invasion has been prophesied, but many of the people on Earth now believe the prophecy to be a myth and the vocation of the Watchers, though sacred, to be a futile one. The protagonist is not initially named (the rules of the guild demand that his name be kept secret) but we later discover that as a Watcher he is called Wuellig.

The first part of the narrative tells how the Watcher comes to the city of Roum in the company of a Flier named Avluela (whom he loves, though he is much older than she and is in any case bound by a vow of celibacy) and a Changeling named Gormon. The three find themselves without lodgings because the Watchers of Roum refuse to take them in, and they go to seek an audience with the Prince of the city in order to ask for shelter. Their request is granted, but only because the Prince is smitten with Avluela and commands her to his bed. Gormon, at this point, is enraged with jealousy, and confesses to the Watcher that he is Avluela's lover (though such a union is strictly forbidden by the laws of the guild-system). He further swears that in time to come he will put out the eyes of the Prince of Roum in order to revenge himself.

Gormon has made a habit of mocking the Watcher's calling and forces the Watcher to confront his own lack of faith by questioning him while the Watcher's hand is inside the Mouth of Truth, a stone hollow which, it is said, will crush the hand of anyone who offends it by lying. When Gormon, in turn, places his own hand in the Mouth so that the Watcher can ask *his* question, he tells the Watcher that despite his conviction of the futility of Watching there *will* be an invasion, and that he is not a Changeling but a military observer for the aliens whose invasion fleet is approaching. The Watcher soon confirms this information, and sounds an alarm which rouses the whole planet to prepare its defenses. Alas, the defenses are quite inadequate, and Earth falls, its conquest little more than a formality.

The ex-Watcher, now guildless because there is no more Watching to be done, decides to leave Roum for Perris in the hope of joining the guild of Rememberers, custodians of Earth's history. He finds company in a man who wears the mask of the guild of Pilgrims, though he does not have a starstone, a jewel which allows genuine Pilgrims to link their consciousness to the divine Will. The false Pilgrim is, in fact, the Prince of Roum, now blinded and fleeing from the invaders, who have ordered the capture of all Dominators. As the two leave the city, the ex-Watcher sees Avluela flying overhead in full daylight, sustained in her flight by Gormon the invader, who flies with her.

The second section of the book tells of the travelers' acceptance by the guild of Rememberers in Perris, sponsored by a female Rememberer named Olmayne. The protagonist, now called Tomis, throws himself into the tedious work of an apprentice, and eventually — by sheer accident — locates an "image-recording" which shows the ancestors of the invaders imprisoned by men of the Second Cycle in a kind of zoo. It is believed that this historical act called down the wrath of the Will upon Earth to destroy the civilization of the Second Cycle. The invaders have finally come to take the revenge which they swore in the distant past — to complete the humiliation of man. The invaders desperately want to recover and destroy this particular image-recording, which has been concealed by the Rememberers, and Tomis eventually betrays its whereabouts to them in order to win the freedom of the Prince of Roum, who is threatened with exposure by Olmayne's husband Elegro. Tomis wins an amnesty for the Prince, but gains nothing, because the Prince is murdered by Elegro, who is himself slain by his adulterous wife.

In the third part of the book both Tomis and Olmayne become Pilgrims, bound for Jorslem as possible candidates for rejuvenation by means of a process administered by the guild of Renewers. Not everyone is accepted for Renewal, and some of those to whom the process is administered fail to meet the spiritual requirements. While *en route* to Jorslem Tomis and Olmayne become involved with a Surgeon who expresses his opinion that the invasion not only marks the consummation of the punishment inflicted upon mankind by the Will for the sin of pride, but also provides a sign that the time is now ripe for the redemption of the race. Tomis discovers when he reaches Jorslem that a new guild has been formed, a guild of Redeemers, which will accept members from all other guilds, including Changelings. He meets Avluela again, and finds that she already belongs to the new guild.

Tomis and Olmayne are both accepted for Renewal, and Tomis is successfully rejuvenated; but Olmayne, a jealous and intolerant woman entirely selfish in her outlook, proves unable to adjust to the requirements of the treatment and regresses to early childhood, in which condition she dies.

The means by which the members of the new guild obtain personal redemption — and seek redemption for the whole race — is a mutual attunement of minds made possible by a combination of the instruments once used by the Watchers and the starstones used by the Pilgrims. Together, the two devices permit users to attune themselves to the Will and literally to enter into one another's spirit. All men can now be reunited, no matter what their status or occupation, and the despised Changelings are to play the role of scapegoats no longer. The conquest of Earth ceases to have any real importance: "When all mankind is enrolled in our guild, we will be conquered no longer. When each of us is part of every other one of us, our sufferings will end. There is no need for us to struggle against our conquerors, for we will absorb them, once we are all Redeemed."

Nightwings was written by Silverberg in the months following the destruction of his home by fire, an event which in his autobiographical essay "Sounding Brass, Tinkling Cymbal" he characterizes as traumatic and confesses to having seen as a kind of judgment, redressing an imbalance resulting from his enjoyment of good fortune in the past. Clearly, there is within the book considerable depth of personal feeling and an entirely private significance. Its symbolism often seems less than subtle, but there is no mistaking the authenticity of the emotion underlying its allegorical features. There is much in the novel which can best be interpreted by reference to Silverberg's personal experience. It clearly reflects, for instance, the fact that during the 1960's he traveled extensively in Europe and that his visit to Jerusalem was of particular personal significance. But it is also a futuristic recasting of traditional Judeo-Christian salvation myth, and as such has much more general allegorical claims.

Nightwings, especially the first section, is in some ways a deeply nostalgic work. The situation described there — the decadent Earth strewn with the quasi-magical flotsam of an ancient and all-powerful technology, threatened by invasion from the stars — is highly reminiscent of the scenarios which Silverberg employed habitually in the days when, as a prolific young science fiction writer, he used to fill the pages of *Science Fiction Adventures* with novelettes bearing titles such as "Slaves of the Star-Giants" and "Vengeance of the Space Armadas." *Nightwings* recalls this conventional scenery in the service of a very different ideology; the romanticization of extravagant violence and tough-minded heroism is here replaced by a very different set of values emphasizing the virtues of empathy and pacifism. The theme which runs through virtually all of Silverberg's novels of the second phase of his career (post-1965) is the healing of states of alienation: the reconciliation of "outsiders" of various kinds to their fellow human beings, very often by a direct contact of minds, frequently involving processes of rebirth both literal and metaphorical. *Nightwings* approaches this theme in reverse of the pulp-fiction scenarios which Silverberg had abandoned in order that the scenario itself might be, in a sense, renewed.

Everything that Silberberg does in *Nightwings* he went on to do much better in other novels. The mythology of rebirth is much more powerfully developed in *Downward to the Earth*, while the allegorical qualities of the plot helped prepare the way for the brilliant *Son of Man*, by far the most significant allegorical novel to use the vocabulary of symbols developed by the literature of the scientific imagination.

Nightwings is inferior to much of Silverberg's work of the 1970's, but it is nevertheless an important work. It cannot be described as a transitional work, for Silverberg had already abandoned the habits of his earlier career some years before writing it, but it is a novel which constructs a kind of bridge between the mythology of his early work and the ideological concerns of his mature work. The Second Cycle of the book is an imaginary historical era which was once central to the futuristic imaginings of science fiction writers, but which has now passed from fashionability — an invalidated dream. *Nightwings* is a novel which recognizes the redundancy of that mythology while remembering that it once seemed so marvelously appealing. Contemporary science fiction — of which Silverberg's later work is such an important part — is now into its own "Third Cycle" of tattered dreams and spiritual questing, and for this reason *Nightwings* has a certain paradigmatic status. It is hard to find the story wholly convincing, and its message is awkwardly over-obvious in its presentation, but the novel remains very much in keeping with the ideative climate of recent science fiction.

NORSTRILIA

Author: Cordwainer Smith (Paul M. A. Linebarger, 1913-1966)
First book publication: 1975
Type of work: Novel
Time: Approximately A. D. 16,000
Locale: Norstrilia (Old North Australia), Mars, Earth

The adventures of Rod McBan, who buys the Earth but gives it up and returns to his native Norstrilia when he learns the real meaning of life

Principal characters:
> RODERICK MCBAN, CLI, a very rich, very bright, very eccentric young Norstrilian
> LORD REDLADY, his first protector
> THE CATMASTER, his guru
> ELEANOR, his stand-in
> LAVINIA, his patient true love
> C'MELL, a fabulously beautiful, wise, and trustworthy cat-woman
> LORD JESTOCOST, a powerful chief of the Instrumentality and ally of the underpeople
> E'TELEKELI, spiritual leader of the underpeople

Like Frank Herbert and J. R. R. Tolkien, Cordwainer Smith dreamed a world into being. In his twenty-seven "Instrumentality of Mankind" stories, Smith developed one of the most elaborate and extensive imaginary universes in science fiction — a universe of several thousand planets, each with its own weirdly appropriate creatures, culture, and terrain. Moreover, he linked these myriad planets by more than fourteen thousand years of history, in which the Instrumentality is the dominant, unifying force. Because it encompasses such breadth of space and depth of time, Smith's dream world has a captivating density and a richness of detail which have engrossed readers since the series began to unfold in the 1950's.

Norstrilia, which is the longest and one of the last of the "Instrumentality" tales, provides a particularly illuminating perspective on Smith's inventiveness with settings. It is the only novel in the group (the other twenty-six "Instrumentality" works are all short stories) and, although Smith died before he could complete his grand design for the whole series, we know that he intended *Norstrilia* to serve as a major focal point. In *Norstrilia* Smith amplified and explored many of the themes he had introduced in his short stories; by centering his novel on the contrasting cultures of two especially important planets in his system, Earth and Old North Australia (or Norstrilia), he pointed up the dynamic antithesis that shapes all one hundred and forty centuries of his fictional history.

Most simply, this basic antithesis is between logical positivism and intuitive spirituality. Most Lords and Ladies of the Instrumentality, and indeed most people throughout Smith's vast planetary system, are logical positivists; they believe that life is precisely what the physical senses declare it to be, wholly material. From their point of view the planet Norstrilia is one of the universe's great resources, because it is the sole producer of "stroon," a life-prolonging substance which gives almost all humans a life span of several hundred years. Thanks to "stroon" and other technological improvements, the human condition in the seventeenth millennium when *Norstrilia*'s action takes place, is no longer the nasty, brutish, and messy sort twentieth century readers must endure.

Surprisingly, however, the Norstrilians themselves quietly but systematically resist the effects if not the premises of the enlightened materialism to which Norstrilian "stroon" so significantly contributes. Instead of adopting the luxurious hedonism favored by Earth's humans, Norstrilians live in spartan simplicity, denying themselves fleshy comforts in order to protect and heighten what they believe to be their truest, most important resource — Norstrilian strength of character. Because it deliberately reintroduces discomforts, uncertainties, and even dangers into the materialistic Utopia designed and administered by the Instrumentality, Norstrilian culture epitomizes the "Rediscovery of Man" movement which forms a large part of Smith's world history. To Rediscovery people, exemplified in this novel by the Norstrilians, the "perfection" engineered by the Instrumentality's technocrats can only corrode and destroy human nature and human societies, for such notions of Utopia inaccurately assume that material ease is the one object of human desires.

But to Roderick McBan, CLI, *Norstrilia*'s central character, Norstrilian asceticism and Earthly hedonism alike fail to meet essential human needs. McBan first turns to the holographic image of Shakespeare's Hamlet, then to "Reconstituted Late Inglish Language Verse," for the wisdom he finds lacking in his native Norstrilian culture. These ancients instantly show him that the human condition is fundamentally, not incidentally or secondarily, psychological — that what one thinks determines what one experiences. Energized by this radically antimaterialistic sense of things, McBan exiles himself from Norstrilia and flies to Earth, which he has bought in the initial manic flurry of his new self-assertiveness. And on Earth he completes his personal version of rediscovering mankind: he enters the underpeople's mysterious subculture and is converted to their revolutionary religious outlook:

> Now it was all different. . . . He had his own problems, but they were no longer the problems of wealth or of survival. Somehow he had a confidence that a hidden, friendly power in the universe would take care of him, if he took care of others.

McBan gains this intuitive world view by undergoing a sort of primal scream therapy under the direction of the underpeople's principal spiritual teacher, the Catmaster. Much of what he learns in the Catmaster's "Department Store of Hearts' Desires" we are plainly meant to learn for ourselves in the pages of *Norstrilia*, which recounts that each place McBan visits really signifies a psychological rather than a physical locale. So Earth represents humanity's divided consciousness, split between the pragmatic, rational thinking which dominates Western civilization and the intuitive, emotional thought processes which Westerners have traditionally associated with women, (some) animals, and the inscrutable Orient. For the first several millennia of its existence the Instrumentality, symbolizing the organizing force in human consciousness, has allied itself with pragmatic intellectuality (whose philosophy is logical positivism) and suppressed the instincts and feelings (according to Smith, the core of intuitive spirituality); now, in the time of Roderick McBan, CLI, the psychological balances are shifting, and especially astute Chiefs of the Instrumentality, such as Lord Jestocost and Lady Alice More, are beginning to liberate the underpeople — to reaffirm the value of intuitions, instincts, and feelings in the psychological universe.

Read from this perspective, *Norstrilia* provides a vivid map of what Julian Jaynes has termed the broken-down bicameral mind. Smith appears to have anticipated Jaynes's theory that all human history originates in and is explainable by the breakdown of communications between the verbalizing, rationalizing, "sensible" left lobe of the human brain and the non-verbal, intuitive right lobe. But Smith, unlike Jaynes, argues that this split can be healed. This is the significance of Norstrilia, which stands for the mind on the verge of reintegration. By emphasizing simplicity, self-reliance, and family-centeredness, Norstrilian culture requires the balanced exercise of both left-lobe and right-lobe traits, and at the same time prevents too enthusiastic an attachment to the values of either half of consciousness. Insofar as it proposes that the Norstrilian life-style is the necessary preparatory discipline we, too, must follow if we hope to become whole, *Norstrilia* is a tract, not a map — Smith's sermon on what we must do to be psychologically saved.

Unfortunately, this novel, which sets forth the case for integration with many beguiling images, memorable characters, and dramatic incidents, fails to practice the very virtue it most insistently preaches. *Norstrilia*'s plot is conspicuously disunified. In fact, the book reads less like a novel than like two imperfectly joined novellas, strikingly dissimilar in focus and style. Excluding the obviously tacked-on "Theme and Prologue," *Norstrilia*'s first seven chapters form a unit dealing with the Old North Australian rites of passage which initiate McBan into manhood; this section centers on the personality of Rod McBan, whom it convincingly portrays as a youth with enormous psychological potential. The plot of these seven chapters consists of a series of harrowing ordeals which compel McBan to acknowledge, develop, and test his capabilities as an intuitive, rational, pragmatic, and feeling person; and the seventh chapter concludes with McBan in the midst of the most difficult challenge of all — testing whether his psyche can survive when his brain has been transplanted into a new body.

Then, following three jarringly choppy "bridge" chapters which remove

McBan to Mars and introduce us to numerous new, undeveloped characters, *Norstrilia*'s second sequence of eight chapters begins. Here McBan's role is primarily that of passive observer touring exotic Earth, while the plot centers on the intrigues of Lord Jestocost, C'Mell, and other underpeople. The function of this half of the book is to explore characters and themes from "The Ballad of Lost C'Mell," "The Dead Lady of Clown Town," and "Drunkboat." Indeed, *Norstrilia*'s second half is far more a sequel to these three short stories than a coherent continuation of *Norstrilia*'s original plot. In these eight chapters McBan's initiation experiences dwindle to minor, peripheral incidents, and his initiators are infinitely more interesting than he is. As a matter of fact, the Rod McBan who visits Earth is so limp and ordinary a young man that one is tempted to conclude that his great experiment has failed, and that his grandly promising psyche died on the surgeon's table.

Paradoxically, the problems with *Norstrilia*'s overall plotting spring, it seems, from the book's strongest and most attractive feature — the intense imaginativeness which vivifies individual scenes. Both here and in his short stories, Smith's best scenes dramatize the sense of wonder — the soul's encounters with an amazingly various, intriguingly numinous universe. McBan's moments in the Garden of Death, the Gap, and the Palace of the Governor of Night all represent his retreat from the world of Norstrilian received wisdom and common sense to the private place of his own interior selfhood; by focusing on McBan's expanding consciousness and building these scenes wholly out of the images in McBan's active intuition, Smith brings his character's adventures straight into our own minds. In the scenes involving the underpeople Smith is even more demanding of himself and us: instead of working through McBan's mediating consciousness, he compels us to perceive the meanings of the underpeople's words and actions for ourselves. Smith's utter fidelity to each imaginative vision — his insistence that every such vision live on its own terms — makes *Norstrilia* an extraordinarily fascinating and suggestive — although inconsistent — work.

Smith's emphasis on imaginative vision at the expense of intellectual outline is all the more interesting when one considers his formidably intellectual background. Actually "Cordwainer Smith" is the pen name of Paul Myron Anthony Linebarger, who was until his death in 1966 one of America's most expert authorities on the politics, history, and literatures of the Far East, as well as on psychological warfare. Fluent in six languages and intimately conversant with several Oriental and Occidental cultures, he used his science fiction chiefly as a vehicle for escaping any single culture's mindset, synthesizing his extraordinary wealth of information into an almost mystical search for a transcendent understanding of human nature and human history. Because its basis is intuitive rather than intellectual, *Norstrilia*'s numerous references to mythological, literary, historical, political, and scientific figures do not exclude most readers, as scholarly allusions usually do: for example, we know C'Mell to be an earth mother goddess because *Norstrilia*'s action forces us to appreciate her primal fertility, not because we happen to remember the role of Semele in Greek mythology.

Although Smith composed *Norstrilia* as a single, novel-length work, it was not published in that form during his lifetime. Smith himself divided *Norstrilia* into two shorter units and added a little explanatory padding to each, but it is not entirely clear whether he did this simply in order to get the story quickly into print by bringing it out in science fiction magazines (which did happen; these edited portions of *Norstrilia* were published in the 1960's), or in order to improve the story's form and focus. Whatever the case, the novel-length *Norstrilia*, which Smith's widow published almost ten years after Smith's death, expresses the vitality and openendedness of a good work-in-progress. And it challenges us to speculate on what Smith might have done with it, had he lived to explore his fictional universe more completely.

OMNIVORE

Author: Piers Anthony (1924-)
First book publication: 1968
Type of work: Novel
Time: An unspecified future
Locale: The United States and the planet Nacre

A novel about first contact with an alien species beyond human comprehension, which shows how the human characters and the aliens are products of their different biological and social structures

> Principal characters:
> SUBBLE, an investigator for the central government
> VEG (VACHEL SMITH), one of the three members of an exploration team on the planet Nacre
> 'QUILON (AQUILON), the second member, and only woman, of the team
> CAL, the third member

Ever since the publication of Stanley G. Weinbaum's "A Martian Odyssey" in 1934, science fiction has been filled with intelligent aliens that pose not a threat to mankind but a puzzle. Such aliens are not the brutal invaders of the Earth that can be found in H. G. Wells's *War of the Worlds* or Robert Heinlein's *The Puppet Masters*, but rather they usually take the form of beings who are interested in observing and communicating with humanity. Such creatures, moreover, are often used by science fiction writers as a means of comparison by which shortcomings in the human race are pointed out. Theodore Sturgeon's "Affair with a Green Monkey" uses aliens in this fashion, as does *Omnivore*.

To say that *Omnivore* presents the aliens so that statements can be made about mankind does not sufficiently characterize the novel nor does it do justice to Anthony's accomplishment. In trying to present both the aliens and the humans, Anthony has created an outstanding example of how a good science fiction writer is able to create new worlds with consistent systems of biology, physics, and environment. His portrayal of the planet Nacre is both convincing and pleasing, and, furthermore, his description of a future Earth is equally consistent and believable.

It is important for the novel that the worlds of Nacre and Earth be credible because the point central to the work is that the aliens of Nacre and the humans of Earth are a result of their physical structures. Anthony takes the old maxim, "we are what we eat," and carries it to its ultimate conclusion. Thus, how each creature lives within its environment, how each constructs its social institutions, and how each lives with its individual identity are all determined by the biology of that being. With such a theme Anthony must carefully construct his world so that each feature will fit.

Omnivore is divided into four chapters. Within each of the first three chapters, the investigator, Subble, interviews a member of an exploration team to Nacre that has returned to Earth. The final chapter concerns Subble's own confrontation with the aliens from Nacre. Anthony has created in Subble one of the more interesting secret agents in literature. He is a human being who has been so modified that he is, for all practical purposes, identical with all the other investigators in his agency. After each assignment, moreover, all individual memories are erased so that the reaction of all investigators to any one case will be identical. This identity of form and mind should not, however, be seen as an equality in mediocrity. All of the agents share a high degree of intellectual achievement, an advanced state of concern for the people they become involved with, and a fine sense of how to use the physical capabilities they have been given through biological modifications. Subble, therefore, is not an oversexed, amoral agent incapable of making independent judgments, nor are any of his fellow agents.

The first of the exploration team that Subble interviews is Veg, a character who in every way fits the description of a rugged outdoorsman, except that he is a vegetarian with a fierce respect for the sanctity of life. Veg is not a pacifist; he is willing to take life if he or his friends are threatened; but aside from such a situation, he insists on the right of all animate creatures to live.

During the course of the interview the reader learns that Subble only knows that he must interview the three explorers and determine if any threat exists to Earth. Subble does not have any idea who these people are or what form a potential threat might take. Each agent is given only the barest details, so that any conclusion he draws will come directly from what he learns on the case. Anthony, thus, uses Subble's complete ignorance of the facts as an excuse for the exposition of the plot; by and large, the device works well.

Subble learns through the interview why Veg became a vegetarian. When he was young, Veg's older and more promising brother died of cancer. Veg could not understand why the brother had died rather than he himself. His only method of resolving this dilemma was to conclude that there was no reason for death in general, and that nothing should die. Thus he resolved to avoid killing all animate creatures. Veg, in other words, has chosen his style of life out of a need to respond to a personal crisis. His choice reflects an attempt to answer a question that has no solution, and, in this way, it is not an answer but an escape.

Once Veg has told Subble about his earlier life, he is able to speak about his part in the exploration of Nacre. Instead of simply having Veg relate his experience, Anthony uses a flashback method, with Veg as the point-of-view character. In this way he recreates the entire episode, complete with Veg's reactions to it, without having to keep up the pretense of a conversation as well. Thus, the planet can be fully described without interruption by Subble.

As Veg describes Nacre the picture emerges of a luxuriant mushroom world filled with colorful, divergent types of fungus, and Anthony's style is equal to the lush nature of the planet. Aside from the "plantlife" Nacre has three species of animate creatures: herbivore, omnivore, and carnivore. Veg's interview describes the exploration team's first encounter with the carnivore, the last of the three varieties the team encountered. The carnivores are mantalike creatures that fly at great speeds and use their thin tails as whips. The tails are extremely sharp, capable of cutting the bodies of the omnivores to shreds. The omnivores appear to be their sole source of food; however, Veg, 'Quilon, and Cal were not aware of the mantas' eating habits, and, therefore, fled the first one they saw. In fleeing, the team's vehicle burned out and the three were stranded on Nacre, forced to return to their base on foot.

Veg relates only the first stage of their journey. He tells Subble that it will be up to 'Quilon and Cal to finish the story. Clearly, the tripartite division of the adventure is geared to the three characters. Each part ends with a climactic moment for the teller. For Veg, this moment occurred when he killed one of the carnivores, believing that his and 'Quilon's lives were in danger. In order to save 'Quilon, in particular, he was forced to destroy the creature. The death of the manta at the hands of Veg ends the first chapter of *Omnivore*. From Veg's earlier conversation with Subble, the reader can be sure that this killing has had a deep and disturbing effect on Veg, but it is an effect that Veg must work out for himself. Having all the information he will get from Veg, Subble moves on.

In Chapter Two Subble and the reader are introduced to 'Quilon. After the interview with Veg it has become obvious that there is a love triangle between Veg, 'Quilon, and Cal. According to 'Quilon, the reason that the three of them are now separated is so she can make a choice between the two men. Subble, however, and the reader as well, suspects that the cause of the separation lies deeper. The killing of the manta has hurt Veg, and one starts to look for an equal injury in 'Quilon. She tells Subble that she too has become a vegetarian, but unlike Veg, her food preference seems to be an emotional response to her stay on Nacre. 'Quilon is a remarkably beautiful and intelligent woman who, as a child, was somehow made to feel guilty about her beauty. As a result, she has convinced herself that her smile is both ugly and revealing of her inner worthlessness. When she finally trusts Subble sufficiently, the episode she relates to him is centered around these feelings of self-hate.

'Quilon's story begins after the killing of the manta. Later on the trip, another manta began escorting the three explorers. It did not threaten them except when 'Quilon approached Veg. Veg was able to touch Cal and 'Quilon was able to touch Cal without any reaction from the manta, but 'Quilon was driven off each time she neared Veg. While experiencing this mysterious behavior on the part of the manta, the team was attacked by an omnivore. On Nacre it is the omnivore that is the most vicious of the creatures. It attacks all things with senseless brutality unconcerned with the destruction it causes. The omnivore is only concerned with sustaining its own life, and anything that will contribute to that single and immediate end will suffice.

In the battle against the omnivore, Veg fell over a ledge. 'Quilon quickly followed and, happy to see Veg unharmed, she smiled. Veg was immediately aware of the significance of the smile and rather than call attention to it tried to control his own expression. The result appeared to be a sneer, which 'Quilon interpreted as confirmation of her inner ugliness. Thus, Nacre has proved climactic to 'Quilon as well. At that moment her most unhappy thoughts about herself were reinforced.

'Quilon's attempt to be a vegetarian is part of her self-punishment. Before her episode on Nacre is related, she takes Subble to see an automated "farm" in her living complex. It is a nightmare of machinelike efficiency in which animals are caged, fattened, and slaughtered with complete indifference. To 'Quilon, the human race is the equivalent of the omnivore of Nacre; it destroys brutally for its own self-indulgence with no concern for the environment it must live in. It is in this chapter that Anthony portrays the overcrowded life of Earth in detail.

Life has become intolerable to many humans because of the compromises that have had to be made for the sake of overpopulation. 'Quilon is a fitting spokeswoman for this description because she strongly feels an affinity with the omnivore of Nacre and sees in the human omnivores a distinct parallel. Where Veg has turned to vegetarianism because of his guilt for not dying in place of his brother, 'Quilon turns to it because of guilt for being a human.

In the first two episodes, Subble has been a concerned and interested listener as Veg and then 'Quilon tell their stories, but when he interviews Cal, Subble must assume a new role. Veg referred to the threesome as brawn, beauty, and brains, and Cal is definitely the "brains" of the group. He becomes Subble's teacher as Subble prepares to face the mantas. Cal confirms Subble's suspicion that the three explorers have brought some mantas back to Earth. It will be Subble's task to confront them and learn from the mantas as well.

Before Cal begins his lessons, however, he ties together the story of the expedition on Nacre. Cal has a rather gruesome dietary quirk. Both previous to and during the adventure on Nacre, Cal had convinced himself that he could "eat" nothing but blood. 'Quilon had told Subble of this and included the fact that during their trip back to their base she had bled herself in order to sustain Cal. Furthermore, after the attack by the omnivore and its subsequent death at the tail of the manta, Cal had drunk the "blood" from the body of the creature.

He then explains to Subble the reasons behind each of the characters' eating habits: each of them is seeking to establish a separate identity, one that denies their humanity. Life has become far too burdensome as man, and, therefore, such habits become both a denial of the human characteristics so abhorrent to them and a claim to individuality. Cal, however, has also learned a lesson on Nacre which involves a fundamental difference between humans and the creatures of that planet. The three species of Nacre are inexorably characterized by their place in the food chain, while humans can transcend their position.

Before Subble understands Cal's point, Cal leads him on a hallucinatory dream through the fungus kingdom. Subble learns to allow the vision to shape his thought as he comprehends the importance of various types of fungi for life on Earth. Unfortunately, while the description of the dream and the events that take place are rich in detail, Anthony never fully justifies its length or most of the information that comes from it. Subble must learn something of the type of creature represented by the mantas and he must learn to control his vision under the influence of the drug. But much of the dream exists for its own sake and does appear to slow down the novel at its crucial point. The dream sequence is intensified when the Cal part of the episode on Nacre is finally brought into the chapter as an afterthought. The dream simply seems to be too long for its stated purpose and it interrupts the more important part of the chapter.

Cal's episode begins with a description of how the manta killed the omnivore by cutting it to shreds with its tail. Cal then continues by explaining the manta's attempts to keep Veg and 'Quilon separated. The manta classified Veg as a herbivore, 'Quilon as an omnivore, and Cal as a carnivore. On Nacre the herbivores are entirely peaceful, feeding off the "vegetation" of the planet. The carnivores, while not so peaceful, feed strictly off the omnivores and preserve the herbivores as a vital link in their food chain. The omnivores, however, disrupt the food chain because their food preferences are not limited. Thus, they are totally destructive, and the carnivores, by making the omnivores their sole source of food, keep them in check. Given such biological organization on Nacre, the mantas did not see Cal as a threat to Veg because carnivores do not eat herbivores. 'Quilon, moreover, could not be a threat to Cal because carnivores are fully capable of destroying omnivores. But the omnivore 'Quilon was a threat to the herbivore Veg; therefore, the manta tried to protect Veg from her.

It was this revelation that has so disturbed 'Quilon, but an even worse one was in store for Cal. For years Cal had tried to destroy any interest in preserving his own life. He had deliberately cut himself off from any positive friendship and had formed self-destructive habits. Cal was not only sick of his own life, he was sick of the human race itself. Thus, when 'Quilon bled herself for him, Cal's whole aim toward annihilation was shaken. His friends were willing to die rather than abandon him to his long-sought goal. As a gesture of his love for his friends, Cal gave up trying to die on the journey back to the base.

A second event occurs before they return which makes Cal put off his own death indefinitely. Toward the end of the adventure the three explorers encountered a group of mantas. At that moment, the cloud cover of Nacre opened and bright sunlight broke through. Since the mantas evolved in a world usually shaded by the clouds, this light blinded one of the creatures. 'Quilon ran to aid it, but the light had done its damage and the manta was completely disabled.

The other mantas quickly put the helpless one to death, and then one of them lightly punished 'Quilon for interfering. Although she was not aware of it, 'Quilon's actions prevented the freeing of the dead manta's spores into the atmosphere. The mantas, however, recognized 'Quilon's motive as compassion, and as an act of faith they gave her eight baby mantas. These are the mantas that the team has brought back to Earth with them.

What has so deeply disturbed Cal about this whole event is that he understands that the mantas see in 'Quilon a nobler quality than he has seen in his fellow man. The mantas have every reason to hate any omnivorous creature, but they are willing to trust what they have seen. Cal has refused to place any such trust in people, even his friends. Thus, the mantas have undercut the very basis for Cal's death wish, and as Cal implies in his conversation with Subble, he has learned that simple classifications will not do. But such a lesson is a hard one to absorb fully, and, like 'Quilon and Veg, Cal has needed time to appreciate what his experience on Nacre has done for him.

The final chapter of *Omnivore* is Subble's confrontation with the mantas. In many ways it is an unsatisfactory chapter. Anthony equips Subble for this confrontation with electronic gear and with a hallucinogen, and Subble does establish contact with them. But the mantas insist that Subble fight one of them to the death to prove his worthiness to "speak" with them. They are aware of the personal problems which inhibit Veg, 'Quilon, and Cal; they are also aware that they are dealing with a race of omnivores that can be compassionate. But they have refused meaningful contact with the humans because they are in doubt as to how far the race has advanced. Unfortunately, Anthony never really gives a convincing reason as to how Subble's killing of one of the mantas will prove human worthiness, nor does he explain on what criterion the mantas base their concept of advanced civilization.

Thus, while the reader is treated to a very effective battle between Subble and one of the mantas, the question as to why all this is happening is never clear. The question, moreover, changes from why to what as the chapter continues. Subble takes the hallucinogen and goes through a series of visions that start with an exposition of the manta life cycle and end with the death of the manta at Subble's hands. Subble is then killed by his own hallucination.

At this point it would appear that Anthony got tired of his work. The ending comes fast and it leaves too many questions open. Evidently the mantas have learned to respect Subble. As a gesture of such respect they radio his report to his superiors and end with a description of the mantas and the fact that Subble has killed one of them. The superiors, fearing what the spores of the dead manta will do to the ecology of the Earth, round up the remaining mantas, as well as Veg, 'Quilon, and Cal and ship them all off the Earth; and it is at this point that the novel closes.

Throughout *Omnivore* Anthony has carefully compared the products of two different biospheres. Cal, Veg, and 'Quilon, with all their hopes and fears, are perfect products of their environment. The mantas, moreover, are equally perfect representatives of a parallel evolution that has taken place on a planet with a very different ecology. But having made the comparison Anthony leaves the reader to wonder what the experience has done for any of the characters. Beliefs are shaken, but that is all. Such an ending is unfair to the reader because he has become involved in the lives of these characters. It is hard not to care about them. Thus, a lack of resolution is frustrating.

Veg, 'Quilon, Cal, and the mantas appear in two other novels which follow *Omnivore*. It is interesting to note, however, that in neither of these novels does Anthony go into the same depth of detail in characterization as in the first, nor does he ever resolve the inner problems for his humans. Perhaps this is the problem of working on a series of novels involving the same characters. A complete resolution in one novel defeats the series, but too often a series that deals continually with the same characters exhibiting the same personal problems becomes boring. Whatever the cause for the weak and unsatisfying ending to *Omnivore*, one can only regret it. Piers Anthony created two credible worlds, fascinating aliens, and sympathetic humans. Such creations deserve better treatment.

THE OPHIUCHI HOTLINE

Author: John Varley
First book publication: 1977
Type of work: Novel
Time: Approximately six hundred years in the future
Locale: Luna, Earth, Saturn, Poseidon, Pluto, and a position seventeen light-years
   from the Solar System

*Forced to flee the Earth because of the invasion of superior aliens, mankind will
soon be forced to leave the Solar System*

   Principal characters:
      LILO-ALEXANDR-CALYPSO, an unwilling agent of Boss Tweed
      BOSS TWEED, former president of Luna and leader of the Free
         Earthers
      VAFFA, Tweed's child, multiple clones of whom serve as Tweed's
         soldiers
      CATHAY, a disbarred teacher and unwilling agent of Tweed

The fictional world of the future presented in *The Ophiuchi Hotline* is one
of the finest examples of what science fiction does best: create self-consistent,
alternate worlds that address present-day concerns. John Varley portrays a
world replete with dazzling technological innovations, mysterious aliens,
advanced human cultures, and exciting space opera; yet each of these elements
is kept in balance with one another and with the statements the author makes
concerning the future of humanity.

Just how fine an accomplishment the novel is can be seen in how much
Varley packs into the world of *The Ophiuchi Hotline* without destroying either
its inner consistency or the reader's credibility. At some point during the end
of the twentieth century, aliens had entered the Solar System. They are of a far
greater level of intelligence than humans, but seemed, at first, uninterested in
the planet Earth. A race similar to these aliens exists on the planet Jupiter,
where the aliens first went. However, after these aliens learned of the existence of sperm whales, killer whales, and bottlenosed dolphins on Earth, creatures which the aliens consider of an order of intelligence second only to themselves, they invaded the Earth to free it from the control of man, a creature of
only third-level intelligence. Mankind had no adequate defense, and those who
survived the famine brought on by the invasion fled to eight planets and satellites in the Solar System.

This dispersal of humanity took place some five hundred and fifty years
before the opening of the novel. Between the invasion and the first action of
the novel, a second significant event had occurred: about four hundred years
earlier radio signals started to be received from what was believed to be
Ophiuchi 70. These signals have been constantly monitored since then. They
contain scientific information thousands of years in advance of human science,

and while only about ten percent of that information is understandable to man, it has caused significant innovations. Among these innovations are an exact method of recording the entire content of a human brain, procedures for gene manipulation, processes for using minute black holes as sources of energy, and force fields that allow humans to exist in the vacuum of space. Thus, while the human race has lost its home planet and exists in fear of what the Invaders might do next, it has continued to develop complex technologies that allows it to mold new environments.

One particular technological innovation, however, stands out from all the rest: man has learned how to clone exact duplicates of himself. The clones are not used as slaves or as colonizers; in fact, no clone is allowed to live if a person with the same genetic code is alive at the same time. Clones plus the brain recording device are used to ensure the immortality of the originals. Every citizen of the Eight Worlds has the right to this eternal life. Their brains are periodically recorded, and if one should chance to be fatally injured, a clone of that person is awakened and the brain record is implanted in it. In such a way, the original may die, but a type of immortal life is given to the mind of that person.

Three elements are woven together in the well-structured plot. The novel opens in the cell of Lilo-Alexandr-Calypso, who has been condemned to permanent death for a crime against humanity. Because of the universal use of cloning and of cosmetic surgery, the Eight Worlds are faced with the difficult task of defining exactly what constitutes a human being. This problem has been resolved by using as the basis of the definition the fundamental human genetic code; that is, humans are defined by their DNA. Given such a definition, human DNA becomes one of the taboo areas for genetic manipulation because, for this society, that would be tampering with the equivalent of the soul.

Lilo, however, was interested in trying to reverse the effects of the inbreeding of the race caused by the limited stock of human survivors of the alien invasion. She was aided in her research by the belief that much of the untranslated information gathered from the Ophiuchi Hotline outlines methods of manipulating DNA. But Lilo was caught with her research notes and now faces eternal death.

Because of the severity of her sentence, Lilo becomes a prime candidate for Boss Tweed's Free Earthers. Tweed sees her as useful to his plans to retake the Earth, and, immediately before her execution, he substitutes one of her clones for the original Lilo. Even though Lilo is freed through Boss Tweed's machinations, however, she has simply changed one death for another, although this one is far less permanent. Tweed is obsessed with the desire to return to Earth and throw out the Invaders. This obsession has gone so far that he has taken his only child, created multiple clones from it, and turned them all into highly efficient killers. Lilo wants no part of his schemes, and it takes the death of the original Lilo and one of her clones, before the third Lilo agrees to at least play along with Tweed for awhile.

What follows this agreement is a fine example of what a science fiction writer is able to do that a mainstream writer cannot. Varley develops three parallel elements by creating three different Lilos. Through a series of events, one Lilo ends up on Earth, and through her the reader learns of how the planet and a small remnant of humans has fared since the dispersal. By the end of this episode, it is clear that Earth can never be home for mankind again. The second Lilo becomes part of a successful rebellion against Boss Tweed. No matter how admirable his intentions, Tweed's actions are both unrealistic and inhuman. They are unrealistic because the aliens' superiority to man is not just a myth — there really is nothing the human race can do against them. They are inhuman because he has created what is in effect a prison camp on Poseidon, a satellite of Jupiter, and peopled it with condemned criminals and illegal clones. All of these people face instant obliteration if any of the Eight Worlds learns of them, and Tweed holds this over their heads as a whip to make them do his bidding. By the end of this episode the reader's sympathy is on the side of the prisoners.

It is finally left to the third Lilo to solve the problem of the Ophiuchi Hotline. Whoever is responsible for the hotline has sent a message to the humans that there is a charge for use of the hotline and that the bill is now due. No one, however, knows what that charge is or what the threatened consequences of nonpayment might be; this information is left to Lilo, Cathay, one of the Vaffas, and a pilot named Javelin to discover. Javelin has learned that the hotline originates not at Ophiuchi 70, as had been supposed, but at a point seventeen light-years from the Solar System. The trip out to this point takes ten years, and when they reach it, they meet the Traders, the "Ophiuchis" themselves, and learn that the message was meant to accomplish two things. First, the Traders wanted the humans to get to the sending station so that they could be informed of what their future holds. Second, they wished to propose to the humans a form of payment for use of the hotline.

As to the first of these goals, Lilo and her fellow travelers are told that the fate of the human race is no different from that of other land-dwelling, tool-using creatures. The Invaders are far superior to them all and has a past history of displacing these other intelligent races. All one can do is accept the displacement and find another home. Even Tweed's rebellion against the Invaders is nothing more than a repetition of what has been tried by many other species in the past. It is inevitable that the displaced race will try to regain their lost home, and it is equally inevitable that the Invaders will destroy the race as a result of the attempt.

The Traders' advice to the humans as to their future actions is painfully clear: man must change so that he can fit into the wandering life that his future holds. It is the function of the Ophiuchi Hotline to inform the endangered race of the knowledge needed to survive. The most important part of that information is the manipulation of human DNA. If man is to wander the stars, he must be physically prepared for it. The human resistance to the necessary genetic manipulation is one of its most serious handicaps, for in order to live a race must be willing to change. Thus, William, one of the Traders who runs the hotline, says to Lilo and the others:

> You can no longer afford that quirk. You will have to cease defining your race by something as arbitrary as a genetic code, and make the great leap to establishing a racial awareness that will hold together in spite of the physical difference you will be introducing among yourselves. And you *must* define your race more successfully than you have done so far. Today, you could not tell us what it is that makes one a human being.

These words summarize, in fact, much that has happened in the novel. Tweed, for example, dreams of a return to the original homeland, but he has no feeling of remorse for the ways in which he has used people and caused them to suffer. What good is the homeland if there is no humanity in it? Certainly the Earth has only a pitiful few humans living on it. But just as certainly Tweed's methods lack humanity.

Even more to the point, however, is the position of the people of Poseidon. They are given no right to life; they are not considered human by the laws of the Eight Worlds. Yet, after the reader learns their histories and their hopes, they are seen as very human indeed. Thus, Varley ends *The Ophiuchi Hotline* with one of the most often-asked questions in science fiction: what is a man? While he never gives a direct answer to that question, it is obvious that the definitions used by the majority of the characters in the novel are not acceptable.

By introducing the Traders at the end of the novel, Varley is able to tie all his elements together. The Invaders, the hotline, and the cloning are now seen as a whole. The Invaders are not just a unique event in the lives of a single race; they are a cosmic phenomenon that many, many races have had to learn to cope with. The Ophiuchi Hotline follows these Invaders, giving the knowledge necessary for survival to those races that will learn.

Finally, Varley examines the cost of such knowledge. The development of cloning has narrowed the human race's definition of what constitutes a human to a technical one limited in scope to what humans were in the past. The Traders offer humanity a chance to change that definition. In return, the Traders demand that they be allowed to enter the minds and bodies of human individuals to learn about human culture. Through the acquisition of new cultures, the Traders have been able to maintain a racial vitality. Without change a race will stagnate and die.

In both races,.human and Trader, change is essential, for neither will exist long without it. In the presentation of this quintessential science fiction theme,

Varley has dramatically described a world of vast changes that is merely the prelude to further changes.

OUT OF THE SILENT PLANET

Author: C.S. Lewis (1898-1963)
First book publication: 1938
Type of work: Novel
Time: The present
Locale: England and Malacandra (Mars)

> *The first book in the Ransom trilogy — the others being* Perelandra *(1943) and* That Hideous Strength *(1945) — in which Lewis uses science fiction as the vehicle for a mythopoeic discussion of good and evil*

> *Principal characters:*
> RANSOM, a Cambridge philologist
> WESTON, a physicist
> DEVINE, a materialist
> HROSSA, seal-like Martians, poets, singers, and dancers
> SERONI, angular, human-shaped Martians, thinkers
> PFIFLTRIGGI, toadlike Martians, artists and artificers
> ELDILA, lesser spirits which do Oyarsa's bidding
> OYARSA, the spirit which governs Mars
> MALELDIL THE YOUNG, the Creator
> THE OLD ONE, the being with whom Maleldil lives

Combining religion and science in the same narrative can be a difficult task. Early science fiction writers, for the most part, either ignored religion or claimed that future man would no longer need it. In many cases, where both science and religion had thematic import in the same story, religion was depicted as a haven for the deluded, the foolish, and the unrealistic. However, more recent science fiction, especially that written since the beginning of the 1950's, has been able to bring science and religion into a working, if not always harmonious, literary relationship. C.S. Lewis was one of the writers who demonstrated how this could be accomplished; in *Out of the Silent Planet*, he uses the genre as a means of bringing the reader to a thoughtful contemplation of the mythic nature of the universe.

Dr. Elwin Ransom, a Cambridge philologist on a walking tour of the English countryside, is kidnaped by Weston, a physicist, and Devine, a former schoolmate whom Ransom dislikes. The two are making their second journey to Malacandra (Mars) and take Ransom along in the mistaken belief that the ruler of the planet wants a human for sacrifice. This mistake is typical of Weston's and Devine's inability to perceive what they find on Malacandra. Ignorant of his role in this enterprise, Ransom is delighted to find that space is not a cold and dark emptiness but an "ocean of radiance" which should be called "the heavens." He finds himself mystically attuned to what he sees, and his thoughts turn to images from Greek mythology and to lines from Milton. At this early point in the book, Lewis is already changing the focus from the scientific vehicle in which the three are traveling to the mystical realm through which they are voyaging.

When the ship lands on Malacandra, the scientific portion of the book is virtually over. Weston and Devine are about to hand Ransom over to six *seroni* when a larger water beast attacks. Ransom, who has overheard the other two discussing his fate, uses this moment of confusion to escape. From this point on, Lewis develops a mythopoeic fantasy in the manner of David Lindsay (*Voyage to Arcturus*) and George MacDonald (*Phantastes* and *Lilith*), both of whom Lewis acknowledged as formative influences. Ransom's journey, then, becomes not a journey to discover new places, things, theories, or people, but a journey to discover the self and its relationship to the rest of creation. In addition, Ransom will discover the mythic nature of his own planet, Thulcandra (Earth), and its place in the Field Arbol (the solar system).

For almost two days, Ransom flees every living thing he sees. While resting on a riverbank, he comes face to face with a *hross*, Hyoi. They attempt to communicate, and Ransom finds that his philological knowledge enables him to decipher the Malacandran language. Hyoi takes Ransom by boat to a *hross* village down in a *handramit* (valley) where he spends several weeks getting to know the *hrossa* and learning about Malacandra from them. He also discovers that the *hrossa* know of his own planet, which they call Thulcandra, the silent planet. He learns that Malacandra is ruled by an Oyarsa, a different order of being, and that everything was created by Maleldil the Young who lives with the Old One, two spirits of the highest order without "body, parts or passions." But the *hrossa* cannot tell him more than this; they are but poets, singers, and dancers. For answers to his questions, he must ask the *seroni*, who "would know such things," or Oyarsa himself.

Ransom's life among the *hrossa* is idyllic, and he finds them living the kind of life to which men and women on Earth aspire but rarely attain. Since Ransom spends little time with either the *seroni* or the *pfifltriggi*, the inhabitants of Malacandra must be judged by the actions and attitudes of the *hrossa*. These creatures are by nature temperate, monogamous, and peaceful. The Malacandrans do not even have a word for evil in their language; the closest Ransom can come to a term for such a concept is "bent." That the *hrossa* are the microcosm of Malacandra is made obvious by Hyoi. He links all three major groups — *hrossa*, *seroni*, and *pfifltriggi* — together as *hnau*. What is true of one group, insofar as moral or ethical standards are concerned, is true of all. Lewis, as is made clear later in the book, seems to be presenting a picture of what Earth might have been like if the Edenic state had not been lost by the Fall.

Ransom journeys to meet Oyarsa at Meldilorn guided by a *sorn* named Augray. Ransom and Augray spend several days traveling together, they learn much from each other. Ransom discovers that Oyarsa has ruled Malacandra for all of its existence and that each planet, including Thulcandra, is ruled by an Oyarsa with the help of many *eldila*. Augray also explains that Earth is called Thulcandra, the silent planet, because no communication comes from it. Ran-.

som learns even more about his own planet's singularity when he is questioned by a group of younger *seroni* who are greatly puzzled by Earth's violent histroy; an older *sorn*, who cannot conceive of a bent Oyarsa, suggests that Earth is as it is because the people there, in trying to rule themselves without an Oyarsa, are like someone trying to lift himself up by his own hair. Ransom, like so many literary travelers before him, finds his own world and race somewhat difficult to explain to these superior beings.

Once in Meldilorn, an island of great beauty inhabited by many *eldila*, things move much faster for Ransom. It is within these pages that Lewis brings the major social and mythic themes to their climax; this climax, however, is not so much a climax of action as a climax of thought and philosophy. It is here that Lewis states the ideas for which he has been constructing examples in the previous chapters. These ideas are articulated in a confrontation between Oyarsa and the other two Earthmen, Weston and Devine, who have been brought before Oyarsa for killing Hyoi and two other *hrossa*. Ransom acts as translator during this encounter and attempts to explain Weston's and Devine's comments to Oyarsa.

Weston and Devine are the spokesmen for attitudes which Lewis find abhorrent. Devine's reason for coming to Malacandra is materialistic; gold is abundant and easy to acquire there, and he plans to make his fortune. His previous speech to Ransom about expensive boats, women, and vacation homes and his lack of anything but a working knowledge of Weston's space vehicle were preludes to this. Devine is evil because he is willing to step on anyone, as evidenced by his earlier willingness to sacrifice Ransom in order to make his fortune; to Devine, making money is the most important thing in life. Oyarsa recognizes Devine for what Lewis believes him to be, a talking animal whose body should be "unmade" since the spirit in it is already dead.

Weston's evil is much more serious. Weston believes in sacrificing anything for science and for the future of the human race in general. He believes that it is science and technology which make humans superior and which will enable them to spread throughout the universe; he believes it is the right of humans, as superior beings, to supersede such lesser beings as he perceives the Malacandrans to be. Ultimately, he believes in a Life Force, but he believes it to be evidenced solely in the humanity of Earth which, as a race, will live forever. Weston does not even care for his personal fate and says that if Oyarsa kills him the spread of humanity will take place all the same.

Weston's philosophy seems to be taken almost directly from J.S.B. Haldane's *Possible Worlds* (1927) and Olaf Stapledon's *Last and First Men* (1931), both of which depict future man taking over adjacent planets for himself and slaying the natural inhabitants to make those planets more like Earth. Lewis has prefigured Weston's speech here; earlier in the book, Weston was contemptuous of Ransom's branch of learning, suggesting that such studies used money which should go to science, and Weston was quite willing to sacrifice Ransom to proceed with his scientific inquiry. Ransom's translation of Weston's speech into Malacandran shows just how parochial Lewis finds such a philosophy; moreover, Ransom has already learned from Hyoi, from Augray, and from Oyarsa that Maleldil the Young did not create these worlds and races to last forever. Weston comes off as a nineteenth century nationalist in scientific trappings. His lack of concern for his own fate raises him above Devine's animal status in Oyarsa's eyes, but Oyarsa still judges him bent. It is ironic that Weston, as an agent of the bent Oyarsa of Thulcandra, has made this journey to Malacandra; the journey breaks Thulcandra's quarantine and will cause the bent Oyarsa serious defeats.

On both sides of the confrontation with Weston and Devine, Ransom has time to discuss matters with Oyarsa, and it is here that Lewis delineates the mythic dimensions of the solar system. From the *hrossa*, Ransom has learned of the Old One and of Maleldil the Young, the Creator. Ransom now learns that all of the planets except Thulcandra are united under Maleldil. The Oyarsa of Thulcandra, however, became bent and was subsequently bound to his planet. The Oyarsa of Malacandra explains to Ransom that the bent Oyarsa and the *eldila* who serve him are largely responsible for the state of affairs on Thulcandra, but he also believes that Maleldil the Young has not given Thulcandra up to the Bent One. In fact, there are rumors that Maleldil has "dared terrible things" and may have appeared on Thulcandra at some point to struggle with the Bent One. Thus, Ransom discovers not new truths but the one, universal truth of which Thulcandra's philosophies and religions glimpse or remember only a part.

This theme is the basis for the Christian readings of this book and of the rest of the trilogy. However, students of comparative religions will see that Lewis' structure is so generalized that it could well be interpreted as the basic structure of a number of religions. In fact, this structure can also be observed in many of the world's ancient myth-systems, and this is why the novel is mythopoeic — it reaches beyond a specific doctrine and toward the awe-inspiring and the numinous. Ransom learns a great deal about the "true" nature of the universe. By extension, Lewis seems to be hoping, so also does the reader.

The ending of the book retreats, temporarily, from these considerations as Weston, Devine, and Ransom are allowed to return to Thulcandra. The conflicts are left unresolved and are to be continued in *Perelandra* and *That Hideous Strength*. Critical opinion on *Out of the Silent Planet* and the rest of the trilogy varies considerably; the harshest critics, however, still acknowledge it as an important book, while those who favor it find it extremely moving. In any case, it is a well-written, thought-provoking novel which attempts to deal cogently with the "greater truths" behind or beyond our everyday affairs.

Criticism:

Devoe, Alan. "Scientifiction," in *American Mercury*. LXXVII (August, 1953), pp. 26-29. Devoe discusses the work of Lewis and compares it to that of Ray Bradbury and other major figures in science fiction.

Green, Roger Lancelyn. *Into Other Worlds: Space Flight in Fiction from Lucian to C. S. Lewis*. New York: Abelard Schuman, 1958. Green establishes Lewis' work as the prototype for other science fiction writers dealing with the theme of space flight.

Hillegas, Mark. *The Future as Nightmare: H. G. Wells and the Anti-Utopians*. New York: Oxford University Press, 1967. Hillegas makes a concise but acute analysis of the influence of Wells's "cosmic pessimism" upon C. S. Lewis.

Hilton-Young, Wayland. "The Contented Christian," in *Cambridge Journal*. X (July 1952), pp. 603-612. This critic views *Out of the Silent Planet* as an allegorical depiction of the three parts of man.

Moorman, Charles. "Space Ship and Grail: The Myths of C. S. Lewis," in *College English*. XVIII (May, 1957), pp. 401-405. Moorman comments on the function of Lewis invented mythology in the Ransom trilogy.

PELLUCIDAR

Author: Edgar Rice Burroughs (1875-1950)
First book publication: 1923
Type of work: Novel
Time: 1914
Locale: At the Earth's core

*David Innes returns to Pellucidar, rescues Dian the Beautiful, reunites his empire,
and begins bringing the benefits of civilization to the people of the interior*

Principal characters:
  DAVID INNES, a wealthy young mine owner and Emperor of Pellu-
    cidar
  ABNER PERRY, his elderly companion, an inventor
  DIAN THE BEAUTIFUL, his mate, princess of Amoz
  HOOJA THE SLY, his principal adversary

Pellucidar is the second of seven novels that Edgar Rice Burroughs situated
on the interior surface of a hollow earth. The history of the "hollow earth"
theory, whose most notable recent adherent was Charles Manson, is outlined
in more detail in the first work of the series, *At the Earth's Core* (1914).
Burroughs, never one to let a good idea lie fallow, continued to use the setting
in *Tanar of Pellucidar* (1929), *Tarzan at the Earth's Core* (1929), *Back to the
Stone Age* (1937), *Land of Terror* (1944), and *Savage Pellucidar* (1963).

As the dates show, Burroughs' second use of the setting closely followed
the publication of *At the Earth's Core*. *Pellucidar* was finished in January of
1915, and published as a five-part serial in Frank A. Munsey's *All-Story Cavalier* that same year. Although it did not see book publication until 1923, it has
been reprinted frequently since, as have most of Burroughs' novels. It formed
part of the author's incredible early productivity: *Pellucidar* was the sixteenth
novel-length work published since he had begun writing in 1911. Even more
astonishing is the variety of the work that Burroughs turned out in that short
span. In four years he used African settings five times (three of them with
Tarzan as the central figure) invented the world of Barsoom, and employed his
celebrated Martian setting in three novels. He wrote two novels with contemporary settings, one realistic and one adventurous, wrote two set on Pacific
islands, wrote a Ruritanian romance, set a historical novel in thirteenth century
England, and adapted the hollow earth theory for the world of Pellucidar inside
the Earth.

Although Burroughs did not long maintain this level of productivity, he
always lavished his imagination on his settings, as this remarkably diverse
record shows. In fact, one might say that the center of interest of a Burroughs
novel is not the taciturn hero or the nubile and courageous heroine, not the
stereotyped chase-and-grab-'em plot, not the usually workmanlike but often
wooden dialogue, but the setting. And if we take the slight liberty of consider-

ing his exotic aliens as part of the furniture, then the setting is certainly the star.

The typical Burroughs adventure is enclosed within a frame story designed to ease the transition from the reader's world to the strange tale to come, and *Pellucidar* is no exception. It has a magnificent framing device, one which the critic Richard A. Lupoff believes to be one of Burroughs' finest creations. The frame begins, as many of the author's works do, not in *Pellucidar* itself, but in an earlier book in the series. Burroughs was as much a conservationist of plot as of setting, and he provided many of his novels with a hook at the end to which the narrative of a sequel could be linked if desired. For example, *The Gods of Mars* (1913) ends with John Carter's wife, Dejah Thoris, caught in a cell with a sort of timelock, the supplies in which will be exhausted before the cell will open again. Her rescue comes in the sequel, *The Warlord of Mars* (1913).

In the same cliff-hanging way, *At the Earth's Core* concludes with David Innes stranded in the Sahara; he has brought the mechanical prospector that had taken him to Pellucidar back to the surface. But as a result of treachery, he has not returned triumphantly with Dian, his mate, but with a Mahar, one of the reptilian creatures that rule the lands of the core. Determined to return to Dian, he plans at the novel's end to load the prospector with gear of various sorts and technical works, and burrow through to Pellucidar once again, stringing a five-hundred-mile telegraph cable behind him as he goes.

As *Pellucidar* opens, an unnamed narrator — Burroughs himself, it is implied — tells of receiving a letter from a traveler, Cogden Nestor, in Algiers. In Nestor's Saharan travels he has discovered a box buried a few inches in the sand. It contains a telegraph key clicking away, and a wire running from it downward into the sand. Since Nestor cannot understand the Morse code, the noise means nothing to him. But he has read *At the Earth's Core* — he considers it "impossible trash" — and he realizes the significance of a small piece of paper within the box, bearing the initials "D. I." He writes to the narrator for urgent confirmation that *At the Earth's Core* is pure fiction. In one of the admirably laconic responses in literature, the narrator cables: "Story true. Await me Algiers." The narrator and a telegrapher join Nestor, and they begin communicating with the person at the other end of the wire, who is indeed David Innes, and the messages they receive form the major part of *Pellucidar*.

As a story, *Pellucidar* is inferior to *At the Earth's Core*; its plot is fast-moving but predictable. At the end of the earlier novel, Innes had united the nearby tribes into an empire with himself at its head. Since his return to the surface, however, the union has fallen apart, and Dian has been captured by Hooja the Sly. Innes' task is therefore twofold: first to put his empire back together, and second to rescue Dian from a villain whose sole purpose in both novels seems to be the frustrating of the hero. With the aid of Abner Perry, the inventor of the mechanical prospector, Innes succeeds at both endeavors, and at the end of the novel he is busily engaged in bringing more and more cultural advantages to Pellucidar. Having given the stone age inner world bows and arrows, the cannon, and the like, he is dismayed to realize that Perry's and his chief function has been to increase the efficiency of warfare, making it possible to kill more Pellucidarians at a much faster rate. So in addition to his earlier gifts of the sailing vessel, the compass, and other peaceful innovations, Innes establishes regular trade, invents a Pellucidarian writing system, founds shipyards, coal mines, colleges, and printing presses — everything but money, which he refuses to institute. The story ends with no obvious hook for a sequel, chiefly because Innes has taken a fatal step for the hero of an adventure novel: he has settled down.

There are signs of haste that help to diminish the standing of *Pellucidar*. When Innes enters the territory of the Thurians, he sees one of their villages, and describes it as being walled by logs and boulders; it lacks a gate, but "ladders that could be removed by night led over the palisade." Burroughs has forgotten that only in the previous chapter he had situated the Thurians in "The Land of Awful Shadow," where it is always night.

One innovation does brighten the novel (again, one concerned with setting), but even that change raises problems. A frequently occurring theme in *At the Earth's Core*, one which continues in *Pellucidar*, is a meditation on the nature of time. The interior of the earth is perpetually lighted by a central miniature sun; hence, Pellucidar enjoys a continuous noon. There are no months or years, because the motion of heavenly bodies, by which people of the upper Earth can measure accurately and repeatedly long periods of time, are absent in Pellucidar. Innes and Perry make conjectures about the passage of time being subjective. Innes takes part in adventures that seem to him to last weeks, even months, yet when he returns to Perry, the old man has been reading the whole time, and perceives Innes' absence as consisting of a matter of minutes. Again, when Innes returns to the surface, he is amazed to find that his journey, which he believes to have lasted at most one year, has in fact taken ten.

To be sure, there is some kind of biological clock that continues to function: characters eat and sleep (though not with any regularity), the natives of Pellucidar are born, grow old, and die. But neither Innes nor Perry (nor the natives, who have no conception of time) can be sure of duration. This uncertainty irritates Innes and Perry, and in *Pellucidar* they discover a way to measure time objectively.

It turns out that Pellucidar has a satellite, a "pendant world" that hangs eternally suspended about a mile above the inner surface. Because this moon rotates upon an axis parallel to the surface, and because its topography is clearly visible from Pellucidar, Innes decides to establish an observatory to note the recurrent appearance of a marked surface feature and to use the period of rotation of the pendant world as a measure of time. Later, after he has developed radio transmission, the observatory broadcasts time signals to the rest of his empire.

Although the pendant world can give Pellucidar an objective standard of time, it presents a problem for some of the inhabitants, who must live in darkness. The period of rotation for the pendant is the same as that of the earth-shell, so it hangs suspended always over the same spot ("The Land of Awful Shadow," covered always by a dusky gloom). Burroughs never gives an estimate of the magnitude of the satellite, but it is obviously of considerable size because from the surface Innes can see mountains, valleys, rivers, forests, plains, and even oceans.

Perhaps Burroughs himself was beginning to weary of Pellucidar, or to feel his invention flagging within the Earth. The second novel in the setting had capitalized on the popularity of *At the Earth's Core*, yet *Pellucidar* was not to see book publication for eight years, preventing immediate comparison between the two novels. Whatever the reason, a full fourteen years passed before Burroughs had Tarzan visit the setting. Despite the pendant world, despite the use of dinosaurs as mounts (á la Alley Oop), despite a newly invented race of agricultural apemen, *Pellucidar* shows a falling off from the inventiveness of the book to which it was a sequel. *Pellucidar* does not show Burroughs at his best.

Criticism:

Green, Roger Lancelyn. *Into Other Worlds: Space Flight in Fiction from Lucian to C. S. Lewis*. New York: Abelard Schuman, 1958. Green attempts to place Burroughs' science fiction writing in its proper critical perspective.

Krneger, John R. "Names and Nomenclature in Science Fiction," in *Names*. XIV (1968), pp. 203-214. This interesting article reveals Burroughs' systematic pattern of indicating rank and occupation through names.

PERELANDRA

Author: C. S. Lewis (1898-1963)
First book publication: 1944
Type of work: Novel
Time: The early 1940's
Locale: England and the planet Venus, called Perelandra

The saving of the planet Venus from an Adam and Eve-like fall from grace

> *Principal characters:*
> DR. ELWIN RANSOM, a Cambridge philologist
> EDWARD ROLLES WESTON, a physicist
> THE GREEN WOMAN, the "Eve" of Perelandra

The second novel of the famous space trilogy is certainly C. S. Lewis' most beautifully written book. Given his genius, it should have been, for Lewis had set himself the incredibly difficult task of writing a novel, the setting of which is Paradise itself — a fresh, just-born innocence on the planet Venus before the Fall — before sin, death, corruption.

The last novel of the trilogy, *That Hideous Strength*, is a remarkable fantasy, a satiric study of our own very fallen planet. The first, *Out of the Silent Planet*, introduces the main character of the trilogy, Dr. Elwin Ransom, a Cambridge philologist, in a novel which is formally a fairly traditional voyage-to-Mars work of science fiction. Ransom is kidnaped by an evil physicist named Weston who wants to colonize and corrupt the planet Mars. Ransom helps to foil Weston's scheme as he learns about Mars, a planet coming to the end of its life. Ransom also learns to overcome his human fears of the alien — a key theme in Lewis' work — as well as to accept death, his own and even the death of a whole world.

Ransom's education takes place within a very traditional Judeo-Christian cosmology: God's creation of the worlds and their inhabitants, their later fall from innocence and the role of the fallen angels led by Satan, and the consequences of that fall are all part of the scheme Lewis employs. He renames the angels *eldila*, gives the planets other names (Mars is Malacandra; Venus, Perelandra; and Earth, Thulcandra) and calls God Maleldil; but generally his universe, for all its spaceships and modern physics, would be readily familiar to, say, John Milton or Dr. Samuel Johnson.

The kidnaping that took Ransom to Mars was an apparent accident. But the *eldila* send him from Earth on his second space voyage and the difference is important. The second novel is concerned, philosophically, with the question of free will and predestination. Ransom is sent to the young planet of Venus in order to help prevent, if he can, the fall from innocence of its first morally responsible creatures. He meets a Green Woman, who is, of course, the "Eve" of this planet. She is tempted by Satan who has taken — literally taken, in diabolic possession — the body of Weston, still determined to preserve his limited conception of life (that is, simply human life as it is known on the planet Earth). On Mars, Weston had tried merely to subdue the natives, like a conquistador, to make room for Earthlings. But on Venus, he cooperates with Satan to reduce the Green Woman, and thus the children she will later have, to the fallen moral level of his own species. Though a fallen mortal himself, Ransom is given the extraordinary chance to do battle with Weston-Satan for the soul of the Green Woman and the destiny of Perelandra. This chance also enables Ransom to learn about the nature of destiny and to ask, in both a general and profound way, what kind of thing life itself actually is.

Perelandra can be seen as seven separate but unequal sections (or movements: Lewis himself described the book as "operatic" — even Wagnerian). Indeed, it has something in common with the epic. It involves a long journey by a single man, who, after a hand-to-hand battle, receives an Achilles-like wound in his heel. Moreover, it is told in a kind of epic flashback. The first section offers the "frame" for the rest of the work. A narrator, identified as "Lewis" himself, learns of Ransom's mission in the first two chapters. Ransom asks him to assist in his departure from and his return to Earth. Thus "Lewis" must wade through, almost literally, a swamp of fear — the basic human condition — and learn that the fight with Satan could be a real, that is physical, fight. (Lewis insists that moral realities are not to be regarded as "merely" spiritual.) In the second chapter, Ransom returns to Earth, tells his story to "Lewis," who then describes for us the journey.

The second section describes Ransom's arrival and first days alone on Perelandra. In fact, Ransom lives in Paradise: Lewis' description of this Paradise has a beauty so rapturously intense as to suggest almost a drug- or dreamvision. Ransom finds himself on an island which floats upon the surface of the seas like a rush mat or giant lily pad. On the floating island — there are other such islands which sometimes come together to form small continents and then break apart in a ceaseless flow of changing beauty — Ransom eats, drinks, smells, and absorbs such pleasures as to bring him to the edge of consciousness. He eats a globed fruit, for example, which is so delicious it redefines for him the very meaning of the word *pleasure*. A drink releases in his brain such fantastic sensations that he is nearly delirious with the realization of what sensations his own body is capable of in so wondrous a place.

It is no wonder that Ransom thinks this reality must be a dream and that he feels he is not merely having an adventure but is enacting myth. He wonders why he does not desire merely to consume the fruit or drink the drink and do nothing else. In particular, he wonders about the very idea of repetition and speculates on the possibility that the real root of all evil is the desire to have things again, to repeat experiences. Perhaps, he thinks, even money is valued chiefly as a means of keeping things so as to have them again.

This speculation becomes important, even central, to the novel's development of its principal theme. Interestingly, Ransom strongly desires to wake from a dream, even a pleasant dream; it is Reality he is in search of. (Indeed, much later in the novel he eats a drugweed and rejects it: Reality is not to be found that way.) The Green Woman, whom he meets in the third section, helps him to understand the possessiveness implied in our human hankering for repetition. They discuss time and the order of things, concepts she deals with easily. From her he learns that one must, in effect, know how to choose the given, not necessarily the expected good. But he can help her as well. In her innocence, she cannot understand why she is so separate from God (Maleldil); of course, as a fallen human, Ransom is able to enlighten her.

The Perelandran equivalent of the forbidden fruit in Genesis is Maleldil's prohibition against the Green Woman's sleeping on the Fixed Lands; she is to make her home on the ever changing floating islands. Ransom comes to understand the moral implications of this. First, Maleldil makes any such command in order to bring the necessary virtue of obedience into the world. Second, He makes this particular command to show the importance of accepting change and flux and to resist the impulse (born of fear and lack of trust) for permanence and its near-relation repetition.

The Green Woman is looking for the King, her Adam, and knows that Maleldil is preparing her for this marriage. She learns and thus grows less "young," that is, innocent. In this world, growth and knowledge are possible without experiencing evil. However, the maturity she needs for her destiny — to be the Queen-Mother of Venus — is not possible without knowing and rejecting evil.

Evil arrives (in the fourth section) in the person of Weston. "Westonism" — the mad dream of space colonization — is now put into a moral perspective larger than the one offered in *Out of the Silent Planet*. Westonism is the ultimate desire for Permanence and Repetition, a refusal to accept change, growth, development, even death as part of that process, an insistence that life always and everywhere be what we know on Earth. Lewis' development of Westonism, then, has cosmic implications (outward) and moral implications (inward). It can be both the dream of a mad scientist traveling through space and the temptation to save one's soul from fear and despair by taking refuge in a false hope of permanence.

It might be said that Lewis gives a very new meaning to the "Eternal Triangle" in the crucial (and longest) fourth section of the novel. Ransom and Weston (progressively taken over, however, by Satan) fight — in this part by argument — for the soul of the Green Woman. Behind Weston, as both man and devil, there lies a slowly revealed evil which is utterly imbecilic and pointless. As a particular man, he represents a vague sort of scientific religion, clearly based on the Creative Evolution devised by Henri Bergson and popularized by Bernard Shaw: Weston is always talking about the "thrust" of Life and the need to worship "Spirit." As devil, his temptations to the Green Woman are slightly perverted versions of roles — the tragic queen, the long-suffering mother, the misunderstood woman — which might be good in themselves but here are bad because they are self-obsessed and unreal. Since there is no evil yet on Perelandra there is no need for tragic resignation — although the tragic pose might be attractive in and of itself.

Ransom responds in different ways to different arguments and temptations, and all his responses have to be searched for, sometimes with difficulty, sometimes even through pain and near-despair. To the "scientific" argument that "spirit" should be worshiped, Ransom can only respond that "spirit" has no particular value in itself; as always, the question is of value itself, its source and its location. Of course, Ransom has learned, so to speak, from his own body. On Perelandra taste and pleasure are positive sources of knowledge. When Weston-Satan tempts the Green Woman with the allure of various roles, Ransom can only appeal to Reality itself. But behind it all lies pure evil, an evil which must, however, attach itself to physical bodies and which must, therefore, be fought physically.

The brilliant climax of the fourth section is a long soliloquy (in Chapter 11) in which Ransom goes through a despairing search for the Real by considering the relation of myth and history, change, and even the importance of his own name. He realizes that he is the ransom which must be paid, that there are no accidents, and yet moral actions are possible; he represents God on Perelandra, just as Weston's body is the devil's only foothold on this planet.

The fifth section is the epic fight between Weston and Ransom, rendered with surprising violence. As Ransom has learned earlier the joy that comes through physical pleasure, so he now learns the uses and the joy of righteous hatred. In addition to the physical fight, Ransom is tempted by many of the fashionable twentieth century philosophies. He deeply feels the fear of madness, of death, of pain, and is tempted to surrender (as a hunted man is tempted to give up) to despair itself. There are times when life seems what "Weston" says it is — a bit of pleasure, mostly misery, and, beyond a moment of conscious life, nothing but an eternity of nothing. Ransom must order these thoughts out of his brain even as he kills Weston.

The transitional sixth section shows Ransom alone, recovering from his fight and beginning to experience again the wild physical pleasures of Perelandra as preparation for the closing section of the novel, in which he sees myth become reality. He sees Ares and Aphrodite. He sees the marriage of the King and Queen, saved from a Fall by his action and trust. Tor, the Adamite King of Perelandra, explains to Ransom that he and his Queen did learn of evil — but directly from Maleldil, not through the experience of the Devil. Ransom learns that it is only "cold love and feeble trust" which prevent one from living with each wave that life brings and the even more profound truth that "The best fruits are plucked for each by some hand that is not his own." Ransom asks if everything is without plan. No one can answer, but the conclusion of the novel is a great dance in which Ransom seems to see a Reality in which everything is contained in everything else, in which there are so many interlocking plans that only a mystic could comprehend them all.

And so this novel, an intensely interesting philosophical fantasy and beautiful prose poem, comes to an end with a celebration of movement, order, and love and these noble words: "The splendour, the love, and the strength be upon you."

Criticism:

Hilton-Young, Wayland. "The Contented Christian," in *Cambridge Journal*. X (July, 1952), pp. 603-612. Hilton-Young explores allegorically the myth of the beginning and ending of the human race as it is depicted in *Perelandra*.

Moorman, Charles. "Space Ship and Grail: The Myths of C. S. Lewis," in *College English*. XVIII (May, 1957), pp. 401-405. Moorman utilizes Lewis' own statements on mythmaking in an examination of the authors invented mythology in *Perelandra*.

Norwood, W. D. "C. S. Lewis, Owen Barfield, and the Modern Myth," in *Midwest Quarterly*. VIII (Spring, 1967), pp. 279-291. Lewis' study of the "true Christian myth," is the central concern of *Perelandra*, according to Norwood.

Spacks, Patricia Meyer. "The Myth-Makers Dilemma: Three Novels by C. S. Lewis," in *Discourse*. XI (October, 1959), pp. 234-243. Spacks traces Lewis' treatment of Christian and classical myths in the Ransom trilogy.

PICNIC ON PARADISE

Author: Joanna Russ (1937-   )
First book publication: 1968
Type of work: Novel
Time: The indefinite future
Locale: A winter resort planet called Paradise

Trans-Temporal Agent Alyx leads an odd group of tourists across a strange and dangerous "resort" planet

> Principal characters:
> ALYX, a thief, time-traveler, and survival guide
> MACHINE, a rationalist and Alyx's lover
> GUNNAR, a wishful-thinker and self-serving coward
> MAUDEY, a beauty and youth cultist
> IRIS, Maudey's daughter
> THE NUNS, religious fanatics and drug users

In 1968 when *Picnic on Paradise* appeared, very few writers of science fiction bothered to create believable female characters, and even fewer readers noticed. Women in science fiction novels were one-dimensional stereotypes — seductresses, stony ice-maiden scientists, or an occasional housewife who, as Joanna Russ remarked in her essay "The Image of Women in Science Fiction" (1970), might accidentally solve a galactic crisis by mending her slip. In part, science fiction writers did not need women characters — or so they thought — in the golden age of science fiction when menacing robots, fantastic cities, or monstrous extraterrestrials were the stuff of the novel. Usually, the plot involved the male hero who prevailed against these forces of evil. In part the audience who read science fiction would not notice or might expect female stereotypes, since science fiction readership has been overwhelmingly male, and often adolescent male at that.

Joanna Russ not only is among the first science fiction writers to recognize these caricatures of women, but she has also developed compelling female characters in her own fiction. A prize-winning short story writer and a poet, Russ also holds an MFA from Yale Drama School. This diverse literary background serves her well; her works are consistently vigorous, terse, and timely. She is considered to be one of the writers of the "New Wave" of science fiction, a movement characterized by social consciousness and stylistic innovation. *Picnic on Paradise* is her first novel, and while it is not her best — *The Female Man* (1975) is stylistically more smooth and thematically more mature — it is an important novel for anyone wishing to understand both the role of woman in science fiction and Russ's works in particular. Moreover, in its own right, *Picnic on Paradise* is compelling reading.

The action of the novel occurs sometime in the future on a winter resort planet called Paradise. But Paradise is not without peril, as the heroine of the novel, Alyx, discovers. Snatched out of her own time and planet, Alyx is selected to lead a group of vacationers across the planet. The caravan meets with external threats — bears, the harsh environment — but the real journey occurs within, and the real perils are of the soul, not the flesh. The travelers reveal themselves as they step deeper into an unknown, hostile environment; in particular, the novel follows Alyx on her metaphorical journey into the crevasses of her mind.

The portraits of the other travelers allow Russ to evaluate various aspects of her own society in the late 1960's. The novel mocks the culture which values youth and beauty, uses mood-altering drugs, and devalues emotionally intimate and familial relationships. For example, Maudey has dyed her eyebrows blue and has had extensive cosmetic surgery to retain the appearance of youth; she and her daughter Iris have molded themselves into plastic sex-goddesses. Yet when confronted with the extreme conditions of their journey across Paradise, Maudey despairs that she has made herself into a doll, and Iris reveals that Maudey is indeed her own mother, a fact she has concealed partly to shield Maudey from being thought old, and partly because family relationships are not considered fashionable in the society of that time. Two other tourists are called nuns, devotees of some nouveau-mystical religion whose major ritual seems to be the popping of pills. The nuns have a pill for every emotion, even those which eliminate the grief that the death of a loved one brings. Proffering their hallucinogenic pills to Alyx, the nuns change little in the course of the journey; their path through reality is a dead end.

Alyx herself is one of the first fully realized female protagonists in science fiction. Born in ancient Greece on the planet Earth, she was a murderer and a thief before becoming the tour guide on the planet Paradise. Her presence on the planet was occasioned when she was snatched out of her time and place by the Trans-Temp, a group of anthropologists who study other cultures by interviewing their members in person. In her last moments on Earth, Alyx was about to be drowned, having been cast into the Bay of Tyre while tied to a huge boulder, as a punishment for stealing a chess set. Since she was about to die, the Trans-Temp could ethically remove her from her time without disrupting the stream of events, a problem they scrupulously avoid. Alyx is particularly interesting to them because of her "special and peculiar skills," mainly her ruthlessness, her overwhelming instincts for survival, and particularly her talent which makes her an expert murderer: she hurls a knife expertly, silently, and lethally.

Alyx's attitudes and emotions, however, are the real interest of the novel. Her personality defies the traditional female traits; she is aggressive, fierce, and unmaternal. Her history reveals a woman who had abandoned three children, who was the lover of many but loved no one. In the course of the journey she slaps recalcitrant travelers, eliminates a huge bearlike animal, and finally kills a fellow-traveler, Gunnar, whose cowardice was responsible for the death of Machine, the man who had become Alyx's lover. Moreover, Alyx is a small, compact, dark, not at all the voluptuous stereotype. She is the sexual aggressor in that she initiates the relationship between herself and Machine, but she is not a seductress who ensnares him — the usual stereotype in science fiction. On the contrary, she and Machine have a developing relationship through which both are changed and yet through which both must learn to appreciate the ways in which each of them will not change.

The portrait of Machine parodies stereotypical notions of what a man should be. The name *Machine* itself mocks the emotionless exterior that too often characterizes the science fiction hero. The stereotype preaches that a "real" man should be cool, aloof, and remote, like the traditional Western hero, like the popular film hero played by Clint Eastwood. Too often the science fiction hero has simply been a cowboy transplanted into another time and place; an adventurer who has no woman (or leaves her) and who loves or at least prefers the company of his machine (be it robot, starship, or computer) just as the cowboy preferred his horse. In *Picnic on Paradise*, Machine has named himself because as an "adolescent rebel," he prefers to wear a television-like device called a "Trivia" on his head twenty-four hours a day; plugged in to his drug, he avoids feeling altogether.

Alyx and Machine both move from their isolationist stances and come to a full sharing. In scenes that are sexually explicit yet tender and erotic, Machine allows himself to feel passion, even love, and Alyx, far from being the meek partner of the stereotype, is his teacher and helper.

Russ's purpose throughout her fiction is to depict radical life styles, to present individual portraits of humans who are characterized as much by the way they change as by the way they remain the same. In *Picnic on Paradise* she fulfills these purposes so well that even the climax of the novel (Machine's death and Alyx's stabbing of Gunnar) is acceptable. Machine's accident came as a result of his newfound spontaneity, and Alyx's action, consistent with her former life as a murderer, was no longer criminally motivated but was in an ultimate way motivated by a primal sense of justice and caring. Modern morality does not condone such acts, to be sure, yet one of the successes of this novel is that the reader accepts the rightness of the act.

Some reservations about the novel are its rather brusk exposition and slow pace after the journey commences. A more conventional description of the characters would help involve the reader in the story. Generally, however, Russ has displayed considerable courage in her writing, particularly in her attempts to present themes and characters associated with tragedy. Until recently, science fiction has by and large avoided the truly tragic for the sad or the unfortunate. The death of Machine, while not classically tragic, brings about a kind of redemption in Alyx. She had never lost anything she really wanted, she said, and so had not until then understood her fellow humans or indeed experienced the profound emotions of anger, grief, and acceptance that such events bring.

Ultimately, then, *Picnic on Paradise* presents an assemblage, not merely of travelers but of pilgrims, who journey at first as an escape from their daily lives, but then as seekers and discoverers of their own selves. As Alyx realizes at the end of the novel, her "special and peculiar attitudes" are what define her — not what she can do or even what she can think, but what she is.

PILGRIMAGE: THE BOOK OF THE PEOPLE
AND
THE PEOPLE: NO DIFFERENT FLESH

Author: Zenna Henderson (1917-   )
First book publications: Pilgrimage (1961) ; *The People* (1966)
Type of work: Novelization of short stories
Time: The present and the late nineteenth century
Locale: Southwestern United States

   Both books detail, in a series of loosely connected stories, the attempts of a group of extraterrestrials, possessing psionic powers and stranded on earth after their own planet is destroyed, to find the surviving members of their own race and to forge relationships with earthlings

   Principal characters:
   MARK AND MERIS EDWARDS, a young earth couple in *The People*
   LEA HOLMES, a depressed and suicidal young earth woman in *Pilgrimage*
   KAREN, Jemmy's sister, a teacher and one of the People
   JEMMY, an "Old One" of the People, though young in years and Valency's husband
   VALENCY CARMODY, a teacher who possesses an unusually large amount of the People's psi powers
   BETHIE MERRILL, one of the "sensitives" of the People
   DR. CURTIS, an earth doctor who learns to work with Bethie

   Zenna (Chlarson) Henderson is a schoolteacher who has spent most of her life in Arizona teaching young children. She is also a very gifted storyteller. Her stories are basically stories of hope, of understandings reached often after potentially tragic misunderstandings, or of new discoveries that lend hope to a seemingly hopeless future. They assume that all intelligent life, human and alien, is morally good and shares similarities that make understanding possible. Henderson started writing her stories about "the People" in the early 1950's, a more optimistic and innocent generation, and stubbornly continued on during the 1960's, untouched by the disillusionment and cynicism of that decade. She has written only four books of science fiction. Two of them, *The Anything Box* and *Holding Wonder*, are undisguised collections of short stories previously published in science fiction magazines. The other two, *Pilgrimage: the Book of the People* and *The People: No Different Flesh*, are thematically connected collections of similar short stories. What differentiates the latter two books is not so much the fact that they are tied together by linking narratives or common themes, but that their concern is with a very special group of people.

   "The People," as Zenna Henderson describes them, are a group of extraterrestrials (and their earthly descendants) who emigrated to earth sometime during the nineteenth century when their planet was destroyed (in "Deluge"). They are very similar to native earthlings except for their psionic powers (which must be concealed from most earth humans) and their genuine goodness. They settle in an isolated region of the southwestern United States and the stories tell of their adventures from the time of the destruction of their planet to the late 1960's when they often travel by flying in their pick-up truck. Since they are blessed with a kind of racial memory, those of the People alive in the 1960's have no difficulty remembering and relating a story "narrated" by one of their great grandparents.

Each story is narrated in the first person by one of its major characters. If the character has died, the story is related by one of his or her descendants, still in the words of the person who lived it, by means of the aforementioned racial memory. In *The Pilgrimage* this feat is accomplished by calling a gathering of the people to record their history on earth with a newly invented recording device. They have recently been contacted by another group from their home world who found and settled an empty planet, and they must now decide whether to join this group on their new home, or remain on earth. Three of the six stories in the second book, *The People*, take place a few generations before the stories in the first book, and concern the destruction of the home planet and the tragic first contacts between humans and members of the People. All of these stories are related to an earth couple, befriended by the People in the first story, and the only excuse necessary for such storytelling is the couple's natural curiosity about their new friends.

All of the stories (with the exception of "Deluge") take place in isolated desert country in the southwestern United States. Here Henderson's stories are too compactly written for her to spend much time describing the scenery, but when she does, the canyons and flats, rocky slopes, "scrub-covered foothills," and "pinepointed mountains" are all authentically presented. Authentic, too, are the backwoods characters that people these regions: the country doctors, miners, sheriffs, old-timers, and Mexicans who add local color to her stories. Glory and Seth, the old mining couple in the story "Return," seem as genuine as the land itself.

Unfortunately, not many of her characterizations are that vividly drawn. Her stories often concern young children and their parents and schoolteachers (generally young women). The schoolteachers are interchangeable, as are most of the mothers and fathers. The schoolteachers, whether they are earthlings or members of the People, are sensitive, intelligent, unfailingly patient and understanding of their young charges, and generally a little too good to be true. The fathers are all strict yet kindly and understanding, and the mothers are all warm and loving. Karen's mother and father in "Ararat" are almost completely interchangeable with Bruce and Eve Merrill, the parents in "Gilead"; Melodye Amerson of "Pottage" and Perdita Verist of "Wilderness," both teachers, have very little in their personalities to differentiate them. Henderson is concerned with the similarities between people and between humans and aliens, not with their individual differences. Still, after reading two books in which a great many of the characters are overly similar, one begins to wish that she stressed individual differences more.

All of the stories in *Pilgrimage*, including the thread of narrative that knits them together, explore the problems of lost people, alienated from the rest of their world because of some difference which they sense inside themselves. In most cases the difference is a real one; the People do have powers that earth humans do not possess, and their landing on earth caused many of them to become lost and isolated. With others (many of whom are earth humans) the difference they feel is one they have fashioned out of their own suffering and discontent. It is this problem alone that alienates them and makes them feel lost and alone. These lost ones range all the way from Lea, a normal earthling who is so disillusioned with the futility of her life that she wants to end it, to the whole group of People in the story "Pottage," who are so afraid of revealing their differences from earth humans that they not only deny themselves all use of their powers but all normal enjoyment of life as well. In *The People*, too, the stories are about lost and troubled individuals. In "Deluge" the People lose their home planet, and in subsequent adventures the few who survive the landing on earth are truly lost and alone. Mark and Meris of "No Different Flesh" each suffer greatly because of the destruction of an important manuscript and the death of a baby. Their individual misery alienates them from each other and the world around them. And yet all of these lost people eventually find solutions; there are no unhappy endings. Despite the tragic deaths of some loved ones and the occasional discovery that what one had earlier sought was no longer wanted once it was attained, the stories all end hopefully, full of the optimistic expectation of a bright future.

Zenna Henderson's preoccupation with a bright future for everyone, for happy endings, is tellingly stressed in a story called "Turn the Page" which appears in *The Anything Box*. In it a first-grade teacher teaches her charges about good and evil and that "everyone will finally live happily ever after because it is written that way." Unfortunately her students fail to learn the lesson, which is the same lesson that Zenna Henderson wishes to teach us through her stories: we must believe, because through believing, we can solve our problems and achieve happiness. The People do not have to struggle to believe as we earthlings do; one of their powers consists of the instinctive knowledge that there is a "Presence" that gives great joy, from whom they are separated at birth and to whom they are called back at death. They also know with a certainty that all the events on inhabited worlds must coincide with His grand plan.

Henderson does not present her religious ideas with a heavy hand. Instead she tries to show us that there is still wonder, magic, and miracles in our world. The People themselves seem magical; they can fly and "platt" sunbeams and moonbeams. And in one of the stories, "Wilderness," an earthling is discovered who has developed some of the same powers, as well as some special ones of her own. But the real magic in the stories of the People is worked by human love and understanding. This is the religion that Henderson advocates. It is the love and understanding that Glory and Seth show Debbie and her own love for her newborn child that end her cruel selfishness and assuage her grief in "Return," not any magic performed by the People. And it is the understanding of a human teacher and the love of a human girl that save the Francher child from delinquency in "Captivity."

The author's message is one of Christian love and tolerance for those who are different, for those who may not look or act like the rest of us. In "The Closest School," a story from her latest book, *Holding Wonder*, she makes this tolerance clear when she describes a new child registering for school, a child who is purple and fuzzy but who is as much a shy child as any human six-year-old entering school for the first time. If we can accept a fuzzy purple child as being essentially similar to ourselves, shouldn't it be that much easier to accept the basic similarity of children and adults of other races, religions, and nationality groups? If we can sympathize with the People and feel the pain they are made to suffer because of human intolerance, shouldn't this teach us to be more tolerant ourselves?

The People suffered greatly from human intolerance in some of their first contacts with earth humans. Lytha's family were burned as witches in "Angels Unawares" by people who were religious fanatics — the kind of fanatics who "pervert goodness, love, and obedience and set up a god small enough to fit their shrunken souls." It is the goodness, love, and tolerance that the People exhibit that Henderson would have us emulate.

The People, aside from their special powers, are very human. There are a few customs they remember from their home planet which they no longer follow, some native fruit they brought with them that they still grow and cherish, and a few words and expressions from their native language that are the only clues we are given to the life they lived before they traveled to earth. There is no detailed creation of another culture in these books. "Cahilla," the word Timmy used to refer to the little box of things he brought to earth, comes from the Spanish word *cajilla*; and the expression of surprise and exasperation used by the people, "A donday veeah," seems to come from a Spanish expression which literally means "where are you going?"

Zenna Henderson's books are not profound works nor are they great literature. They were written, as she has said, "for fun" and to make us wonder, and dream, and perhaps learn a few lessons. Her books might be faulted by some readers as being unfailingly optimistic and a bit naïve. But for those who have not become unshakable cynics as a result of the many disillusionments of the last fifteen years, for readers who still have the strength and courage to hope and dream, her stories can be quite touching and enchanting and well worth reading.

A PLAGUE OF DEMONS

Author: Keith Laumer (1925-   )
First book publication: 1965
Type of work: Novel
Time: The future, perhaps thirty or forty years from now
Locale: Algeria, the United States, and a far distant planet

An American agent discovers that aliens have infiltrated human society and are carrying on some scheme that involves stealing the brains of fallen soldiers

> *Principal characters:*
> JOHN BRAVAIS, a spy for an American intelligence agency
> FELIX SEVERANCE, Bravais' superior and member of the Ultimax group

Although Keith Laumer has made a career in the American Air Force, he has found enough time to become prolific as a writer of science fiction. He is probably best known for his stories about Retief, an interstellar diplomat, but in *A Plague of Demons* he has written a novel that is often richly inventive. (*A Plague of Demons* first appeared as a shorter serial in *If* magazine in November and December of 1964, but it is the fuller book version, published in 1965, that will be discussed here.)

The novel opens with the atmosphere of a next-generation James Bond story: John Bravais, a reserve Army officer and agent for an organization referred to as CBI, is in Algeria on a mission, and in preparation for it he is equipped with as many gadgets as Ian Fleming might have used in three novels. To begin with, he has an optical-effect suit, a garment that makes him the next thing to invisible; when the time comes for him to go into action, he wears a device the size of a canteen — a focused phase field generator — that neutralizes gravity around him, enabling him to fly through the air. The goggles of his suit can be tuned to adjust the magnification of its lenses and to allow him to see by infrared. His is also armed with a gun that fires poisoned darts. But this technological plenty finds use in just a single scene. After surreptitiously observing a battle and seeing some very strange things, he reports to his superior, Felix Severance, who decides he needs to be fitted with PAPA: Power Assisted Personal Armament.

Imagine a person wearing a suit of armor, with motors attached to make him faster and stronger than normal muscles can. Suppose further that the person were provided with various sorts of radio equipment and laser weaponry. Assume finally that devices could speed up his reflexes and improve his eyesight. Now imagine that all this is implanted beneath the skin, that outwardly the man looks no different than he did before, and you have PAPA.

As interesting as these innovations are, the gadgetry is not the most fascinating concept of the first third of the novel. Rather, the most provocative idea is one that Isaac Asimov would call "social science fiction," a concept of the kind that *Galaxy* was noted for, in particular: the battle that Bravais is to observe is an infantry-and-armor clash between Algerian and Moroccan forces, one that has been arranged and is being supervised by the United Nations.

Laumer hypothesizes a general agreement among the nations of the world to resolve conflicts in which diplomacy has failed by means of wars that are indeed limited: these small-scale conflicts serve as an outlet for aggressive tendencies at the same time that they settle disputes. They are carefully overseen and confined by United Nations forces, with each side apparently submitting its battle plans in advance to the U. N. Monitor-General. The system is much like a war-game with live ammunition. But those readers who find the notion a fascinating sociological concept will not be satisfied by a full treatment in *A Plague of Demons*: the whole scheme of controlled conflict serves only as a backdrop for the main action — what Bravais does when he sees alien creatures removing and carrying off the brains of fallen soldiers.

Bravais learns that the aliens, who look like large dogs, have infiltrated the United Nations Command, and he suspects that their influence may be much wider. They employ a telepathic control to keep humans from seeing them, a control from which Bravais is immune thanks to one of the implants PAPA provided him. His escape from Algeria, once the aliens have noticed him, begins the middle third of the novel, and its weakest part. As Severance dies, he tells Bravais of a hideout in Kansas in which he can find refuge, and here again Laumer supplies a novel-sized idea only to drop it without development as the plot moves on.

This second idea is the existence of an organization, the Ultimax Group; it consists of about a hundred people as rich as Croesus, as wise as Solomon, as inventive as Edison, and as secretive as Howard Hughes. Since its founding by a circle that included Benjamin Franklin, Ultimax has watched over the rest of us, nudging human events this way and that in order to bring about desirable results. Among other things, it helped to defeat George III, Napoleon, Kaiser Wilhelm, and Hitler. That Ultimax also aided in the modernization of Japan and the unification of the German and Italian states suggests that it must be composed of confirmed, though fallible, nationalists.

Somewhere beneath Coffeyville, Kansas, Ultimax has built one of its Survival Stations, and Bravais gains entrance to it. Almost bomb- and detection-proof, it contains, among other equipment, a completely automated device for the diagnosis and treatment of human ailments. The robot-doctor sedates Bravais, amputates his badly infected left arm, and replaces it with a prosthesis. After recovering from surgery (in an astonishingly short time), Bravais fears that the aliens, still on his trail, may begin to dig down after him. He contacts the other Survival Stations, but there's nobody home — at any of them. He makes his escape from another exit, and orders the station to blow itself up.

The Ultimax Group is another provocative idea, but its necessity to the plot is nonexistent. Although Felix Severance is a member of Ultimax, he sets Bravais to work in Algeria as an agent of the Defense Department. Although Severance suspects that an inordinate number of people have been missing lately, these nagging doubts reside beneath his Defense Department, not his Ultimax, hat. Although he gives Bravais the information needed to enter the Survival Station, it is hard to see why. It heals Bravais' wounds, but since he had met a human doctor on the ship which brought him to the United States, that function was not necessary. Although Severance has suggested the trip to the States for the purpose of organizing reliable individuals into a counter-alien group, the Survival Station never puts Bravais in touch with any other member of Ultimax. When Bravais leaves the station, he goes to the nearest diplomatic post, the British Consulate in Chicago. Had he been cured of his infection by the human doctor and gone directly to Chicago after landing in America, the outcome of the story would not have been affected in the slightest. The Ultimax Group neither helps nor hinders him; it simply occupies space.

Nor is there a convincing reason for Bravais to go to the British Consulate. Presumably, he wants to test the degree of alien infiltration into human society, and when he discovers that the consul is one of the aliens' androids, his suspicions are confirmed. But what purpose is served by the trip? In what way is the British Consul in Chicago more important to alien success than, say, the governor of Kansas? Or the head of the Kansas State Police? Or, for that matter, the customs inspector at Jacksonville, Florida, where he landed? The outcome of the middle part of the book is Bravais' capture by the aliens, and given their omnipresence, that could have happened anywhere. Perhaps the most convincing evidence of the disjointed nature of the middle part is this: the Ultimax Group has given Bravais their emergency number, but despite the spy-eye detector in his upper left canine, the CBI emergency band receiver in his right lower incisor, and a radar pulser transmitter in his right lower third molar, he cannot contact the Ultimax Monitor when the aliens overwhelm him: he has to use a public phone for that.

The third part begins as Bravais regains consciousness to find that he has turned into a huge fighting machine, a super-tank battling unknown forces on an unfamiliar planet. He correctly assumes that the aliens have removed his brain after overpowering him, and installed it as a small but efficient computer in one of their war machines. The aliens, like selective Valkyries, have been taking the brains of the fallen from battlefields in this way for at least 1,500 years, judging from the other units he meets. Bravais finds himself part of a galactic conflict that has been waged since before the human race evolved. Clearly, Laumer's attention in this third part is on the marriage of man and machine, and the replacement of legs by treads and senses by sensors.

The feeling of this new environment is well drawn and has a fascination of its own, but whereas the background of the first and second parts was detailed, almost oppressively so, the background of the third part, the galactic war, is extremely sketchy. The issues at stake are never clear, if they exist at all. What we have is a picture of a kind of Manichaean struggle between opposing forces that are locked in perpetual battle simply because it is their nature to do so.

Bravais, thanks to PAPA's hypnosis, remembers his past. The personalities of the rest of the brains (except for one) lie dormant beneath the control of the aliens. Yet Bravais finds it a simple matter to wrest control of his fellow units from their superiors, return them to self-consciousness, and enlist their aid in a rebellion. At the climax, he transfers his consciousness to a small housekeeping robot, kills the supreme commander on the planet, and takes over. Yet through all the rebellion and apparently after it, the enemy forces that the aliens had been locked in battle with are nowhere in evidence. After Bravais and his comrades (all of whom like nothing better than a good fight) begin their revolt, we hear no more of the enemy. Either they have been defeated just before the revolt began (unknown to the alien commander), or they have conveniently withdrawn.

After Bravais is in control, he contacts Earth and tells Ultimax about the alien menace. The humans start seeking and eliminating the aliens, and expect no great difficulty in the task. Ultimax offers to the human brains the bodies of the alien androids that they have captured on Earth, yet all of them decide that as long as there is a battle out there among the stars, they will keep on as tanks. Their decision is based on love of combat, it would seem, since nothing we have been told about the galactic war presents the slightest reason why humans should involve themselves in it.

In the final analysis, *A Plague of Demons* is three well-made short pieces that do not fit together. Parts were written in 1964, only about four years after Laumer began writing a great deal of science fiction, and Laumer's more recent works show a competence and sureness in the handling of plot that are not displayed in this early work. Similarly, the balance between foreground and background is not always under control: the first and second parts are richly detailed, almost beyond the needs of the story, but the third part seems sketchy and trite, peopled as it is by a grab-bag of unknown soldiers from the conflicts of the Western world. One wonders why, for instance, the aliens choose only male brains, not female ones; it is never asserted that something in the experience or personality of the owner of the brain is made use of once the brain is hooked up in the machine. Quite the contrary: the aliens make every attempt to suppress the consciousness of the brain. Why do we meet only the brains of soldiers, not the man or woman on the street? Why do we meet the brains only of those fallen in battle, not those endangered by accident or disease? If the first and second parts of *A Plague of Demons* are detailed down to the makes of the cars and the calibers of the weapons, why are the motivations of the third part so cloudy?

Whatever the reason for the faults of the whole, the book nevertheless contains scenes that are memorable: Bravais' night observation of the battle in Algeria, his passage on the undersea freighter, and his awakening to consciousness on the alien battlefield are noteworthy. *A Plague of Demons* will most likely be remembered for these well-realized and vivid scenes.

THE POLLINATORS OF EDEN

Author: John Boyd (1919-   )
First book publication: 1969
Type of work: Novel
Time: The twenty-first century or later
Locale: The Earth and the planet Flora

A beautiful and intelligent woman scientist struggles to be reunited with her fiancé on a planet where flowers rule, and in the process discovers astounding things about herself and her relationship to nature

Principal characters:
> FREDA CARON, a beautiful and intelligent cystologist
> HAL POLINO, a handsome young student
> PAUL THEASTON, Freda's fiancé
> HANS CLAYBORG, a friend of Freda, also a cystologist

John Boyd continues in *The Pollinators of Eden* what he began in *The Last Starship from Earth* — a science fiction treatment of the mythic connotations of man's fall from grace — this time borrowing from the myth of Phaedra and Hippolytus. In that myth Phaedra falls in love with her stepson Hippolytus. She erects the Temple of Peeping Aphrodite overlooking the gymnasium where Hippolytus conditions himself by running, leaping, and wrestling, stark naked, and watches him with incestuous desire. She sends him a letter professing her love, suggesting that they go away and live together for awhile at least. Hippolytus is horrified and vehemently reproaches Phaedra. After leaving a note accusing Hippolytus of ravishing her, she hangs herself. When he reads the note, Theseus, Phaedra's husband and Hippolytus' father, prays to Poseidon for Hippolytus' death. His prayer is answered when a huge wave dashes Hippolytus' chariot against some rocks, and Hippolytus is dragged to death by his horses.

With the Phaedra myth as a springboard, Boyd presents his readers with Freda Caron, the protagonist of *The Pollinators of Eden* and a character he himself once described as the thinking man's ideal woman — one who could quote Shakespeare while making love. A beautiful woman whose intelligence has been attested by computers, Freda may well be the thinking man's ideal woman; but she is also a woman capable of being aroused and responding in a sensual manner.

As the novel begins, Freda, Administrative Director of the Cystological Section of the Bureau of Exotic Plants, is awaiting the return of Paul Theaston, her fiancé, from Planet Flora. He is not aboard the spaceship returning from the Planet of the Flowers, however, because he has been given an extension of duty to continue his study of the pollination process of the unique orchids discovered on the planet. In his place comes Hal Polino (Hippolytus), carrying two pots of tulips as a gift to Freda from Paul. Hal is a handsome student assistant, who is much more interested in twentieth century folkways and his guitar than he is in scientific methodology and bureaucratic authority. The tulips Hal has brought are striking in that they are heterosexual in their development, and they can also reproduce sounds that are made against their bulbs.

Freda listens to the briefing that Dr. Hector, the project's scientific director, presents. Dr. Hector, whose lectures are ordinarily marked by a flow of precise, valid, and constant data, now speaks in a passionate and irrelevant fashion that borders on the poetic. From the briefing, which includes a filmed report from Paul on his orchids, Freda learns that not only are the flowers on Flora heterosexual, but that there are no insects on the planet to help with pollination. But more than that, Freda notes that Paul, at one point in the film, inspects an orchid he has named Sally not with the eyes of an empirical scientist, but with the longing of a lovesick adolescent. Indeed, in his own private note to her, he refers to the orchids as lovable and as capable of loving him.

Freda, however, exists wholly in civilization as it has developed and is proud to be a part of its machinery. She attributes much of what Paul has written to her about his work on Flora as simply fanciful speculation that has been encouraged by Hal Polino. Even more shocked when Hal explains that Paul actually believes the orchids of Flora to be ambulatory, she begins to think that her fiancé is in need of institutional care. Nevertheless, with Hal's help, she begins a series of experiments with the tulips sent by Paul to see if she can discover the secrets of their pollination.

As Freda and Hal carry on their experiments, the line between teacher and student begins to blur, and it becomes obvious that Freda is drawn physically to the young Latin. He in turn plays the seduction game from his end. Boyd handles this aspect of the novel with a dexterous combination of subtle innuendo and not so subtle multilevel punning — all of which results in an interesting parallel to the loving flowers of Flora.

Hal's view of Flora is that beneath its beauty lurks a malevolence toward humans. He believes that the plants once destroyed all carnivorous creatures on the planet and that, if given the chance, they will do so again. Freda, though, is not ready to accept such a theory. Nor is Dr. Hans Clayborg, who supports the plan to put a permanent experimental station on Flora. His theory is that the flowers on Flora have learned to survive the death and rebirth of universes — something that man has not learned.

Freda and Clayborg are part of the deputation to Washington to testify before a Senate committee on the value of the experiments a permanent station could carry out on Flora. Confessing to him that she is afraid of being touched, she permits him to conduct a martini experiment. After four doubles, they feel she is ready for sexual adventures. It turns out, however, that Clayborg is too drunk to calculate correctly the point at which her desire to be loved balances her fear of being touched — and they end up in a cold shower.

One of the more interesting scenes in the novel takes place following the

Senate committee's rejection of the plan to construct an experimental station on Flora. Senator Heyburn, Chairman of the Senate Committee on Plant Classification, states off the record that ease, order, intellect, and enlightenment have combined to destroy the moral fiber of the United States. Echoing Wallace Stevens' view of death as being the mother of beauty, Heyburn argues that man has progressed only because he was cast from Eden. Like Captain Ahab of *Moby Dick*, he hurls curses at the dying sun and blasphemes the name of God. In short, what Heyburn would do is to rev up a starship to a velocity that would send it out of time — beyond God — and then to return after the explosion of the present universe to a new and virgin universe. Clayborg responds by saying that man cannot go beyond God, but must accept the Law of Morality and work within the cycles of creation. Only in that way can man achieve the New Jerusalem.

The experiments that Freda and Hal carry out with the tulips convince them that the plants can actually think and are, in fact, more intelligent and adaptable to their surroundings than is man. Thus, says Hal, they along with the orchids on Flora, pose a danger to men. Together, he and Freda begin to incorporate their findings into the thesis that Freda is writing on the possibility of intelligent plant life.

As they proceed with this work, Freda — like her namesake Phaedra — is attracted to Hal. She does not build a temple from which to watch him, but she is aroused by his working around the tulips in only a pair of shorts. She realizes her emotional weakness in this situation but is helpless to do anything about it and finally reconciles herself to an approaching sexual tryst with Hal. Before this tryst can occur, however, Hal is killed by a high-frequency sound wave sent off from the tulips.

Freda, aware that if it is found out that the tulips killed Hal they will be destroyed, confides in no one. Moreover, she also recognizes that the danger that Paul faces on Flora is not that of being killed, but that of having his libido taken over by the orchids. Her motivation now is not that of a scientist, but that of a woman fighting to keep her man. Her problem is how to get to Flora. Reminding herself that the best administrator is one whose symbol of authority is the second finger extended vertically from a clenched fist, Freda cleverly extorts from her superior, Dr. Gaynor, approval to join a small group leaving for Flora.

Thus Freda and Paul are reunited on Flora, where the latter delights in showing his fiancée his groves of orchids. He is unmoved when she tells him that the tulips killed Hal, and he explains to her that both he and Hal knew that the tulips could emit dangerous high-frequency sound waves.

During her first night on Flora with Paul, Freda dreams she is offered up "breech foremost" to an orchid high priest and seduced amidst "exquisite agony and searing rapture." The next day Paul takes her to a female orchid, and Freda is once more "lifted to heights of adoration," this time knowing well "what was up and who was down." Freda awakens the following morning to find Paul gone and three men approaching her with a tranquilizing gun. Because some of their private conversations have been overheard, they have been branded as defectors.

Back on Earth, Freda, confined to a kind of mental institution for officials, gives birth to a chubby, perfectly oval-shaped seed, which is sent to Santa Barbara to be planted. Using her wiles and her body, she enlists the aid of a psychiatrist, who, with the help of Hans Clayborg, obtains her release and a permanent assignment to Flora. So the novel ends.

When one recalls how Darwin devoted two volumes to orchid pollination, the plot of *The Pollinators of Eden* seems not so strange after all. But Boyd in this novel is not interested primarily in the scientific aspects of orchid pollination. What he is interested in is man's perennial desire to recapture Eden or something like Eden; but he is interested in an ironic way. While obviously there could have been no pollinators of the original Eden, Boyd does have pollinators on Flora, his new Eden. The irony is that it is man himself (woman herself) who becomes an instrument of pollination. Freda, the true Earth Mother, is gloriously deflowered by a flower and gives birth to a seed. If ever there were a culmination of the back-to-nature motif so prevalent throughout literature, here it is. A human world hopelessly ensnared in technology, bureaucracy, and behavorial psychology, and selfishly intent upon raping nature has, in some sense at least, had the favor returned.

While Boyd, as mentioned previously, uses the myth of Phaedra as a springboard for his story, a search for strong parallels between the two yields little. Freda can in a limited way be seen as Phaedra. The names are similar, as are the names Hal Polino and Hippolytus; and Freda seems to fall in love with Hal as Phaedra did with Hippolytus. Even (Paul) Theaston sounds like Theseus. But there the similarities seem to end. Anything more requires a wrenching that can only distort and diminish a rather fascinating story, a story with optimistic, not tragic, overtones. Freda has achieved her goal: to be sent back permanently to Flora, where presumably she will be reunited not only with Paul but also with nature, in the truest sense. For her, Eden will exist again; and man and nature will be one, working within the cycles of creation.

A PRINCESS OF MARS

Author: Edgar Rice Burroughs (1875-1950)
First book publication: 1917
Type of work: Novel
Time: The late nineteenth century
Locale: Arizona and Mars

The heroic adventures of John Carter, first American on Mars, who rescues a beautiful Martian princess from a series of villainous Martian captors of various races and tribes, wins her love, and saves the planet from extinction

> *Principal characters:*
> JOHN CARTER, the hero
> DEJAH THORIS, the heroine
> TARS TARKAS, the best green Martian man
> SOLA, the best green Martian woman
> SARKOJA, the most dangerous green Martian woman
> WOOLA, Carter's devoted Martian watchdog
> KANTOS KAN, Carter's red Martian sidekick
> SAB THAN, Carter's red Martian rival

A Princess of Mars was Burroughs' first novel. Although he went on to write seventy more books — including ten additional Mars novels, five Venus novels, and twenty-eight Tarzan novels — *The Princess of Mars* remains one of his most popular works. The reasons for its enduring popularity are instructive; for, with a freshness, exhilaration, and clarity not always found in his later writings, this novel addresses some of the most widespread hopes and fears in modern Western culture.

The novel opens in 1866 with the coming of modern times to the United States. To the narrator-protagonist, Captain John Carter of the Confederate Army, life seems to have lost most of its meaning now that the Gilded Age has begun. No longer the chivalric champion of the Old South, he has been reduced to self-centered money-grubbing as a prospector in the Arizona desert. Alone with his partner and former comrade-in-arms Captain John Powell, Carter quickly discovers that even his limited goal of restoring his personal fortune is probably not attainable. Their living death in the desolate wilds turns into total death as first Powell and then Carter are pursued and apparently killed by savage Apaches.

Up to this point, Burroughs' novel uses the melodramatic elements of Western popular fiction to represent familiar terrors of the modern industrialized world. There is the ordeal of discovering who one is and what one can do in this world, where many find, with Carter, that traditional familial and social roles no longer provide workable answers. There is the bedeviling suspicion that neither society nor nature concerns itself about any individual, however prudently, morally, or gallantly he may behave, and that all individuals are likely to be victimized by brutal, essentially impersonal forces which they can neither understand nor control. In the grimly realistic modern world view, no earthly frontier affords escape from these distresses. Nor can modern man outrun death, against whose triumphs work, fame, and love are pitifully, utterly ineffective, and in whose onmipresent shadow good and evil lose all significance.

For Burroughs' hero there is a way out. Carter inexplicably jumps out of his clothes, out of his apparently dead body, out of the cave which has become his tomb, out of Earth's imprisoning atmosphere — and finds himself in a strange environment which he instinctively knows to be Mars. Superficially, the Red Planet is quite a contrast to Earth: under its two moons, Carter meets his first Martians — six-armed, oviparous green people who tower an intimidating fifteen feet in height. Yet on closer examination these green Martians, the Tharks, reveal themselves as extreme embodiments of the same cruel, predatory spirit which menaced Carter and Powell in Arizona. On Mars Carter learns that even one good man can make a great difference. He begins by astounding himself and the Tharks with his Earthman's ability to leap extraordinary Martian distances, and goes on to display other physical skills with which he successfully combats one belligerent green giant after another. But his crucial superiority is his sense of decency; by awakening the same sense in Tars Tarkas, a green Martian prince, Carter is able to subvert Thark society, so that at the end of the novel, when Tars Tarkas has been voted the Tharks' new leader, there seem solid grounds for hoping that Carter has started the green Martians on the road to reform.

In battling and subverting the Tharks, Carter represents civilized humanity, seeking out and destroying the "huge and terrible incarnation of hate, of vengeance and of death." The reader identifies with him as the idealized master of derring-do who is the standard hero of adventure stories. But Carter does not remain simply a heroic warrior assailing green monstrosities; because he must also confront the red Martians, who represent humanity imprisoned by civilization, he grows into a new dimension of heroism. As he labors to restore the red Martian princess, Dejah Thoris, to her family, Carter becomes a romantic hero whose actions are directed solely by his love for this ideally beautiful, wise, and virtuous woman. The new Carter is a superheroic savior who preserves all Mars — and, by implication, all humanity — from otherwise inevitable destruction. For Carter the superhero, incorporating both the adventurous and the romantic stereotypes of heroism, defeats the most difficult enemies in his world: alienation and purposelessness.

Apparently Burroughs himself, like his fictional Martians, found Carter's superheroism irresistibly inspiring. In each of the ten sequels to *A Princess of Mars* the original formula recurs — the hero of adventure and the hero of romance fuse and conquer. Moreover, Tarzan of the Apes and Carson of Venus also follow this pattern throughout the thirty-three volumes devoted to them. In other words, Burroughs' best-known books tell one essential story over and over: the perennially popular myth of his brand of superhero.

The details do vary from book to book, however, and such differences in detail are especially marked in the eleven Mars novels. Mars was Burroughs' first imaginary world, and he invested it with a much more complex history, geography, zoology, and anthropology than he invented for any other fictional environment. Burroughs' Mars is not merely a place where Carter can develop the heroism denied him in Earth's Gilded Age; it is a richly exotic haven to which Burroughs' reader can imaginatively escape from humdrum reality. Most of the fascinations of Mars are disclosed in *A Princess of Mars* and in its two immediate sequels, *The Gods of Mars* and *Warlord of Mars*; all three novels were written and published between the years 1911-1914. In these volumes, which Burroughs intended as an epic trilogy, Carter rises to be Warlord of Mars, and as he does so, he explores the Red Planet from pole to pole. He meets members of Mars's five major races — green, red, black, white, and yellow Martians — as well as the bizarre plant people; he ranges over Mars's deserts, forests, rivers, mountains and polar regions; he encounters various strange and horrible Martian creatures, including white apes, thoats, siths, apts, banths, and calots; he learns the complex Martian language and social etiquette; he demystifies Mars's mystery religions; and he masters Martian science, technology, and politics. Much of the suspense in the three novels derives from the fact that neither Carter nor the reader knows what to expect in this emphatically unearthly realm.

In presenting his fictional Mars, Burroughs displays considerable skill. He provides vivid, particularized, highly specific descriptions, so that the reader cannot help but visualize precisely the images called up. And this visual information is supplemented by audible clues, for the Martian language which Burroughs invented for his Mars stories is onomatopoeic — its terms sound like what they mean. Moreover, Burroughs' Mars tantalizingly combines the fantastic and the familiar; its elements differ enough from everyday reality to be consistently amazing, yet often they also externalize images which every man can recognize as the stuff of his own daydreams and nightmares, and which are integral to Western popular culture.

For the most part Burroughs seems to have churned out these images without considering their symbolic or mythic significance. The unpremeditated, spontaneous quality of his writing is a pronounced characteristic of popular fiction, which energetically eschews the intellectualized approach of the highbrow author. Burroughs' spontaneity undoubtedly charms many among his worldwide readership. Unfortunately, it also mars his novels with serious artistic flaws. His plots usually lack focus and climax, but are instead episodic ramblings along vaguely defined thematic tracks; furthermore, they frequently reproduce Burroughs' few favorite stock situations, rather than presenting a new line of action. So, for example, the last half of *A Princess of Mars* deteriorates into a repetitive sequence of pitched battles among diverse opponents and noticeably lacks the dramatic intensity which distinguishes the novel's first half. And so many Martian princesses undergo capture — there is at least one such kidnaping or imprisonment in every Mars volume — that Mars seems to be populated mostly by past, present, and would-be princess-stealers and princess-savers. Of course all of Burroughs' books, including this one, were composed for serial publication and understandably express the serial writer's typical preference for immediate thrills and shortterm climaxes. It seems likely that Burroughs' lifelong orientation toward magazine publication reinforced his tendency toward slapdash plotting, and kept him from trying very hard to write unified novels.

By contrast, he appears to have been deeply troubled, even obsessed, by something else which he did not think through in *A Princess of Mars*. Carter's superheroism is implicitly self-contradictory, for he must simultaneously demonstrate that he is Mars's most sensitive lover and its most efficient killer. Popular fiction often blends clashing images in this manner; the stereotypical Western hero, bringing law and order by his violent individualism, is an obvious example. But Burroughs, who perpetually glorified the loving warrior, evidently could not help examining, reexamining, and repeatedly trying to explain and harmonize the inherent conflicts in his concept of heroism. Despite the numerous explicit moralistic statements in this novel that true heroes must be loving, Burroughs does not quite establish that Carter's compassionate soul dominates his perfectly muscled physique — particularly since Carter's "love," not to mention the exigencies of action-oriented serial fiction, impels him from one gory exertion to another. Although Burroughs extends Dejah Thoris' ordeal of captivity through *The Gods of Mars* and *Warlord of Mars*, bestowing her on various Martian fiends all over the planet, he keeps relying on Carter's sword to save her from her several captors. As Carter's daughter explains in *The Chessmen of Mars*, fifth novel in the series, Carter has a credibility problem: her lover reminds her that

> "It has been long ages since the men of Barsoom [Mars] loved peace."
> "My father loves peace," returned the girl.
> "And yet he is always at war," said the man.
> She laughed. "But he *says* he likes peace."

While the first three Mars novels articulate the paradox in the lover-warrior image of superheroism, volumes four through seven attempt to resolve that paradox. In all four novels Burroughs replaces Carter with alternate protagonists, each of whom combines warmaking and lovemaking in a slightly different personality. These new protagonists — Carthoris, Gahan, Paxton, and Hadron — confront what is really a single enemy in diverse incarnations: all four must prove that brawn does not matter more than brain. Burroughs represents the mind-body conflict by strikingly original, memorable images — phantom bowmen, whose existence is purely hallucinatory; the symbiotic rykors and kaldanes, complementary races of bodiless heads and headless bodies, brain transplants, dazzlingly beautiful villains and unimaginably hideous heroes and heroines. Possibly because of the power this theme held for its author, the Mars series displays a focus, color, and dramatic intensity in its four central volumes which it had not shown since the first half of *A Princess of Mars*; *The Chessman of Mars* is especially strong.

These four novels also re-create the rebirth and redemption pattern which is so important in *A Princess of Mars*, where the miraculously reborn Carter redeems Tars Tarkas, Sola, and even Woola the watchdog from the spiritual death enforced by the brutish Tharks. Similarly, Carthoris, Grahan, Paxton, and Hadron must each undergo the regenerative experience of finding and winning his princess, or soul-mate; and each helps at least one token "convert" to free his or her true souls from materialistic impediments. By contrast, the final four volumes of the Mars series center on death, the king of terrors, which Carter defies but cannot completely conquer in *A Princess of Mars*. Images of death abound in the last four Mars novels: the "rat," a professional assassin in Mars's labyrinthine criminal underworld; synthetic thugs, created out of uncontrollably expanding ooze; walking, talking corpses; skeleton men. In the eleventh volume, *John Carter of Mars*, death-images coalesce in the culminating horror of a synthetic man who becomes a mad scientist and manufactures the super-weapon to end all super-weapons, a gigantic, synthetic white ape. Death envelops Carter in *A Princess of Mars*, which begins by killing him off and concludes by returning him to his Arizona tomb under such ambiguous circumstances that everything Carter has fought for — his own life and that of the Red Planet — seems lost. Carter does survive, of course, and the Mars series continues, but death haunts his efforts and in the last four Mars novels gathers a terrible, concentrated force. Burroughs may have been seeking a way out of the apparently mortal danger to his first hero when he sent Carter briefly to Jupiter in the last half of *John Carter of Mars*. But death came for Burroughs himself before he could pursue this possible escape route, so that Carter is at the last, as he was from the first, true to his greatest love and one real home — Mars, the warrior's world.

Criticism:

Hillegas, Mark. "Martians and Mythmakers: 1877-1938," in *Challenges in American Culture*. Edited by Ray B. Browne, Larry N. Landram and William K. Bottorff. Bowling Green, Ohio: Bowling Green University Popular Press, 1970, pp. 150-177. This is the most detailed discussion of Burroughs' treatment of the "myth of the superior Martians." It also compares Burroughs' use of the myth to other major writers.

Kyle, Richard. "Out of Time's Abyss: The Martian Stories of Edgar Rice Burroughs," in *Riverside Quarterly*. V (January, 1970), pp. 110-124. Kyle believes that Burroughs' Martian stories are heavily indebted to the influence of H. Rider Haggard.

Moskowitz, Sam. *Under the Moons of Mars: A History and Anthology of "The Scientific Romance" in the Munsey Magazines, 1912-1920*. New York: Holt, Rinehart, & Winston, 1970. Moskowitz traces the influence of Burroughs on Martian themes in science fiction.

Mullen, Richard D. "The Undisciplined Imagination: Edgar Rice Burroughs and Lowellian Mars," in *SF: The Other Side of Realism*. Edited by Thomas D. Clareson. Bowling Green, Ohio: Bowling Green University Popular Press, 1941, pp. 229-247. Mullen, through an examination of the Martian novels, attempts to show the sources of Burroughs' descriptions of the planet.

THE PUPPET MASTERS

Author: Robert A. Heinlein (1907-   )
First book publication: 1951
Type of work: Novel
Time: Probably the twenty-first century
Locale: The United States

A novel of education in which a young secret agent, fighting against aliens who possess their human hosts, learns to make full use of his mind and capabilities

> Principal characters:
> SAM (ELIHU NIVENS), a secret agent
> THE OLD MAN (ANDREW NIVENS), head of the secret agency and Sam's father
> MARY (ALLUCQUERE), a secret agent and later Sam's wife

The Puppet Masters is a perfect example of what is referred to as "golden age" science fiction. In the novel, Robert A. Heinlein presents a world under seige by an alien life form that attaches itself to human hosts and effectively controls all the actions of that host. Except for the hump caused by the alien body connected to the back of its victim, the possessed human appears to most people to be acting quite normally and freely. Other than accepting the aliens and the colony on Venus, Heinlein asks no further act of faith on the part of the reader. And even in the case of the aliens, all features of the novel are carefully presented in sufficient detail to create a credible world. Thus, while the fantastic is very much part of the novel, fantasy is not. All actions, all events, all solutions have explanations within the work itself.

But the world of *The Puppet Masters* is only part of the justification for calling the novel golden age science fiction. Of far more importance than the fictional world itself is what is done with that world. Heinlein has chosen his aliens carefully because he has a particular theme in mind, a theme that recurs in several of his works: mankind is threatened by a form of life that is absolutely uninterested in compromise. In such a battle there can be only one victor, and the victory must be complete. Like the bugs in *Starship Troopers* (1959), the slugs of *The Puppet Masters* appear one day, start to possess humans, and set out to enslave all of humanity. Heinlein clearly presents the alien slugs as intelligent, brutal, singleminded creatures bent on their own design of cosmic rule. No accommodation or compromise can be reached because they are simply not interested.

It the utter ruthlessness of the puppet masters is not accepted by the reader, an important part of the novel will be lost, as it is all too often lost by readers of *Starship Troopers*. Heinlein is not a simpleminded militarist who glories in calling the enemy names, in describing futuristic military hardware, or in portraying gory battle scenes. Rather, like John W. Campbell, Jr., in "Twilight," he is interested in defining those features of the human race that enable it to survive and to develop. Unlike Campbell, however, Heinlein is not satisfied with merely calling man an "animal with curiosity." He is interested in survivors, in successful and idealistic men. The puppet masters, therefore, are not only aliens that threaten humanity; they are also the excuse for Heinlein to explore with the reader definitions of survival, success, and idealism. And it is this exploration that makes the novel so successful as science fiction.

The aliens, since they completely control the hosts that they attach themselves to, become a graphic symbol of oppression. Yet ironically, the human host, who knows that he is being controlled, derives a certain amount of pleasure from the takeover. Because the slugs think and make decisions for their hosts, they offer a degree of peace and joy that arises from a freedom from responsibility. But for Heinlein, such peace and joy prevent human survival and success. Moreover, people willing to surrender free will in order to experience *nirvana* endanger not only themselves but also the entire race. Survival, success, and idealism must depend on a different type of man, represented in the novel first by the Old Man and then by Sam.

It might be difficult to imagine the head of a supersecret agency as idealistic, but the Old Man clearly is. Sam, one of his agents as well as his son, says of him:

> Not that he was a soft boss. He was quite capable of saying, "Boys, we need to fertilize this oak tree. Jump in that hole at its base and I'll cover you up."
> We'd have done it. Any of us would.
> And the Old Man would bury us alive too, if he thought that there was as much as a fifty-three-per-cent probability that it was the Tree of Liberty he was nourishing.

While such an ideal may seem out of touch with our present, it is an essential belief to Heinlein. Man must be free; the Old Man believes first and foremost in this single dictum. But his idealism alone is not sufficient to qualify the Old Man as either a survivor or a savior of the human race; it must be tempered with a practical wisdom which allows him to judge the gravity of a situation, to determine the possible solutions, and to decide which of the probable solutions is best for the immediate case. Thus, the Old Man is an idealist, but more importantly, he is a *competent* idealist. The term "competent" is very important here because, on the one hand, it defines the limits of idealism and on the other, it is synonymous with survival and success. By the end of *The Puppet Masters*, there are two competent men: the Old Man and Sam.

In many ways the novel presents the education of Sam into a competent man. At the beginning, Sam acts out of a double loyalty, as an agent of the United States and as the son of the Old Man. But that loyalty is not always sufficient to guide his actions, especially during those times when Sam must act for himself. Thus, when he returns to Des Moines, Iowa, to obtain filmed evidence of the slugs in control of humans, he is anything but successful. He first picks on a man who is not possessed, and then, when he does invade a stronghold of possessed humans, he fails to get the needed proof. Finally, when he returns to the agency, he returns with a fellow agent who is, unknown to him, possessed. Sam has done the best job he is capable of under the circumstances, but he has not done a competent job. In these early chapters, Sam still has much to learn from his father; he is still a young man learning how to cope, and competency will only come with the experience of age.

Sam's education begins in earnest after he has been possessed by a puppet master and then rescued by his father. At this point a personal crisis forces him into competency: the Old Man needs a volunteer to be possessed by a captured master so that information can be obtained from it; Sam is in no mood to volunteer, especially since the captured master is the one from whom he has just escaped. However, when he finds that the volunteer is Mary, the woman he loves, he steps forward and allows himself to be placed under the slug's control once again. Despite his fears and his nightmares, he gives himself up to the one thing that he most abhors. Such an act is necessarily a step in his education because, up to this time, Sam has acted only out of blind faith in his father. In order to continue to develop into a competent man, however, he must act on his own for people other than himself. Here is the beginning of the idealism that his father already has. It is a small beginning, but one that will fully develop as the novel progresses.

As Sam gains more experience in fighting the puppet masters, he starts to act in a more informed way. While he still does not have his father's ability to reason through to concrete conclusions with the use of limited information, he does exhibit a fine ability to act conservatively on the facts he has. Thus, when he scouts out Kansas City, a puppet master stronghold, he is able to avoid the traps set up for him. In this particular case he makes fewer mistakes than in his earlier ventures and is actually able to bring back valuable information. However, Sam's information is too late to help an attempted invasion of the territory held by the slugs, and the information is already known through other sources. Again, Sam cannot be blamed for the outcome; he has done a good job, but he is not yet up to the standards required of the competent man.

Two events lead to the final step in Sam's education. The first is his marriage to Mary, and the second is the revelation of Mary's earlier life on Venus. The marriage, in a world that defines itself in terms of temporary "contracts" between men and women, represents Sam's final necessary commitment to others beyond himself and his father. Mary, as an infant, was part of the first settlement on Venus. The settlers were possessed by the slugs, who for some reason died; and Mary survived both the possession and whatever caused the death of the puppet masters. So shocking was the experience, however, that she has blocked the entire period out of her consciousness.

The Old Man and various military officials realize that if Mary can recapture the memory, the solution to their problem might be at hand. Something must be found that will kill the masters but leave their human hosts alive. An elaborate procedure is therefore begun in which Mary relives her entire experience under hypnosis. To spare her the pain of the memories, she is instructed at the end of each session to forget what she has remembered under the probing of the scientists. Furthermore, Sam is not allowed to participate in the sessions because his lack of expertise and his emotional involvement with Mary would make him a hindrance.

After many fruitless sessions, Sam does insist on joining the group. He reasons that others with even less at stake than himself are participating, and that, given his knowledge of his wife, he might very well be of some help. He goes even further than this, moreover, and orders his father and all nontechnical people out of the session. Then, once the scientists are about to begin, Sam insists that all previous tapes relevant to the search for the solution be played for him, and that his wife be allowed to see them as well if she wishes.

The result of Sam's action is an immediate solution: Mary sees the tapes and quickly identifies the disease that had killed the puppet masters. Thus, acting out of love for his wife and using his understanding of her personality, Sam is able directly to attack the problem and resolve it. As later problems arise, such as the danger that the disease poses for the human hosts, the method of transmitting the disease, and the timing of the spread of the disease, Sam uses the same combination of compassion for others and practical wisdom to find answers. It is at this stage that Sam has become a truly competent man. He now acts with both mind and heart in perfect accord. As proof, furthermore, of just how far Sam has progressed, when the Old Man is possessed by a slug, it is Sam who saves him.

At the end of *The Puppet Masters*, Sam has grown into a man ready to face his destiny with full confidence in his ability both to fight for the right reasons and to fight well. He is now ready to carry the battle to the home of the puppet masters, and his final speech summarizes not only the lessons he has learned but also those that Heinlein has sought to teach the reader throughout the work:

> Whether we make it or not, the human race has got to keep up its well-earned reputation for ferocity. The price of freedom is the willingness to do sudden battle, anywhere, any time, and with utter recklessness. If we did not learn that from the slugs, well — "Dinosaurs, move over! We are ready to become extinct!"

While the idea of the competent man can easily be lost in much of the rhetoric found in the novel, the reader would be doing a disservice to himself and Heinlein to do so. The simplistic expressions used in reference to the Soviet Union and the female characters are certainly most annoying to readers of the present. *The Puppet Masters*, however, must be judged in terms of the genre, and, as science fiction, is it successful.

Criticism:

Sarti, Ronald. "Variations on a Theme: Human Sexuality in the Work of Robert A. Heinlein," in *Robert A. Heinlein*. Edited by Joseph D. Olander and Martin H. Greenberg. New York: Taplinger, 1978, pp. 107-136. Sarti calls this a new twist on the invaders from space theme.

Slusser, George E. *The Classic Years of Robert A. Heinlein*. San Bernardino, Calif.: Borgo, 1977, pp. 42-49. Slusser calls this a classic tale of intrigue.

THE RAKEHELLS OF HEAVEN

Author: John Boyd (Boyd Upchurch, 1919-   )
First book publication: 1969
Type of work: Novel
Time: 2228
Locale: The Earth and the planet Harlech

Two space scouts, one a con man and the other a carrier of God's Word, set about changing the patterns of tolerance and permissiveness that mark a planet conceived of by its inhabitants as heaven

> Principal characters:
> JOHN ADAMS, a space scout
> CARA, his wife
> KEVIN O'HARA, a space scout
> BUBO THE DEAN, the leader on Harlech

In the Preface to the Penguin Edition of *The Rakehells of Heaven*, John Boyd states that the ideal reader of the novel "should have the mentality of a Southern stock-car racer, be a Baptist with a sense of detachment, have a well-developed sense of the absurd, and be fascinated with the quirks and accomplishments of the human animal." What he meant by the first two characteristics, perhaps only he knows; but certainly the last two are understandable and, indeed, applicable. *The Rakehells of Heaven* presents a story that is on the one hand a hilarious satire and on the other a tribute to man's never-flagging efforts to change the *status quo*, for better or worse.

The third novel in a trilogy, *The Rakehells of Heaven* was begun, according to Boyd, as a science fiction version of the myth of Prometheus, that Titan condemned by Zeus to be bound forever to a jagged cliff for giving man the knowledge of fire, numbers and letters, and happiness and evil. Defiant in spite of his punishment, Prometheus insists that his action was no crime but merely an effort to help man, to teach him to hope — in other words, to change the *status quo*. In the end Zeus shatters the Titan's rock with a bolt of lightning which hurls Prometheus to an abysmal dungeon deep in the Earth. As Boyd himself admitted, he does not carry the myth through to the end of the novel. In truth, it is doubtful, without Boyd's comments in the Preface, that the reader would recognize this particular myth as the point of departure for one of the most entertaining fictional trips into space.

At the opening of *The Rakehells of Heaven*, the hero of the novel, Space Scout John (Jack) Adams returns from a mission earlier than scheduled and without his companion, Space Scout Kevin (Red) O'Hara. The narrator of the story, a psychiatrist at the Mandan Naval Academy, debriefs Adams with the specific purpose of finding out why Adams has aborted the mission and what has happened to O'Hara. The official theory prior to Adams' arrival is not only that he has violated regulations by returning early, but also that he has suffered stalker's fever — a condition in which one spaceman, because of prolonged confinement on a spaceship, stalks his partner and kills him. What the psychiatrist learns is the tale of the novel.

Jack Adams, a Southerner from Alabama, and Red O'Hara, a shanty-Irishman from County Meath, were classmates at Mandan Naval Academy. O'Hara, nicknamed King Con, succeeded at their first meeting in conning his roommate Adams out of the lower bunk, in spite of which they developed a close friendship. Upon graduation, because their separate but equal personalities interlocked, they were assigned a space mission together, but not before O'Hara married, and Adams received a Call to carry the Lord's Word to other galaxies.

The purpose of their mission is to scout the universe for undiscovered planets that are similar to Earth, explore them, and classify *homo sapiens*. To be thus classified, an alien inhabitant must, among other things, possess an opposing thumb, believe in a Supreme Being, practice coitus face-to-face, be able to crossbreed with humans, and have a gestation period of from seven to eleven months. If these conditions cannot be met, then the planet in question is to be occupied by the Interplanetary Colonial Authority.

Adams and O'Hara find a promising planet, land their ship, set up a tent, and arrange numerous Earth exhibits. Soon a large crowd of humanlike beings gather in a nearby field for a game similar to soccer, in which, with their exceptionally long legs, they demonstrate superiority to humans. One other aspect that Jack and Red are quick to notice is that under the very short tunics, the only clothing worn by the planet's inhabitants, there are no "shorts or panties."

The two space scouts soon learn they are on the planet Harlech, which is made up of an association of self-governing universities. Because all industry is automated, the Harlechians spend their time in scholarly pursuits. Jack and Red, having landed in the area of University 36, receive an invitation through Bubo, Dean of 36, to offer courses at that institution. Jack offers to teach Earth customs, philosophy, government, and religion; Red offers to teach Earth folklore, poetry, drama, and biology. They become known as Jack the Teacher and Red the Teacher.

While the two new additions to the faculty of 36 learn the language of Harlech and prepare their courses for the coming summer session, they discover Harlechian distinctions: Harlechians live primarily underground because of the violent electrical storms that frequently sweep the planet's surface; they practice free love; they show no emotions; they have no word for God; and their word for heaven is Harlech. Red, with his virulent interest in sex, feels he really is in heaven and soon earns a reputation for sexual prowess. Jack, on the other hand, vows to remain aloof from such activities and to bring the Word to the Harlechians.

Con man that he is, Red convinces Dean Bubo that the courses he and Jack are to offer should be in a new department, Liberal Arts. Then he conducts a

publicity campaign with large posters urging that the students "Thrill to lepre-
chauns!" and "Experience the miracle of Salvation!" The classrooms are arranged in tiers, with the students sitting on high stools, and the large number
of female students wearing no underwear; Jack and Red witness a new view of
academe. Jack struggles vainly to keep his eyes away from temptation by looking at the ceiling while he lectures and hoping that such a posture will be
thought of as a strange Earth custom. Red, far from distracted by the nudity of
his students, uses it to call the roll, "since all their faces look alike."

Finally conditioning himself to look not at the faces of his students — a
Harlechian taboo — but at their "forfended places," Jack lectures with zeal
on the virtues of modesty. But he falls victim to Cara, his golden girl, whose
"mound of Venus swelled as a perfect ovate spheroid tassled with cornsilk
curls," and whose "curve gave it an air of joy blended with a feeling of peace
which seemed to exude happiness and serenity." His lectures, however, soon
take effect; his golden girl, along with her classmates, begins to wear underwear.

Red sets out to present a television adaptation of Shakespeare, in which he
amalgamates *Romeo and Juliet*, *Hamlet*, *Macbeth*, and one or two other plays
— a true Elizabethan soap opera. A great success, the production causes the
Harlechians to do something they never have done — show emotion. In fact,
Bubo the Dean, acting as the God who punished the sinner Prometheus, decides that those who played the roles of villains should be expelled from
school; and they are. This act infuriates Red (Prometheus), who now says that
Bubo must be taught a lesson in justice, and he stages a cultural battle of the
Titans in this particular Heaven. He plans to present another drama, this one a
Christmas extravaganza focusing on another Prometheus, Christ, complete
with Herod, centurions, the Maids of Bethlehem (prostitutes), angels, a virgin,
and the Christ child. He hopes to get Bubo the Dean to expel more villains so
that he, Red, will have the nucleus of a revolutionary force.

Jack and Red have accomplished several changes on Harlech: modesty has
taken hold; emotional responses are apparent; a legal system prevails; a police
force exists; and sexual possessiveness has taken over from the earlier concept
of free love. In short, Jack and Red have turned Harlech into a mirror of Earth;
the change becomes evident when a Harlechian man is murdered in a dispute
over a woman. The murderer is found to be Nesser, a young man that Jack has
been using as an altar boy in his religious classes.

Things look bad for Nesser despite his being defended by two students who
have studied in Jack's legal class. At the last minute, however, they come up
with a wrinkle worthy of a Clarence Darrow. Since the murdered man's organs
have, according to Harlechian custom, been transplanted to other Harlechians,
Nesser's lawyers maintain that the victim is alive and well in various parts of
Harlech. Nevertheless, Nesser is sentenced to hang. He beats the hangman by
hanging himself.

On first falling in love with Cara, Jack refuses to take her, saying the flesh is willing, but the spirit says no. The spirit, however, soon gives way to the flesh. Here the roles of the two space scouts are reversed: Jack, always the defender of regulations and duty, becomes the one willing to give in to the pleasure principle; and Red, usually a hell-raising con man, argues that to defect would be stupid. He suggests that Jack, as commander, appoint him, Red, as chaplain to their crew so that he can marry Jack and Cara. Soon, with Cara pregnant, Jack hopes that her gestation period will qualify her as a humanoid, but she gives birth in the fourth month. She explains, however, that Red used her as an experiment in his class on love and courtship and, since the baby is his, she meets the deadline with two months to spare.

Jack sets out searching for Red to kill him and angrily tells Bubo the Dean that Red should be crucified in his own Passion Play. Before Jack can intervene, Red is crucified, and his body is burned by lightning.

To prevent the students from making Red a demigod, Jack reveals that his and Red's mission had been military not educational; Bubo has Jack put in his spaceship and sent back to Earth. Jack attempts to accelerate to the point that he can beat time and arrive on Earth prior to the time that he and Red actually left, thereby saving Red's life; but this fails. The psychiatrist comments that Red O'Hara, con man that he is, cannot be dead. If there was a crucifixion, then there was a resurrection. After all, Red is an Irishman. And who should know Irishmen better than Dr. Michael Timothy O'Sullivan?

The book, then, satirizes higher education and the egotistic compulsion to make other worlds like our own — to rake our hell over their heaven. The Harlechians may think their society, tolerant and permissive as it is, is heaven; but Jack and Red know better. For Jack Adams, with his Southern Baptist Puritanism, tolerance and permissiveness lead away from God's word. For Red O'Hara, with his Irish Catholic Puritanism, those qualities take away the sense of victory that comes from a hard-fought seduction. Though these apparently divergent views cause conflict between the two space scouts, they add up to the same thing: with no goals — holy Words or earthly seductions — there can be no heaven. For heaven is not a place where one arrives; it is a place toward which one strives.

Some readers may complain that Jack and Red serve as serpents in the garden, destroying the idyllic innocence of the Harlechians, much as missionaries did to the inhabitants of the South Seas or other places. At another level, Red and his fate may be seen to exemplify one of the types of hero that Joseph Campbell describes in *Hero with a Thousand Faces*; like Prometheus, Red darts to his goal and unbalances the established powers so that they react sharply, and he is "blasted from within and without — crucified, on the rock of his own violated unconscious."

But the humorous element remains uppermost. Boyd has written that while writing *The Rakehells of Heaven*, he often woke his wife in the middle of the night, chuckling over some incident from the book. Boyd commented that if the books of his trilogy were named after characters from Shakespeare, *The Rakehells of Heaven* would have to be Edmund from *King Lear*, because it "was a whoreson of science fiction, but there was great sport in its making." And, to be sure, there is great sport in its reading.

RENDEZVOUS WITH RAMA

Author: Arthur C. Clarke (1917-   )
First book publication: 1973
Type of work: Novel
Time: 2031
Locale: Rama, an alien spacecraft, the Lunar headquarters of United Planets

The grandly exciting story of the human exploration of a giant, uninhabited alien artifact which enters the solar system from interstellar space

> Principal characters:
>   COMMANDER WILLIAM T. NORTON, Commanding officer of *Endeavour*
>   SURGEON COMMANDER LAURA ERNST, ship's doctor and Norton's sometime mistress
>   LIEUTENANT COMMANDER KARL MERCER, *Endeavour*'s second officer
>   LIEUTENANT JAMES PAK, *Endeavour*'s most junior officer
>   LIEUTENANT BORIS RODRIGO, religious fanatic and expert saboteur
>   DR. BOSE, Chairman of the United Planet's Rama Committee

Rendezvous with Rama is one of those novels obviously destined to become instant classics. The combination of authorial reputation, imaginative use of setting, likable characters, and exciting action brought the book immediate success, including the then-rare accolade of both Hugo and Nebula awards, along with several other less prestigious honors. It has remained a large seller in the several years since its first publication, for it combines adventure, mystery, and scientific gadgetry in an extraordinarily pleasurable way. No heavy philosophical work, the book nevertheless poses important questions and, significantly, leaves the answers open at its end. Furthermore, it moves rapidly and easily through scientific marvels and alien wonders with the grace and assurance possible only for an author who really knows what he writes, yet can present it in a lucid manner acceptable to a novice. *Rendezvous with Rama* is thus a *tour de force* of a kind possible only in the best of hard science fiction.

At first blush, the novel is an example of the traditional sense-of-wonder, technologically oriented science fiction. It postulates steady progress by the human race in technical fields, so that in the year of its setting, there is a United Planets Headquarters on the moon, from which are administered the external affairs of the seven member bodies (the planets Earth, Mars, and Mercury; and the moons Luna, Ganymede, Titan, and Triton). Obviously, colonization and commercial space travel are commonplaces. Other technical advances are also presented: the Earth is defended, for example, by Project Spaceguard, an extensive tracking and missile network (based on the ABM systems its name recalls). This marvel is designed to prevent Earth's collision with any wandering space bodies whose impact on the surface could cause major damage; it is this system, ostensibly put in place after a disastrous meteorite strikes northern Italy, which detects Rama and sets the events of the novel in motion. Spaceships are plasma-powered, large, long-range, and equipped for all sorts of missions; they carry space scooters for short-range missions in deep space. War and weapons are strictly controlled, but the Hermians (inhabitants of Mercury) use fusion bombs in their mining operations and have the capacity to launch them at interplanetary distances. Some terraforming has been attempted, but most human settlements on the bodies of the solar system are marvels of life-support engineering — probably nowhere more so than on Mercury. Nor are the biological sciences neglected: the caretakers aboard Clarke's spaceships are "simps," living products of the Superchimpanzee Corporation's experiments with natural and synthetic genes. These animals possess an IQ of about sixty and can comprehend several hundred words of English; but weighing less than thirty kilos, they consume only half the food and oxygen of a human being while replacing 2.75 persons in routine jobs.

Thus, the author gives us no romantically conceived solar system, with terrestrial locales and indigenous life forms; we see a rigorously extrapolated one, employing the best scientific knowledge available to Clarke at the time of writing. Note the accuracy, for instance, of the astronomical observations used in the depictions of uninhabitable Venus and the barely habitable Mercury. Clarke is, of course, optimistic in his predictions of the solutions to the engineering problems involved in exploring and colonizing the solar system, but the rules of this subgenre require him to be. He is also playful at times, in such notions as a Lunar Olympics structured to take advantage of the low gravity and airless surface of that world; even his playfulness is purposeful, however, for the sky-bike used in the Olympics by one of the officers of the cruiser *Endeavour* is also used to explore the interior of Rama. Unfortunately, sometimes Clarke provides a conventional rather than a genuinely necessary extrapolation, as in providing his spacemen with the legal right to multiple wives and families on different planets; and sometimes he is merely topical, as when he has the commander of *Endeavour* echo Neil Armstrong's first words on the moon as he lands his ship on Rama. On balance, however, Clarke provides a sound technical novel, resembling in its plausibility of detail his own earlier works, such as *A Fall of Moondust* and *Earthlight*.

But *Rendezvous with Rama* is not only like that particular sort of earlier Clarke novel; it has some affinity as well with his less conventional *Childhood's End* and *2001: A Space Odyssey*. Like those earlier works, *Rendezvous with Rama* is a "first contact" story (there is even a chapter entitled "First Contact"). The aliens of this novel, however, are not physically present; Clarke depicts only their handiwork, Rama, named by human observers for the Hindu god. This artificial planetoid, a gigantic hollow cylinder fifty kilometers long and twenty kilometers in diameter, intrudes on the solar system, leading to the exploratory mission which occupies the bulk of the novel. The explorers are the crew of the Solar Survey research vessel *Endeavour*, commanded by

William Tsien Norton, providentially one of the more experienced and more competent space commanders. Norton's mission is to land on Rama, gather as much information as possible, then abandon the giant vessel as it swings past the sun on a parabolic orbit which will take it forever back to interstellar space.

To accomplish this, Norton has a talented and imaginative crew well versed in the dangers of space, alien worlds, and unexpected events. The mission is no cakewalk — for one thing, *Endeavour*'s fuel will be exhausted in simply making the rendezvous, and the subsequent rescue of her personnel will be difficult — but it will be, presumably, an archaeological expedition, for there is no sign of life to mankind's first visitor from the stars. Consequently, *Rendezvous with Rama* reads like a grand and colorful adventure. The superiors who send *Endeavour* to Rama think in terms of Schliemann at Troy and Mouhot at Angkor Wat and Norton twice compares himself to Howard Carter at the opening of Tutankhamon's tomb, thus emphasizing the archaeological aspect of the mission. But more often Norton thinks of Captain James Cook, after whose ship his is named, and the lonely exploration of the vast wastes of the Pacific, amidst storm, cannibals, reefs, and disease. Clarke's plot deftly incorporates elements of both kinds of voyage of discovery.

In the rousing plot, Norton and his crew explore the interior in a series of compact, often tense incidents. While these are often stereotyped — Opening the Door, Seeing the Vast Interior for the First Time, Descending into the Unknown Dangers — Clarke's concrete detail and laconic, even understated, style keep the reader turning the pages. The writer becomes a verbal magician, pulling a series of ever more complex tricks out of his hat. Etched on the reader's mind is a sequence of vivid sketches; for all that Rama is an enclosed artifact, this is a novel of vistas and scenery. The grand staircase leading from the center of the end to the wall; the cylindrical sea encircling Rama at its waist, flanked by sheer, metal cliffs; the six giant artificial suns, linear lights shining from deep valleys across to the other side of the cylinder; the different colors and textures of portions of the interior; the shapes of the "cities" and "towns" which dot the interior — all these are stunning concepts, fully realized in Clarke's wholly appropriate prose.

Along with these static scenes are the dynamic events which take place against them: the first breath of Raman air, stale with the disuse of eons; Norton and a small party sailing a makeshift boat across the Cylindrical Sea; Jimmy Pak flying his sky-bike to the far end of the interior to explore the mysterious peaks there; most memorable of all, the grand surge of all Raman things toward the Cylindrical Sea as the great machine shuts itself off. These are heady moments indeed. Yet, they are as soundly grounded in extrapolation as the scenes sketching the human achievements of 2030. Clarke has worked out a logical — even necessary — sequence of events, given the probable origin and intent of a ship such as Rama, and he has deduced the sorts of technology that its builders would have needed to accomplish their ends.

The novel, then, is a tour of the wonders of technology, ours and theirs. But though it resembles some of the opening events in *Childhood's End* and the scenes of *2001: A Space Odyssey* set in the computer-driven spaceship, both the quasireligious awe of the Overlords and their masters of the former book and the anthropological analysis and Eastern mysticism of the latter are missing. The first contact in this most recent Clarke speculation on the theme is only with the products of alien minds, never with the beings themselves. Hence, the earlier novels' insistence on alien interference with human affairs is also missing. Here there are no aliens helping mankind to move to a higher state of being; Rama and its absent builders are cosmically indifferent to the human impingement on the planetoid's journey — even unaware of it. The early fears of some members of the Rama Committee, and especially the paranoia of the Hermians, are never actualized; Rama is no Pandora's box.

This is not to say that Rama is empty of mysterious beings, even if they are not quite the evils released by Pandora. When Rama reaches a (predetermined?) distance from the sun, it switches on. Out of the rich chemical soup which is the Cylindrical Sea, the chemical complexes which resemble Earthly cities manufacture *biots*, the crew of Rama. These are creatures which are a hybrid of machine and living organism — biological robots, as the acronym hints. They come in all sizes and shapes, each uniquely configured for its task (some of the tasks are, of course, incomprehensible to Norton's party). In general, they seem to be making Rama ready for the habitation of its controlling race, which may or may not be the eight-foot-tall, three-armed, three-legged, spiderlike creature for whom was designed a sort of spacesuit found in the Raman place called London. Since Rama, for all its age, looks new when Norton first enters, can it have been programmed as a robot ship to seek the proper place to set up housekeeping for its prodigiously advanced builders? Where then are the Ramans? Have they all died in the millennia Rama has spent in interstellar space? Or will they be rebuilt, like the biots, at the proper time? None of these questions is answered; nor are the even more grand questions behind them: where do we humans stand in relation to the other beings in the universe? Do we matter? Can we ever know? The mystical but perhaps too pat answers of the earlier Clarke "first contact" books are wholly absent here.

Unfortunately, Clarke's substitutions for the profundities of the earlier works are the weakest portions of *Rendezvous with Rama*. The arch hints about Norton's sexual entanglement with his ship's doctor add a sporadic romantic subplot which is, finally, only trite. Even worse is the melodramatic attempt by the Hermians to destroy Rama with a nuclear-armed guided missile. True, the Hermians would have the most to lose should Rama settle down in the solar system — as it appears to be doing at one point — for they will be closest and their hold on their planet is the most precarious in the solar system. But Clarke depicts them as paranoid frontiersmen who, in the best Western mode, think xenophobically and reach for their guns. The Hermian ultimatum and missile, Norton's decision to disarm the missile, Rodrigo's brave dismantling of the weapon — all these are hyped-up incidents in a space opera subplot which is ill-matched with the grandly simple and genuinely exciting scenes of exploration. These are the flaws which, combined with the lack of mystical answers, keep the Rama novel from achieving the almost cult status of Clarke's other works about aliens; although all three books are to some extent contrived, this one *seems* so. Nevertheless, the reader takes away from it a sense of wonder and a quickened pulse as the result of contemplating Rama and its implied builders. These emotions are only heightened by Clarke's constant reminders — even to the closing line — that the Ramans do everything in threes. There will probably not be two more Ramas; but the one, and its novel, are very grand machines indeed.

Criticism:

Scholes, Robert S. and Eric S. Rabkin. *Science Fiction*. New York: Oxford University Press, 1977, pp. 85-86. These pages contain a brief discussion on Clarke's themes and style of writing.

RINGWORLD

Author: Larry Niven (1938-   )
First book publication: 1970
Type of work: Novel
Time: Approximately one thousand years in the future
Locale: "Ringworld," a huge artificial sphere two hundred light years from Earth

Four space travelers journey to, and explore the surface of, Ringworld, an artificial sphere approximately three million times the size of Earth

> *Principal characters:*
> LOUIS WU, a two-hundred-year-old Earthman of mixed human ancestry
> NESSUS, a Pierson's puppeteer
> SPEAKER-TO-ANIMALS, a young kzin
> TEELA BROWN, a twenty-year-old Earthwoman
> PRILL (HALROPRILLER HOTRUFAN), a bald woman at least fifteen hundred years old
> SEEKER, a native of the Ringworld

By 1970, "hard" science fiction had become passé, but Larry Niven provided the exception to prove the rule. His *Ringworld* is an incredible, sometimes hilarious, and thoroughly entertaining *tour de force*.

The four main characters — Louis, Nessus, Speaker, and Teela — are in themselves interesting and believable enough, but their chief function is to act and react in such ways that the Ringworld and a few other bits of Niven's hardware become familiar enough to be accepted as probable. The other two, Prill and Seeker, are present to give the reader a perspective on the Ringworld that only native beings can; besides, each is needed for the conclusion of the plot. The plot exists merely to get the main characters on and off the Ringworld, and to provide a series of incidents each of which makes the hard science fiction explanations integral parts of the novel and plain imaginative fun.

The plot is utterly simple. Nessus chooses three other persons to travel with him to the Ringworld (though he says nothing about the place itself and admits only that it is about two hundred light years from Earth); in return for their part of the expedition, the humans and the kzin will get a working model — and detailed plans for constructing more — of an incredibly faster-than-light vehicle. The four travel to Nessus' destination, crash on its inner, habitable surface, explore by traveling about 300,000 miles, meet the two other major characters, and finally succeed in escaping from the Ringworld. More accurately, the four participate in the adventure through the exploration stage, then Teela decides to remain with Seeker, and Prill decides to leave with the other three.

There is, however, some background information that lends interest and credibility to the plot. The action takes place roughly a thousand years from now. For about two hundred years, there has been peace between the kzinti and the Earth-type humans; during those two centuries, the Earth's population has been controlled in part by means of a birthright lottery (the winners are allowed to have children), and the kzinti have grown markedly less aggressive. Pierson's puppeteers, an intelligent race known for its main occupation of trading, its refusal to reveal the whereabouts of its home world, and its members' conspicuous cowardice, have all but disappeared from Known Space during the same two centuries. That is no coincidence: Nessus himself was the one who engineered the birthright lottery system, and few puppeteers wanted to be around when and if the humans discovered that they were being bred, like laboratory animals, for the genetic characteristic of luck. Nor is it a coincidence that the kzinti-human wars occurred in the manner that they did, for in allowing them to continue the puppeteers were helping nature to de-select the most aggressive of the kzinti.

The remote motive of the plot is this: the central core of this galaxy went nova more than ten thousand years before the temporal setting of the book, and the "explosion" of lethal subatomic particles would reach Known Space in about twenty thousand years. The puppeteers, so cautious that only the "insane" among them dared to leave the surface of their home world, had two needs: to escape the result of the supernovae before it reached them, and to find enough habitable planetary surface for their enormous population. Something like the Ringworld might answer the latter need, but because the race was so very cautious, it had set its very planets in motion — just a bit under lightspeed — in order to reach the Clouds of Magellan with a temporal margin of safety. Since no one but a crazy puppeteer — or a kzin or a man or a woman — would dare to explore the artifact called Ringworld, the crazy Nessus finds the most socialized and amiable of the kzinti, a man who has lived long enough to prove that he has excellent judgment with regard to fatal risks, and a woman with six generations of good-luck genes bred into her and takes them off to visit the Ringworld.

Louis Wu goes along because he is bored, having just celebrated his two-hundredth birthday. Speaker-to-Animals goes because it would be an absolute failure of courage not to go. And Teela Brown goes because she is on Nessus' list of lucky humans and, for the time being, she loves Louis and refuses to leave him. Nessus is there to lead the expedition, of course, but also to perform a heroic duty so that he may be granted the right to be a parent.

The four adventurers leave the solar system aboard a puppeteer-designed vessel named the *Long Shot*, which is powered by a quantum II hyperdrive that can move it along at the rate of one light year every one-and-a-quarter minutes (the best starships in use at the time take three days to travel the same distance). Though the *Long Shot* is claustrophobically cramped as regards passenger space, the humans and the kzin are assured that it is merely an experimental model and that their pay for the voyage will be a ship of the sort that will enable the two races to evacuate their planets' and colonies' populations quickly enough to escape annihilation, reach an extragalactic destination, and set up housekeeping by the time the cautious and crafty puppeteer worlds arrive.

Just before the group begins its journey, Speaker — showing at least a remnant of his fierce heritage — attempts to cut the two humans out of their share of the profit and allows Niven to introduce a behavior-modification practitioner's dream. Nessus stops Speaker with a tasp, a surgically implanted device that can be aimed as precisely as a glance and that overwhelms the pleasure center of the brain of its target. As Louis notes after the incident, only the puppeteers would use a weapon that causes its victims to feel *good*.

At the end of the *Long Shot*'s journey, the humans and the kzin discover that the "system" of the puppeteers — four planets terraformed for agriculture in addition to the home planet — is in fact a Kemplerer rosette. In theory, such a formation should be possible by putting three or more objects of equal mass in place equidistant from one another and imparting to each the same angular velocity so that they will revolve forever around the center of gravity their motion creates. In fact, no one had ever seen one; that the puppeteers had made a Kemplerer rosette in cosmic scale causes Louis to decide again to live forever (as he had once when awed by Mount Lookitthat's forty-mile-high waterfall) so that he will not miss seeing everything there is to see.

One of the richly humorous aspects of Niven's imagination is revealed by his juxtaposition of incredibly complex scientific theory and technology with utterly mundane names like the one above. Here, perhaps, lies one secret of the success of his fiction: he provides the reader with considerably more scientific detail than most hard science fiction novels did even when they were in fashion, but he knows human nature well enough to let his fictional places and artifacts bear names that frontier-type humans would be likely to give them. There is the planet We Made It, obviously the site of a successful colonizing venture. The Long Fall River is, logically, the one that has the cataract higher than any other in Known Space. The *Long Shot* is a double pun; the *Lying Bastard* — shortened to *Liar*, the spacecraft that takes the four adventurers to the Ringworld — is given its name because it is as weaponless as any puppeteer could wish yet most of its instruments, like the "flashlight" utilizing a variable-beam laser, are of the sort that have an alternative lethal practicality. "Ringworld" itself is an utterly prosaic name, yet it is perfectly accurate; and on that world are a thousand-mile-high mountain called Fist-of-God and a floating building called Heaven. Needless to say, at age two hundred, Louis did not come by his twenty-year-old's body naturally: he has been taking "boosterspice" for one hundred and thirty years. The result of Niven's nomenclature is a delightful surprise; the lack of respectful terminology for his scientific wonders relieves them of a good deal of jargon and almost automatically causes his readers to feel easy with them.

The four adventurers aboard the *Liar* soon leave the puppeteers' system behind, and, coming out of hyperspace at what would be the outer limit of a star's planetary system, they see a G2 star as a brilliant point of light with a halo around it. The Ringworld is so huge that it is visible at a distance from which a star cannot yet be perceived as a disk. Louis Wu was right: it is a sight worth living two centuries to see.

The Ringworld is an artifact; it did not happen the way the rings of Saturn did — it was constructed by human, though not Terran, engineers. Its dimensions are impossible to comprehend: a million-mile-wide flat circular strip of matter, its flat side facing its sun, the Ringworld revolves around its primary about one astronomical unit out, so that a straight-line journey along its circumference would be almost 600,000,000 miles long. Its inner surface — that facing the sun — is a bit less than 600,000,000,000,000 square miles, and that much area is simply too much for one to imagine concretely; hence the necessity of *Ringworld* the novel, with its comprehensible characters and their actions, to make Niven's exciting abstract concept something that can be experienced concretely and vicariously by its readers.

Evidently, the builders of the Ringworld had not discovered any kind of hyperspatial mode of travel; limited by the speed of light, they could not colonize the planets of distant stars in order to deal with the pressures of overpopulation. But they evidently had discovered a fairly inexpensive and practical means of transmutation, so they could — and did — transform the matter of planets and asteroids and anything else they could come upon into material forms necessary to make and maintain a world that is identical with its orbit, a world with approximately three *million* times the area of Earth. The race that built the Ringworld had three basic problems (after they had taken care of gravity by spinning the ring at 770 miles-per-second, and handled the problem of atmosphere by erecting thousand-mile-high rims to keep the air from falling off the edges).

First, since the Ringworld's habitable surface always faced the sun (which is always in noonday position), the Builders had to arrange for alternating periods of light and darkness; this they did by putting "shadow squares" — rectangles a million miles wide and two-and-a-half million miles long, held in place by invisibly thin wires six million miles long — in orbit between the Ringworld and its sun, at a velocity sufficient to have night-length shadows pass over each part of the Ringworld with precise regularity. Second, because their artificial world was immense beyond imagining, the Builders needed even more energy than that caught from the sun by the Ringworld's area; this they solved by using the "shadow squares" — utterly black and thus most absorbent — to capture solar energy, which could then be beamed down to the surface in usable form. So successful were the Builders at this that they had enough energy at their disposal to make cities with buildings that floated, against gravity, in the very air. The third problem arose from the transmutation itself: once the available matter had been made into the Ringworld, there were no heavy elements left to be "natural resources"; if the great artifact malfunctioned, there would be nothing with which to repair it. And, about fifteen hundred years before Louis, Nessus, Speaker, and Teela arrive, the Ringworld had an energy-breakdown.

While the members of Nessus' expedition begin to view the interior surface of the great ring, their craft is (but for the phobic caution of puppeteer engineers) practically destroyed by still-functioning automatic laser cannon, apparently designed to prevent meteors from reaching the Ringworld's surface. Because of the *Liar*'s design, its living compartment remains intact and crashes on the Ringworld almost exactly between the world's two rims, near the foot of the Fist-of-God. So the four adventurers unload the *Lying Bastard*, mount their ingeniously designed flycycles, and set out to find some civilization. They find ruins instead.

Eventually, the luck of Teela Brown finds a city with a resident "goddess": Prill, who is persuaded by Nessus' tasp to help him and Louis and Speaker to get the *Liar* off the Ringworld. Not until they get her police station "palace" floating of its own accord and moving by the power of Nessus' flycycle do they rediscover Teela Brown. She was getting off her flycycle just as Prill's police machinery overpowered it, so she, lucky as usual, stayed outside the building until she met Seeker. Together they pursue the flying building and catch up with the others, take part in a fight with barbarian natives during which one of Nessus' heads is cut off and Speaker manages to grab the fallen piece of "shadow square" to which its incredibly thin and strong wire is attached, and then they leave the others. Seeker, given some very potent antigeriatric drug more than fourteen centuries ago, must continue his quest: to reach the base of the great arch (the other side of the Ringworld always looks like a blue arch over the flat land). Teela, who now loves the barbarian hero, decides to accompany him — and it is her luck that makes this quest her destiny, for only on the Ringworld are there dangers against which, on Earth, her good luck would have protected her; only on the Ringworld will she ever mature.

About two months later, the flying building reaches the *Liar*. Nessus, kept alive by his flycycle's first-aid kit, is put into his "autodoc" (the puppeteer builders of which had provided a couple of spare heads just in case). The others, using the wire from the "shadow square," tow the *Lying Bastard* up the slope of Fist-of-God, which, like most things even remotely connected to the luck of Teela Brown, has a fortunate aspect: the mountain is actually the scar of a moon-sized meteor, hollow at its core and thus the port of escape. As Speaker and Louis maneuver the flying building so that it will pull the *Liar* down toward them and empty space, they realize that the Ringworld, the outer side of which can stop forty percent of neutrino bombardment, is angled just so that its flat surface will prevent the major part of the galactic explosion from affecting the inner side; Teela and her hero will probably be safe forever.

This is the end of the book, but not the end of fascination with the Ringworld. As certainly as Louis and Speaker plan to return to that artifact someday, the readers of *Ringworld* are imaginatively reexploring the concepts in and the implications of Niven's verbal artifact.

Criticism:

Jameson, Frederic. "Science Fiction as Politics: Larry Niven," in *New Republic*. XXX (October, 1976), pp. 34-38. Jameson gives a discussion of Niven's work, including *Ringworld* in a political context.

Niven, Larry. "The Words of Science Fiction," in *The Craft of Science Fiction*. Edited by Reginald Bretnor. New York: Harper & Row, 1976, pp. 178-194. Niven writes on his own contributions to science fiction literature and analyzes the field generally. The book as a whole is an important work of science fiction criticism.

RITE OF PASSAGE

Author: Alexei Panshin (1940-   )
First book publication: 1968
Type of work: Novel
Time: 2205
Locale: Aboard one of the seven Great Ships left after the destruction of the Earth in 2041

A sensitive portrayal of a pre-adolescent girl's growth to maturity as she qualifies for adult status in her nomadic spaceship society by passing a survival test in the wilds of a barbaric planet

Principal characters:
> MIA HAVERO, the young heroine in her twelfth to fourteenth years
> MILES HAVERO, her father and chairman of the Ship's Council
> JIMMY DENTREMONT, her closest friend
> JOSEPH L. H. MBELE, Mia's and Jimmy's tutor

Rite of Passage was written both as a deliberate response and an attempt to improve upon Robert Heinlein's teenage heroine in *Podkayne of Mars*, for Alexei Panshin is not only a serious student of the earlier science fiction author, but a perceptive critic of his work as well.

In his critical study, *Heinlein in Dimension*, Panshin examined the character and depiction of Podkayne and concluded that although there was a need in science fiction to portray characters other than young men in their twenties, Heinlein had not successfully done so. Panshin then proceeded to do this himself in his 1969 Nebula Award-winning first novel.

Because Panshin had especially faulted Heinlein for the use of the first-person journal, which he felt was an awkward and sometimes confusing technique, he began *Rite of Passage* with a flashback. The heroine, Mia Havero, looks back seven years after the action to evaluate what has happened to her and to examine her growth to maturity as it occurred between the ages of twelve and fourteen. This reflective technique adds a note of verisimilitude to the work. Panshin's technique not only provides an aura of truth, but in addition places the focal point of the novel where the author wishes it: on the process of change. Panshin has Mia note that the changes which occurred *within* her were more important than the events which happened *to* her.

In Panshin's future world, Mia Havero lives with her father, Miles, on an enormous spaceship which, while originally designed to transport colonists, has been reequipped as a self-contained world. It is now one hundred and sixty-four years since the destruction of Earth by wars which were principally caused by overpopulation and its attendant evils (in 2041 there had been an Earth population of more than eight billion). Mankind has evolved in two directions. One hundred and twelve colonies in a like number of star systems have been settled by manual laborers who struggle to wrest a living from an often hostile environment. Seven enormous ships populated by professionals

— primarily scientists and technologists — travel from planet to planet trading limited amounts of scientific knowledge in return for specific, needed natural resources. Mutual hostility exists between the two groups as evidenced by their slang terminology for each other: the Ship inhabitants consider the colonists "Mudeaters," while the latter, in turn, see those on board the Ships as exploitative "Grabbers."

In addition to occasional trade, another major contact between the two groups occurs at Trial, when groups of fourteen-year-olds are dropped from the Ships for thirty-day survival tests. This is the "Rite of Passage" of the novel, comparable to the familiar rites of contemporary society: baptism, confirmation, marriage, and the like. But this rite has more primitive and more serious overtones because it determines who will survive to be accepted into the adult world aboard Ship. It ensures that members of the space-bound society are able to function and survive on a planet, and — even more important — provides an additional check on the population since some fail the test and do not return.

Trial looms before Mia, but there are other trials that she must face before the ultimate one: she must face leaving the Ship and leaving the comforting confines of her "quad."

Panshin handles Mia's development most realistically. She is, in many ways, a typical adolescent with a typical fear of any change: change of residence, of friends, or of her own anatomy as she develops towards adulthood.

As a jest, her father whimsically has "frozen" Mia, so that she will stay a little girl (the fantasy of many little girls), and while she envies the bodily development of her peers, she has more than a little desire to really stay a child, safe and protected. Mia was reared in a communal dorm until age nine, when she fled it to live with her father. Her mother, although alive, is absent from the story, living alone to pursue art (although Panshin also gives some psychological justification for her behavior later in the tale).

As the story opens, Mia is about to meet the first of the changes which she fears, and which shape her: the change of residence to a new quad where she will have to adjust to new friends, new neighbors, and a new tutor. None of these challenges is accidental: they have all been arranged by Mia's father, who now recognizes how reluctant she is to face new situations. Thus, her new best friend is Jimmy Dentremont, who is a potential mate according to the Ship's Eugenist, and her tutor is Joseph Mbele, who had once tutored her father (but who has a more humanitarian ethical code than her father). Her father continues his program for Mia when he invites her to accompany him on a trade visit to the planet Grainau, where Mia makes the startling discovery that the Mudeaters she has scorned in turn look down upon the Ship's people and disparage their way of life.

Other essential changes occur in Mia's character. For example, when she explores the air ducts of the ship, she learns that her companion, while initially a coward, can rise to the occasion and overcome fears. This teaches her empathy, and she begins to see parallels between herself and other persons challenging and conquering the unknown. As she meets ever more difficult tests, she comes to learn about herself, her values, and her ethical philosophy.

Ultimately, there is Trial, and Mia and Jimmy, with others, are singly dropped upon the planet Tintera. The ensuing adventure scenes are unfortunately the weakest part of the novel. Mia meets the inhabitants of Tintera, struggles with evil men, sees her pick-up signal (essential for return to the ship) destroyed, and rescues Jimmy from prison. By salvaging his pick-up signal, she not only survives, but also manages to have her first sexual experience with Jimmy in the midst of all the danger.

More important to Mia's development than the dangers she meets and surmounts, is her change of heart about the Mudeaters whom she had hitherto scorned. She mellows and becomes ever more tolerant throughout the novel as learning about herself connects her to the larger world. However, even though Mia grows into a humane and sensitive individual, the note on which the book ends is falsely optimistic. Panshin hints that the new generation will implement humanitarian programs, yet, at the same time, the entire planet of Tintera is destroyed.

Nevertheless, if Panshin's denouement is weak, the major portion of his narrative is sound and interesting. His descriptions of life aboard the multi-leveled Ship are fascinating. Level Three, a vast area simulating Earth, has three divisions. One sector is utilized for cultivation and production of food, oxygen, and fodder for the cattle being raised. (Beef is the only meat raised naturally; other meat products are grown in vats). A second area contains a lovely park with trees, lakes, flowers, and picnic and riding areas, and the third sector is reserved for a wilderness designed for hunting and used as a training ground for survival lessons prior to Trial. The sheer size of Level Three is so vast that the roof is over three hundred feet above the ground and the area extends for miles before either roof or ground meet the sides of the ship.

Panshin also takes great care to present detailed character descriptions. The populace of the ship, primarily mercantile entrepreneurs, are presented deliberately, with care and attention given to their unique educational, political, and ethical systems. Family life is presented as it is affected by specific space phenomena. For example, the Ship people enjoy extreme longevity. Mia's parents have been married fifty years (although they have lived apart for the last eight). Siblings may be spaced as far apart as forty years.

Another mark of the author's craftsmanship lies in the brief but essential stories he couches within the main story. At several points in the novel, one character tells a fairy (or folk) tale to another. Not only are these vignettes charming in their own right, but they additionally serve to illustrate ethical problems and solutions for Mia, to aid in her development, and also to reinforce the conservative philosophy of the majority of the Ship's adults. For example, Panshin explores sociology and politics, drawing comparisons between the "haves" and the "have nots."

Moments in the plot of *Rite of Passage* may ring untrue, but Mia as a character is believable. Since 1968, other science fiction authors may have matched Panshin in creating a realistic teenaged heroine, but they have not, as yet, topped him.

ROADSIDE PICNIC
(PIKNIK NA OBOCHINE)

Authors: Arkady Strugatsky (1925-   ) and Boris Strugatsky (1933-   )
First book publication: 1972
English translation: 1977
Type of work: Novel
Time: The near future
Locale: North America, probably Canada

A "first contact" novel about aliens who leave their refuse behind after a brief visit to Earth, and about the life and career of Redrick Schuhart, a black market collector of artifacts

> Principal characters:
> REDRICK SCHUHART, a "stalker"
> GUTA, his wife
> MARIA, their daughter, also called "The Monkey"
> KIRILL, a laboratory assistant at the Foundation
> BURBRIDGE, another "stalker"
> THROATY, a black marketeer

The Strugatsky brothers are, together with Sakyo Komatsu and Stanislaw Lem, the most widely read science fiction authors in the world today. Most of their novels have been best sellers in their native Soviet Union, and they have been published all over the world. Several of their novels (including this one) and short stories have also appeared in English translation. Arkady Strugatsky has a background as a linguist, specializing in Japanese, but has been a full-time writer since 1964. His brother Boris was originally an astronomer, then switched over to computers and advanced mathematics and is now a professional science fiction author, also since 1964. This makes for a uniquely broad background, extending from the humanities to technology, an excellent basis for good science fiction.

The authors' diverse backgrounds certainly show in this tale of mankind poking about in the junk left by extraterrestrial visitors, like primitive tribesmen sifting through the refuse left on their shores by passing ships from other continents. The theme of first contact with aliens, with man playing the part of the ignorant savage, the pariah of the universe, as it were, facing a superior and basically incomprehensible culture, is not entirely new: Algis Budrys wrote a minor classic on this theme, *Rogue Moon* (1960), and one year after *Roadside Picnic*, Arthur C. Clarke published his award-winning novel *Rendezvous with Rama* (1973). A more recent example of the theme is seen in Frederik Pohl's *Gateway* (1977), in which mankind uses the artifacts left by an earlier race without really comprehending them or benefiting from even a fraction of their potential.

The Earthmen in *Roadside Picnic* are even worse off. Aliens have visited

Earth and left behind what are called the "Zones" — areas littered with objects of a strange and often dangerous nature. The Zones are in some way contaminated; all the usual natural laws do not apply, and they are deadly for trespassers. Death in the Zones can be swift or lingering, but it always lurks there, and the scientists of the research foundation, who are trying to explore the Zones, have learned to be extremely cautious.

The aliens made a brief visit to Earth and departed, leaving behind what is, perhaps, the cosmic counterpart of empty beer cans, dirty napkins, and the like — but some of this refuse is unusual, to say the very least, and some of the artifacts prove to be of immense value to Earth. A power pack has already revolutionized Earth civilization, although it is almost certain that the aliens did not use if for that purpose; Earthmen's use of it is probably comparable to a savage's use of a pocket calculator as a hammer. A number of artifacts, some of them never seen, give off unpredictable radiation which kills or changes people, while others offer a strange and deadly bliss.

Needless to say, a flourishing black market in these alien objects has sprung up, with "stalkers" sneaking into the heavily guarded Zones to steal things and, if they survive, sell them to private buyers or the Foundation. The story centers around one of these stalkers, Redrick Schuhart, probably a Canadian in his early thirties, who makes a rather dangerous living by getting artifacts out of the Zone outside his home town. A very convincing character, Redrick is far removed from the usual science fiction hero. The story, which alternates between his journeys into the Zone, which he regards with a mixture of longing and intense fear, and his life with his wife Guta and their daughter Maria, called "The Monkey" on account of her fur (probably the result of genetic damage to Redrick in the Zone), reflects very effectively various sides of his personality as he irrevocably moves on toward his dream of salvation in the Zone.

Redrick searches for salvation, as does everyone in this novel, each in his own way, and maybe he finds it in the end — in the mythical Golden Ball, the most mysterious of all the alien objects, never seen but much whispered about, which is said to fulfill all wishes. This rumor is an obvious case of wishful thinking, of course; but in an age where old gods have fallen, new ones must be found. The aliens and their mysterious objects are as close to modern gods as anything likely to be found; and besides, the Golden Ball might really be able to grant wishes. All stalkers, and in effect the rest of humanity, beseech the unknown aliens to act as their saviors, and many of them appear to get just what they ask for — not from the aliens, who probably never even noticed that Earth was inhabited, but from themselves. Much of the novel is actually a tale of self-fulfilling prophecies, with the aliens acting as catalysts, untouchable and incomprehensible gods who can only be glimpsed through the effects of their unpredictable litter.

This is a rather ironic view of humanity, groveling before the discarded trash of unknown cosmic travelers and finding esoteric meaning in this junk. The authors have put forth views like this before, notably in their celebrated novel *Vtoroe nashestvie marsian* (The Second Martian Invasion, 1967), a wry comment on H. G. Wells's *The War of the Worlds*, in which mankind learns to live with the Martian invaders, acting as milch cows and selling their digestive juices to the aliens, who conquer not by heat rays, but by modern business practices. *Roadside Picnic*, however, is more subtle, and the satire is less heavy. As in Clarke's *Rendezvous with Rama*, the aliens are never seen, and, although their strange refuse has very tangible effects on human civilization, the real effect grows out of the expectations of people. People have glimpsed God, or at least His refuse, and are ardently anxious to give themselves to Him. The only problem is that God is not interested: He does not care for them, and has passed them by without even noticing them.

One perceives that this might be a rather daring statement for two authors who have had their ups and downs in the official Soviet eye, since it depicts people behaving unheroically when faced with uncomfortable truths, and, moreover, suggests that ideals are not always to be trusted. When Redrick finally finds the Golden Ball, which is as close to God or salvation as he ever will come, he is overwhelmed and cannot bring himself to make the wishes he has planned to make — money, a long life, health for his daughter, and so on — surely a god cannot be bothered with things like that. He ends up lamely wishing for happiness for all, which is about as vague a wish as anyone could make. Nevertheless, it is an altruistic wish, and as such might be interpreted as a sign of moral growth. In any event, it ends Redrick Schuhart's quest for salvation and eternal happiness.

European — and especially East European — science fiction writers have long made an art of subtle hints, allusions, puns, double meanings, and seemingly innocent remarks understood only by those who are intended to understand. This approach is not used solely for political reasons, as many Westerners are prone to believe, but for intellectual and literary ones. Stanislaw Lem is very adept at this, as are the Strugatskys; their works are like onions with layer upon layer of meaning beneath the overlaying plot. European readers are practiced at peeling off these layers, but in translation and in the transition to another cultural and historical environment, some of this complexity is lost. Perhaps the Strugatskys' works can be appreciated to their full extent only by a Russian; the same might also be true of Stanislaw Lem and the Polish authors. The Strugatskys are especially talented at satirizing the official government, Party language, and behavior of the Soviet Union; unfortunately, however, much of this sort of satire can be rather incomprehensible to a Western reader who has not experienced life in the society being described.

Perhaps the Western reader, brought up on standard British or American pulp magazine fare, with its sterling heroes, nubile heroines, and loathsome monsters, is in a similar position to Redrick in *Roadside Picnic*, finding his own truths where there are no such truths and using the marvelous objects differently from what was intended.

Still, good science fiction is good science fiction, and even to a Western reader, *Roadside Picnic* remains a forceful story with all the good qualities one would hope to find in the genre: vision, irony, and above all, literary excellence.

SHADOWS IN THE SUN

Author: Chad Oliver (Symmes Chadwick Oliver, 1928-   )
First book publication: 1954
Type of work: Novel
Time: 1950's
Locale: Jefferson Springs, Texas

One of the first novels to introduce serious anthropological themes in science fiction, and to present a more mature and sympathetic view of alien "invaders"

> Principal characters:
> PAUL ELLERY, a young anthropologist
> ANNE, his fiancée
> JOHN, an alien leader
> MELVIN THORNE, a rancher in Jefferson Springs
> CYNTHIA, a teacher at the Jefferson Springs high school

As much of science fiction deals with imaginary cultures and contact between radically different civilizations, it is something of a surprise to note that before Chad Oliver, anthropology had been one of the more neglected sciences in the genre. Perhaps this is because of the engineering and physics biases of many of the editors and readers in the 1940's, who may have regarded anthropology as something of a "soft" science. Perhaps it took the rise of what has been called "social science fiction" in the early 1950's — science fiction that deals with social and cultural issues — tc enable writers to make the all-too-logical connections between the issues treated in anthropology and those treated by science fiction. Perhaps, even, many science fiction writers simply did not *know* enough anthropology to use it as a basis for speculation in fiction.

Chad Oliver did much to change this in the ealry 1950's, and *Shadows in the Sun* draws much of its historical importance from the fact that it was one of the first serious works of anthropological science fiction, a subgenre which now boasts works by some of the major writers in the field, such as Ursula K. Le Guin. Oliver, himself a practicing anthropologist with a Ph.D. from UCLA, approached the problem of aliens taking over the Earth as an anthropological problem, and *Shadows in the Sun* is loaded with expository summary of anthropological theory and technique. What if, he posits, the Earth were being colonized in much the same way many "backward" areas of the Earth had been colonized by European explorers — such as North America or Africa — without the "natives" ever being fully aware of what was going on? What if we were the Indians rather than the Europeans, and what if such broad social movements as the migration to the cities were secretly being engineered by an alien civilization with advanced propaganda techniques, in order gradually to confine us to "reservations"?

Such questions, of course, may reflect the early 1950's paranoia about conspiracies as much as they reflect genuine anthropological concerns; and indeed, some of the major themes in the novel are characteristic 1950's themes. The notion of aliens taking over a small town with no change in the outward appearance of the town was common during this period, probably reaching its most famous manifestations in the first version of *Invasion of the Body Snatchers* (based on a Jack Finney serial which appeared the same year as *Shadows in the Sun*); and even if Oliver's aliens are portrayed as essentially indifferent to the welfare of Earth, the fear of a fifth column within our culture, controlled by some distant foreign power, is pervasive in the novel.

The presence of the aliens is also related to another favorite fear of the period — atomic war. While the aliens are forbidden by their own law to intervene in human affairs, they rather hope and expect that Earth will reduce its population and level of civilization through such a war, thus making room for more colonists. A political faction among the aliens even advocates intervening to promote war among the natives. Furthermore, when anthropologist Paul Ellery discovers the presence of the aliens, who have gradually supplanted the entire population of the small town of Jefferson Springs, Texas, he is invited to undergo a period of education and training which will enable him to join them — a process which sounds suspiciously like sophisticated brainwashing techniques which, during the 1950's, Communist nations were widely suspected of using. All this serves to remind us that the novel is very much of its time; still, the work does not seem especially dated.

The major reason the novel still holds up well is the ingenuity with which Oliver formulates his anthropological problems and the clarity which characterizes the exposition underlying these problems. In fact, in many ways the book is more of an intellectual exercise than a novel. The narrative is thin, the characters sketchily drawn, and the focus is consistently on the thought processes of Paul Ellery as he tries to formulate and solve the problems facing him. This focus on formulating the problem — on learning to ask the right questions — is remarkably sophisticated for a genre which had characteristically presented clearly drawn puzzles that could be unlocked by ingenious scientific deduction or, failing that, heroic action. Paul Ellery's initial problem is that Jefferson Springs is too normal, that it conforms too precisely to what an anthropologist would expect from a community of its size and location. But this, Ellery realizes, is not much of a problem: why is a normal community so normal? The mystery of Jefferson Springs is one he could hardly explain to anyone intelligently.

But like the typical dogged scientist of science fiction, Ellery persists in trying to unravel the mystery — and here is where Oliver's ingenuity in plotting enables him to depart from formula. While the reader, perhaps familiar with stories of this type, expects the solution to this problem to coincide with the resolution of the plot, instead we find the problem solved before the book is one-fourth over — and the answer is simply given to Ellery by the aliens. Realizing that Ellery cannot really do anything with the information once he has it, the aliens offer it to him freely — thus creating a new problem for him and in the process elevating the level of the overall puzzle another notch. Ellery's next problem is more complex: what is the nature of this alien civilization, and what, if anything, is its weakness? Oliver introduces suspense into this latter portion of the narrative by imposing a deadline on Ellery: he must answer these questions before he makes the final decision as to whether to undergo the aliens' training program and become one of them.

Again Ellery's problem, essentially, is formulating his problem, and again he is somewhat frustrated in his detective work by having the answer handed to him by the alien leader John, who has come to like and value Ellery as a friend, even though by his standards primitive. Only a week before Ellery must make his decision to join the aliens or remain on Earth, John invites him aboard the spaceship which seems to serve as an administrative center for the Earth colonies and shows him a vision of some amorphous, truly alien beings called the Others. Again, Ellery is forced to shift his perspective: compared to the Others, John and his fellows colonists are not really aliens at all, but fellow humans who happen to be born into a far more advanced civilization than our own. The unity of humanity as a species needs to take precedence over loyalty to specific political or cultural units, which are after all only structures within which humans operate.

It is here that the central theme of the book finally becomes clear — the relationship between the individual and the culture. Despite the advanced technology and science of the alien colonists, the individual colonists are no more advanced than ordinary humans. In fact, they are ordinary humans, not brilliant scientists or intellectual supermen. Ellery had seen some evidence of this earlier in his relations with two of the aliens other than John. One was Melvin Thorne, whose "cover" in Jefferson Springs was that of a cheerful redneck Texas rancher. Ellery eventually comes to realize that Thorne's personality is really like that; his disguise is his role rather than his personality. The other was Cynthia, the high school teacher who has a brief affair with Ellery; he finally realizes her sexual attraction to him was real, even if it did involve for her an element of decadence, of making love to a "primitive." John, however, finally enables Ellery to see that it is not he who is primitive, but rather his culture, or more accurately, his culture's science and technology. For the political structure of the aliens' government is really not much different from that of many colonial governments in Earth's own history. Furthermore, Ellery comes to realize, the colonists are alienated from the mainstream of their own culture, condemned to living in a kind of galactic backwater and as resentful of that fact as colonials always are.

Morally and politically, then, the aliens are no more advanced than we are; their culture is not genuinely alien from ours, it is simply more developed. Oliver's characterization of individual aliens is in keeping with this point: they write bad poetry, tell jokes, make political deals, and generally behave not at all as one would expect from science fiction aliens. As individuals, they are no different from us. When Ellery is finally made aware of this, he realizes that to join the aliens would be merely to trade one set of cultural problems for another, and not really to gain much in the process. In the end, he rejoins his fiancée, Anne, and decides to devote himself to the betterment of his own society on Earth.

As a novel, *Shadows in the Sun* has its weaknesses. Most of the characters are rather hastily drawn, though the characterization of Ellery himself provides an insightful portrait of a young scientist grappling with problems beyond his grasp and, more importantly, facing the real difficulty of formulating these problems. The alien John is a fine antidote to the usual run of humorless intellectuals that so often represent advanced societies in science fiction, though his motives are never made quite clear. Other characters, such as Thorne or the dour editor of the local newspaper, are stereotypes — though we cannot be sure whether the stereotyping is on Oliver's part or is a wry comment on the aliens' attempts to simulate small-town life in America. The style of the novel often tends to be frustrating, as Oliver repeatedly leads us through Ellery's thoughts in interior monologues so single-minded that we begin to lose patience. And the exposition of anthropological ideas, though entertainingly written, adds a note of overt didacticism to the book and gives it a slightly patronizing tone. In 1954, however, it may be that such didacticism was useful in bringing anthropology into science fiction. *Shadows in the Sun* is neither great nor greatly ambitious, but in many ways it achieves the entertaining blend of idea and action toward which so much science fiction strives.

THE SIRENS OF TITAN

Author: Kurt Vonnegut, Jr. (1922-   )
First book publication: 1959
Type of work: Novel
Time: The future
Locale: The United States, Mars, Mercury, Titan

The satirical and comically visionary account of one man's odyssey through the solar system as he searches for the meaning of life and the destiny of man

> *Principal characters.*
> MALACHI CONSTANT, the richest American and a notorious rake
> WINSTON NILES RUMFOORD, a space-time traveler
> BEATRICE RUMFOORD, wife of Winston, wife of Malachi
> CHRONO, son of Malachi and Beatrice
> SALO, an eleven-million-year-old Tralfamadorean messenger

Kurt Vonnegut's deceptively simple and seemingly unsophisticated style reveals a lucid vision of the modern age.,His books are restrained in a manner which lures the reader on with unaffected prose and surface humor. It is only when the reader is thoroughly enmeshed in the web of character and incident, and is chuckling to himself about the situation of some fictional being, that his self-satisfied grin begins to fade. Indeed, with the recognition of his own face in the group portrait of humanity, the reader comes to understand Vonnegut's depth and insight. As his characters pursue their own truths and eventually discredit themselves, his readers find themselves inextricably wired into the proceedings. The undertow of his humor pulls the reader down, forcing him to confront cherished dogmas and entrenched values. Kurt Vonnegut has been the gadfly of modern existential man, and has only recently emerged from the literary "underground" into the mainstream of contemporary letters.

The Sirens of Titan represents an early stage of Vonnegut's writing; written in 1959, it is an occasionally heavy-handed attempt at "social significance" satire. Here, in his second novel, the writing is more clearly science fiction than either his earlier or later work. The genre lends itself to the breadth of Vonnegut's vision and is a compatible form for his treatment of such broad subjects as war, religion, human contingency, and other existential problems. His use of science fiction enables him to draw upon many of the progressive beliefs man has developed through science itself, allows him to take the reader through space and time, and encourages him to create deranged worlds which are actually the logical extension of contemporary American values.

With a style free of esoteric mystification, Vonnegut telegraphs his punches. While there is much to be discovered between the lines, his major targets are clearly delineated. In *The Sirens of Titan*, Vonnegut wastes no time in presenting his themes. His comic, nightmarish vision is an honest portrayal of man-in-the-world which attempts to affirm hope for mankind in general. If there is a major thrust to this book it is the relentless convergence upon the question of life's ultimate meaning or the purpose of life itself. The story is constructed in a manner which forces the reader to encounter both internal and external realities of an absurd, chaotic universe. It is a look backwards to an unenlightened time, one described by the narrator as "the nightmare ages." This was a time of outward searching. Mankind wanted to know who was in charge, what life was all about. Since the actual search of the heavens yielded nothing, all that remained was inner reality, a new frontier which would eventually yield "goodness and wisdom."

Nevertheless, the action of the novel begins in a time of spiritual impoverishment. Not only does the author set out his themes early in the story but he also outlines the course of events. Winston Niles Rumfoord, a man whose private spaceship chanced a collision with an "uncharted chronosynclastic infundibulum," and his dog, Kazak, are about to materialize within his palatial mansion somewhere in Newport, Rhode Island. Because of their intrusion into this time-funnel, the man and his dog exist as a type of "wave phenomenon — apparently pulsing in a distorted spiral with its origin in the sun and its terminal in Betelegeuse." Traversing the universe in this Einsteinian time-space warp, they exist simultaneously in all times and places with which the wave-phenomenon makes contact. This simultaneity of existence enables the man to experience the future, the present, and the past all at once. Because he can predict the future, his periodic materializations are significant.

If Winston Niles Rumfoord could effectuate change in the course of cosmic events he would be much more than a fortune teller. Unfortunately, he, like everyone else, is subject to the whims and fancies of the meaningless universe. As the story begins, Vonnegut's existential hero, Malachi Constant, is present for one of the materializations. In this meeting Constant learns that his ultimate destiny will take him to a satellite of Saturn called Titan; but first he will marry Beatrice Rumfoord on Mars, go to Mercury, and come back to Earth again. The remainder of the book is a gradual unfolding of this design. The plot of *The Sirens of Titan* follows Malachi Constant through a series of interrelated events that tempt the reader to interpret Vonnegut's universe as predetermined.

Yet, as the narrative develops, it is clear that the author's underlying concern is really with man's incapacity to master his own destiny in spite of insight into the overall design. Many paradoxical elements in Vonnegut's plot development create the basis for comic irony or black humor. Through the exposition of characters and events he takes issue with the comfortable belief that there is a benevolent force in the universe rewarding the good and punishing the bad. For some, organized religion provides a preordained purpose to existence; these people are a recurring target of Kurt Vonnegut's trenchant wit.

Malachi Constant, soon to be involved in a rather difficult trek throughout the universe, is the "richest American — and a notorious rakehell." An unim-

pressive character born into greath wealth, he inherited a fortune from a physically and morally unattractive man whose only explanation for his great success was that he had had an enormous quantity of "dumb luck." Noel Constant, through an investment technique that consisted of breaking down sentences of the Gideon Bible into capital letters, dividing the letters into pairs,
putting periods between the letters, and then investing in corporations that had
those initials, had become a millionaire. In the end, without ever understanding why his method worked, he died and passed on his money and investment
technique to his son. Malachi, singularly unconcerned with understanding the
nature of his good fortune, completely accepts both his good luck and his
riches without question.

Cosmic irony, as seen in the success story of Noel Constant, is continually
on hand in Vonnegut's books. Vonnegut's characters often find themselves
questioning what is real, what is imaginary, and whether or not the difference
really matters. Although they are equally trapped in a world which provides
little in the way of purposeful order, a conflict arises between those characters
who embody passive acceptance of reality, and those who demand meaning in
a world that has none to offer. Neither Malachi nor his father understand the
nature of their luck. They passively accept it, recognizing that some people are
lucky and some people are not. The belief that God or Harvard Business
School is responsible for great wealth or luck is rejected outright. The issue of
an absurd universe cannot be evaded by reaching out for higher appeal or hope
that transcends humanity. Vonnegut irrepressively satirizes those who believe
that there is a definitive relationship between being good and doing good,
between good works and rewards, and between bad works and punishment.
The universe is indifferent; that is simply the way it is. There is little reason
behind it, and what reason there is is far from holy.

When Malachi's luck leaves as mysteriously as it had arrived, his fortune is
lost. Not understanding his bad luck any more than his good luck, he opts to
go to Mars with two recruiters for the Martian army. Simultaneously, Beatrice
Rumfoord, knowing her husband's prediction that she would marry Malachi on
Mars, is insulating herself against every contingency. Nevertheless, she is ab-
ducted.

The second segment of *The Sirens of Titan* is a continued assault on rationality. Although the setting has changed to Mars, Vonnegut's vision remains
focused on the existential constructs of an absurd universe. The lack of cosmic
understanding is as predominant on Mars as on Earth. Recruits from Earth
have been systematically relieved of their memories, fitted with antenna implants which control actions and induce great pain for disobedience, and are
being trained for an impending invasion of Earth. Just who is in command and
why the invasion is to take place is not known. What is clear to the reader is
that the invasion is doomed to failure — it will be, in essence, a mass suicide.

Vonnegut's creation of an anti-Utopia on Mars is a vehicle of situational satire. His abhorrence of war is made clear in all of his work, and the military is one of his consistent targets. Here, in *The Sirens of Titan*, the meaningless invasion of Earth and its concommitant death and destruction parallel the Dresden experience, a theme to be found directly or indirectly in each of his books. The lack of freedom, the blind obedience, and the arbitrary control of thought and action are somewhat exaggerated, yet not entirely unlike our traditional military values. Furthermore, the brainwashing and implantation of pain-inflicting devices are metaphorically similar to our own uninitiated recruit's experience.

Up to this point, most of Vonnegut's characters either acquiesce in the human condition or deceive themselves through belief in some cosmic absolute. The thesis that people cannot bear freedom to any large degree is not a profound literary pronouncement. Likewise, the heroic resistance of one individual to societal oppression is old hat. Through the use of the Martian anti-Utopia and the creation of Unk, Vonnegut seems to be parodying the Orwellian mode.

Malachi Constant's identity on Mars is Unk. Unk is a resistor who, in spite of continual punishment and brainwashing, attempts to maintain his individuality through the forbidden process of remembering. Learning that his wife, Beatrice, and son, Chrono, are on Mars, Unk attempts to desert the invasion force, find his wife and son, and fly off somewhere to find some meaning to it all. Unfortunately, his attempt is thwarted and he ends up on a spaceship that is programed to take both Unk and his "buddy," Boaz, to Mercury.

Winston Niles Rumfoord, the true force behind the suicidal invasion by the Martian army, is successful in the first phase of his plan to reorganize the values of people on Earth. Capitalizing on the Martian army's total defeat on Earth, Rumfoord creates a new religion built on collective guilt, which is named "The Church of God the Utterly Indifferent." Since the religion is based on "luckless" equality, all persons are required to handicap themselves so as to avoid any advantage over others. Against this background, the major tenet of the religion is that man does not need, nor will he get, help from God.

Vonnegut's characters go through various forms of torment as they are unwittingly used by superior forces. Unk is brought back to Earth through a series of Rumfoord's contrivances only to find himself the long-awaited "Space Wanderer." As a pawn to Rumfood's purposes, Unk is now the Messiah figure of the new religion which paradoxically is unified around the defilement of that most pernicious of persons — Malachi Constant. In a religion that denies luck as a force in human life and has a world view based on everyone being a victim of a series of accidents, Malachi Constant represents the unfair advantage obtained by so many prior to the Martian War.

The idea that there can be a "religion" based on the belief that there is chaos in the universe and that everyone is equally victimized by a series of accidents is an example of Vonnegut's use of bitter irony. It is in the last segment of the novel that the author lands the *coup de grâce*. After being united with his family and learning his true identity, Malachi Constant sets out for Titan with Beatrice and Chrono. Here they meet Salo, a robot messenger from Tralfamadore, whose mission had been to deliver a message from his planet to the end of the universe. Unfortunately, Salo's spaceship malfunctioned and he became grounded on Titan. For 200,000 years, Salo waited patiently for his replacement part to be delivered to Titan. Since Salo had the ability to watch events on Earth, messages from his home planet were transmitted to him by way of tremendous structures which civilizations had built on Earth. Stonehenge, for example, was actually a message in Tralfamadorian meaning "replacement part being rushed with all possible speed." The replacement part, Chrono's good luck piece, after fifty thousand years of human history, had arrived.

The resolution of *The Sirens of Titan* answers the question set out at the beginning of the book. The meaning of human history, the ultimate destiny of mankind, resides in the pragmatic design of the distant planet Tralfamadore to deliver a replacement part to one of their spaceships. Even for Salo, whose whole purpose for existing was to deliver the message across the galaxy, and who was instrumental in helping Rumfoord bring about the Martian War, there is a grimly humorous discovery. After waiting so long for the replacement part, Salo, who had faithfully followed his orders not to open the message, tears the container open in a fit of rage. The message contains a single dot which, when translated into English, means "Greetings." Upon discovering this, he takes himself apart, throwing his parts in all directions.

Vonnegut, by the end of the story, presents the reader with a teleological universe that remains fitfully chaotic and uncontrollable. Even with insight into the future, man is powerless to control his own external destiny. The events that take place appear to be subordinated in a hierarchical fashion to pragmatic circumstances which, although not predetermined, remained fixed in time. Yet the events do not fit into any overall structure of cosmic pupose. Malachi Constant is the pawn of Winston Niles Rumfoord; Winston Niles Rumfoord is the pawn of Salo and the Tralfamadorians; the Tralfamadorians seem to be pawns themselves. None of Vonnegut's characters seem to have more than a limited ability to see and an even smaller ability to understand why things are the way they are. But Vonnegut's final judgment is not one of despair. Malachi Constant's utterance to Salo after Beatrice's death that "a purpose to life, no matter who is controlling it, is to love whoever is around to be loved," indicates the author's ultimate faith in mankind's ability to create meaning. The only possible solution is the discovery of an internal center of meaning. The truth must be found within each individual.

The Sirens of Titan cleverly succeeds in the ironic juxtaposition of the comic spirit and Existentialism. The ultimate cosmic joke, that all Earthly events from Stonehenge to the Great Wall of China to the Martian War were the result of direct intervention by the inhabitants of a distant planet trying to transport a spare part to one of their spacecraft on Titan, is the darkest of humor. Vonnegut's universe is born of paradox. There is an intermingling of mystery, chaos, and predetermination. His use of comic irony helps the reader tolerate the painful apprehension of an absurd universe.

There is no question that Vonnegut, in *The Sirens of Titan*, tends to moralize. In his overwhelming concern for humanity he is sometimes guilty of oversimplifying many complex issues. It might even be said that he includes too much in the story — various side issues and discussions might just as well have been skirted or left alone. Satire and irony are themselves wonderful vehicles of social commentary, but in using them, the author runs the risk of being potentially obscure, misunderstood, or boring. Vonnegut may or may not be guilty of any combination of the three, but the uncertainty in judgment perhaps speaks for itself. Yet, an analysis of *The Sirens of Titan* must be concluded with praise. In spite of criticisms made, the overall effect of the novel is to assert a positive belief in humanity. *The Sirens of Titan* is the product of a skilled artisan who is able to point out the problems of man and society without negating man as an individual.

Criticism:

Ketterer, David. *New Worlds for Old; the Apocalyptic Imagination, Science Fiction, and American Literature*. Bloomington: Indiana University Press, 1974, pp. 296-333. Ketterer discusses *The Sirens of Titan* in comparison with other novels of the same genre.

Lawler, Donald J. "*The Sirens of Titan*: Vonnegut's Metaphysical Shaggy Dog Story," in *Vonnegut in America; an Introduction to the Life and Work of Kurt Vonnegut*. Edited by Jerome Klinkowitz and Donald L. Lawler. New York: Delacorte, 1977, pp. 61-86. This is an excellent analysis of *The Sirens of Titan*, and probably in more depth than any work yet written.

Schatt, Stanley. *Kurt Vonnegut, Jr.* Boston: Twayne, 1976, pp. 30-42. This major work of criticism on Vonnegut gives some discussion of *The Sirens of Titan* as a part of his major novels.

THE SKYLARK SERIES

Author: Edward E. Smith (1890-1965)
First book publications: The Skylark of Space (1946); *Skylark Three* (1947); *Skylark of Valeron* (1949); *Skylark DuQuesne* (1966)
Type of work: Novels
Time: The twentieth century
Locale: The Earth, various worlds of other stars, other galaxies

The story of a group of friends who, with the aid of spaceships of ever-increasing size and power, roam the cosmos and save nations, worlds, and galaxies from threats of conquest

Principal characters:
  RICHARD BALLINGER SEATON, PH.D., a young scientific genius
  DOROTHY VANEMAN, his fiancée, later his wife
  MARTIN REYNOLDS CRANE, a multimillionaire explorer-archaeologist-sportsman
  MARGARET SPENCER, his eventual wife
  MARC C. DUQUESNE, PH.D., a brilliant but blackhearted scientist
  BROOKINGS, President of World Steel
  DUNARK, Crown Prince of Kondal

The Skylark of Space was written by Edward E. Smith some ten years before it was published in *Amazing Stories*, the early chapters including some contribution by Lee Hawkins Garby, who helped him out with the romantic interest. It failed to find a market until Hugo Gernsback created a magazine specializing in "scientifiction" — a home that might have been made specially for this novel. It was serialized in Gernsback's magazine in 1928, and proved to be a great hit with the readers — it was the most popular story Gernsback's *Amazing Stories* ran, and became an important influence on the direction taken by the science fiction pulps.

A sequel, *Skylark Three*, was serialized in *Amazing Stories* in 1930, and the third part of the trilogy, *Skylark of Valeron*, appeared in *Astounding Stories* in 1934-1935. *The Skylark of Space* was first published in book form in 1946, *Skylark Three* in 1947, and *Skylark of Valeron* in 1949. After *Skylark of Valeron*, Smith began work on the Lensman series, and it was not until the 1960's, after a string of failed novels, that he decided to return to the *milieu* of his first triumph by writing *Skylark DuQuesne*. This fourth novel was serialized in *If* in 1965 and reprinted in book form the following year, by which time Smith was dead. His work has enjoyed a spectacular posthumous boom, with paperback editions of his major series being frequently reprinted in the United States and Great Britain, and with two series of pastiches being developed by other writers around characters from minor novelettes.

It is difficult today to appreciate the effect *The Skylark of Space* had on its original audience. We are now familiar with space opera on a grand scale, and that familiarity very rapidly bred contempt when it was realized that a preoccupation with scale for its own sake provided only a tenuous illusion of inventiveness and ideative extravagance. Galactic empires are now conventional stage sets for exotic futuristic romance, and no longer inspire awe. We have grown used to the idea that the universe is so vast that our entire galaxy is merely an insignificant speck within it, and we are so far past the stage of being excited by it that we can casually cultivate a disregard for its implications.

In 1928 it was different. It was only in 1912 and the years following that Slipher discovered the galactic red-shifts, and Leavitt, Hertzsprung, and Shapley calibrated the yardstick that made measuring interstellar distances relatively simple (via their work on Cepheid variables). The general theory of relativity had been published as recently as 1917, and Millikan had popularized the idea of "cosmic rays" in 1925. Edward E. Smith understood none of these things (despite his Ph.D.) — and, indeed, he seems even to have been unaware of the difference between velocity and acceleration — but such news nevertheless had some impact on his imagination, causing an excitement which he found it possible, albeit in a rather crude manner, to communicate to other readers equally naïve. To Smith and to his readers, the knowledge of the immensity of the universe was new and inspiring, and there was a new and special delight in the thought of exploring that immensity.

In the first paragraph of *The Skylark of Space*, a copper bath containing an unknown metal whose properties Richard Seaton is attempting to discover takes off and flies at enormous speed into the unknown. When he awakens his friend Martin Crane to the possibilities opened up by this event, the two make haste to obtain legal control over the metal and to set up business on their own, building a spaceship. Their scheme is bedeviled by the exploits of one of Seaton's ex-colleagues, Marc DuQuesne, and his allies in the crooked cartel known as World Steel, who are determined to seize the discovery for themselves. Brookings, the president of World Steel, wants to take over the world; DuQuesne wants to take over the universe.

Seaton and DuQuesne each build a starship. DuQuesne uses his to kidnap Seaton's fiancée, Dorothy Vaneman, but ends up in deep trouble, marooned in the gravitational grip of a dead star hundreds of light-years from Earth. Seaton rescues them, but has to search for new supplies before he can return to Earth. He becomes embroiled in a war between Kondal and Mardonale, the two nations of the planet Osnome, and wins it for Kondal, being then acclaimed as the Overlord of Osnome. These encounters set the pattern for the whole series: Seaton and DuQuesne are locked in a long battle, which Seaton always wins by having the bigger and more powerful ship, and in the intermissions between rounds of their personal conflict, Seaton takes time out to fight more extravagant battles involving whole worlds and entire races.

In *Skylark Three*, Seaton saves his Kondalian friends again, this time from invaders from Urvan. After threatening to blow up Urvan and annihilate the

Urvanians if they refuse to capitulate to his demands, he forces a peaceful resolution, and is hailed as Overlord of Urvan. This petty squabble fades into insignificance, however, when he has to face the threat of the Fenachrone, who have just set out to conquer the universe. After absorbing the scientific knowledge of several friendly races, including the extremely advanced humans of Norlamin, Seaton is ready to confront the new threat, and duly does so. The Fenachrone are too nasty to join his burgeoning galactic club, so he annihilates them to the last alien (though a few escapees are invented in order to play a minor role in *Skylark DuQuesne*).

In *Skylark of Valeron*, DuQuesne, after duping the Norlaminians into giving him a ship as good as *Skylark Three*, takes over Earth. Seaton cannot stop him because he has had to escape an attack by disembodied intelligences by entering the fourth dimension, where he is temporarily inconvenienced by a race of sea horselike aliens. When Seaton (now back in *Skylark Two*, having abandoned *Skylark Three* to the attack of the pure intelligences) returns to normal space he is a long way from home, and is further delayed by having to intervene to save the human inhabitants of Valeron from the depredations of some chlorine-breathing amoebas. Eventually, though, he builds himself a new and even bigger *Skylark* (this time the size of a small world), saves Earth, and packs DuQuesne and the disembodied intelligences off on a trip to the edge of the universe in a prison of force. There, for thirty years, the matter rests.

The spirit of these early books is one of sheer exuberance. The forces at Seaton's disposal grow mightier as he conquers new "orders" of radiation and absorbs into his own brain the knowledge of other races. By the end of *Skylark of Valeron*, he seems all-powerful, able to materialize more or less anything he wishes by the power of thought. This is wish-fulfillment fantasy taken to the ultimate, and the other aspects of the series also reflect the childish mode of thought where wishes are everything: the lavish violence, the incessant narcissism, and the sharp and easy distinction between *us* and *them* all reflect his juvenile phase. Smith delights in blowing up stars and annihilating whole races, and has no difficulty in selecting his targets: "Humanity *über alles* — *homo sapiens* against all the vermin of the universe!" cries Seaton enthusiastically as he embraces Valeron's cause. This is hardly adult thinking — indeed, it is hardly thinking at all. The "science" in the stories is, of course, all pretense, a jargon of apology for the development of an absolute power fantasy. Smith is not merely careless of authentic science, but actually contemptuous of it; when Seaton pauses to wonder why there are human beings on so many worlds, Crane puts on his anthropologist's hat and explains that "the ultimate genes must permeate universal space itself."

Skylark DuQuesne is not cast in quite the same mold as its predecessors. The style is more flippant, the plot is sprawling and confused. Curiously, the book is infected by a strong mock-feminist ethic and is brimful of liberated ladies — even Dorothy, who exists in the original trilogy mainly to be kidnaped and constantly to reassure Seaton that he is utterly wonderful, takes to going into battle, packing a pair of long-barrelled .38's beneath her bouffant skirt. The elements of the plot, however, are unaltered. There are more races of menacing aliens to be annihilated in the batlike Llurdi, and there are more chlorine-breathing amoebas; there are millions of enemy worlds to be destroyed, though they cause no more than the usual trouble:

> They died in uncounted trillions. The greeny-yellow soup that served them for air boiled away. Their halogenous flesh was charred, baked and desiccated in the split-second of the passing of the wave front from each exploding double star, moments before their planets themselves began to seethe and boil. Many died unaware. Most died fighting. Some died in terrible, frantic efforts to escape. . . .
> But they all died.

The only major change made in this scenario is that it is DuQuesne who replaces Seaton as the savior of humanity's universe — Seaton (who was always a bit squeamish) finally wilts under the pressure. DuQuesne's reward is to be given his own little galactic empire to rule according to his own principles, which seem to comprise little more than rigid autocracy and a strict program of eugenic selection. He accepts his rule gracefully, explaining that he no longer wants Earth, which is hopelessly decadent, or the home galaxy, which is now filled with "damned sissies."

The fact that Smith was prepared in the end to favor DuQuesne over Seaton came as no more than a mild surprise in view of the political ethics implied by his earlier novels, but it would be too harsh to criticize him unduly on these grounds. Even at the age of seventy-five, Smith retained an outlook in his fiction that was too naïve to permit questions of moral philosophy to have any real meaning. His stories, like the games played by small children, are actually totally isolated from the concerns of the real world. They have exactly the same virtues as such games, and should be considered in the same light. Their brutality is the innocent brutality of fantasy — a safety-valve for the expression and release of impulses which have to be repressed in real life. They are not (mercifully) any kind of a prescription for real life.

The *Skylark* books are aesthetically and intellectually vacuous, and can no longer offer the same kind of revelatory consciousness-expansion that they once did. This should not, however, prevent us from recognizing the historical importance of *The Skylark of Space* within genre science fiction, the power of its influence on subsequent work done under the label, or the fact that it really did have something valuable to offer its teenage audience in 1928. The contemporary Smith revival is harder to understand, but it seems probable that the audience is still composed mainly of preadolescent teenagers with a considerable appetite for extravagant power fantasy, and that the total lack of intellectual and moral sophistication exhibited by the novels provides them with an advantage in the literary marketplace that more recent works do not have. It must be remembered that, although there is a constant supply of new naïve readers, naïve writers are no longer as common as they were in 1928.

Criticism:

Ellik, Ron and Bill Evans. *The Universe of E. E. Smith*. Chicago: Advent Publishers, Inc., 1968. This book offers a complete discussion and analysis of all of the Skylark and Lensman novels of E. E. Smith.

SLAUGHTERHOUSE-FIVE

Author: Kurt Vonnegut, Jr. (1922-   )
First book publication: 1969
Type of work: Novel
Time: Before, during, and after World War II, and the future
Locale: The United States, Germany, Tralfamadore

   The Dresden fire-bombing from the point of view of Billy Pilgrim, the Tralfamadorians, and Vonnegut as narrator

> *Principal characters:*
> "VONNEGUT," the narrator
> BILLY PILGRIM, a man who becomes unstuck in time
> VALENCIA MERBLE, the girl he marries
> MONTANA WILDHACK, his mate on Tralfamadore
> PAUL LAZZARO, the man who kills Billy
> ROLAND WEARY and
> EDGAR DERBY, would-be heroes
> BERNARD V. O'HARE, Vonnegut's World War II buddy
> MARY O'HARE, his wife
> THE TRALFAMADORIANS, green creatures from outer space

Slaughterhouse-Five, on first reading, may seem an uneasy blend of the realistic and the science fiction novel. As Vonnegut explains in the opening chapter, he at first planned an epic novel about the fire-bombing of Dresden by the Americans in World War II. Realizing that war is confused, anticlimactic, and antiheroic, Vonnegut expresses this confusion in the experience of his protagonist, Billy Pilgrim, who comes "unstuck in time" and in disconnected episodes travels to his past, his present, and his future, not necessarily in that order. Only when he is captured by the Tralfamadorians, strange green creatures from outer space that are shaped like plumber's helpers, does he achieve any kind of unity and coherence of perception. For the Tralfamadorians, every moment is like any other moment, for they can see all experience at once. "So it goes" is the response to death and destruction, and the phrase recurs again and again. Even the fire-bombing of Dresden becomes bearable when seen as one of a series of random events, when the Oz-like Dresden that was destroyed still exists in another moment of time.

   The "present" of the novel and the focal point of the action is World War II, an event, for Billy, now in the past. Written in 1969, *Slaughterhouse-Five* is a commentary on all wars, but especially on the Vietnam War. There is no heroic action. Eighteen-year-old Billy, along with Roland Weary, also just eighteen, is captured by the Germans. Weary constantly jeers at Billy for his lack of heroism and constantly romanticizes his own role in the war. He dies on a prison train from gangrene of the foot, but not before he convinces Paul Lazzaro that Billy is responsible for his death and elicits Lazzaro's promise of revenge. From prison camp they are sent to Dresden, where they are lodged in underground slaughterhouses, Billy in the Slaughterhouse-Five of the title.

There they survive the fire-bombing to emerge into a science fiction-like "moonscape" haunted by death, including the incongruous shooting of "poor old Edgar Derby" for "looting" a Dresden teacup that has somehow survived the bombing.

The war action develops on a reasonably straight chronological level, with flashes of Billy's past and future juxtaposed to related events in the war. Billy becomes an ophthalmologist (reinforcing the main themes of vision and perception) and marries the fat and hideous Valencia Merble, daughter of the richest ophthalmologist in Ilium, New York. They have two children, Barbara and Robert. Billy's life is relatively uneventful until after his daughter's wedding, when he is kidnaped by the Tralfamadorians and taken to live in a geodetic dome on exhibition on a simulated Earth environment. Billy is provided with a mate, Montana Wildhack, a luscious model for, among other things, pornographic pictures; the two have a child. But Billy also continues his life on Earth, coming back to preach the Tralfamadorian philosophy. He dies when he is shot by Paul Lazzaro as he addresses a huge crowd in Chicago in 1976. The juxtaposition of past and future events with the action of the war creates an ironic perspective on both.

Perhaps the most important and complex character in the novel is "Vonnegut," for in *Slaughterhouse-Five* he has not one, but two *personae*. There is the narrator of the framework "with his memories and his Pall Malls," and the Vonnegut who interacts with the characters in the novel, who was also in World War II: "That was me. That was I." Vonnegut observed in the preface to *Happy Birthday, Wanda June* (1970) that he is a character in all of his novels; in addition he has at least one alter ego per novel. These characters move from book to book, and so do places (like Ilium, the name deliberately ironic) which reinforce his Tralfamadorian vision of life, which in *The Sirens of Titan* (1959) he calls the *chrono-synclastic infundibulum*. That is, according to the Tralfamadorians, who also appear in *The Sirens of Titan*, a point in the universe where all contradictory opinions, be they ever so disparate, meet and harmonize. It is this point of view that the Tralfamadorians teach Billy Pilgrim.

Yet despite this personal identification, Vonnegut treats characters — and they treat one another — with a great deal of detachment. People are "machines"; they are referred to in abstract terms. Robert, Billy's son, is usually referred to as "the Green Beret," reflecting also the dehumanizing effect of war. A Russian soldier, also a prisoner, who encounters Billy views him as "a curious scarecrow" and attempts to talk to "it." Two of the very few people capable of real love or hate are Mary O'Hare, Bernard V. O'Hare's wife, and Paul Lazzaro. Neither is willing to accept death as "so it goes." Both try to change "the past, the present, and the future" which Billy cannot change, Mary by refusing to accept the heroic view of warfare, and Lazzaro by his insistence on personal hatred. Paradoxically, through his hatred he arrives at an antiwar stance: it is ridiculous to kill someone *unless* you hate his guts. "Vonnegut" accepts Mary's view that wars are made glamorous by "dirty old men" and fought by "babies" and alters his original concept of his novel. Billy accepts Lazzaro as simply an agent of the inevitable.

"Vonnegut" himself observes, despite his assertion that all the characters are based on real people, that there are "almost no characters" in *Slaughterhouse-Five*, and very little drama, because the people in it are "so sick" and so much the "listless playthings of enormous forces." War, he continues, discourages people "from being characters." But the major reason there are "almost no characters" is that *Slaughterhouse-Five* is a novel of ideas. Characters function as explanation and often have symbolic names, such as Roland Weary, whose name is a combination of a once heroic name and an accurate description of his real state. In *Slaughterhouse-Five*, what is to be explained is that life and death are inexplicable.

It is no accident that the alter ego closest to Vonnegut's own identity is Kilgore Trout, the "cracked Messiah" with a genuine incapacity for hatred, whose novels Billy has read and whom he seeks out. Trout is an obscure, mad, misunderstood science fiction writer. Yet his madness is that of the sacred idiot. Interspersed through *Slaughterhouse-Five*, as well as through Vonnegut's other novels, are the plots of Trout's novels, "prophetic books" within prophetic books. *Slaughterhouse-Five* even includes a novel by Trout with a plot similar to its own, a glimpse of the situation from Trout's bizarre point of view. In like manner, earthly reality and history appear in *Slaughterhouse-Five* in part from the use of real and imaginary books and documents — *The Execution of Private Slovik*, a history of Dresden, Bertram Copeland Rumfoord's history of World War II — not for the illusion of realism, but as another kind of "prophetic book" commenting on the action. *Slaughterhouse-Five* is thus about the inexplicability of all wars, from Biblical to Vietnamese. One of Trout's novels, *The Gutless Wonder*, tells of a robot who pilots a bomber, remarkable in 1932 for predicting "the widespread use of burning jellied gasoline on human beings." Trout's novels add another of Vonnegut's perspectives to *Slaughterhouse-Five*.

Yet another perspective appears in the difference between characters appearing in *Slaughterhouse-Five* and their appearance in other novels: Bernard V. O'Hare, Rumfoord, Eliot Rosewater, and Howard W. Campbell. O'Hare and Campbell appear in *Mother Night*, a black comedy about tracking down Nazi war criminals, in which O'Hare is the villain, or as much of a villain as Vonnegut ever creates; and Campbell, we learn, was an undercover agent for the Allies — the American Nazi pose was his cover. Rumfoord appears in *The Sirens of Titan* as a benevolent if eccentric millionaire and so does Eliot Rosewater in *God Bless You, Mr. Rosewater*. Their presence implies other views and perspectives on the events described in *Slaughterhouse-Five*.

This is the Tralfamadorian perception, to which Billy Pilgrim is converted.

Tralfamadorians have an Emersonian perception of reality, a Blakean fourfold vision. Their metaphor for Earthling vision is apt: a man who is able to perceive the world only through the hole at the end of a six-foot piece of pipe. Earthling time is opposed to Tralfamadorian time, and Billy Pilgrim becomes unstuck in Earthling time. Though he has complete perspective of his life from start to finish, he has no control over what moment he will experience next. Billy first appears in the novel as a possibly mad middle-aged man, writing letters to the editor about his Tralfamadorian experience, letters which state the theme and structure of the novel. Billy thinks of himself as "prescribing corrective lenses for Earthling souls," "Earthling" in this context implying the Tralfamadorian view of man.

While praising Trout's ideas and the Tralfamadorian perspective, Vonnegut at the same time criticizes the idea of science fiction as prophetic book or salvation; thus, when Billy Pilgrim and Eliot Rosewater turn to science fiction to find some meaning in life, Vonnegut parodies their attempt. Kilgore Trout is eager to see evidence that the things he writes about actually exist. Billy dies in 1976, and Lazzaro is then an "old man"; actually, both would be in their fifties. Parodying future prophecy novels, Vonnegut notes that by 1976, "He [Billy] has to cross three international boundaries in order to reach Chicago" from New York. When Billy makes a speech to the Tralfamadorians, pointing out how terrible Earthlings are and what a threat they are to the universe, the Tralfamadorians are not impressed. "Science fiction had led him to expect" that aliens would be terrified of Earthling "ferocity" and "spectacular weaponry." But the message of science fiction is all wrong. The Tralfamadorians know that one of their own test pilots will press a button and the whole universe will disappear. Nor will the Tralfamadorians attempt to prevent it. It has always happened, and it always will. There is, of course, the paradox that it is the characters who could only exist in science fiction who point out the flaws in science fiction; and Vonnegut's own attitude is equally paradoxical. He dislikes being put in the category of science fiction, yet he is sharply critical of writers who refuse to be aware of the twentieth century technological ethos.

When Billy finally accepts the Tralfamadorian vision, he tries to get others to accept it and is at first thought insane. He becomes a prophet, himself a "cracked messiah." Only in the future is he taken seriously. Billy is in some ways a Christ-figure, but Christianity is not enough of a solution for modern man's dilemmas: *The Brothers Karamazov* contains "everything there was to know about life," yet "that isn't *enough* any more." As "Vonnegut" observes, the epigraph of "the little Lord Jesus,/ No crying he makes" applies only to Billy's singular lack of tears at the unhappy moments of his life. Characters in the novel are searching for some meaning in life, though they have no common solution. Billy's mother, like many Americans, is "trying to construct a life that made sense from things she found in gift shops." Kilgore

Trout writes *The Gospel from Outer Space*, a reinterpretation not so much of the Gospels as of people's attitudes towards them. Billy's "Tralfamadorian adventure with death" is strongly reminiscent of the resurrection as described in St. Luke's Gospel, in which Christ demonstrates his reality by eating. The difference between Tralfamadorian and Christian interpretations is that the idea of resurrection and heaven is comforting, whereas the idea of endless repetition is not — at least, as Billy discovers, not as an idea coming to the average person out of the blue. Nor is the concept pleasant to "Vonnegut," who observes toward the end of the book that he does not relish the idea of spending eternity perpetually visiting various moments; though if it is true, he is "grateful that so many of those moments are nice."

Billy does not always attain or keep his Tralfamadorian vision. He is the alter ego who is furthest from the "real" Vonnegut, appearing in the novel primarily as a young man or as an innocent. Yet his awareness is occasionally Vonnegut's. He does not have entire foreknowledge or self-understanding, and his foreknowledge can inhibit another's actions. When Valencia offers to lose weight and wants to become attractive to him, he tells her he likes her the way she is, not because he really believes so, but because he has the foreknowledge that the relationship will be "bearable." He accepts with like passivity life with Montana Wildhack in the geodesic dome.

Vonnegut's outlook might be described as Calvinism in reverse gear. A similar sort of determinism appears in his other work. In *Slaughterhouse-Five*, Vonnegut says, "I was the victim of a series of accidents, as are we all," and the Tralfamadorians assert, "Only on Earth is there any talk of free will." But what is determined is not cosmos but chaos. As the Tralfamadorians put it, man should not ask "why" — "There is no *why*."

If there is no *why*, then what moves the artist to create, to say as Vonnegut does repeatedly through the novel, "Listen!"? At the beginning of *Slaughterhouse-Five*, Vonnegut compares himself to Lot's wife, who did look back, "because it was so human," and refers to the novel as a "failure," inevitable since it was "written by a pillar of salt." The flaw in the concept of the chrono-synclastic infundibulum and the "so it goes" philosophy is that one cannot go back in time, except in art, nor even in art if books are written by a "pillar of salt." Dresden will always be like Dayton, now, and not like Oz. Kilgore Trout's final desperate cry to Vonnegut (in *Breakfast of Champions*, 1973) is *"Make me young."* "Mustard gas and roses" is throughout *Slaughterhouse-Five* the smell of death, but it is also the breath of the artist.

Vonnegut creates cosmic and darkly comic chaos, luring the reader into the awesome emptiness of space, peopled with the bizarre creatures "science fiction had led him to expect" there, to demonstrate that there is no comfortable escape — whether past, present, or future — from reality, and that only from a point of vision completely outside Earth can man attempt to live with or account for such horrors as the Dresden fire-bombing. Yet the novel ends on a tentatively hopeful note, at the moment in time with Billy in a horse-drawn wagon after the bombing, lying relaxed in the sun and listening to a bird call. Even though both Billy and the reader are aware that soon someone will discover the pathetic condition of the horses and that when Billy sees them he will weep for the only time in the whole war, this moment of peace will still remain, the bird will still question *"poo-tee-weet?"* happily. By journeying into the cosmos for a perspective on incomprehensible Earthling warfare, Vonnegut has created one of the best of the twentieth century's war novels.

Criticism:

Festa, Conrad. "Vonnegut's Satire," in *Vonnegut in America; an Introduction to the Life and Work of Kurt Vonnegut*. Edited by Jerome Klinkowitz and Donald L. Lawler. New York: Delacorte, 1977, pp. 133-149. Festa analyzes Vonnegut's satire.

Harris, Charles B. "Time, Uncertainty, and Kurt Vonnegut, Jr.: A Reading of *Slaughterhouse-Five*," in *Centennial Review*. XX (1976), pp. 228-243. Harris gives a good analysis of the entire novel.

Schatt, Stanley. *Kurt Vonnegut, Jr.* Boston: Twayne, 1976, pp. 81-96. This major work on Vonnegut places *Slaughterhouse-Five* in perspective with his other works.

Tilton, John W. *Cosmic Satire in the Contemporary Novel*. Lewisburg, Pa.: Bucknell University Press, 1977, pp. 69-105. This work, although dealing with a number of other authors, discusses *Slaughterhouse-Five* at great length, citing it as a major American novel.

SOLARIS

Author: Stanislaw Lem (1921-   )
First book publication: 1961
English translation: 1971
Type of work: Novel
Time: An unspecified future
Locale: A space station hovering over the planet Solaris

A detailed and ingenious description of the human efforts to come to grips with the problems posed by the mysterious ocean covering the surface of Solaris, attempts which end in bitterness and frustration

> *Principal characters:*
> KRIS KELVIN, a psychologist
> RHEYA (HAREY in the original), his dead wife, materialized by the Solaris ocean
> DR. SNOW (SNAUT in the original), a cyberneticist
> DR. SARTORIUS, a research physicist

Whatever else Lem's fiction might be, whether in the realistic or in the humorous, absurd mode, there is one thing central to it: particular models of thought relating specific incidents to a larger design — a style that leads from particulars to universals. This fact is perhaps nowhere clearer than in *Solaris*, which is, in terms of the number of translations it has had, and the critical comment it has evoked, Lem's most important novel. Andrei Tarkovsky, the Soviet director, has rendered it into a widely discussed film that shifts the focus from Lem's burning curiosity about pure knowledge to the human problems of the characters confronted with the Solaris phenomena and to some rather general sentiments about the responsibility of science and scientists. While Tarkovsky's film has received wide critical acclaim, Lem himself does not approve of it, since it totally neglects the cognitive aspects of his novel, and concentrates on things that are at best of secondary importance to him. He has, in fact, never seen the film in its entirety.

The central thematic and philosophical interest of the novel concerns the attempt to solve the riddle of the planet Solaris. The planet revolves around a blue and red double-sun somewhere in the galaxy, and its surface is, aside from some bare islands, entirely covered by a colloidal ocean. This ocean gives rise to a wealth of different formations, which almost never repeat themselves. They are classified and described by the Solarists, the scientists engaged in the exploration of this biological phenomenan. Scientific interest was first aroused when Solaris' orbit was found to be stable, although this contradicted the fact that it revolved around a double sun. The stabilizing factor could only be the ocean, which somehow influenced gravitational fields and stabilized the path of the planet, a feat well beyond the scope of terrestrial science. This astronomical discovery led to a flourish of scientific literature about the planet, but not to any generally acceptable results. Investigation suggested that the ocean was a biological, not simply a physical phenomenon, and even that it was possibly a sentient being. As a result of this rather vague conclusion, the scientists became frustrated, and at the time of the novel, Solaris studies have declined.

The research station on the planet is manned by three people. When the novel's hero, the psychologist Kris Kelvin, arrives on the planet, he finds Gibarian dead of suicide, Dr. Snow half-crazed with fear, and Sartorius in seclusion. Snow greets Kelvin suspiciously, and Kelvin has a hard time convincing him that he is not a phantom. The scientists have begun to observe the materialization of their deepest psychological secrets, things suppressed and forgotten, because they are invariably shameful. Gibarian was plagued by a giant Negro woman; that which haunts the other two is not revealed to the reader, although Snow suggests some fetishistic objects, aberrations of the mind that have become flesh and blood. For Kris Kelvin it is Rheya (Harey in the original), a young woman who killed herself after a quarrel between them, who is materialized by the ocean.

She first appears in the station, not knowing what happened to her, and, they resume their relationship where it left off. To the hero, the return of a person he knows to be dead is horrifying. She has aspects of a succubus, a demon of hell, sent to torment him, which is all the more cruel since she herself is perfectly innocent and does not know her true nature. Quick-witted Kelvin packs her off into a rocket and blasts her into space, only to find her soon returned, still loving him, and with no recollection of his attempt to dispose of her. The duplicate Rheya is a creature formed of neutrinos instead of atoms (though down to the molecules not different from another woman), and she is inextricably bound to the psyche from whose deepest memories she has been created; she cannot stand being separated from her beloved for even a few moments, and when separated she is capable of tearing her way with superhuman strength through steel doors. When injured, her torn tissue has an extraordinary regenerative power, renewing itself in a very short time. Even a suicide attempt with liquid oxygen proves ineffective. Apart from that, she is psychologically quite human, hurt where a normal woman would be hurt, loving as the real Rheya would have loved. If she is a tool created by the ocean for some sinister purpose, she herself does not know what that purpose is. This innocence is what makes her situation so tragically poignant. Whatever the ocean may have intended her to be, she is a woman deeply in love, and the longer she is near Kelvin, the more human she becomes.

Contrary to his first horrified impulses, panicked into murder by her appearance, Kelvin comes to love the replica of his dead wife, though she is incorporated in another material substratum. For Lem, love appears to be something spiritual, more a matter of the mind than of the flesh, with fulfillment rarely possible. Years later, he was to reverse the Rheya situation in the dazzling novella "The Mask," told from the point of view of the woman, a killer-robot programed to pursue and kill the man she has come to love. Sexual fulfillment again being impossible, she is united with her beloved only in death. She finds him covered by an innocent sheet of white snow, not knowing whether she would have killed him if she had found him alive. These are highly romantic affairs with death close by, based on spiritual affinity rather than on physical attraction. This aspect of *Solaris* is presented as a tender, though feverish, high strung love story that shades over into the visionary. It is a science-fiction version of the romantic theme of love beyond death, with the dead female returning not as a vampire, and indeed quite without necrophilic overtones, but by the scientific marvel as a "Phi-creature" or phantom of the ocean.

She is, however, not an exact copy of the dead woman, for she knows things, reconstructed from Kelvin's memory, that the real Rheya could not possibly know. The core of her being remains a mystery, for beyond the normal human tissues and cells that mask the true purpose of the Phi-beings, the electronic microscope reveals only the emptiness of space. When Rheya learns that she is not a normal human being, she is shattered. She reacts to the situation with noble self-sacrifice, knowing that her love for Kelvin has no future. When the physicist Sartorius finally discovers an anti-field for the destruction of the neutrino fields, and the new demons can be exorcized by physics, Rheya asks Snow for her own destruction. Tragic as the story is, and as painful as it is to Kelvin, it is nevertheless one that can be communicated to others without shame. What Snow and Sartorius have to hide must be more horrifying, and Lem wisely refrains from giving more than hints and suggestions. What the ocean reveals to human beings is, in Snow's words, their deepest shame, their folly and their ugliness; it acts as a psychic mirror for the "knights of the Holy Contact" who set out to discover other worlds, and yet encounter only themselves.

In *Solaris*, Lem has successfully combined his central epistemological position with the individual story of a love transcending the limits of life. Of course, the tender and tragic love story remains secondary to the philosophical problem, and the characters are basically building blocks in Lem's epistemological construction. There is also no social environment in the book; the only thing the reader learns about the society that sends scientists to Solaris is that there is a UN convention against the use of X-rays (which is broken by the Solarists). Lem establishes a "pure" experimental situation, undiluted by any social interference, that is concerned with human essentials, not with social accidents. This ideal situation allows him to study his abstract characters and their problems in depth, as representatives of the cognitive situation of mankind.

Interesting as the planet Solaris is in all its particulars, it is only an illustration of rather abstract problems, a concretization of highly unusual and distinct particulars that, as always with Lem, goes beyond the specific case and points towards the general predicament of mankind: the limits of human knowledge, and what takes its place when no final knowledge is possible. "Genius and mediocrity alike are dumbfounded" by the teeming diversity of the oceanic formation of Solaris, some short-lived and explosive, others regular and relatively stable; some superficial formations, others giant structures reaching miles into the atmosphere. At their simplest, they reproduce things that are brought into contact with their surface; at their most complex, they perform complicated functions, bizarre metamorphoses and movements. Sometimes they are thought of as gigantic limbs or organs of the colloid ocean, but all such comparisons are futile. Most interesting of these forms are the symmetriads with their property of illustrating, sometimes contradicting, various laws of physics, and which seem to represent spatial analogons to transcendental equations.

These descriptions and classifications fill thousands of volumes in the vast Solaris library. They became especially numerous after the enthusiasm of the theory-formulating fathers of Solaristics became frustrated, because of their auspicious lack of success at arriving at any explanation, and their failure to achieve contact with the ocean. Then the routine workers came and began observing and filing away masses of repetitious information. However, all the data remain frustratingly phenomenal, while the meaning remains as hidden away from human understanding as ever. The phenomena are described with lucid clarity, but the essence is deeply mysterious. This abyss between observation and interpretation provides the central tension not only of this novel, but of Lem's whole work. This is no variation of the "there are things not meant for man to know"; man is meant to know everything that he can, but there are things that he cannot know, because of the structure of his mind and body and the structure of the universe.

The apparent futility of the Solaris studies does not result in facile despair. The effort is not wasted; experiments must be made, even if they yield no immediate results, but only raise man's failure to understand to a higher level of nonunderstanding, a frequent occurrence in the pursuit of scientific truth. Man must go on hoping and acting on incomplete data. In this respect, Lem is somewhat of an existentialist; in spite of a positive attitude toward science, he is well aware of the absurdity of existence. Although there are reviewers who prefer the banal conviction that he is antiscience, this is very unlikely in view of the intimate knowledge of scientific theories he displays in his fiction and nonfiction.

Thus, Lem is not so much concerned with results as with processes and ways of thinking. This approach gives his writing its energy and dynamism, despite a general lack of plot action. All the descriptions of the Solaris ocean are merely phenomenal and aesthetic, not even scratching the surface of the phenomenon. Explanations are metaphors and similes rather than literal descriptions of processes. This is the deep paradox of Solaristics: man can only resort to the terminology and conceptual apparatus available to him, totally inappropriate though it is for grasping the essence of the situation. In seeking the truly alien, man must always rely on himself and what is familiar to him, because there is nothing else. His cognitive situation is comparable to that of a creature inescapably caught in a net; he may expand that net somewhere, deform it, but try as he might, he will not get out. The mountains of data collected on the Solaris ocean over nearly a hundred years prove unable to answer the innocent question of a schoolgirl: "And what is it for?" There is no lack of theories, but all are equally unproven if unrefuted.

It has come to be generally accepted that the ocean is sentient but the nature of that sentience remains a mystery. From the early optimistic theories about imminent contact, Solaristics has branched into various subfields, with a scientific orthodoxy, heroes, authorities, heretics, and the features of a cult rather than a science. All these theories share, however, one thing: they can neither be refuted nor validated, and any explanation merely replaces "one enigma with another, perhaps even more baffling." This reflects the normal progress of science, made poignant here by the extremity of the situation, by the very size and grandeur of the problem that inevitably leads from the physical into the metaphysical.

In dramatizing the problem, Lem polemizes both the physical and metaphysical against the intellectual pretensions of man, who merely wants to extend his rule over the cosmos and refute the banal solutions offered elsewhere in science fiction. As a rule, other science fiction worlds are purely phenomenological, alien only in appearance, but essentially anthropomorphic: xeno-biological oddities, exotic as they may be in their forms, are psychologically as close as the people in the supermarket next door. For Lem, the true alien has alien principles, laws and purposes not accessible to human reason; this requires a program that is contradictory and unrealizable. So, with a mighty effort, he tries to describe what cannot be understood by man, and which therefore always turns into a mirror, onto which man projects his own thoughts, hopes, and fears. No matter how far the voyage, we meet only ourselves, projecting our own meaning into the alien world. Where science must be silent, its surrogates step in. Not willing to accept the irrevocable loss of Rheya, Kelvin constructs for himself the metaphysical comfort that Solaris is an imperfect god, and he waits for another miracle, the return of Rheya. The essence of that which cannot be grasped intellectually, can nevertheless be accepted emotionally through a quasi-religious belief and appreciated aesthetically. Kelvin's final contact with the ocean is an aesthetic acceptance. Faced with the absurdity of existence, man must nevertheless continue the struggle and at least preserve his dignity. Kelvin's anguish is similar to that of Berton, the helicopter pilot, who was the first person to confront the psychic emanations of the ocean when he saw the face of a giant child. Berton makes all his statements dependent upon whether the commission investigating his case will take him seriously, "because the contents of my hallucinations belong to me, and I don't have to give an account of them, whereas I am obliged to give an account of what I saw on Solaris." There are not many characters in science fiction who speak like this and not many authors who achieve such a convincing fusion of intellect and emotion as Stanislaw Lem does in *Solaris*.

SPACE LORDS

Author: Cordwainer Smith (Paul M. Linebarger, 1913-1966)
First book publication: 1965
Type of work: Thematically related short stories
Time: The remote future
Locale: Earth and various other planets, in and out of the solar system

Reprints of five stories originally published in magazines in the early 1960's, an important segment of Smith's "future history" of the Instrumentality of Man

In the 1970's Cordwainer Smith became recognized as one of the most original writers of science fiction, as well as a man whose life was hardly less interesting than his stories. "Cordwainer Smith" was only one of several pseudonyms used by Paul Linebarger. Although Linebarger was born in the United States, much of early life was spent in China, where his father was an American adviser to Sun Yat-sen, nationalist leader and first president of China. As a result, Linebarger, who was Sun Yat-sen's godson, spent his formative years in a culture that must have seemed as exotic to Americans of the time as his stories were to a later generation. He traveled extensively both in the Orient and in Europe, learning six languages and finding time to take a doctoral degree in political science. His writing began as a sideline to his several vocations as university professor, government executive, and officer in U.S. Army Intelligence.

According to J. J. Pierce, a recent editor of his stories, Smith's writing of science fiction began in his teens with a short story now lost. But readers of the genre first noticed his work with the publication of the story "Scanners Live in Vain" in 1950. In the 1950's and early 1960's stories followed which made it clear that in Cordwainer Smith a major talent had appeared. One important component of that talent was Smith's ability to establish an atmosphere unique to science fiction, that of the alien society, and to create that atmosphere in a unique way. Some background in the methods of the science fiction genre is necessary to understand Smith's particular technique.

As a method, the role of extrapolation in science fiction has been widely discussed; through its use, writers create a setting in the future by assuming that some present trend will continue or intensify, while they hold other factors in society constant. For example, in one series of stories, Larry Niven assumes that human institutions, desires, and abilities will remain as they are now with the single exception of perfected procedures for transplanting bodily organs; thereafter the effects of this single variable are explored.

But ultimately such explorations of the future are limited. When we look at the span of human history in the past, we realize that at some point not only will abilities and institutions change, but human desires themselves will be different, creating a society as odd to us as ours would be to an Egyptian peasant from the days of the Pharaohs. Of course, these changes will occur not only in the large components of society, but in trivial ones as well. Whatever diversions may exist ten millennia from now, we may well doubt that people will light up tobacco cigarettes in their spare moments, as a character does in Isaac Asimov's Foundation series. Therefore, the writer who sets a story in the far future has a massive task before him, one in which extrapolation will not be of much help. The canvas of the far future society will be much broader than that of, say, George Orwell's *Nineteen Eighty-Four*, yet every detail must be something strange and wondrous.

Several methods are useful for depicting a setting that is radically rather than slightly different, and exotic in many ways, not only in one. The first uses familiar words and terms but in odd juxtapositions, as in Robert Heinlein's celebrated sentence, "The door dilated." The noun "door" and the verb "dilate" are familiar words, but when we read them as subject and predicate we know that the story in which they are contained presumes a society different from ours in a fundamental way. The reader receives much the same feeling in a Robert Silverberg story in which the bartender has one for himself, not by drinking the alcohol but by transmitting it directly into the bloodstream. Here again, all the parts of the action are familiar, but they are combined in an unexpected unity.

Another method of establishing an exotic setting is that favored by Cordwainer Smith. It starts with terms that are strange in themselves. Some of these terms are recognizable deformations of words changed by time: thus the place-name Meeya Meefla hints at its origin as Miami, Florida. Other terms become clear as the story unfolds: we learn that "underpeople," a word found in many of the tales, is the name for human-shaped intelligent beings derived from the lower animals. C'mell, for example, is a character whose name shows her feline ancestry by its initial letter — for "cat." And still a third group of terms is never explained, contributing strongly to the air of mystery, to the sense of a deep and hidden background that marks the work of Cordwainer Smith. Alpha Ralpha Boulevard, for instance, is a name that tantalizes, since its first part is familiar, and the reader has the feeling that the whole would make sense if perhaps just one piece of its history were known. Or again, a strange machine is known as the Abba-dingo. The definite article makes the name sound like a title, like something unique, yet the source of its name and even its original purpose are hidden from us. As these examples suggest, Smith is especially masterful at evocative and haunting names — C'mell, Lord Jestocost, Charlie-is-my-darling, Mother Hitton — they seem to come from another world, which is just the effect the author is aiming for.

This sense of a mysterious background is crucial to the success of Smith's fiction, since many of his stories (including all those in *Space Lords*) take place in the remote future, perhaps ten or fifteen thousand years hence.

Smith's stories, like those of the early Heinlein or Ursula K. Le Guin, form a connected future history operating through a single vision. Mankind has spread throughout the stars in that scheme, but unlike many centuries-spanning epics, Smith's interstellar society is not static. Over the series of his tales, changes continue to occur in technology, human relations, and politics. In only the field of technology, for instance, starships propelled by the pressure of light on huge sails give way to planoforming — travel through something like that science fiction standby, hyperspace. The planoforming concept is especially rich in details: the go-captains whose subconscious minds navigate the ships, the pin-lighters whose telepathic perceptions guard the ships, the cat-partners who serve the pin-lighters. Yet even all this gives way to something like teleportation.

Nostalgia is a common human response to technological change; people feel sentimental, for example, about the obsolescence of gleaming transcontinental passenger trains and regret seeing the profession of railroad engineer lose its luster and prestige. Yet it is a measure of the skill of Cordwainer Smith that he can make us feel nostalgic about the passing of a profession that is entirely fictional and located in a future far beyond the extent of our lives, as he does for the scanners, spaceship pilots in "Scanners Live in Vain."

Political institutions change as well as technology. In "Alpha Ralpha Boulevard" we see a lasting (and boring) Utopia yield to a world in which the human need for challenge has been rediscovered. In several stories, the under-people, little more than slaves, press for and eventually achieve freedom and respect. Methods of judicial proceedings change, ways of punishment change.

This variety of changes allows most of Cordwainer Smith's stories to be placed roughly in chronological order in his outline of future history. The order of the five stories in *Space Lords* coincides neither with their order of composition nor their arrangement in the book. Following Pierce's chronology, the order of the stories should be "The Dead Lady of Clown Town" first, "Drunkboat" second, and then three stories whose order relative to one another is difficult to determine: "Mother Hitton's Littul Kittons," "The Ballad of Lost C'Mell," and "A Planet Named Shayol." In this order they span most of the changes noted above.

Despite all this change, Cordwainer Smith can hardly be called a writer of hard science fiction; his emphasis is not on technological advance. Nor is he a sociological writer; institutional changes are not his prime concern. Rather, through all his stories, through all the exotic and even bizarre settings, we understand his characters and sympathize with them because he is concerned with the human heart — even when that heart lies within the body of a beast.

It is no disparagement to say that in the main Smith has only one theme: love. That theme, in its varied forms, is so rich a subject that thousands of years of storytellers have not exhausted it, but it is rare to science fiction. When one thinks of writers in the field who have dealt with the subject, Theodore Sturgeon and Ursula Le Guin come to mind, but past them, the list is not very long. No writer in the genre exercises greater skill in characterization or motivates those characters in mature human relationships better than does Cordwainer Smith.

The three central stories in *Space Lords* clearly show Smith's favorite theme. "The Dead Lady of Clown Town" places a simple love theme within a larger plot about the resistance of the underpeople to their oppressed status. At the center stands D'joan, a girl of dog ancestry, whose resemblance to Joan of Arc goes deeper than her name. But unlike the maid of Orleans, D'joan leads an army of underpeople whose only weaponry is love for mankind. We see her struggle through the human eyes of Elaine and the Hunter, whose comparatively mild punishment for their part in the uprising points up the savagery of D'joan's martyrdom at the stake. The story displays love between man and woman, love between intelligent species, and, in the mechanical person of the Lady Panc Ashash, even the love of machines for humans, all against a background of civil insurrection.

The caring of being for being in these stories suggests that Smith proposes a definition of humanity based on the expression of kindness and affection: beings who can do that, whatever their nature, share in humanity.

"Drunkboat" shows the power of the bonds of love; they fuel the teleportation of a traveler through space to the side of his beloved, whose life he believes to be in danger. Here love triumphs not only over distance, but over technology as well, since the story hints that a controlled form of teleportation will replace the planoforming ships.

"The Ballad of Lost C'mell" deals again with the underpeople. It concerns only a single incident in their long struggle to be treated as intelligent beings, and in that sense can be thought of as a companion piece to "The Dead Lady of Clown Town." C'mell's love is returned; the seventh Lord Jestocost, a member of the shadowy but powerful Instrumentality, allows himself to be used to penetrate the Instrumentality's secrets because of his affection for C'mell, and he later on becomes a champion of the rights of the underpeople. Their largely unstated love is made the more poignant by being illegal, by being repressed by both of them, and by being to the last unconsummated.

Perhaps Smith's most interesting concept, one that appears in story after story, is the Instrumentality of Man. While not a government, the Instrumentality exercises a supreme power, even over planetary governments. It is something like an aristocracy, and is perhaps hereditary. Its members are telepathic, intelligent, but not supermen. Their most outstanding characteristic is their collective dedication to a set of ideals that remains shadowy, and there is something about them more like a religious order than a country gentry. In the end, the suggestion of a religious dimension to the Instrumentality may be the most revealing, for an instrument is designed for a purpose, designed to be used for something. And there is an ambiguity about their name: are they an instrument through which mankind works, or is mankind the instrument, the tool through which a divine providence achieves its purposes? Smith, a sincerely religious man, may have answered yes to the second question. His theme of an all-pervading and all-conquering love fits comfortably within the Christian conception of divine benevolence. His raising of beasts and even machines to a share in the communion of people of good will suggests the coming of a new creation. Had Smith lived longer, we might have seen in his work an imaginative picture of the end, in St. Paul's words, towards which all creation strives. As it is, he has given us unforgettable stories of incidents that occur along the way.

STAR MAKER

Author: Olaf Stapledon (1886-1950)
First book publication: 1937
Type of work: Novel
Time: From 1937 to the death of the last galaxy
Locale: England and the cosmos

Using his "hypertelescopic imagination," the Narrator transcends the limitations of time and space and searches for the ultimate source of creation (the Star Maker) and for answers which relate man to this creator and the rest of the universe

> Principal characters:
> THE NARRATOR, an Englishman living in the suburbs of London
> BVALLTU, his traveling companion

Except as a prose narrative drawing from the author's imagination more than from sources in history, *Star Maker* scarcely meets the requirements of a novel. In his Preface to the work, Stapledon remarked that *Star Maker* "is no novel at all." Plot is nonexistent; there are no characters. The Narrator, seemingly a rather prosaic married Englishman, becomes a mere disembodied point of view ultimately identified as "I, the cosmic mind." The setting is the entire cosmos and the time frame is approximately five hundred billion years, from the creation of the cosmos to the complete physical quiescence of the universe.

Stapledon described his book as "an imaginative sketch." And while there is some reference to various scientific principles and theories — the Big Bang theory of creation, relativity, the Dopler effect, and so on — it is primarily a work of fantasy rather than science fiction. Perhaps *Star Maker* is most appropriately described as Stapledon's attempt to construct a myth based on known or plausible attributes of man and his universe, a myth consistent with scientific understanding. In the Preface to his earlier novel, *Last and First Men* (1931), Stapledon described a "true myth" as a vision which, given a specific culture, attempts to give voice to the loftiest ideals of that culture.

This is Stapledon's purpose in *Star Maker*. The myth takes the form of a quest, a search not so much for knowledge about the cosmos and man's relationship to it, as for the proper attitude which should come as a result of this knowledge. The Narrator begins in isolation, ignorance, and bitterness. With an act of will and "hawk-flight of the imagination," he becomes both part of a community of questors, and eventually an aspect of the cosmic mind as he makes the spiritual voyage to confront the Star Maker (the "absolute spirit" in all things) in order to have the meaning of the universe revealed. He "awakes" back on earth, enlightened with knowledge which will help him and the rest of mankind to endure the dangers of the present and furnish guidelines for the future.

In something resembling a mystic trance, the Narrator moves away from earth. Traveling at speeds much faster than light, this "disembodied, wandering view point" visits innumerable worlds and establishes telepathic contact with various beings. This mental intercourse allows him to live through the experiences of his hosts and to grasp the reality of the alien worlds. Moving initially to worlds essentially similar to his own, he and his traveling companion, Bvalltu, are able to travel through time as well as space and visit many strange worlds, staying sometimes for days, sometimes for centuries — observing the cycles of progress and regression, lucidity and ignorance, love and hate, civilization and barbarism.

One of the more interesting worlds they visit is a sea-world inhabited by a symbiotic race of fishlike creatures, "ichthyoids," and spiderlike crustaceans, "arachnoids." After eons of competition and war, these creatures "moulded" one another to create a "well-integrated union." The Narrator compares this society to the human race and argues that it was mentally more flexible and had a greater capacity for community. The complete union of the dual race came about when it developed telepathy and genetic research, two essential activities which the Narrator suggests are necessary for man to overcome his limitations, to achieve true community, and to "wake" to the meaning of the cosmos. The themes of telepathy and genetic research recur in Stapledon's other works also.

In his travels, the Narrator comes upon worlds populated by sentient beings whose collective personality is the consequence of a group rather than a single individual. In this world, the basis of intelligence is sometimes a flock of sparrowlike creatures whose individual bodies are linked as a single individual with human intelligence. The Narrator visits other worlds composed of plant-men, organisms simultaneously animal and vegetable. In many of the worlds he visits, he finds situations and problems similar to those which threaten the Earth. These worlds are able to solve their problems only by overcoming both a pernicious individualism and a traditional "tribal spirit" (nationalism). In the fortunate cases, these societies "awake" — a central image in all of Stapledon's works — to a "new lucidity of consciousness and a new integrity of will" in order to create a world community, communistic in essence and permitting the expression of the general will of the inhabitants. The Narrator observes that this awakened stage is perhaps the happiest of all the ages throughout the existence of a world. In turn, these societies develop into galactic Utopias whose inhabitants work to "awaken" themselves more fully, contact and "awaken" other galaxies, and increase the self-awareness of each individual "world spirit." All this is accomplished through telepathy, which unites the whole galaxy.

At one point, the Narrator and his companions merge to form a "single mobile view-point" and travel back in time to the birth of the stars. In the beginning, it is discovered that stars somehow are alive after some worlds attempt to move their neighbor stars out of their customary orbits, only to have the stars nova. The Narrator says, "Stars are best regarded as living organisms." Each star is conscious of other stars as conscious beings. The stars' purposes are basically twofold: to participate in discovering the nature of the cosmos, and to "execute perfectly their part in the communal dance." This latter activity recalls the medieval and renaissance notion of the music of the spheres. In his *Religio Medici* (1643), Sir Thomas Browne (1605-1682) writes,

> For there is a music wherever there is a harmony, order or proportion; and thus far we may maintain the music of the spheres; for those well ordered motions, and regular paces, though they give no sound unto the ear, yet to the understanding they strike a note most full of harmony.

The stars dance to this music. Ultimately, they connect telepathically with the minded worlds and establish the galactic mind. Finally, the Narrator discovers that even the nebulae are "conscious," and that they relate to one another by gravitational action and light pulsation. Indeed, the entire universe is one interconnected organism, all part of the Star Maker's creation. In the initial explosion creating the millions of galaxies, each galaxy was hurled apart, but each remembers and feels itself a part of the single spirit of the whole.

In coming to this understanding, the Narrator seeks to confront the source of all creation, the Star Maker, and, for an instant, manages to get a glimpse of the star of stars:

> I saw, though nowhere in cosmical space, the blazing source of the hypercosmical light, as though it were an overwhelmingly brilliant point, a star . . . this effulgent star was the centre of a four-dimensional sphere whose curved surface was the three-dimensional cosmos.

The Narrator is crushed by his love and longing for a union with this infinite spirit. He worships the Star Maker, but is not loved in return, as the Star Maker neither loves nor needs love. The Narrator realizes the "rightness" of this experience. It is appropriate for the creature to love the creator, but it would be narcissistic for the creator to love its creature, for that would be merely to love part of itself. The Narrator finally realizes that "the virtue of the creature was to love and to worship, but the virtue of the creator was to create, and to be the infinite, the unrealizable and incomprehensible goal of worshipping creatures."

Continuing with the metaphor of the Star Maker as artist, the Narrator tries to relate "the myth of creation," and here he is at an even greater loss for words. His description must be symbolic and take the form of myth and parable; yet he relates the activities of the Star Maker moving from juvenile and immature creation to mature creation. His first cosmos is a "toy" of mere rhythm; others follow, some nonspatial, some without time, some with simultaneous temporal dimensions which might or might not overlap, and some with life. In his mature creations (of which our cosmos is one), he made creatures which were free and recalcitrant to his own purposes. This marked a climax of sorts in his creative activity — "And he saw that it was good." However, the Star Maker moves on to create cosmos after cosmos, some almost totally inaccessible to the mind of the Narrator. Finally, he has a chance to see the ultimate cosmos — a cosmos standing in relation to our cosmos as we stand in relation to a single atom. Even here, however, its creatures suffer grief and agony; but as he protests, the Narrator understands that this is as it should be, and he is filled with mixed emotions — horror and anger, yet acceptance, and even praise. He learns that the Star Maker's temper is not one of sympathy but of contemplation. His creatures live not to be loved or hated — although this is included — but to be appraised by their maker. This is as it should be; this vision of the eternal spirit compels adoration.

The climactic encounter over, the Narrator wakes up back on his hill in the suburbs of London. The anxieties and uncertainties remain. The world's madness is closing in upon him, and he understands that the magic circle of community built up in his relation with his wife is the only certain foundation upon which to build. In lines reminiscent of Matthew Arnold's poem "Dover Beach," the Narrator sadly describes the world's delirium as it seems to be rushing headlong into a new, more horrible catastrophe than World War I. How does one confront such times? The Narrator has learned that he must be guided by two principles: first, to strive for a human community and second, to awake to the "hypercosmical reality" revealed in the Star Maker, to struggle to win some additional increment of lucidity before "the inevitable darkness."

The movement of the novel is in the Narrator's attempts to overcome his sense of spiritual crisis, to come to a state of wakefulness. This crisis has essentially two dimensions: the need to overcome those obstacles which keep man from realizing some kind of true community with his fellow man, and the necessity of putting oneself in harmony, in the correct spiritual attutude toward the universe. It is a movement from protest and rebellion to acceptance and serenity. The mechanism for the resolution of the crisis is the imaginative voyage itself, which lets the Narrator see all of experience from a godlike perspective. Thus, in his visit to the Other Earth and his experience with the Other Men, whose culture is based on taste and gustatory experience, the Narrator is able to witness the horrible effects of racism — each race insisted that its unique "flavor" was the only valid sign of spiritual worth — of industrialism, of ethnic prejudice, and other farcical events which suggested life on earth. The idiotic behavior of the aliens constantly gives the Narrator an opportunity to compare events on this world to events on Earth. The invention of radio-brain-stimulation on Other Earth provides an opportunity for the Narrator to explore the dangers of mass communication and mass culture as it is used for propaganda and brainwashing and for creating the Other Fascism.

Time and again, the Narrator sees race after race struggle to achieve the "bliss of true community" only to fall short because of the folly of either individualism or the mob-spirit. The cyclic pattern becomes universal; a race emerges from barbarism, progresses to a point of lucidity, and then, through some folly or general loosening of will and integrity, civilization takes a downward spiral into almost subhuman savagery, only to begin the cycle again. The Narrator questions the meaning of all that he sees.

Finally, the inability to grasp the significance of man's life, the awareness of man's insignificance compared to the stars, the realization of the ultimate impermanence of Utopia, and the eventual death of all that is valuable, coupled with the vision of his creator coolly contemplating the suffering and ultimate death of his creations, stirs the Narrator into spiritual rebellion. The other movement of the novel is the movement to overcome this protest. In addition to teaching his readers the nature of and need for true community, the Narrator learns how to justify the Star Maker's ways to man. Ultimately it involves questions of evil, suffering, and death, which are resolved when seen from a cosmic perspective.

Stapledon's message was essentially the same in all of his works. Seen from a cosmic perspective, man indeed may be of a very low order of existence, and this point of view makes all the difference. We do not condemn others for not allowing insects to live out their full life because we are not convinced of the intrinsic worth of an insect's life; we are able to accept the death of some animals because we do not credit them with cosmic importance. However, we are convinced of our own importance. But from the cosmic perspective, the assumption that man is the ultimate order of creation seems absurd and based on failure of imagination. As Stapledon explained in his *Philosophy and Living* (1939), it is ridiculous for man to demand that the universe be moral, that God be good. We must learn to deal with the seemingly logical conflict between our two fundamental religious experiences, between moral protest which attempts to alter the universe and the cold clear ecstasy of acceptance, the tragic view of life.

In each instance, the Narrator's moral protest to what he regards as wholly alien to the cosmic spirit is seen to be a manifestation of pride, selfishness, or simply ignorance. He learns to accept the perfection of the spirit. He learns that the Star Maker may seem hostile to the less-awakened, but to those who have attained lucidity, the entire tragic drama is not only necessary but also a source of joy. There is no question that the basic attitudinal frame of *Star Maker* is one of acceptance. The individual accepts, even welcomes the final defeat. On several occasions, the Narrator witnesses the effects of passive resistance and death. Rather than defend themselves or retaliate, in the process wounding their communal spirit, whole worlds choose annihilation. Yet they die praising the universe, the Star Maker, the Star Destroyer. Just before his death, Stapledon published *A Man Divided* (1950) in which he argued that nothing is merely lost in pain and suffering, that the agonies as well as the joys "are gathered up in the whole single music of existence." We must view the human condition from the point of view of the Star Maker.

Yet with its mind-boggling imaginative *tour de force*, this is a rather curious message for a science fiction novel. Published on the eve of World War II and foreshadowing some of the Nazi horrors, the novel abjures the fervor of moral protest in favor of a passive acceptance and a celebration of a detached acceptance and contemplation. Using the Narrator's own metaphor, life is turned into art. The Star Maker is an artist; his worlds are artistic creations. Because they have a structure, a beginning, middle, and end, these universes can be contemplated as aesthetic objects. However, they can be seen as such only from a standpoint outside history, from the standpoint of eternity. From inside the work, from the point of view of history, the final curtain has not fallen. There are still choices to be made and potentialities to be realized. This is the arena of action, not contemplation. Man creates his future; history is nothing but man acting. Can man afford the luxury of viewing life as if it were a complete work of art, as if it were finished?

The tragic view of life assumes the existence of limits, finalities, and absolutes. Science fiction, while recognizing limits, is essentially the fiction of the possible. There are few limits and fewer certainties; there is almost always that not-yet-existing future where almost anything can happen. With all of its incredibly fertile possibilities, *Star Maker* is essentially a conservative work. Like Oedipus, in Sophocles' tragic drama, the Narrator learns that man and, indeed, the entire cosmos are rather limited phenomena. He learns that freedom and even joy come in man's recognition of his "awakening" to necessity; and, in that awakening to lucidity, he will rejoice.

Criticism:

Moskowitz, Sam. *Explorers of the Infinite: Shapers of Science Fiction*. Cleveland: World, 1963. This general sketch examines the themes of Stapledon within the traditions of science fiction.

STRANGER IN A STRANGE LAND

Author: Robert A. Heinlein (1907-   )
First book publication: 1961
Type of work: Novel
Time: The early twenty-first century
Locale: Earth (area once known as the United States), Mars, and "Heaven"

A satirical view of human behavior observed by and involving the first human being born on Mars, who returns to Earth to claim his birthright; he founds a church which combines both of his upbringings and which results in his martyrdom

Principal characters:
> VALENTINE MICHAEL SMITH, the Man from Mars, "archangel Michael"
> JUBAL HARSHAW, a doctor, lawyer, and hack writer who unofficially adopts Michael
> GILLIAM BOARDMAN, a nurse, then Michael's lover and chief apostle
> BEN CAXTON, a newsman who helps rescue Michael from hospital isolation

Stranger in a Strange Land is a curious book which marked the shift in Robert Heinlein's fiction away from the extrapolative, mimetic mode he had helped to develop, toward the querulous philosophizing and garrulous cuteness of his later novels. Though critics might carp, the move proved commercially successful. As social upheavals in the 1960's led to revaluations of life and literature, social organization, and science fiction, Stranger in a Strange Land itself became an underground classic, the first "best seller" to emerge from the science fiction genre.

Perhaps more complicated than complex, the novel depends at least partly for its effect on readers' fastening on to one of its contradictory strands to the neglect of others. While commentary within the book seems to make it "about" any number of things, the central concerns are the conduct of life and the establishment of general authority. Thus the framework of the narrative is the age-old myth of the dying god, on which are strung at least three familiar subsidiary storylines.

The strand which introduces the book is the cops-and-robbers adventure story, with science fiction gimmicks of the 1930's and 1940's (aerocabs, videophones, programed kitchens) constructing a "nostalgic" future. Smith, orphaned child of *three* parents from an ill-fated expedition to Mars, where he was reared by the Martians, is returned to Earth and held in protective custody by the world government. Risking their jobs and lives, Ben Caxton and Gilliam (called Jill) Boardman spirit him away to the mountain hideaway of Jubal Harshaw, who engineers Smith's freedom and begins the task of educating him in human customs.

The second strand is the *Bildungsroman*, the novel of education or development, which takes Mike from social childhood to maturity as he learns about people, laws, customs, money, love, manipulations, religion, and, finally, laughter. Strand three, developed simultaneously, is a satire of human customs, with special relevance to the mid-twentieth century as seen in futuristic guise from the alternating vantage points of Mike and Jubal, each of whom has some claim to be the novel's title character.

The dominant thread, however, is the myth of the dying and resurrected god, surrounded by attendant apparatus. Beginning "Once upon a time" in traditional fairy-tale fashion, the book presents a reworking of the mythical hero: orphaned in infancy and reared by strangers, he is brought back to his rightful kingdom, where he makes peace with his "father," wins the hand of more than one fairy princess, begins to reorganize society, hands down codes of behavior, and prepares for his martyrdom. His adopted father, Jubal, is his toughest convert, but once he has been won over by Michael's self-sacrificing and the efficacy of his teachings, he turns to spreading the gospel by writing a book of roughly the same scope as this one.

Smith's teachings of the Martian language and the magical-mystical powers of the mind it unlocks are sold to the public in the guise of religion, since churches are relatively free from regulation and public censure. In its carnival-like presentations, Mike's church takes its teachings from Jubal's writings and from Mike's life on his own after leaving the safety of Jubal's roof, but it is clearly a delicious parody of mass-marketed Christianity, the Church of the New Revelation (Fosterite). Although Fosterites are burlesqued in Heinlein's presentation, Jubal recognizes their legitimacy as a church which brings about the happiness it promises. Mike's Church of All Worlds promises — and delivers — even more, and is always treated with respect in the narrative.

Although its teachings are supposedly rooted in Martian language concepts, they are very close to literal readings of various human scriptural injunctions. "Waiting is," "I am only an egg" and "grokking to fullness" have the qualities of Eastern wisdom to them, for they are alleged to belong to a long-lived, egg-laying, ghost-dominated, alien race. However, taking literally such Christian commandments as "love one another" and "this is my body; take and eat" leads to consequences which would not have pleased the Church Fathers, much less their cultural descendants. Love and sex are shared in common by members of the church's inner circle; rather than "waste food," moreover, the friends of someone who has departed (such as Mike at the end of the novel) practice ritual cannibalism.

Central to the religion is the verb "to grok," which gained wide currency in the 1960's. Literally it means "to know, completely, holistically," which has traditional mystical associations that Heinlein made use of earlier in his career. Knowing completely, however, seems to mean to know the divine presence in someone else, and in yourself, so that he finally translates the term as "Thou Art God," another catch-phrase made popular by the novel. Assuming such divinity, moreover, gives one the ability to sense good or evil, as ultimates, in a thing or another person and even the right or the obligation to rid the world of that in which one "groks wrongness."

This is the most controversial of Smith's teachings, especially in terms of its effects on the real world of the novel's audience. Granted that in the story Mike is superhuman, perhaps even an angel granted that in the text death is not an ending, but rather a shift or translation to another plane of existence. However, the perfection of his followers, in both the novel and its audience, may be in doubt. They are left with the possibility of actions followed by bloody consequences without the assurance of a comic Heaven offstage. There have been, in fact, followers of the book's purported teachings for whom free love, "water sharing," and even ritual killing have seemed justified. Also, there were fascinated readers in the younger generation for whom this wish-fulfillment fantasy was at least a vicarious answer to a society which demanded their sacrifice in an Asian land war, which opposed their protests against that war, and which tolerated assassinations of political leaders who might have stopped it.

A scriptural acceptance of the novel, however, disregards the strands of parody and satire, the ironic distance between Mike and Jubal and the narrator, and the libertarian patriotism of the author. Since so much is mocked in the novel, and the tone toward Mike's church is almost reverent, it is relatively easy to forget the difficulty such a church would face in the real world — without a fabulously rich "angel" as its founder and patron saint. Even though Jubal becomes a reluctant convert after Mike's martyrdom and apparent spiritual resurrection, Jubal's strictures against organized religion, his sense that this religion is fit only for angels, and his dissatisfaction with the humorlessness of church members all operate to undercut the literal acceptance of Mike's teachings, even within the text.

Outside the text, it should be obvious that there are no Martians, nor is there a bureaucratic Heaven where Fosterite "Archangels" (Church leaders) and Mike himself go after they "discorporate." Furthermore, since the book was written well before the assassination of John F. Kennedy and subsequent massive involvement in Vietnam, its political relevance to the 1960's can be at most that of a parable. And though the author might oppose the draft on libertarian principle, he also opposed pacifism, refusal to fight for one's country, and the kind of organized resistance to "legitimate" authority to which the reading of this book became linked.

Despite Heinlein's attempts to disassociate himself from what the book appeared to stand for, *Stranger in a Strange Land* is a very personal novel. Its structural concern, like those of Heinlein's "juvenile" novels with adolescent heroes, is with education for the proper conduct of life. Like its predecessors, it has two versions of the Heinleinian "competent man," an older and putatively wiser one in Jubal, a younger and supremely gifted one in Mike. But whereas the relationship between the two types was once straightforward, here it is fraught with difficulties. Jubal begins as Mike's mentor, the traditional adviser of hero myths and Heinlein juveniles. But the teacher becomes the pupil at the end; having done his part to create Mike, he is taken over by his creation despite his own skeptical rationality.

The significance of this structural reversal lies in the character of Jubal and his relationship to the author. Whereas in earlier books the focus was on the hero of the action, here the focus is dual. As the archetypal hero, Mike is the story, so to speak. However, Jubal is who it happens to, the major viewpoint character, who reacts to and rationalizes the actions of the Man from Mars. Although there is also an omniscient narrator, Jubal is implicitly the teller of the tale even before he begins to dictate his version at the end.

Jubal parallels Heinlein in a number of ways. He is a writer who revels in his commercial success. He is supremely competent — we are told. He is opinionated about everything, often iconoclastically. For the most part he is an unregenerate individualist. He was also born about the same year as his creator. Other parallels are more conjectural. Jubal is an intellectual who has learned to manipulate, rather than change his society. And he is a victim of *anomie*, rootless, lacking social norms and values, accepting only empirical evidence, and wanting something to believe in.

Michael gives him something to believe in, and Jubal accepts it in the end, but only after a long struggle. Mike's religion requires total commitment, up to and including death, which goes against the grain of Jubal's commitment — and Heinlein's — to the individual ego. For Jubal, as a writer, is a natural solipsist, recognizing his own free will, but not that of his characters or, in practice, that of his employees. Heinlein similarly has trouble breathing life into characters who do not fit his mold of the "competent man," and has shown his fascination with the theme of solipsism in other stories as well as this one.

Reading Heinlein into Jubal gives us a sense of the author's struggle for control of this novel. Knowing his own creative participation, like Jubal's in the forming of Mike, he is led by it to a directive contrary to his own survival as controlling consciousness. A drive to reassert control can then be posited in the mocking openings of chapters told from the long view of the omniscient narrator, the Martians, or the figures in Heaven, which essentially disestablish any ground level of reality, and set the reader free to choose his own.

Such a process might explain, if not excuse, some of the aesthetic failures in the book, such as its vacillating tone, its arbitrary changes of viewpoint, and its indeterminate position on the message that it carries. It suggests, too, why subsidiary characters, even ones as important as Ben and Jill, may not be believable human beings: they are not real to begin with in Heinlein's imagination, so they can simply serve several plot functions for the sake of narrative economy.

But the strength of the story and of the metastory — that subtext of who is to be master, author or material — certainly surmounts many of these problems for the reader who is caught up in the same problem as Heinlein was, of why life is worth living. If one does not accept the essentially authoritarian answer represented by Valentine Michael Smith, there is still plenty of entertainment in the chase, in the satire, and in the longing for omnipotence and omniscience which the book at least partly satisfies on a vicarious level.

Criticism:

Cansler, Ronald L. "*Stranger in a Strange Land*: Science Fiction as Literature of Creative Imagination, Social Criticism, and Entertainment," in *Journal of Popular Culture*. V (Spring, 1972), pp. 944-954. Cansler discusses *Stranger in a Strange Land* as an example of changing cultures.

Christopher, Joe R. "Lazarus, Come Forth from that Tomb," in *Riverside Quarterly*. XXIII (August, 1975), pp. 190-197. Christopher concentrates on the structure of Heinlein's work.

McNelly, Willis E. "Linguistic Relativity in Old High Martian," in *CEA Critic*. XXX (March, 1968), pp. 4-6. McNelly explores the pervasive religious theme of *Stranger in a Strange Land*.

Plank, Robert. "Omnipotent Cannibals in *Stranger in a Strange Land*," in *Robert A. Heinlein*. Edited by Joseph D. Olander and Martin H. Greenberg. New York: Taplinger, 1978, pp. 83-106. Plank calls *Stranger in a Strange Land* "innovative," but not Heinlein's best work in this analysis of the novel.

Slusser. George E. *Robert A. Heinlein: Stranger in His Own Land*. San Bernardino, Calif.: Borgo, 1976, pp. 17-33. Slusser discusses Heinlein's use of personal power in *Stranger in a Strange Land*.

THE SWORD OF RHIANNON

Author: Leigh Brackett (1915-1978)
First book publication: 1953
Type of work: Novel
Time: The near future, and one million years in the past
Locale: Mars

Bearing the mythic sword of Rhiannon, Matt Carse is cast one million years into the Martian past to work out both his own fate and that of Rhiannon, the ancient "Cursed One"

Principal characters:
> MATT CARSE, a well-respected archaeolgist turned renegade and grave robber
> BOGHAZ HOI, an ancient Martian thief of Valkis, companion and ally of Carse
> LADY YWAIN, an ancient Martian princess of Sark, first the adversary and then the beloved of Carse
> RHIANNON, an extremely ancient Martian, known as the "Cursed One" because he gave knowledge and power to lesser Martians

The Sword of Rhiannon is very nearly a paradigm of much of Leigh Brackett's romance-adventure science fiction. Were it not for the mythic elements embodied in the story and the resonance of the major characters and incidents, one might be tempted to categorize the work as "space opera." But the elements of familiar myths are interwoven in original ways and, given the brevity of the novel, the sometimes stereotypal main characters ring true. So, although the work requires a fairly strong "suspension of disbelief" and certainly has enough swashbuckling action, it transcends the limits of "space opera."

There are five attributes which, together, make *The Sword of Rhiannon* a significant work of literature in addition to a well-told story. One is the fine construction of the narrative; Brackett's prose is subtly rich in connotation, so that the brevity of the book results in neither a thin plot with sketchy characters nor a series of telegraphic sentences the meaning of which must remain simple and superficial. The narration is utterly to the point, with no digressions to complicate the plot; what is told is told fully if briefly.

The simplicity of plot and verbal economy result in evocative glimpses of various alien life forms and also in a peculiar variation on the kind of character Brackett seems to prefer in her adventure-narratives. In *The Sword of Rhiannon*, readers discover a number of races which evolved independently on Mars: the native human Martians found in many of Brackett's stories about the Low Canals; the half-human, half-serpentine Dhuvians who become extinct by the end of the tale; the half-human, half-seallike Swimmers who must be the prototypes of the "children of the sea" in the *Ginger Star* trilogy; and the half-human, half-avian Sky Folk who also appear, somewhat changed, in that more recent longer work. Within the world created by *The Sword of Rhiannon*, these halfling races are interesting because they postulate, on Brackett's Mars, a theory of independent evolutions to sapient life and because they reveal the richness of Brackett's imagination.

Most of Brackett's readers are familiar with Eric John Stark, the son of Earthborn human parents orphaned very young and then reared by the non-human natives of Mercury's twilight belt, finally to become a renegade merce-nary with his feral upbringing almost always in conflict with the patina of civilization that is his heritage as a man. Brackett wrote about Stark before she created Matt Carse, but it is apparent that Carse is a variation on Stark, differ-ing from him primarily because of the demands of *The Sword of Rhiannon*. Carse is, if compared to Stark, a bit too civilized (though "the primal ape" in him comes to the surface more than once); but because *The Sword of Rhiannon* tells of an archaeologist's dream as well as an adventurer's, the narrative re-quires a protagonist with a formal education and some success in the discipline of archaeology, for only an archaeologist could recognize the authenticity of the sword of Rhiannon, its inestimable value, and his own subconscious wish to go, literally, back into the past he has studied and imagined.

In addition to a strong, intelligent, resourceful hero, a tight narrative con-struction, and a number of evocative characterizations, *The Sword of Rhiannon* has a fourth literary attribute, its setting, which makes the book a notable one. Implicit in most of Brackett's fictions about Mars is a long and mysterious past (with great cities and kingdoms the ruins of which make grave-robbing a pur-suit of the avaricious and not only the activity of ghouls). The Mars of the not-too-distant future — where the beginning and end of *The Sword of Rhian-non* are set — is an incredibly ancient and still-dying world, where the vertical succession of seaport ruins attests to the inexorable evaporation of a great body of water. All that is left is a vast arid depression, some few canals the only remnants of a great sea, and decadent Martian towns — Jekkara, Valkis, Bar-rakesh — still clinging to life and old ways next to the black waters of the Low Canals. Brackett's *The Secret of Sinharat* reveals the ability of some of the very ancient Martians to perpetuate their individual lives by transferring their life-essences to younger "hosts" when their most recent bodies grow too old and frail. What *The Sword of Rhiannon* adds to this familiar Mars is a vicari-ous experience of its past; when Matt Carse first scrambles out of the tomb of Rhiannon he knows, because of his archaeological background and the evi-dence of his senses, that he has somehow traveled back to a warm, moist, green, fertile Mars that could not have existed fewer than a million years be-fore his birth.

The first ten pages of the novel establish the setting as Brackett's familiar Mars: late at night in the dark streets of Jekkara, Matt Carse hears someone following him and allows his pursuer, an unsuccessful grave-robber of Bar-rakesh, to fall into his ambush in a deserted part of the Low Canal town. When Carse forces Penkawr to take him to the treasure that the little native Martian claims to have discovered, the two make their way into the higher, older part of Jekkara — the long-abandoned seaport — and the setting itself foretells Carse's journey into the past. Seeing the treasure that Penkawr has hidden in the ruins, Carse immediately realizes that the sword is the sword of Rhiannon and that Penkawr has discovered the tomb which many believe to be mere legend; Carse demands a two-thirds share of the profits and Penkawr, angry at the Earthman's arrogance but well aware of Carse's ability to sell artifacts at higher prices than a Low Canal thief, grudgingly agrees to the terms of the partnership.

The influence of setting on plot becomes more apparent when the two arrive at Rhiannon's tomb. Inside, surrounded by artifacts as well-preserved as they are ancient, Carse seems to fall into a trance of archaeological awe. Penkawr takes advantage of the other's inattention, and pushes Carse into a black sphere of nothingness in the actual burial chamber. Helplessly, feeling confusion, disorientation, and some strange probings that seek to force their way into his conscious mind, Carse sinks into what must be a bubble in time; when he emerges from it, still holding the sword that lured him, Carse digs his way out of the tomb and looks out upon the setting of his real adventures, out upon a strangely transformed Mars.

It is the Mars of an archaelogist's dream: greenery surrounds him, the breeze is moist and warm, and the port of Jekkara gleams on the edge of a great sea. Matt Carse has traveled a million years into the past.

Throughout the remainder of the story, this ancient Mars determines most of the strictly arranged incidents of the plot at the same time that it explains away most of the mystery that seems to shroud the Mars of Brackett's more usual temporal settings. What happens is simple enough: Carse makes his way to Jekkara, becomes entangled with Boghaz Hoi of Valkis, and becomes with Boghaz a galley slave on a ship of the Lady Ywain, princess of Sark. Expectedly enough for a Brackett hero, Carse then kills the Dhuvian who was Ywain's chief protection, leads a successful mutiny, and, keeping Ywain as prisoner, heads the vessel west to the home of the Sea Kings of Khondor. There he meets Emer, sister of the ruler of the Khonds, a young woman who spends much time with Swimmers and Sky Folk and who (perhaps because of this association) telepathically detects a trace of Rhiannon in the recesses of Carse's mind. The plan Carse proposed — to go to the tomb of Rhiannon and bring its treasures to Khondor — fails and, because a group-entry into Carse's mind reveals that he does indeed harbor the spirit of Rhiannon the Evil One, Carse is condemned to die and plans are laid for a mass attack by the Sea Kings upon Sark. But trusty Boghaz the master-thief brings Carse the sword of Rhiannon and they escape, taking Ywain with them, just before the news of Carse's "possession" and its threat becomes universal knowledge among the Khonds.

While imprisoned and awaiting his death, Carse permits Rhiannon to communicate with him. He learns that the ancient spirit had been waiting more than a million years to undo his sin, that he cannot except with Carse's consent wholly possess the Earthman's person, and that Rhiannon is the one guise under which Carse may hope to obtain his freedom. So Ywain, Boghaz, Carse, and the non-Khond oarsmen of the Sark vessel leave Khondor; closely pursued by the fleet of the Sea Kings, they barely make it to Sark; once there, with Carse pretending to be Rhiannon reincarnated, they take Ywain's father and go to Caer Dhu so that Rhiannon may reclaim the miraculous technology he gave the Dhuvians. At precisely the crucial instant, Rhiannon does take charge of Carse's being (the Dhuvians knew what Carse did not: that the halflings of Caer Dhu had turned against their benefactor and used his weapons against him), and destroys Caer Dhu and all its inhabitants. In a moment of panic, Ywain's father runs into the field of Rhiannon's weapon, dies, and leaves Ywain the ruler of Sark. But neither she nor her people want her to rule, so, after letting Boghaz use his part in the destruction of the Dhuvians to set himself up as king of Valkis, Carse-Rhiannon and Ywain return to Rhiannon's tomb. They witness the return of the Quiru and the liberation of Rhiannon; they step into the bubble of time, guided by a grateful Rhiannon, and step out into the Mars of Carse's lifetime. Carse has Rhiannon's sword and the woman whose courage never failed her, and Ywain has the man she desires and a world, though now dying, that is still her own.

The story as related here is clearly melodramatic, and so would the book be, if its plot were its dominant feature. But *The Sword of Rhiannon* is more than melodrama: even the plot is structured carefully around Rhiannon and his sword, and two other attributes — its use of mythic elements and its evident influence on subsequent science fiction — raise the novel well above the level of "space opera."

After a superficial reading, one cannot help recognizing the Prometheus myth: rebellious Rhiannon gives to the Dhuvians knowledge and power against the wishes of his fellow Quiru, and for his act is imprisoned alive in a time-defying tomb. Then there is the *Prometheus Unbound* analogy, since Rhiannon does in the end obtain both the forgiveness of the other Quiru and the freedom to join them as an equal. The Dhuvians are quite literally the children of the snake, and not much imagination is needed to connect them with the serpent of Eden. Once this connection is made, Rhiannon's godlike qualities make him into a type of Lucifer, though his return to temporal Mars in order to set things aright once more is reminiscent of the harrowing of Hell. If one seeks meaning from these mythic elements by supposing there to be a one-to-one relation between each myth and *The Sword of Rhiannon*, one will find only confusion. What is notable about the novel is Brackett's use of various myths for artistic reasons — and results — of her own.

At one level, Rhiannon is Prometheus, but he is "bound" by his fellow Quiru and his own mistake in judgment (a tragic character), and "unbound" by his sincere repentance and the will of an Earthman (a comic character in the sense that a comic plot is resolved by reintegration with one's society). That the comic and tragic *mythoi* coexist in *The Sword of Rhiannon* is evidence that Brackett refuses, thematically, to accept and then depict a fictional world wherein good and evil are as simplistically separable as black and white. This thematic ambivalence is also apparent in Brackett's depiction of the Dhuvian halflings; they are children of the serpent, true, but they are the ones who are tempted and succumb — they are hardly, even in their dealings with Sark, Tempters in their own right. If Mars under Dhuvian rule is analogous to some sort of Hell, then the dual-natured Carse-Rhiannon who restores the world to the peoples of good will is analogous to the divine-and-yet-human Christ who released all those souls from the Hell to which only their Original Sin of being human condemned them. As for Lucifer, Rhiannon is his antitype, because his *"Non serviam"* is directed to the luminous Quiru: he disobeys precisely in order to do service to the lesser beings of Mars. And once the technological nature of his service is recognized, a more modern myth appears: "technology without good will and wisdom is a tool of destruction."

Recognizing these mythic elements in *The Sword of Rhiannon*, yet refusing to be detailedly exegetical about them, one can still appreciate Brackett's use of myth. For one thing, she makes each element of myth — not each myth itself and in its entirety — serve its purpose in her narrative. For another, she captures the subconscious attention of her readers by providing characters and incidents very closely related to the psychological truths, the veracity of which are (in Western cultures) universally accepted. Thus, *The Sword of Rhiannon* is at its surface a fast-paced entertaining narrative of adventure and is at its deeper thematic levels a narrative that compels readers' attention because it addresses itself to matters important to the subconscious parts of their minds. In such a thin volume, Brackett's words seem to do a great deal.

A final noteworthy attribute of *The Sword of Rhiannon* is its influence, both on Brackett's subsequent works and on the works of others. Thematically, the destruction of Caer Dhu and the consequent waning of Sark suggest the truth that, though good may conquer evil, some of the good must be lost even in victory (this is the same truth that pervades *The Lord of the Rings*: though Sauron is defeated, Middle Earth must pass away). In the context of Brackett's other Martian fiction, the destruction of Caer Dhu explains the decadence of "modern" Mars. Having the technology of Rhiannon for ages and controlling the empire of Sark, the Dhuvians kept the rest of Mars from developing its own technology; once the Dhuvians were annihilated, the other peoples of Mars had to fall back on their static ways, and these ways were insufficient to cope with the inexorable changes — like the evaporation of the sea — that, for want of intelligent intervention, ground Martian civilization down to the level of the Low Canals. So, *The Sword of Rhiannon* is the distant background in Brackett's other Martian tales.

The cohabitation of one body by two minds (when Carse is literally at the command of Rhiannon within him) and the prevalence of telepathy and other psychic powers (always by the agency of some jewel) would not seem so notable if Marion Zimmer Bradley's *Darkover* novels did not rely so heavily on what is suggested in *The Sword of Rhiannon*. Bradley's Darkovan telepaths each have a matrix jewel or starstone to focus and amplify their psychic powers, and it is a common Darkovan practice to embed a matrix jewel in the hilt of a sword. With just these two facts in mind, it is difficult not to remember the several mentions of a smoky jewel, almost with a life of its own, in the hilt of Rhiannon's sword. It is equally difficult to perceive the incident in which Emer, using her black pearl like a Darkovan telepath, first discerns the presence of Rhiannon within Carse as inconsequential. And when she and six of the wise ones (three Swimmers, three Sky Folk), using a large cloudy jewel — it is even called "the stone of thought" — to bring their minds together, to force the great Rhiannon to admit his presence in the mind of Carse, it becomes clear that the scene is virtually the prototype of Bradley's matrix circles.

By virtue of its finely constructed plot, its appropriate characterization, its rich setting, its use of mythic elements, and its effect on subsequent science fiction, *The Sword of Rhiannon* must be considered an important book.

THAT HIDEOUS STRENGTH

Author: C. S. Lewis (1898-1963)
First book publication: 1946
Type of work: Novel
Time: The mid-twentieth century
Locale: England

The conclusion of C. S. Lewis' Perelandra Trilogy, in which the lords of the unfallen planets intervene on Earth, Merlin reawakens, and Arthur's successor unites their forces to prevent the establishing of a dictatorship in Great Britain

> *Principal characters:*
> ELWIN RANSOM, a former university professor of philology
> MARK STUDDOCK, a fellow in sociology at Bracton College
> JANE STUDDOCK, his wife
> MERLINUS AMBROSIUS, the magician of Camelot
> JOHN WITHER, Deputy Director of the National Institute of Co-ordinated Experiments

C. S. Lewis was in every respect an unusual man: among the many sides of his personality were those of world-respected scholar of medieval and Renaissance literature and avid reader of science fiction. He had little patience with those who saw the two interests as contradictory; he enjoyed science fiction without condescension, applying the same standards to Martian or medieval romances alike.

That Hideous Strength forms the third part of Lewis' "space trilogy," following *Out of the Silent Planet* and *Perelandra.* But the term "space" is misleading: the setting of *That Hideous Strength* is entirely in England, and as Lewis himself pointed out, it can be understood without having read the earlier two works. It demonstrates, better than the first two parts of the trilogy, Lewis' mastery of what might be called synthetic mythology: putting together bits of earlier traditions to form a new, satisfying, and complete whole. Better than any other of his works, *That Hideous Strength* shows that the past, in the hands of an artist who knows and respects it as Lewis did, is alive and powerful.

A prominent skein from the past in Lewis' weave is the picture of the eldils. It is wrong to consider them angels in the sense of the rosy cherubs of quattrocento art. Only if we use "angel" as a generic term meaning any noncorporeal intelligent being, will it serve to categorize Lewis' creations. The author's source for the eldils was medieval angelology, which, following the fourth century writer, Pseudo-Dionysius, reckoned nine orders of angels, each with specific functions. Among the concerns of the angels were the planets, each of which was associated with a spiritual being in a relationship analogous to that of the body to its soul. Far from being only a part of theology, these angels held an important place in the theory of physics. Thinkers before the announcement of Newton's Laws of Motion observed that things kept moving only as long as force was applied; the continuous motion of the planets therefore required a continuous application of force, and the angelic powers were postulated as the source of the motive energy. This idea brought a satisfying symmetry to the picture of the universe: just as humans had individual guardian angels, and as nations had principalities watching their affairs, so also did the planets have their tutelary spirits, or "powers." Lewis borrows some details of this scheme for his trilogy, utilizing the planetary powers as his eldils, beings of great might and energy. But he made some changes, too.

Whereas Dante had suggested that the power ruling Earth was Fortuna — chance — Lewis amended the system to include elements of the Eden story by identifying the ruling power of Earth as Satan. Since that spirit's rebellion, Earth had been cut off from communication with the rest of the beings of the solar system; hence, it is "the Silent Planet." Finally, the use of the powers provided Lewis with a connection to the most popular mythology of our time (although he had no notion that it would become so) — *The Lord of the Rings* by his friend and colleague, J. R. R. Tolkien. The powers, or eldils, of Lewis' Thulcandra, Malacandra (Mars), and Perelandra (Venus) are the same sort of being as Tolkien's Valar.

Like the eldils, who appear in all three parts, the figure of Elwin Ransom serves to unite the parts of the trilogy. Ransom, a philologist like Tolkien, undergoes an astonishing transformation through the three books, as if Lemuel Gulliver were to turn into Lord Wellington. We first see Ransom as a vacationing professor, a little tweedy, between thirty-five and forty years old. During his stay on Mars in *Out of the Silent Planet*, he is fearful, bumbling, and more than a little comic. He is also principally an observer. The second volume, *Perelandra*, turns Ransom from an onlooker to a participant, as he struggles with the possessed body of Weston, his kidnaper in the first work, and succeeds in keeping the Earth's rebellion from spreading to Venus. During that volume Ransom grows considerably in inner strength and dignity, and at its conclusion he receives a wound. Upon returning home, he realizes that his wound, like that of Frodo in *The Lord of the Rings*, will not be healed on Earth.

Already it can be seen that Lewis' imagination worked well at selecting pieces from a variety of sources, borrowing the resonances of those sources, and adapting them to his own purposes. Ransom's wound adds still another mythology to *That Hideous Strength*: that of Camelot. In the final book, Ransom acquires another name, Mr. Fisher-King, bringing us again into the atmosphere of medieval romance. Although Lewis could have had a variety of sources for this detail, the one which most closely resembles *That Hideous Strength* is *Parzival*, a thirteenth century poem by Wolfram von Eschenbach, and the source as well of such diverse later renderings as Wagner's *Parsifal* and parts of T. S. Eliot's *The Waste Land*.

The Fisher King in Wolfram's *Parzival*, Anfortas, is wounded like Ransom, and the fertility of his land suffers as a result. Wolfram makes Anfortas gather around himself both an order of celibate knights (Ransom is unmarried) who carry out dangerous missions, and a group of chaste women who serve the Holy Grail. Like the Fisher King, Ransom is surrounded by an aura of magic: radically changed by his experiences, he now appears as a robust youth of twenty or so; he speaks to animals and communes regularly with the eldils; and throughout the novel he directs the activities of the band he has assembled.

But Ransom is no longer the central figure: his wound has made him immobile, and, more important, his near-apotheosis takes him somewhat out of the human sphere. Because he has become less understandable to ordinary mortals, Lewis has wisely moved him to the periphery of the action. At the center of the story is a more ordinary couple, Mark and Jane Studdock. The structure of *That Hideous Strength* depends on a careful arrangement of opposites in this conflict of good and evil, and that pairing process extends even to the Studdocks. Feeling the emptiness of her marriage and a rising fear of its failure, Jane is drawn with reluctance to the circle surrounding Ransom at St. Anne's-on-the-Hill, while her husband Mark edges toward complicity in the work of the National Institute for Coordinated Experiments (N.I.C.E.) at Belbury. They are each attracted and repelled by what they find in their new surroundings, and we see the progress of the plot to its climax chiefly through scenes in which they figure.

The conflict in the plot is provoked by the villains, the officers of N.I.C.E., who have been as misunderstood by some readers as has the angelic machinery. For instance, J. B. S. Haldane, the eminent biologist, saw N.I.C.E. as a caricature of and attack on science itself. He pointed out that the only real scientist in the novel is repelled by the Machiavellian plans of N.I.C.E., refuses to have anything to do with the organization, and is murdered by its Security Police. Haldane, as innocent of literary insight as he was of political judgment, missed the whole point. Preeminent among the leaders of N.I.C.E. are not physical scientists, whose link with reality is maintained by contact with their subjects, but behaviorists: psychologists, sociologists, and politicians. And even these disciplines are represented by corrupted examples. Lewis' point is not that science *per se* is a threat to humanity, but that any threat to human freedom and dignity will, in these times, present itself as scientific, just as in an earlier age it might have presented itself as religious.

Thus the leaders of N.I.C.E., bureaucrats rather than scientists, seek power, not knowledge. And one source is as good as another. If science will not give them all the power they want, they are willing to turn to magic. The Institute has located in Belbury, near a small college, on the strength of information that Merlin lies sleeping nearby, and is soon to awaken. If they could manage to win the half-demonic Celt to their side, their plans would proceed even faster. But they are frustrated when Merlin revives before they expect and joins Ransom's group at St. Anne's.

Merlin is one of the Lewis' most successful characters. He is soundly and convincingly from another time, barbaric in some ways, yet at the same time direct and more honest. He is both humorous and awe-inspiring, and at the same time manages to cement into place the two myths mentioned earlier. As a living, breathing figure from Camelot, he brings with him all the suggestions of splendor and tragedy from the Arthurian cycle. But he points us in another direction as well: we find out that the language Ransom uses with him is the speech of Atlantis, the True West, the Numenor of *The Lord of the Rings*. While Ransom and Merlin speak, the shades of Arthur and Gandalf hover nearby.

The villains are likewise well drawn. The Devil worship carried on in secret by the leaders of N.I.C.E. represents their total rejection of human values. If their plans succeed, they will form the Inner Party of an Orwellian dictatorship, beginning with England, but eventually clutching the whole Earth, and even the other planets. The comparison with *Nineteen Eighty-Four* is not adventitious; in *That Hideous Strength* we see Oceania in the making. Had Haldane looked clearly, he would have noticed Lewis' plain identification of the real villain: an attitude in philosophy that Lewis traces through Hegel and Hume and the Logical Positivists, an attitude that trickles down to popular thought as the notion that all human behavior is relative, and no actions are good or bad in themselves. Lewis argues that when such principles are embraced, only the ruthless will prevail. What begins in N.I.C.E. as a series of experiments on animals is but a prelude to similar ones on prisoners (in the name of rehabilitation), in which the methods for control of the general population will be worked out.

The brilliant characterization on the side of evil, matching that of Merlin, is Lewis' portrait of John Wither, Deputy Director of the Institute. Wither is the consummate opportunist. Throughout the many scenes in which he appears and the many speeches which he utters, he never commits himself to a statement. With the practice of years he has so guarded himself from engagement with his fellows that he has trimmed away his own being little by little, until his own bodily existence is not much more than a relative thing. As a portrait of evil he reminds one of Screwtape, the senior devil in Lewis' *The Screwtape Letters*, and the picture is all the more frightening when we realize that Wither has done this to himself with his eyes open all the way.

Fortunately, Wither and his henchmen do not succeed. They fail for two reasons. First, Weston's invasions of Mars and Venus in the first two novels have broken the quarantine, and the powers of the unfallen planets can act on Earth in self-defense. The second reason, equally as important, is that despite the philosophy of N.I.C.E., there is a reality beyond situation ethics: nature herself turns against them.

Throughout the novel, the villains, especially Wither, have prostituted language and its outlets: one of the aims of N.I.C.E. is the control of newspapers and radio, and one of Mark's first assignments is the manipulation of public opinion through a campaign of lies. Similarly, inhumane experiments on beasts have formed a major part of their work. At a climactic banquet scene, the directors and supporters of N.I.C.E. are subjected to a second confusion of tongues. As they discover that Babel has come again, the experimental animals escape from their cages and ravage the guests. The narrator points out that their aims have succeeded in an unexpected way: they wanted language divorced from meaning, and now they have it. As they were no respecters of the persons of the beasts, so the beasts return their treatment. The scene closes as it began, with reminiscences of the Old Testament: the village, the site of the new Tower of Babel, now suffers the fate of Sodom and Gomorrah.

In gathering together strands from a variety of sources, the story Lewis weaves benefits from the colorful richness of medieval philosophy, the tales of King Arthur, the Old Testament, and *The Lord of the Rings*. *That Hideous Strength* caps a trilogy that begins on the loom of science fiction, showing, if any further proof were needed, that the genre provides an adequate framework for a tapestry of any subject, especially if the weaver has the skill of C. S. Lewis.

Criticism:

Hilton-Young, Wayland. "The Contented Christian," in *Cambridge Journal*. X (July, 1952), pp. 603-612. Hilton-Young analyzes the mythmaking employed in *That Hideous Strength* and compares Lewis to other modern religious novelists.

Moorman, Charles. "Space Ship and Grail: The Myths of C. S. Lewis," in *College English*. XVIII (May, 1957), pp. 401-405. Moorman looks at Lewis' use of Arthurian mythology in *That Hideous Strength* and compares its treatment to the cosmic myth of the first two novels in the trilogy.

Norwood, W. D. "C. S. Lewis, Owen Barfield and the Modern Myth," in *Midwest Quarterly*. VIII (Spring, 1967), pp. 279-291. Norwood finds that the romantic fantasies of the earlier Lewis novels shift to a historical realism in *That Hideous Strength*.

Spacks, Patricia Meyer. "The Myth-Makers Dilemma: Three novels by C. S. Lewis," in *Discourse*. XI (October, 1959), pp. 234-243. Spacks criticizes the science fiction framework in *That Hideous Strength* for trivializing the Christian meaning for the non-Christian reader.

TWO PLANETS
(AUF ZWEI PLANETEN)

Author: Kurd Lasswitz (1848-1910)
First book publication: 1897
English translation: 1971 (abridged)
Type of work: Novel
Time: The 1890's
Locale: The North Pole, a space station, Mars, Europe

A conflict between Earth and a materially and morally superior Martian civilization organized along Kantian lines, ends in a peaceful reconciliation between the worlds

Principal characters:
> HUGO TORM, the head of a German attempt to reach the North Pole by balloon
> ISMA TORM, his wife
> KARL GRUNTHE, an astronomer and another member of the expedition
> JOSEF SALTNER, a natural scientist, the third member on the balloon trip
> LA, the Martian woman who falls in love with Saltner
> FRIEDRICH ELL, an enigmatic astronomer who advanced the money for the Polar expedition; a Martian-human halfbreed

During his lifetime, Kurd Lasswitz was sometimes compared to H. G. Wells and Jules Verne, but he neither reached the prominence of these two men, nor gained their influence. Although not of their stature, he is nevertheless an important European pioneer of science fiction. His novel *Two Planets* is a genuine interplanetary classic, a book that has been translated into many European languages and is still in print in Germany. His other works have been largely forgotten; he wrote a number of short stories, other fantasy novels, and popular and philosophical essays. Lasswitz's first work of fiction was *Bilder aus der Zukunft* (1878) which combined two tales, one rather short and one longer, the first of which, "Bis zum Nullpunkt des Seins," was first published in a newspaper when Lasswitz was twenty-three years old. This humorous story inspired Claes Lundin to write the Swedish science fiction classic, *Oxygen och Aromasia* (1878).

Lasswitz also wrote one of the first theoretical literary essays on the principles of science fiction, "Uber Zukunftsträume," which is included in his collection of essays, *Wirklichkeiten* (1900). He called such stories "scientific fairy tales," defended the use of science as the subject matter, and set out to write such stories himself, in the volumes *Seifenblasen* (1890), *Traumkristalle* (1902), and the posthumously published *Empfundenes und Erkanntes* (1920). Most of these pieces are quite slight, hardly more than thinly fictionalized popular essays, but some are charming fairy tales and quaintly scientific stories introducing original concepts that recur later in science fiction by other authors. Even Jorge Luis Borges read Lasswitz, and his story "Die Universal-bibliothek" (translated in Clifton Fadiman's *Fantasia Mathematica*, 1958) served as an inspiration for Borges' own "The Library of Babel."

Some of Lasswitz's fairy-tale-like and often sentimental fantasy novels show the influence of the panpsychic ideas of the German philosopher Gustav Theodor Fechner, who even attributed souls to heavenly bodies and plants: *Aspira* (1906), subtitled "the novel of a cloud," and *Sternentau* (1909), "the plant from Neptune's moon," are today almost unreadable. *Homchen* (1902), however, first published together with *Traumkristalle* in a volume entitled *Nie und Immer*, is a spirited animal fable from the prehistoric past of Earth.

The book for which Lasswitz has become famous is, however, the two volume interplanetary novel *Two Planets*, which combines rocketry with Utopian ideas. Lasswitz's principal inspiration in this novel, as well as in his discursive writings, was Immanuel Kant and the German Idealism of writers such as Friedrich von Schiller. It is not a faultless novel; it is perhaps somewhat schoolmasterish, but it is a laudable and largely successful attempt to infuse philosophical ideas into a space novel. Although Lasswitz's novel appeared in book form in the same year H. G. Wells's *The War of the Worlds* was serialized in *Cosmopolitan*, his Martians are not BEM's, but appear quite human. Technologically they are advanced far beyond mankind, and they are above all morally superior beings. They clearly differentiate between duty and inclination, following the Kantian ideal; they do not allow themselves to be governed by their passions, and therefore they are truly free. Their guiding principle is the development of the autonomous individual personality, the free determination of the individual. Martian society is a personal Utopia, a permissive society where happiness and freedom of the individual human being are more important than the organization of the politics. Not the greatest good for the greatest number of people, but the highest possible development of the individual consciousness is the society's goal. Lasswitz had little interest or understanding of the social movements of his time, the problems of the masses.

Mars is a loose confederacy of small and big states — republics and monarchies mixed, capitalist, socialist and even Communist societies coexisting side by side — and the form of government may at any time be changed by a simple vote of the population. Or, since many homes are mobile, a Martian may simply take his house and remove it to a place and a country more to his liking. By penalty of loosing his franchise, every Martian has to read at least two newspapers a day, including one of the opposition. Mars is a truly enlightened community, far above the quarrels and conflicts of backward Earth. In reality, however, the superior Martians are not immune to corruption; they become corrupted by their own power over the humans, arrogant and tyrannical, infected by "Erdkoller." Soon they become divided among themselves into parties: the Philobaten ("Ba" being Martian for Earth; the "Baten" are the humans) consider the Earthmen more or less their equals, granting them the right of self-determination; while the Antibaten are shocked by conditions on

Earth and feel that human beings are a dangerous and inferior breed and must be held in check.

The novel opens with a balloon flight to the North Pole, undertaken by the scientists Saltner, Grunthe, and Torm. It is financed by the enigmatic Friedrich Ell, who has prepared a Martian-German dictionary. Later he is revealed to be the son of a German mother and a Martian spaceship captain who crashed on Earth. This beginning was probably inspired by the Swede Andrée's unsuccessful and fatal attempt to reach the North Pole by balloon in 1896. The three explorers reach the pole without difficulty, but find that they are not the first to be there. The Martians have already erected a circular ground station, while a space station hovers 6356 miles above the pole. Airtight cars move in an "abaric field" or a field of antigravity between the two stations. The explorers are caught in this field, and their balloon is drawn towards the space station. Torm escapes by parachute, and Saltner and Grunthe are saved by the Martians and shown the wonders of their advanced technology. Grunthe later returns to Europe to warn the world of the arrival of the Martians, while Saltner, who soon falls in love with the beautiful Martian girl La, visits Mars.

The Martians are greatly handicapped by Earth's much stronger gravity (a difficulty later overcome by transportable abaric fields). This aggravates the first interplanetary diplomatic incident when, after having captured two Martians, a British gunboat opens fire on a Martian airship built for movement in the Earth's atmosphere. The British refuse to submit to a Martian ultimatum and are captured by the Martians, who have meanwhile transported a whole fleet of airships to Earth. Europe becomes a Martian protectorate, and human beings are subjected to compulsory reeducation after their armies have been disbanded. For practical reasons, Russia and the United States are at first left alone. The Martians, however, are soon corrupted by their own power and begin to behave like petty tyrants, holding in contempt the people they are supposed to raise to their own cultural level.

Discontent grows among the humans. A "Menschenbund," in which Saltner and Grunthe play prominent roles, rallies under the battle cry of "Numenhood without Nume" ("Nu" is Martian for Mars, and the "Nume" are the Martians. Linguistically, the novel is not far advanced; almost all of the Martian proper names are monosyllabic). This party accepts the benefits of the higher culture and the goals of the Martians as their own, but they resent the alien interference and want to develop autonomously. When huge new taxes are to be levied and the United States also becomes a protectorate, a secretly built American air fleet rebels, capturing the Martian polar stations and the Martian fleets on Earth. Rather than resort to genocide (although there was a plan to stop the rotation of Earth around its axis), the Martians return to the moral principles they abandoned, and a peace follows that benefits both worlds.

Thus *Two Planets* was one of the first science fiction novels to explore fully the clash of different cultures. The Martians are not depicted as extraterrestrial monsters but as a more advanced stage of humanity. They serve as a mirror and a promise of what mankind's own future might be to "Ko Bate" (poor humankind), as well as ultimately serving as a warning against arrogance and intellectual pride. This ameliorating aspect of the novel is not quite successful, however, because the book is didactic rather than dramatic, containing flat characters and marred by the clichés of conventional love stories. The novel is much better in its purely discursive passages which have a winning lucidity, and it also presents many technological ideas of note.

Lasswitz may not have been the first science fiction writer to have introduced space stations (both Edward Everett Hall and Konrad Tsiolkovsky were earlier), but independently of the others he arrived at the same idea and went on to develop fully the space station as a sort of stepping stone and relay station for interplanetary travel. His space station is designed like a wheel, which anticipates the satellites suggested by later writers on astronautics. It hovers above the pole, because the rotation of Earth causes no complications. Lasswitz's spaceships, built of the gravity-free material "stellit," move by a combination of the shrewd use of gravitational forces (traveling in astronomical orbits between the planets) and supplementary rocket power ("repulsit" shots that move the spaceship in the opposite direction). The mechanics of space travel are described accurately by Lasswitz, who was by profession a mathematician. The Martians also possess a sort of ray gun, the telelyte, that sets off catalytic reactions of a chosen kind in the target; an interplanetary telegraph using light rays; and a telescope with electrical amplification. Martians can look into the past by observing the light signals produced by the occurrence a long time ago. The "geography" of Mars more or less follows Percival Lowell's ideas: the canals on Mars are used to bring the rare water from the poles. Solar energy is collected in the deserts (and solar plants are erected on Earth later; what the Martians mostly want from Earth is energy), and energy serves as currency. The Martian households are fully automated. The Martians either live in skyscrapers distributed along the canals (which do not, however, form cities) or in small movable houses. Food is prepared synthetically. All Martians are required to labor for one year in the working force, but they have no compulsory military service and possess (until their contact with Earth) only a small police force.

Mars is then, a veritable Utopia, specifically, a technological Utopia where the machine serves man and does not enslave him. Freed from labor, the Martians can pursue artistic endeavors. The ultimate art form on Mars is one that relies on the most intimate and highly regarded sense, the sense of feeling. *Two Planets* thus reconciles science, the arts, and philosophy in a personal Utopia governed by Kantian ideas and presents an important depiction of the clash of two cultures in science fiction. Unfortunately, Lasswitz was at best a respectable but not a great writer. His writings lack the mythic beauty and dramatic immediacy of the best work of Wells. And while the important books of Wells are today as vital as ever, Lasswitz's novel is but an interesting minor landmark in the science fiction tradition, more to be applauded for its ideas and its ambition than its literary execution.

Criticism:

Hillegas, Mark. "The First Invasions from Mars," in *Michigan Alumnus Quarterly Review*. (February, 1960), pp. 107-112. Lasswitz's *Two Planets* is compared to H. G. Wells's *War of the Worlds*.

"Martians and Mythmakers: 1877-1938," in *Challenges in American Culture*. Edited by Ray B. Browne, Larry N. Landrum and William K. Bottorff. Bowling Green, Ohio: Bowling Green University Popular Press, 1970, pp. 150-177. Hillegas presents a penetrating analysis of the myth of the Martians and their invasion of Earth particularly as it was shaped by Lasswitz in his *Two Planets*.

Rottensteiner, Franz. "Kurd Lasswitz: A German Pioneer of Science Fiction," in *Riverside Quarterly*. IV (August, 1969), pp. 4-18. This survey of Lasswitz' work shows that his utopias stressed the happiness of society gained through the development of the individual.

A VOYAGE TO ARCTURUS

Author: David Lindsay (1876-1945)
First book publication: 1920
Type of work: Novel
Time: The 1920's
Locale: England and Tormance

Accepting Krag's challenge to visit Tormance, the only inhabited planet of Arcturus, Maskull undertakes the quest for Surtur, who holds the secret of the ultimate

Principal characters:
   MASKULL, the natural man hero in quest of the ultimate
   NIGHTSPORE, Maskull's spiritual self
   CRYSTALMAN, the great spirit of illusion, the enemy known as Shaping
   KRAG, the guide who brings Maskull and Nightspore to Tormance, revealed finally as Surtur, leader of the sons of Muspel

David Lindsay's *A Voyage to Arcturus* is one of the original, enigmatic works of imaginative literature published this century. Critics have described it variously as science fiction, fantasy, allegory, and a philosophical novel. It is, perhaps, all of these and more. Throughout Maskull's adventure, there is the sense of strange things happening, of experiencing new orders of reality. Lindsay's purposes in the romance, beyond the creation of the extraordinary world of Tormance, are clouded by the vastness of the possibilities inherent in its structure. Lindsay invents such a world on Tormance as the reader has never before experienced. The incredible visual effects highlighted by *jale* and *ulfire*, two new primary colors peculiar to Tormance, the intensity of the character's feelings, and of Maskull's reactions to the ever-changing conditions and strange creatures of Tormance arouse wonder and awe in the reader, creating responses which can hardly be defined but which the reader somehow understands.

The story begins at a seance attended by Maskull and Nightspore, an evening's diversion for a society of dilettantes, at which the materialization of a youth takes place. As if by cue, Krag appears, wrathfully dismissing the spirit who responds with "a smile full of significance which, however, no one could understand." Krag, however, seems to understand and immediately breaks the neck of the youth, whose features twist into a "sordid, bestial grin, which cast a cold shadow of moral nastiness into every heart." Maskull is both appalled and fascinated. Incited by Krag, who promises to take him to a world where such goblins originate, Maskull agrees to go. Strangely, Nightspore identifies the hideous expression on the apparition as belonging to Crystalman and reveals that they are all going to Crystalman's world. Yet another mystery is added when Krag explains that Surtur, an authority figure, has gone before them and requires that they follow.

The three are to leave from Starkness Observatory by means of Arcturian "back rays," rays that travel back to their source. Before departing, three remarkable things happen. Krag shows Maskull through a glass that Arcturus is actually a double sun with a planet, Tormance, circling it. The second is the sound of ghostly drum beats, which are to both lead and pursue Maskull through his sojourn on Tormance. Third is a ritual knife cut on the arm given Maskull by Krag which enables Maskull to ascend the observatory tower, from which he can view Tormance and the dual suns. Prior to the cutting, Maskull was prevented by a strange gravity from ascending very far. At this point Krag cautions Maskull, telling him that he is merely an instrument to be broken, that his fate is connected to Nightspore, who is now asleep but who will awaken at Maskull's death. Krag warns: "You will go, but he will return." When Maskull appeals to Nightspore, he is told that Surtur is the master who knows the meaning of these things. In a storm of anxiety and wonder, Maskull leaves for Tormance.

Maskull awakens on Tormance alone and is not to encounter Nightspore again until he reaches Lichtstorm, although he does encounter Krag on occasion. Maskull is rescued and sheltered by two natives, Joiwind and her husband Panawe. Maskull learns that the dual stars have different names and different natures: the white star is Branchspell and the blue is Alppain. He soon grows three new sense organs which heighten his perceptions of tenderness, kindness, and warmth. Ironically, Joiwind and Panawe for all their kindness do not really have a true understanding of Crystalman's world.

Lindsay's success is extraordinary in rendering the various regions and races of Tormance. Each race has its own vision of truth, its own hierarchy of ideals and values. In different ways each vision has an element of truth, but the understanding is distorted and often misdirected. Maskull, therefore, is allowed a true vision in his journey only from Krag or from Surtur's revelation of himself as a storm and his declaration that Maskull was brought to Tormance to serve. However, neither Maskull nor the reader is prepared to understand these revelations, and they are perceived vaguely as foreshadowings. As Maskull moves from region to region, he finds himself thinking in new ways, developing new senses, experiencing new emotions, and behaving instinctively and at times compulsively according to the customs of the country, however savage or strange.

Maskull's behavior on Tormance is oddly contradictory. Although he is a natural man, a hero of the sort we find in Germanic legend, he seems at the same time strangely detached from his own experiences and actions. Perhaps this is the inevitable result of the allegorical division of Maskull-flesh versus Nightspore-soul. Maskull does learn eventually that Crystalman, the shaping spirit of Tormance, is responsible for the development of all the sense organs and the accompanying modes of being and experience. He also comes to appreciate that Tormance is a world in the throes of early experimental development. Everything seems to be charged with new forms of life and overflowing with energy.

Maskull's inconsistency, his failure to have a mind of his own once on Tormance, the sense of drift in his actions serve to emphasize two themes. First, it appears that it is not only what one believes that changes but also that truth itself, indeed, reality, is various. Maskull's understanding of these processes is fragmentary at best. He develops an uncertain picture pieced together from fragmentary and often erroneous evidence. As Maskull follows the mysterious lead of Surtur toward Lichtstorm, he seems to be moving upward from the physical to the spiritual plane, from love of pleasure to acceptance of pain. Maskull's encounters, therefore, are not so much designed to produce knowledge or understanding as a new state of awareness; for in the end, the great truths he learns depend on suppression of his will, his self-consciousness, and his own identity.

During his journey through Wombflash Forest, Maskull learns from Dreamsinter that he came to Tormance like a Prometheus to steal Muspel fire, "to give a deeper life to men — never doubting if your soul could endure that burning." Indeed, Maskull alone cannot endure, but Nightspore, Maskull's spiritual self, is victorious after Maskull's death. Maskull learns that Crystalman has worked to prevent Maskull's recognition that the world of Crystalman is the false world of Shaping. He learns that the apparition at the seance was actually himself being strangled by Krag and that it was a foreshadowing of his own death.

As Maskull lies dying in the arms of Krag on Surtur's ocean under rising Alppain, he reaches his highest degree of self-understanding — "I am nothing." But Krag, who will be revealed to Nightspore as Surtur, adds the greater truth of revelation — "You are Nightspore." Maskull's destiny was, therefore, to die on Surtur's ocean and to bring Nightspore, his soul, to a rebirth under the blue sun. It seems clear at this point that Tormance is a world in which consciousness and environment are interactive and mutually dependent and that the symbiosis includes both conscious and unconscious faculties.

Under Krag's directive insistence, Nightspore, now mysteriously reborn in Maskull's death, climbs a second tower toward the ultimate revelation that was denied Maskull. He discovers that the spirit light of Muspel passes through the body of Crystalman, who feeds upon it and who transforms the light into all the varieties that make up existence. In short, Crystalman is a small body which casts a great shadow, and the world he shapes changes and dances so that Crystalman may feel joy. Nightspore learns further that there is both a divine reality and a divine plan, that there is a battle going on, a deadly serious one, between the power of Crystalman to deceive and the power of Surtur to make truth known. The Maskull-Nightspore quest confirms that Krag speaks truly when he says that he is mightier than Crystalman.

Just what Nightspore is supposed to make of his new understanding is not clear. He has been reborn and evidently not for the first time. He and Krag are to return to earth to take up the struggle against illusion and the false worship of the world that Crystalman makes. Nightspore will not forget the lesson of Krag-Surtur, whose final revelation is that Surtur is known on earth as pain.

Much of the great imaginative power displayed in Lindsay's work is derived directly from the progression of adventures that carry us through Maskull's quest. The world of Tormance is convincingly brought to light. Its inhabitants are compelling creatures and not grotesques despite their unique sense organs and their allegorical origins. Perhaps not since Edmund Spenser and John Bunyan have allegorical characters been so astutely handled, but Lindsay's characters seem to represent a new iconography. The landscapes are exciting, plausible, and often wild with an alien beauty. Moreover, the geographical and ecological systems are admirably adapted to each adventure. Thus in creating a secondary reality and in compelling our imagined belief in that creation, Lindsay's story is a spectacular success.

The impact of Lindsay's romance depends in part on his treatment of ideas. The victory or the quest achieved by Maskull is the loss of self and the total rejection or repudiation of will in pursuit of the Platonic ideal. It is difficult to say whether Maskull's self-recognition as nothing should be taken as a pun, a kind of religious hyperbole, or the partial truth of a metaphysics rooted in Crystalman's world. Whatever the case, Maskull's release comes from his straining to penetrate that world to reach truth. It is a release that permits Nightspore to carry on the rebirth process.

One view presented numerous times and as often rejected is the sentimental or modern humanist belief in the beauty of the world as an expression of the creator. The Western ideals of beauty, love, goodness have been falsified by Crystalman or Shaping. What is left, it seems, are truth and reality, which are one, and which are really only known to us on earth through pain.

Another important aspect of this romance is the mythic. It seems that Lindsay fabricates his own mythos with its roots drawing on the occult, on classic and Norse mythology, on Western and Eastern religions, especially Christianity and Buddhism, on medieval legend, and on science fiction, presumably seen as a new form of mythology. Lindsay was himself a student of the occult and of Kabbalistic lore. *A Voyage to Arcturus* resists any attempt to fit it into a traditional mythic pattern, although it seems more Germanic than classical, more Manichaean than Christian in orientation. If Lindsay is indeed offering the reader a new mythos, it is a myth of two worlds, of duality and therefore one whose structure challenges the reader's expectations of familiar patterns.

Related to the mythic patterns that Lindsay uses are the elements of allegory. At least the pattern of action seems to be that of a symbolic allegory of man's search for ultimate truth and reality. Maskull and Nightspore represent body and soul, the soul alone achieving ultimate truth after the death of the body, which belongs to Crystalman. In fact, in these terms, the soul would be born to life, purged from the corruption of earth and the flesh; and these are the very terms in which Krag instructs Nightspore at the end. The case for allegory is strengthened by the profusion of allegorical names used by Lindsay. But the names themselves puzzle because they are doubly rather than singly allegorical, oblique rather than direct, many of them suggesting contradictory meanings or strange new forms of metaphor in names like Tormance, Branchspell, Alppain, Wombflash, Ifdawn and so on. They tease us out of thought.

It is risky to venture beyond the basic allegorical frame, but it seems that on a wider scale of measurement the allegory is one of death, birth, and reincarnation, which sets itself to dramatize in symbolic terms the successive states from conception to birth as psychic as well as physical.

If this is allegory, perhaps it represents a new type, blending myth and psychology. Suppose there is a consciousness of another order, gradually forgotten after birth, which is a period of interlife. If that is what Lindsay is giving us here, it seems possible that *A Voyage to Arcturus* is at least in part an attempt to exercise such a racial memory or unconscious recognition by means of a symbolic or archetypal pattern which would therefore seem to us to mean a great deal more than it says.

C. S. Lewis praised Lindsay's achievement in *A Voyage to Arcturus* for generating that idea of "otherness," doing so by drawing on the world of the spirit, the only other real world we know. Who could deny that? Perhaps Lindsay himself best described the grandeur of his work in the words of Earthrid, the music master, speaking of his music to Maskull:

> Now men when they make music are accustomed to build beautiful tones, because of the delight they cause. Therefore their music is based on pleasure; its symmetry is regular and charming, its emotion sweet and lovely. . . . But my music is founded on painful tones; and thus its symmetry is wild and difficult to discover, its emotions bitter and terrible.

Criticism:

Amis, Kingsley. "Adventures on a Distant Star," in *New York Times Book Review*. (November 24, 1963), p. 60. Amis finds *A Voyage to Arcturus* as less science fiction and more religious allegory.

Brophy, Brigid. "Rare Books," in *New Statesman*. XIV (June, 1963), pp. 904-905. Brophy is quite critical of *A Voyage to Arcturus* in which she observes "a displeasing smell of repression."

Russ, Joanna. "Dream Literature and Science Fiction," in *Extrapolation*. XI (December, 1969), p. 6-14. Russ analyzes *Voyage to Arcturus* as a typification of "dream literature," a schematic projection of daydreaming.

THE WANDERER

Author: Fritz Leiber, Jr. (1910-   )
First book publication: 1964
Type of work: Novel
Time: The near future
Locale: The Earth, Luna, the Wanderer, and space

An account of a strange planet's appearance near Earth, some of the violent consequences of that visit, and the reasons for the planet's coming and its going

> Principal characters:
> PAUL HAGBOLT, a publicist for Project Moon
> DON MERRIAM, an American astronaut
> MARGO GELHORN, Paul's friend and Don's fiancée
> DOC BRECHT, a piano salesman and a competent man
> ROSS HUNTER, a Professor of Sociology
> TIGERISHKA, a large feline
> MIAOW, a small feline

In the first sentence of *The Wanderer*, Fritz Leiber associates his novel with "tales of terror and the supernormal." Leiber's precise diction indicates both rhetorical intent and the basis of the novel's odd quality of lucid grimness. Terror, not horror, revulsion, or simple fear, is the chief response which the novel means to evoke; and the terrifying agency is the supernormal, not an incursion from beyond the natural world but a visitor from outside our narrow knowledge of the universe. In the course of the novel the moon is destroyed, cities and countries are devastated, and millions of people die; yet the cause of this appalling disaster is merely the carelessness of some hard-pressed, frightened people trying to free themselves from the policies of a profoundly conservative government. What Leiber tells us is often dismaying and sometimes perverse, but his smooth prose and calm narrative manner tend to mask the disturbing qualities of events until they have become memories rather than immediate observations. The resulting sensation is not unlike the discovery that one has been giving detached and judicious consideration to the aesthetics of vehicular manslaughter.

The central event of the novel is the appearance of a strange planet, the Wanderer, near the moon. Since it is about the same size as the Earth, its tidal influence is as much as eighty times greater than the moon's. The earliest effects felt on Earth are earthquakes and vulcanism. Los Angeles is ravaged by an earthquake and subsequent fires; Krakatoa explodes again. But the most destructive consequence of the Wanderer's approach is the magnification of the ocean tides. The Low Countries (the Imperial Valley, northern Siberia, Virginia, Maryland, the river valleys of England) are flooded. At low tide the Gulf of Tonkin is empty. At high tide, only the tops of Manhattan's tallest skyscrapers remain above water. Lake Michigan's three-inch tide increases to a four-foot tide in Chicago. The Pacific, aided by vulcanism, carves a canal through Nicaragua. Wherever the lands are low and the tides run, people drown.

The Wanderer also completely disrupts electromagnetic communications. The new planet not only has a magnetic field much stronger than Earth's, but it also emanates "influences" that strike Earth in straight lines, causing atmospheric ionization and other effects that render all wireless transmissions impossible. The tital effects are entirely a matter of physics, the result of large masses in proximity to each other. But most of the electromagnetic effects seem to be by-products of the Wanderer's identity and the reason for its visit. The strange new world is actually artificial, a voyager in hyperspace and a ship for the several races who live in its fifty thousand levels. It has entered our solar system to refill its fuel tanks.

The refueling process causes the most spectacular destruction resulting from the Wanderer's visit: the disintegration of the moon. When the Wanderer exits from hyperspace it is — evidently by its captains' design — only twenty-five thousand miles from the moon and captures that body gravitationally. The moon's new orbit soon brings it only twenty-five hundred miles from the larger world. This is well inside Roche's limit, the distance within which a satellite will be broken up by tidal forces, and the moon promptly shatters to fragments. As soon as the fragmentation begins, the crew of the Wanderer begins using some sort of gravitational or momentum fields to suck mile-thick strands of the substance of the moon into their huge vehicle's depleted tanks.

Leiber makes it plain that none of this havoc was strictly necessary; the Wanderer could as well have taken a Jovian satellite. As Paul Hagbolt, one of the major characters, infers, the people of the Wanderer were driven into their blundering actions by the fear of that which pursues them. The unveiling of the nature of that pursuer, together with the concomitant description of the condition of the universe, forms the novel's climax.

The narrative technique Leiber employs for *The Wanderer* is common to many disaster novels: short chapters, a large number of characters, and a frequently shifting point of view always in the third person. The episodic technique has several specific advantages. It suggests the comprehensiveness of the disaster. Since an individual caught up in such a cataclysm would scarcely apprehend much beyond his own situation, the multiple point of view is a plausible and efficient way to provide the reader with information. It also provides a variety of characters to attract the reader's interest and sympathy; thus it tends to sharpen the reader's interest in the question of who will live and who will die, enhancing the suspense. Leiber is careful not to dissipate these advantages by making no conflicting claims of equal importance on the reader's attention.

Clearly the narrative has one main line of development (with several branchings and confluences) and ten or twelve secondary lines, some of which end long before the conclusion of the novel, with the deaths of their point-of-view characters. Leiber puts these secondary lines to a number of uses. For instance, the very first effect of the Wanderer's appearance is the death of Asa Holcomb, whose heart bursts "with the wonder and majesty of it." Over two hundred pages later Leiber counterpoints the useless death of the novel's most competent man in a silly accident by flashing to the Arizona mesa where the vultures are stripping the last flesh from Asa Holcomb's face, "laying wholly bare the beautiful grinning red bone."

As in this instance, Leiber tends to juxtapose rather than connect incidents. Indeed, none of the secondary plot lines ever join either the main line or one another; in the universe of *The Wanderer* communion is never easy, common, or untroubled. But although Leiber refuses to integrate his plot — and by refusing suggests the necessarily fragmented nature of the experiences the novel describes — he insists upon certain other connections. Besides the obvious relationship of "terror and the supernormal" to death, Leiber demonstrates the sexual content of the Wanderer's significance to humans. When the visiting planet appears, Sally Harris is fulfilling her promise to Jake Lesher to "make the stars move" as they ride the roller coaster at Coney Island. The stars spin and shake — or seem to — as the Wanderer exits from hyperspace; Sally thinks she is the cause, and the appearance of the Wanderer itself a moment later is a bonus. For some people, like Richard Hillary and Vera Carlisle, sex is a solace amid tribulations. For others, sex and death seem almost indistinguishable. As they begin to drown in a subterranean military post flooded by the tides, General Spike Stevens and Coloney Mabel Wallingford simultaneously make love and strangle each other.

Leiber is frequently satirical but also not above diverting his readers in ways conventional to modern disaster novels. Yet the sexual incidents of the minor plot lines, together with such other divertissements as the gold-digging of Barbara Katz in Palm Beach, the treasure-hunting of Bagong Bung in the Gulf of Tonkin, the pot-smoking of Arab Jones in Harlem, the madcap terrorism of Don Guillermo Walker in Nicaragua, generate a mood and perspective for the central actions of the main plot line. The perspective is close to stoic, the mood is ironic, and the knowledge that emerges from those central actions is proper cause for melancholy — though not, Leiber's tone suggests, for despair.

The main plot line involves half a dozen primary characters and twice that many secondary figures. It begins in Southern California with Paul Hagbolt and Margo Gelhorn driving toward Vandenberg Two, a U. S. Space Force base, to watch a lunar eclipse. They are diverted by Margo's wish to look in on a flying saucer symposium on a nearby beach. The Wanderer appears while they are with the saucer students, and Margo remains with this little group throughout the rest of the novel. But Paul is taken aboard one of the saucer-shaped auxiliary craft which the Wanderer dispatches in a makeshift effort to alleviate the destruction it has inflicted upon the Earth. The saucer pilot uses a momentum pistol to deflate a tsunami wave threatening the saucer students.

Paul has just rescued Margo's cat, Miaow, from the water when the saucer pilot, dropping the momentum pistol, reaches out and hauls Paul and Miaow aboard the saucer. It is not exactly an abduction; the saucer pilot is a female alien of feline descent. She calls herself Tigerishka, and her interest was in Miaow, whom she assumed to be intelligent, rather than in Paul, the "monkey."

While these events are occurring, Paul's friend and Margo's fiancé, Don Merriam, is flying through the moon. Don, an astronaut, has escaped the quake-wrecked Moonbase U. S. in a Baba Yaga, a small rocket ship. By accident he does not quite achieve escape or orbital velocity, but as the Baba Yaga plunges back down, the moon shatters like a pebble in the gravitational field of the Wanderer. Unable to reverse his course, Don flies between the sundered halves of the moon. Issuing from this prodigious chasm he sees the Wanderer for the first time; he is captured and taken aboard. Later he is taken — or sent — on an odd, rather dreamlike tour of the traveling planet, a brisk survey of structure, crew, and resources that turns into a lesson which Don does not quite understand. Part of the message is clear enough: the sum of all there is and all there may be is very large. Don is shown a series of three-dimensional viewing tanks. In the first he sees our galaxy; in the second, the whole cosmos of which our galaxy is a tiny part. In the third this entire universe, identifiable by its incomprehensibly twisted shape, is represented as one among many universes, all of them appearing to be somewhat hypothetical.

The significance of the last stop on Don's tour is not as obvious to him. In a huge room, designed to resemble a natural planet, Don sees a felinoid (like Tigerishka) chase down and kill a unicorn. He sees a bird with topaz plumage killed and its blood sucked by another felinoid, who smiles at him as she feeds. The killers are strong and graceful.

Don's friend, Paul, would have less difficulty comprehending the scene; he spends two days with Tigerishka in her saucer. Under the influence of her growing sympathy for Paul and prodded by his sometimes pointed questions, Tigerishka eventually tells Paul of the Wanderer's origin and current plight. The planet is a "getaway car" for a cosmic lost generation, sailing the genuine void, hyperspace. Tigerishka's people — many races besides the felinoids — are desperately in flight from the plague of intelligence, the cancer of science, most of all from the ennui that comes when the intelligent application of science has made the cosmos safe for all except the Wild Ones. They run from a social order that envelops stars with artificial planets, whose conservatism is so effective that nearly all the stars are shrouded, their light trapped by the synthetic worlds.

"The universe is full, Paul. Intelligent life is everywhere, its planets darkening the stars, its engineers recklessly spending the power of suns to make mind's environment — burning matter to energy everywhere to make more form, more structure, more mind. The Word — to call mind that — goes forth, and soon there is nothing but the Word. The universe with all its great reaches and magnificent privacies becomes a slum, begins to die of too much mind."

The Wanderer runs for the potential freedom of hyperspace, and the police planets of the universal government pursue. In the end, one of them catches up, the Stranger, much larger than the Wanderer, all steel gray opposed to the Wanderer's flamboyant maroon and gold. A battle ensues; as the Wanderer seems to be losing, it flashes into hyperspace. Moments later the Stranger pursues again, and the incursion of the universe into terrestrial affairs ceases.

Leiber ends the novel flatly, with the touchdown of the Baba Yaga bearing Don and Paul at Vandenberg Two, where Margo and Ross Hunter (who have become lovers), together with the saucer students, have finally arrived. It seems an appropriately inconclusive stopping point; the Wanderer has merely gone on, its quest unresolved, its fate unknown, its only astronomically significant effect on the Earth a tiny lengthening of the sidereal day. In spite of its length, *The Wanderer* has about it somewhat the air of an incident sliced from life and displayed without comment — disaster as found art.

But Leiber has made his judgment of the Wanderer's significance in a characteristically perphrastic manner. Tigerishka's account of the Wanderer and the Wanderer's universe generates emotional tides between herself and Paul Hagbolt. In a welter of unclear but strong emotions, a tangle of loneliness, pity, Weltschmerz, and xenophilia, far and equidistant from Earth and Wanderer, monkey-man and cat-woman make love. Several chapters later, when Tigerishka brusquely refuses to let Paul come with the Wanderer, he asks her what she had felt the night before other than pity and boredom. In reply she slashes his cheek deeply with her claws. Don Merriam, a little dimly, recognizes the paradox: " 'I don't know, Paul, but if I were in love with a cat-lady, that clawing would be the one thing that would convince me she did love me back' "

In the universe of the Wanderer, now shown to be our universe, the intelligence that defines us, by which alone we survive, is also the agency of spiritual death and moral isolation. To live truly, to love genuinely, to encounter others are acts of violence. We must be as intelligent and as beastly as we can be.

WAR OF THE WING-MEN

Author: Poul Anderson (1926-   )
First book publication: 1958
Type of work: Novel
Time: 2426
Locale: The planet Diomedes, a hundred light-years from Earth

Shipwrecked far from the nearest human settlement on an aberrant planet, three people must find a way to survive both natural dangers and a war between two groups of nonhuman indigens

Principal characters:
NICHOLAS VAN RIJN, head of Solar Spice & Liquors
LADY SANDRA TAMARIN, heiress to the rule of the planet Hermes
ERIC WACE, factor for Solar Spice & Liquors on the planet Diomedes
SYRANAX HYR URNAN, Commander of the Fleet of Drak'ho
DELP HYR ORIKAN, his Chief Executive Officer
THEONAX HYR URNAN, son of the Commander
TROLWEN, Commander of the Flock

The adventure on a strange planet, one of the primary conventional science fiction forms, attracts both readers and writers by the freedom it appears to offer from terrestrial history, geography, and, perhaps, natural laws. But the poetic license for the maker of imaginary worlds is usually qualified by various constraints, some of which may be self-imposed by the writer. One constraint may be the sort of relation the other world bears to our own. Strangeness of certain kinds, as in the Barsoom of Edgar Rice Burroughs or the Perelandra of C. S. Lewis, displaces the work toward fantasy. Pretended but inauthentic strangeness, which cannot be exemplified here because the many works displaying it are justly ignored or forgotten, shows the other world to be merely Earth under an assumed name. Another sort of constraint may be the use to which the invented world is put. None of the planets in Isaac Asimov's Foundation trilogy is very exotic because none need be much more than an undistracting background for conversations or disputes among the characters, all of whom are human.

During Poul Anderson's long career as a science fiction writer, one of his most impressive talents has been for the creation of plausibly alien worlds. Although these inventions are based upon conventional astrophysics (and generally accepted biology, when the worlds bear life), none of the dozen or so planets whose features are crucial to plots or themes could ever be confused with Earth, nor could certain events for which they are the settings occur in terrestrial environments. In some of Anderson's fiction, these worlds are employed as devices to energize plots, as pirate gold energizes *Treasure Island*. Sometimes, too, the story seems to be mainly a vehicle for the depiction of an interesting, if hypothetical, cosmic specimen. But in *War of the Wing-Men*, Anderson's concern is the interaction of character and situation;

the plot of the novel is, essentially, the resolution of the confrontation between Nicholas van Rijn and the planet Diomedes.

Anderson devises somewhat artificial circumstances to make Diomedes a problem that van Rijn and his companions must solve if they are to survive. Returning from Antares to Earth, van Rijn and Lady Sandra Tamarin have stopped for a brief tour of some interesting Diomedean scenery. Eric Wace, trading factor on the planet for van Rijn's company, Solar Spice & Liquors, begins to fly them to one of the sites, but a bomb disables the aircraft, which crashes at sea. (The bomb may have been directed against van Rijn by a business rival or against Lady Sandra by a political rival; in either case, it is only a plot device.) The three survivors are ten thousand kilometers from the human settlement, with no way to cross the sea or to send a message for help. Their plight is aggravated by the fact that Diomedean life is based on proteins different from the earthly kinds; humans are, in a sense, allergic to the planet. The only food the three castaways have is what they can salvage from the wreck.

The divergence of biological evolution is unlucky, but it can hardly be unexpected. Diomedes, however, is a freak among planets, freakish in its composition, freakish in its movements. Its axial tilt of almost ninety degrees consigns each of its poles to half a year of darkness and appalling cold; its habitable regions extend only about forty-five degrees north or south of the equator. Its makeup is even less normal than its motion. Because of some oddity in the processes of its formation, Diomedes contains almost no elements heavier than calcium. Thus, although it has nearly five times the mass and over twice the diameter of Earth, its density is only half our planet's, and its surface gravity is only ten per cent stronger. But since the mass of Diomedes determines its gravitational potential, its atmosphere is much deeper and thicker than Earth's, thick enough to support true flying mammals, including some, the dominant species, almost as big and fully as intelligent as human beings.

The cultures of these intelligent Diomedeans have been shaped by the conditions of their planet. It is not a world that favors the development of an advanced technology. Light metals are abundant, but the Diomedeans have no way to exploit them; an electrolytic technology is a prerequisite for refining aluminum or magnesium, and copper or silver — much heavier than calcium — is a prerequisite for an electrolytic technology. The Diomedeans are fixed in an endless stone age.

Two groups of these indigens constitute the remaining element of the survival problem for the humans. The location of the crash is near the area where the land-based Lannachska and the seagoing Drak'honai are embattled. The Lannachska, like most Diomedean tribal groups, are migratory, spending the summers hunting at thirty or forty degrees latitude, flying to the equator for the winter to meet other groups and trade a little, and, chiefly, to mate. The Drak'honai live always on their rafts and boats. Since they have established permanent and continuous, if unfixed, homes, they have been able to develop a somewhat more sophisticated culture than the Lannachska, but the most profound difference between the groups is that the Drak'honai have no seasonal breeding cycle. Each "race" feels that the other is perverted and repugnant — indeed, utterly alien. They are at war because the Drak'honai, following a shift in the habits of the fish that is the staple of their diet, have invaded the sea near the Lannachska's summer home island. When the Lannachska returned from their annual migration, the Drak'honai, anxious for a secure port and detesting the cyclic breeders anyway, were already in possession of the Lannachska towns. For each group, defeat by the other means virtual extinction, and neither can divert any effort from the way to dispatch messengers on a long, dangerous mission for the succor of the humans. Thus Anderson has arranged a three-way struggle for survival, with the human case appearing the bleakest of the lot.

The character and abilities of Nicholas van Rijn provide the satisfactory resolution of the problem. When the novel was published as a serial in *Astounding Science Fiction* (and, later, when it was included in the interrelated collection *The Earth Book of Stormgate*), it was entitled *The Man Who Counts*. Its more familiar title emphasizes the main action of the plot, but the original title, the one Anderson preferred, emphasizes the organizing theme. The war is distinctly subsidiary to the survival effort; van Rijn manages to convert it into the means for saving himself and his companions.

Overtly, van Rijn seems ill-suited to deal with the situation. He is a huge man, tall and broad-shouldered as well as broad-bellied, and his manner is not one to instill confidence in his leadership or his capacity to meet physical dangers. As much gourmand as gourmet, drinker, smoker, wencher, and general sybarite, he honors St. Dismas, patron of thieves, and his entrepreneurial tactics are tempered only by his belief that making enemies needlessly is bad for business. His language is colorful, heavily flavored with tangled metaphors, *mal mots*, and distorted syntax; his dress is flamboyant but seldom neat; he appears heedless of details and method. Eric Wace grows more and more to regard him as a lazy, boorish, bossy, and selfish parasite. But the plot makes it plain (and Lady Sandra, spelling it out, finally, for Wace, spells it out also for the readers who have been along for the action) that van Rijn is the man who counts. From the time of the crash he labors unremittingly, though not always obviously, for survival, and he is able to turn even some of the least apparently tractable elements of the desperate situation effectively to his own purposes.

To emphasize his implicit argument that the most important survival skills may not be the most obvious ones, Anderson employs for most of the novel the obtuse viewpoint of earnest, efficient, competent, and unimaginative Eric Wace. In many respects, Wace is the character whom convention would expect to save the day. He is courageous and skillful; he designs and supervises the construction of the equipment and van Rijn offhandedly demands. He is clearly aware of what he accomplishes himself, since his efforts produce immediate and tangible results, but he cannot see that van Rijn accomplishes anything of substance. He resents van Rijn's brusque and generalized orders; he resents even more his appetite for the rapidly diminishing supply of terrestrial foodstuffs. Until the adventure is safely concluded and Lady Sandra takes an opportunity to enlighten him, he does not understand that van Rijn is both organizer and motivator of all that has been achieved. As van Rijn puts it, " 'My job is not to do what is impossible, it is to make others do it for me!' "

Van Rijn's basic method is an *ad hoc* pragmatism, to use whatever is available, to do whatever works. The most ingenious examples of his tactics are also the crucial events of the plot. For instance, near the beginning of the novel, the Drak'honai, wondering if the humans may be useful in the war, rescue them from the foundering skycruiser. Van Rijn soon realizes that because the Drak'honai already enjoy a strategic advantage, he and his companions will be more valuable to the desperate Lannachska. A Lannach herald and interpreter, Tolk, will carry a message to his commander if some way can be found for him to escape the Drak'ho fleet. Exploiting rivalries and class tensions among the Drak'ho officers, van Rijn sets off a minor civil war to cover Tolk's flight.

Later, using tactics and weapons suggested by van Rijn and developed by Wace, the Lannachska manage an uneasy stalemate with the Drak'honai. The two forces are so evenly matched that neither can overwhelm the other. But the Lannachska need soon to begin their preparations for the autumnal migration to the equator, and the Drak'honai still need fishing grounds. A climactic battle would be irreparably damaging even to the victors and would leave the humans still stranded and starving. Van Rijn's first move is to show, by logical deduction, that Lannachska and Drak'honai are members of a single race. He convinces nearly all the leaders of both groups that the different breeding patterns are cultural adaptations, not racial divergences. Only the irrational and fanatic Drak'honai admiral remains unpersuaded, continuing to insist that the Lannachska must be obliterated. His position is crucial because the rigidly hierarchical Fleet will obey him even if they doubt his wisdom. Van Rijn's last and triumphant ploy is to insult the admiral profoundly by suggesting that he harbors a repressed desire to sample Lannach forms of sexuality. Outraged to frenzy, the admiral, with the reflex of a carnivore, bites van Rijn on the buttock. A few minutes later, the Diomedean dies of a massive allergic reaction to the alien flesh. The admiral's successor then agrees to a peaceful compromise with the Lannachska, and the former enemies send a joint embassy with a message to the distant human settlement. Van Rijn, Wace, and Lady Sandra are saved.

Anderson makes no claim to major significance in *War of the Wing-Men*, but its interest is genuine and substantial. Diomedes figures effectively as an exemplum of the challenges a complex universe may pose, and Nicholas van

Rijn is a cogent exemplar of intelligent response. The novel is reassuring but not comfortable: a world that demands a van Rijn to equiponderate it is not a world made for man, however successfully some men may live in it.

THE WAR OF THE WORLDS

Author: H. G. Wells (1866-1946)
First book publication: 1898
Type of work: Novel
Time: The early twentieth century
Locale: Woking (West Surrey), London and environs

Seeking a refuge from their dying planet, Martians invade and conquer a helpless Earth, only to be destroyed by a bacteria for which their systems are unprepared

Principal characters:
THE NARRATOR
HIS YOUNGER BROTHER, a London medical student
THE CURATE, a nearly hysterical clergyman who shares the Narrator's hiding place
THE ARTILLERYMAN, a surviving soldier who vows to restore human supremacy
THE MARTIANS, invaders and would-be conquerors from a dying planet

In *The War of the Worlds*, H. G. Wells's fourth "scientific romance," he fixed the image of the hostile alien invader in both the science fiction genre and in the popular mind. When Orson Welles adapted the novel to radio for his famous 1938 Halloween prank, the resulting chaos gave Wells's tentacled Martians, their Heat Ray, their giant tripod vehicles, and their black poison gas the status of modern myth. Every Bug-Eyed-Monster, giant insect swarm, activated primordial beast, and extraterrestrial invader that had dominated the screen, the comic strips, the Big Little Books, the pulps, and the less sophisticated science fiction publications of the 1930's, 1940's, and 1950's, paid dubious homage to Wells's doomed Martian monsters.

However, as is frequently the case when a book has such a thorough and enduring influence, the original has been distorted and lost behind the images and popularizations it spawned. While in simple summary *The War of the Worlds* may resemble many of its trite, simplistic offsprings, it is actually a forceful, sophisticated novel that remains original, intense, and provocative today.

Because of the enduring power of its images and influence, it is easy to forget the extent to which *The War of the Worlds* was a product of its own time and culture. The notion of the collapse of moral order and the general dissolution of society and culture was a generally pervasive one in that *fin de siècle* period. The more particular idea of an invasion from the Continent was likewise common, and had generated its own body of writings with which Wells was familiar. Indeed, it is possible to see *The War of the Worlds* as a variation on the "imaginary future wars" novel — the most notable example of which is George Chesney's *The Battle of Dorking*, 1871, in which Martians replace the Germans or French.

Nor was the identification of Martians as the probable alien invaders an unlikely one in the 1890's. Initially stimulated by Schiaparelli's "discovery" in 1877 of the Martian "canals," public speculation about the possibility of intelligent life on Mars grew into what one newspaper labeled the "Great Mars Boom." The notion of an advanced civilization on Mars peaked with the publication in 1892 of Camille Flammarion's *La Planete Mars*, as well as the books written by United States astronomer Percy Lowell in the middle of the decade.

Wells's own interest in Mars considerably predated the "boom." From his early college days onward, Wells had puzzled about the possibility of life on Mars, and his early writings contain several references to it, notably an early lecture entitled "Are the Planets Habitable" (1888) and a later article, "Intelligence on Mars" (1896). The particular inspiration for a Martian invasion came, however, from his brother Frank, to whom the book is dedicated. As Wells recorded in his *Autobiography* (1920), "We were walking together through some particularly peaceful Surrey scenery. 'Suppose some beings from another planet were to drop out of the sky suddenly' said he [Frank] 'and began laying about them here!' "

His brother's idea was a natural. Wells knew the countryside well, and he carefully orchestrated the details of his novel to particular sites. As he said in a letter quoted in Bernard Bergonzi's *The Early H. G. Wells:*

> I completely wreck and destroy Woking — killing my neighbors in painful and eccentric ways — then proceed via Kingston and Richmond to London, which I sack, selecting South Kensington for feats of particular atrocity.

The apparent, almost loving glee Wells took in unleashing such fictional carnage on his neighbors probably came from his satisfaction in attacking the complacency and arrogance of the late Victorian bourgeoisie, in terms of their narrow social awareness, their petty materialism, and their false cosmic security.

Yet, for all of its turn-of-the-century topicality, *The War of the Worlds* is an enduring work of art. In focusing many of the preoccupations of his own day, Wells succeeded in creating a modern myth of compelling and sustaining power. When Orson Welles and Howard Koch adapted it, they naturally altered the novel to suit the new medium, times, and geography, but the degree to which they remained faithful to the original is surprising. The images, situations, and themes that panicked the American listeners came from the original, sharpened and given a dramatic immediacy in the 1938 radio copy.

Wells divides the novel into two neatly labeled books, "The Coming of the Martians," which chronicles the landing, emergence, and takeover by the Martians, and "The Earth Under the Martians," which examines postholocaust reactions to and implications of the invasion, depicts the death of the Martians from unseen biological causes, and, finally, describes humanity's efforts to return to normality.

Unlike the protagonist of most of Wells's other writings, the narrator of this novel is almost totally passive. His only act, the killing of the hysterical curate, is a desperate gesture of self-preservation. He simply reports, dryly, with a faint irony at times, the evolving situation as he observes it. He is a bit more sensitive and thoughtful than his neighbors, but no more able to affect events than they. And that, of course, is the point; no human agency can affect the course of events. Much of the power of the novel comes from this sense that mankind — even the Martians, for that matter — are being swept along by forces they cannot even see, much less understand and deal with.

Unlike the radio version of the story, in which the threat is perceived almost immediately and military defenses — albeit inadequate ones — set up at once, in Wells's original, the civic reaction (to the extent that there is a reaction at all) is casual, a combination of curiosity and mild concern. The populace seems to doubt even the possibility that anything really unusual could come into their environment, or, in the unlikely event that it did happen and that the intruders turned out to be hostile, that they could quickly and easily be contained by the local militia. Even after the Martians have unleashed the first of their hideous weapons and destroyed all within viewing distance, people are only mildly interested. As the Narrator's neighbor muses to him in the midst of gardening: "It's a pity they make themselves so unapproachable. . . . It would be curious to know how they live on another planet; we might learn a thing or two."

This combination of apathy and cockiness gives Wells's book some of its most memorable qualities: the bitter irony of seeing the trivial overwhelmed by the awful, the growing sense of horror and helplessness that slowly, painfully takes over, and the sudden frenzy that sets in once the situation is fully understood. Particularly successful is Wells's careful pacing, and his handling of the moment-to-moment details of the invasion.

Obvious incongruities in this swift transition from complacency to panic are almost humorous. "The respectable inhabitants of the place, men in golf and boating costumes, wives prettily dressed, were packing, riverside loafers energetically helping, children excited, and, for the most part, highly delighted at this astonishing variation of their Sunday experiences." It is with such careful choice of detail, rather than by attempting to describe large numbers of frenzied people, that Wells is able to present convincingly this "liquefaction of the social fabric."

Overwhelmed by the panic, buffetted by the crowds, dazed by collapse of all resistance, and narrowly escaping death himself, the Narrator finally finds himself trapped in a house on the edge of one of the pits containing a Martian space vehicle. At this point, Wells shifts the book's point of view to the narrator's younger brother, a medical student in London. The shift is structurally awkward, but understandable. Having documented the launching of the Martian attack, Wells needs to show its climax in London, but there is no way he can believably transport his disheveled Narrator to the action. Moreover, the Narrator is too slow and passive to act as a convincing focus for the more dramatic action that takes place in London. The younger brother is a more positive character; he even exhibits some Victorian gallantry in rescuing a pair of ladies from the crowd. But the Londoners as a whole are neither courageous nor effective against the devastating Martians.

> . . . this was no disciplined march; it was a stampede — a stampede gigantic and terrible — without order and without a goal, six million people, unarmed and unprovisioned, driving headlong. It was the beginning of the rout of civilization, of the massacre of mankind.

In the second half of the book, the rhetorical Wells, who was to do such damage to the later books, takes over, although not so intrusively as to hurt the novel. Indeed, after the intensity of the destruction scenes, the talk comes as a welcome respite and the ideas do, ultimately, reinforce the implications made by the actions of the book. In the course of his wanderings, the Narrator encounters two neatly labeled characters, the Curate and the Artilleryman, who embody two basic reactions to and attitudes about the holocaust.

The Curate most obviously represents the collapse of the old order and, more centrally, its values and belief systems. Since the Curate's behavior borders on hysteria, Wells's satiric thrust is almost too broad to be taken seriously. The Curate simply deflates, along with his doctrines, into a gibbering, trembling wreck; he views the Martians as a divine judgment. When the Curate's near insanity threatens to expose them to the Martians, the Narrator, in his only aggressive action of the novel, kills him.

The Artilleryman, whom the Narrator meets as he wanders back toward Leatherbend in hopes of finding his wife, is a more complex figure with a more ambiguous message. The Narrator had met him previously, in a thoroughly demoralized state, immediately after the initial Martian attack. By this second meeting, however, the Artilleryman has apparently mastered his feelings and developed a new sense of resolution. He presents the Narrator with a coherent and comprehensive analysis of the Martian strategy and then offers his own blueprint for the survival — and eventual return to supremacy — of the human race. In his view, the Martians "haven't begun on us yet." He describes the manner in which the Martians will catch and cage humans for food, amusement, and pets, and he envisions an alien-dominated world in which human beings, relegated to a subspecies, will actually come to enjoy their lot: "The Martians will just be a godsend to them. Nice roomy cages, fattening food, careful breeding, no worry."

Evident in the Artilleryman's speech is his contempt for most of his fellow creatures and their usual activities: "There won't be any more blessed concerts for a million years or so; there won't be any Royal Academy of arts, and no nice little feeds at restaurants." To him, the invasion has become an experiment in survival of the fittest, and he has cast himself for leadership among the fittest. Ultimately, he believes that the strongest men will be able to capture the Martian machines and turn them against their inventors; he revels in the potential carnage.

The Narrator is carried away by the logic and intensity of the Artilleryman's vision until he examines the man's actual condition more closely. The Narrator looks at the burrow he had been digging for ten days as the first step in his plan: "such a hole I could have dug in a day." He watches the would-be leader lounging about and gorging himself on leftover luxury items. Finding himself drifting into the easy complacency of immediate pleasures, reinforced by dreams of future omnipotence, the Narrator leaves saddened and annoyed at himself for falling into such an easy emotional trap.

Thus, the primary reason that Wells's rhetoric does not damage the fabric of this parable is that he carefully undercuts what the characters say by what they do, thereby ironically qualifying the elitest theories of his would-be hero. Yet, the ideas the Artilleryman promulgates are not actually refuted and were to persist and grow in Wells's subsequent writings. Indeed, the idea of an elite of highly disciplined, morally, intellectually, and aesthetically superior men as the only salvation from the progressive chaos of the twentieth century was to become one of his primary convictions qualified by the deft ironies present in this work.

Disillusioned by his experience with the Artilleryman and still hopeful of somehow finding his wife, the Narrator wanders in the direction of London. He encounters no more people, but he does notice some odd things: the red weedlike plant that had come with the Martians is dying off; he sees a dog run by with a chunk of black meat in his mouth; and, he hears the frightening cry: "Ulla, ulla, ulla, ulla." Finally, upon entering London, he comes upon a group of stilled war machines, and, beyond them the dead bodies of Martians who have died of unaccustomed bacteria. This quick, neat dispatching of the Martians by convenient germs comes with shocking suddenness and produces a feeling of contrivance. Can this conclusion be justified in literary and thematic terms? Dramatic intensity and effectiveness of the storytelling notwithstanding, a final value judgment of the novel probably depends on the validity of this ending, and any proper analysis of the fate of the aliens requires, first of all, a more careful analysis of their nature and history.

On the first pages of the novel, the Martians are described as having "minds to our minds as ours to those of the beasts that perish, vast intellects vast and cool and unsympathetic. . . . ," but the first thing about them that impresses the reader is not their intellect, but their physical appearance. The creature is a monster, a primordial thing with qualities both of land beast and sea monster. This view is reinforced when the narrator watches it feed. Lacking digestive organs, it drinks blook directly from its living human victims — it is not only a beast, but a vampire as well. Thus, while the reader understands that it is the mind of the Martian that is to be feared, he is subjectively repulsed by its bestial physical qualities.

Roughly speaking, there are three images of the alien invader that provoke fear in the reader (leaving aside the more contemporary benign invaders who want only to help, study, commune with, or merely puzzle us). First is the picture of the bestial invader — B.E.M.'s of all sorts, giant insects, Cthulhu-like primordials, dragons, blobs, and the like — everything that touches our innate fears of animals and insects. Second is the mechanical invader image of creatures who come with machines to render us impotent and to beat us at our own game, technological superiority. The third image is that of the interior invader, the alien, usually unseen, who takes us over before we know it, who is so much like us that we cannot usually see it, much less deal with it. Wells utilizes elements of all three images but most obviously the first two.

Although the Martians appear bestial, they are relatively helpless. The greater gravity of earth renders them almost immobile, and early in the novel the Narrator almost pities them for their physical infirmities. It is only when they utilize machinery that they become invulnerable. "Yet though they wore no clothing, it was in the other artificial additions to their bodily resources that their great superiority over man lay." From their glistening cone-shaped metal rockets they burn up spectators with a Heat Ray. Once settled, they enter gleaming metal tripods and stalk about the countryside raising havoc and releasing poison gas. There are hints that they are beginning to launch flying machines. Thus, the second fear, that their machines will destroy us (a fear which extends also to machines of our own making), has emerged forcefully by the middle of the book.

On the surface, the third kind of fear, the fear provoked by the idea that the *human* qualities of the alien make him so frightening, would seem to be the one element that Wells's aliens lack. They certainly do not look like humans, and their basic biological functions and activities are totally dissimilar. Their behavior, however, cannot be accurately called inhuman. They do nothing to man that he has not already done to lesser species, or even, in fact, to his own kind:

> The Tasmanians, in spite of their human likeness, were entirely swept out of existence in a war of extermination waged by European immigrants, in the space of fifty years. Are we such apostles of mercy as to complain if the Martians warred in the same spirit?

Left at that, the point is merely satirical, a biting comment on human nature in general and imperialism in particular; but Wells has more in mind than that. Crucial to the nature of his Martians is their reason for coming to Earth in the first place. Their invasion is no expression of wanton cruelty or even calculated aggression, but is a desperate act of racial survival. "The immediate pressure of necessity has brightened their intellects, enlarged their powers and hardened their hearts." The Narrator tells us this in the first pages of the book, thus explaining the rationale of the invasion, thereby not only preparing the reader for the action to come, but also foreshadowing in a profound and subtle way the novel's climax.

Two related assumptions commonly held in Wells's time underlie both the reasons for the invasion and the nature of the invaders: first, that the sun was cooling off and consequently that our solar system was dying gradually from its extremities inward; and second, that Darwinian notions of evolution would apply to any organic creature living anywhere in the universe. In addition, Wells accepted the moral attitude toward evolution of T. H. Huxley, his old teacher, that evolution and progress are not synonymous: that, in the long run, evolution is likely to be regressive, however positive it might appear to a late-Victorian humanist.

Thus, the planet Mars has reached its stage of exhaustion. Cooling rapidly — a condition that will ultimately be repeated on Earth — it will soon be uninhabitable. The *logical* place for the Martians to go is, of course, the Earth, the only habitable planet that is closer to the sun. The Martians' superiority is merely the result of time; Mars is dying sooner because it became habitable sooner, and, since its creatures have had much longer to evolve, they have developed their civilization to a much higher degree.

During the period when he is trapped with the Curate in a house overlooking one of the Martian pits, the Narrator studies the aliens at close range, and realizes that, for all of their (to us) grotesque physical peculiarities, they are models of efficiency. Unnecessary or irrelevant physical characteristics — sexual organs, digestive tracts, elaborate muscular and nervous systems — have been evolved out, leaving only the essentials: eyes, hands (tentacles, usually), a hearing mechanism, a strawlike appendage for draining the blood, and, above all, a brain. Wells summarizes the creatures in a key passage:

> . . . in the Martians we have beyond dispute the actual accomplishment of such a suppression of the animal side of the organism by the intelligence. To me it is quite credible that the Martians may be descended from beings not unlike ourselves, by a gradual development of brain and hands . . . at the expense of the rest of the body. Without the body the brain would, of course, become a mere selfish intelligence, without any of the emotional substratum of the human being.

Thus the Martians are well-equipped with all the apparatus needed to analyze, to plan, and then to act, unhampered by such considerations as feelings, desires, or values. Wells seems to ask whether this will be the logical direction for development of the human species as well — progressive evolution with a vengeance.

Whether the aliens' vulnerability to germs was the result of a natural absence of such bacteria on Mars, or was due to their success in eliminating them from their environment, is left ambiguous by Wells, but the implication of their deaths is clear: cosmic process and evolution are impersonal, unavoidable, and, the Narrator's musing about God notwithstanding, amoral and mechanistic. Artistically the demise of the Martians is not only justified, but necessary; philosophically it is consistent with the dark vision of the author's other scientific romances.

The final victory of mankind over the Martians, particularly since it is coupled with the Narrator's reunion with his wife, should end the book on an optimistic note, but quite the opposite is true. At best, the final mood of the book could be called pensive. The lesson about man's vulnerability to the vagaries of forces outside of his control has been made too forcefully for the Narrator to feel any continued sense of security. The outcome of the invasion, he suggests, is more of a reprieve than a victory, and even if the Martians do not return, there are probably other beings out there.

But perhaps what the invasion has suggested about man himself is even more responsible for the bleak mood of the book's ending. In the human reaction to the aliens, we have seen apathy, selfishness. confusion, pettiness, blind fear, hysteria, disdain, and arrogance, but very little heroism. On the other side, in the Martians we see what man could become — inhumanly rationalistic and barbarously efficient. Nor does Wells present this as a choice. The novel is no exhortation to cultivate the humane side of man. The brain and the hand are the parts of man most likely to survive in the evolutionary process; the humane qualities are ultimately expendable. The initial shock in reading *The War of the Worlds* is produced by the strangeness and grotesqueness of the Martians as compared to man, but the lasting impression is of their similarity. Or, to paraphrase Walt Kelley's comic-strip 'possum, Pogo: "we have met the alien and he is us."

Criticism:

Borrello, Alfred. *H. G. Wells: Author in Agony*. Carbondale: Southern Illinois University Press, 1972, pp. 14, 81-82. Borrello provides a general thematic analysis of *The War of the Worlds* as part of a larger study of the author.

Costa, Richard H. *H. G. Wells*. New York: Twayne, 1967, pp. 43-46. This general study of the author takes a brief look at the plot concerns of *The War of the Worlds*.

Gilbert, James B. "Wars of the Worlds," in *Journal of Popular Culture*. X (1976), pp. 326-336. Gilbert analyzes the style of *The War of the Worlds* and surveys its impact on the literature of science fiction.

WAY STATION

Author: Clifford D. Simak (1904-   )
First book publication: 1963
Type of work: Novel
Time: The 1960's
Locale: A farmhouse near Millville, Wisconsin

A character study of a man who operates a Way Station in Wisconsin for aliens who are passing through the area unbeknownst to anyone else on Earth, and of this man's ultimate choice of loyalties between his native planet and his alien friends

Principal characters:
> ENOCH WALLACE, the custodian of the Way Station
> ULYSSES, Enoch's superior from Galactic Central
> CLAUDE LEWIS, an Intelligence agent spying on Enoch Wallace
> LUCY FISHER, a deaf-mute girl
> WINSLOWE GRANT, Enoch's mailman
> MARY, an apparition

Clifford D. Simak is one of the more pastoral writers in the science fiction field. His stories tend to be works of gentle beauty rather than the fierce action/adventure romances that predominate in the genre. The fate of the world may hinge upon the events in his work, as it does in *Way Station*, but the decision comes across as the personal revelation of one man rather than a result of chest-thumping heroics by a larger-than-life-sized figure.

Way Station is without question one of Simak's greatest works, a masterpiece that received the Hugo Award as the best novel of 1963. It deals with concepts so large that they span the entire galaxy and explore the essence of religion, and yet Simak keeps it all in perspective by focusing virtually all the action within a few square miles around a farmhouse in rural Wisconsin. The intricate interplay of vast cosmic forces is dealt with through the soul of one lonely, troubled man.

That man is really the product of another age. Enoch Wallace was born in 1840 and served in the Civil War — and yet in the present, when by all rights he should have been dead and buried decades ago, he only appears to be thirty years old. He lives by himself in his old family farmhouse, venturing outside it only about an hour a day and having no communication with anyone but his mailman. The country folk in his community have long since accepted him as one of the local oddities, but he has now attracted the attention of U. S. Intelligence, which wants an explanation for this phenomenon.

Very simply, Enoch Wallace is the keeper of a Way Station for beings from all over the galaxy as they travel from one place to another. Their method of transportation is to transmit their life patterns across space to their destination, with occasional stopovers on long trips to avoid beam dispersal. Enoch's station is one such stopover, but because Earth is considered too backward to join the galactic community, the station must operate in secret. To perform the job for which he was recruited, Enoch must cut himself off from the rest of his species. He subscribes to newspapers and magazines, and talks to the mailman who delivers them, but other than that he is a stranger in his own world. As compensation, he receives a gift many would envy — virtual immortality. Time stands still within his house, and he only ages during the hour or so a day that he takes his walk to the mailbox.

One of the strengths of a really good science fiction story is that it tickles the reader's imagination, leaving vast empty areas that he can fill in for himself. Simak does this admirably in *Way Station*. The concept of such a place, wherein one ordinary person can meet and converse with all sorts of beings from all over the galaxy, conjures up different images in each individual reader's mind. Simak gives tantalizing glimpses of the exotic throughout the book — enough to stimulate the reader's dreams of wonder without giving him all the answers predigested. Each reader can dream for himself of the marvels he would see if *he* were the stationkeeper.

But for all the excitement of his job, Enoch Wallace is a very troubled man. Despite the glimpses he is given of galactic civilization, he lacks the companionship of his own people. He befriends the sensitive deaf-mute, Lucy Fisher, and he talks with his mailman, but they cannot give him all the company he needs. Long ago, in desperation, he used some alien magic to "create" some shadow people of his own, friends who could be conjured at will and sent back to their private limbo when he was tired of them. One of these is the beautiful Mary, with whom he has gradually fallen in love. But they can never touch because she is not real. In a way, she symbolizes his greater plight, for his whole existence is a shadow; he dares not touch the real world for fear of finding that *he* has become unreal.

But, like it or not, the real world is encroaching on Enoch's hitherto private existence. There are the watchers, headed by Intelligence agent Claude Lewis, intent on discovering his secret. There is Lucy, who is forced to take refuge in the Way Station to escape a homicidal beating by her loutish father. But most of all, there is Earth itself. Using statistical principles taught him by some alien travelers, he can tell from the trends reported in the newspapers that human society is headed toward a nuclear holocaust. Enoch feels that some of the knowledge he has gained from his alien contacts might help relieve the situation if he could communicate it to people of importance — but to do so would be to betray Galactic Central and especially his boss, and closest friend, Ulysses.

But the galaxy, too, has its own problems. Up until recently it had been guided by its knowledge of a basic force which people could actually feel through a mechanism known as the Talisman. This certain knowledge of the true spirituality pervading the universe was a moderating influence on galactic civilization. But the Talisman has disappeared and been out of touch for many years, and with it has gone the spirit of reasonable debate within galactic society; factionalism is the order of the day. When Claude Lewis, in his attempt to discover the secret of the Way Station, accidentally tampers with something he should not have touched, he sets off a chain reaction that pits galactic partisanship squarely against Earth.

Enoch Wallace becomes the nexus of the competing forces. He is a peaceful man who wants to avoid war on Earth, and had hoped that someday his native world would be admitted to the galactic brotherhood of planets. But Lewis' action has jeopardized that, and there are forces at work in the galaxy that would love to see the Way Station on Earth permanently shut down. Enoch is caught in a conflict of loyalties; should he stay with Galactic Central and leave Earth when this station is shut down, or should he be true to the world of his birth? Over the past century he has accumulated knowledge and artifacts that might revolutionize the world — but does he dare tell anyone?

Simak's story succeeds so marvelously because he is able to deal with these cosmic issues through the problems of a single, very sympathetic character. The world's problems are Enoch's problems, and the factionalism of the galaxy is mirrored in his own conflict. Enoch becomes the crucible; the decisions are his, and a crisis of major proportions in galactic relations becomes understandable as a crisis within one man's soul. Slowly but surely, all Enoch's attempts to retain a semblance of normality are breaking down. The ghosts he has conjured have developed a strange sort of half-life of their own. They are sentient and aware that they have no reality outside Enoch's existence, and the pain of that is too great for them to bear. They desert Enoch, asking him not to call them up again. This is hardest for Mary, who has fallen as much in love with Enoch as he has with her. That love only makes her existence doubly painful, and she too flees back into her shadow of unreality.

Being a man in the long run is a matter of the choices one makes, and Enoch Wallace has hard ones to face. Not the least of these choices is whether to accept the one possible method Ulysses can suggest to stop the nuclear holocaust on Earth, a method that has worked on a few occasions before: stupidity. Earth's people can be made to forget all they know about technology for several generations. Many people will die that way too, and chaos will reign on Earth for decades, but the total disaster of all-out nuclear war would be averted. As the sole member of the human race in contact with Galactic Central, Enoch must represent his planet and take the responsibility for that decision. But how can anyone make the choice for all the people on Earth?

If there is any flaw in *Way Station*, it is the enormous *deus ex machina* that Simak uses at the end to clear up these problems. The being who stole the Talisman tries to hide out on Earth by traveling through the Way Station. Enoch kills him, and then it transpires that Lucy Fisher is the perfect new custodian for the galaxy's symbol of spiritual attainment. All the loose ends are thus wound up: the planet that produced such a custodian could scarcely be denied admittance to the galactic fraternity; contact with other races will help stabilize the political climate on Earth; Enoch need no longer be cut off from his own race by the secretiveness of his job; and the galaxy has its Talisman back again to stop the petty bickering that has plagued it since the object's disappearance. It is a solution that resolves all the major problems without Enoch's having to make the final choice of loyalties, and it leaves the question open as to what he would have chosen. The ending is emotionally satisfying, but dramatically ambivalent.

This flaw, though, is merely a bow to convention. It is the *asking* of the questions that is important, not how they were resolved in this one particular case. Through Enoch's dilemma, the reader himself is made aware of the harsh choices that sometimes exist — choices of self-doubt, of loneliness, and of conflicting loyalties. Each reader is forced to face those choices as the book progresses, and to come to grips with how he himself might react under those circumstances. By showing how another man deals with the conflicts, the reader may learn something about his own values and judgments.

Simak is a stylist. He is not quite as flowery as, say, Ray Bradbury, but there is still the attention to descriptive detail and the use of lyric language to evoke the desired mood. Time and again he will minutely describe the settings that Enoch passes through, but his descriptions are more than mere boring catalogs of the character's surroundings. The author captures the essence of places and feelings, transforming his words into complete visual images. Simak has always been a writer attuned to the depths of human emotions, and nowhere does he display this talent better than in *Way Station*.

Way Station is, in the final analysis, a probing and sensitive look at what makes a person human. It examines an intelligent, thoughtful man and reveals his inner core — his loneliness, his friendship, and his love. By the end of the book, the reader may realize that the human race has been in a way station of its own, and is now ready to move ahead to its ultimate destiny — whatever that may be.

THE WITCHES OF KARRES

Author: James H. Schmitz (1911-   )
First book publication: 1966
Type of work: Novel
Time: The far future
Locale: Among the stars and planets on the fringe of a galactic Empire in the Milky Way

A galactic "space opera," social comedy, novel of education, and highly entertaining example of science fantasy

> *Principal characters:*
> CAPTAIN PAUSERT, a commercial traveler from the Republic of Nikkeldepain
> MALEEN, eldest of the three daughters of Threbus and Toll
> GOTH, her slightly younger sister
> THE LEEWIT, her youngest sister
> THREBUS AND TOLL, important and powerful witches from Karres
> HULIK DO ELDEL, an Empire spy
> VEZZARN, an ex-safecracker and undercover agent for the Daal of Uldune
> SEDMON THE SIXTH, Daal of Uldune
> LAES YANGO, the Agandar, an infamous pirate
> LORD CHEEL, untrustworthy Prince of the Lyrd-Hyrier

James H. Schmitz's *The Witches of Karres* was judged one of the four best science fiction novels of 1966 by the twenty-fifth World Science Fiction Convention, and it is not hard to see why. It is a superior entertainment which provides equal doses of comedy and adventure while never once challenging either the conventions of the genre or the ethical and philosophical precepts which underlie them. It is, indeed, a fine example of science fantasy, or what is called space opera, yet it is sophisticated enough in style and characterization to stand up under more than one reading.

The Witches of Karres began as a novella of the same title, published in John W. Campbell, Jr.'s *Astounding Science Fiction* in 1949. Obviously popular, for it was the one Schmitz story included in *The Astounding Science Fiction Anthology* published in 1952, it became the first two chapters of the novel. Aside from dropping the chapter divisions of the novella, Schmitz made only a few changes in its final few pages, in order to make a smooth transition into the additional narrative.

The original story is an almost perfectly cohesive whole: its conclusion implies that because Captain Pausert has now "found himself" as a person with a taste for and an ability (including latent Psi-talents) to handle adventure, he will, in the company of a young Karres witch, definitely lead a rich and adventurous life. The essential changes in his character have already taken place, for he has learned that there are larger, richer, riskier, and more genuine ways of life to follow out in the universe than stuffy, "proper" society on

Nikkeldepain will acknowledge, so narrowminded and hypocritical are its mores. Thus Schmitz's extension of his original story adds little to our knowledge of Pausert's character though it fills in its far future galaxy with a wide variety of fantastical creatures and dangerous places and provides a number of paradigmatic and conventionally suspenseful "escape fiction" adventures.

Indeed, unlike those works which attempt, in however small a way, to realize the as yet untapped literary potential of science fiction and thus somehow push the boundaries of genre definition outward, *The Witches of Karres* is interesting precisely because it is so obviously popular genre science fiction, an example of "good old science fantasy storytelling." Schmitz is obviously writing in the A. E. van Vogt mode and this explains both the power and the weaknesses of his novel.

The power is imaginative, though essentially derivative. As J. R. R. Tolkien once pointed out, the very act of casting a story into the long-ago has a magical effect, the sense of "distance and a great abyss of time" transforming the ordinary. The same effect occurs when a story is cast into the far future, a universe as potently magical (even if the "magic" is the result of technology) as any ancient Middle-Earth. Thus, science fiction stories set in an almost-too-huge-to-imagine galactic Empire automatically speak to the average reader's "sense of wonder" unless they are absolutely cretinous in execution. *The Witches of Karres* is written by a professional: it invokes and makes use of all the proper science fiction conventions, and it does so with high comic energy; but it never challenges the conventions on an ideological plane.

The weakness of *The Witches of Karres* lies in its imaginative failure as social extrapolation, a point best examined in relation to the fact of slavery within the Empire. The three young witches are picked up in their galactic wanderings by an "Imperial Slaver." Later sold on Porlumma, they are "rescued" — that is, bought — by the captain, and that is the end of any reference to the Imperial Slave Trade. Schmitz is not truly interested in speculating on the kind of galactic civilization which would require slaves, so he sets his adventures on the edges of the Empire. To begin to question the concept of slavery in this galactic Empire, however, is to confront a series of poorly thought-through assumptions. Schmitz has posited incredible technology for his future and, as Asimov and others have argued in recent years, technology more than anything else has made individual slavery obsolete.

When Pausert finds them, the three witches are working in unnecessary jobs and obviously driving their "owners" crazy. Of course, this triggers the narrative and provides for much comedy. For, although the captain "rescues" these poor lost children, he in fact needs them more than they need him since it is through them and their people that he will begin to grow into the tough, resourceful person with ESP faculties who will later help to save the universe.

As others have pointed out, such science fiction "power fantasies," as Brian Aldiss calls them, tend to deal with pseudoproblems in an unreal societal and psychological context. After all his adventures, the captain is going to work for Karres (which Threbus tells him is "a set of attitudes, a frame of mind" rather than a particular world) and for the "good" Empress who is trying to improve the Empire despite the "evil" Emperor and others in his court. The captain could be defined, as could Schmitz and most of his readers, as a small-l liberal: he acts out of personal compassion and obviously tries to be a "good" man. Thus he decides to refuse, no matter what the cost, to join the Agandar's pirates, but in fact he gets out of that tight spot before he actually has to suffer for his beliefs.

What is missing here and throughout the novel is any complex structural sense of how politics and economics might work in such a civilization. Rather, Schmitz has transplanted a fairly simple and superficial vision of how big governments, pirates, capitalist businesses, and traders operated in the nineteenth century into his imaginary future, and then told a fine, old-fashioned sea adventure set against that backdrop.

Of course, Schmitz is not really interested in creating a complexly realized society; he wants to tell the story of how one individual (with whom we identify) discovers in himself possibilities for heroic behavior he never knew he had. And he does this with both verve and a certain saving ironic comic perspective.

Though sympathetically presented from the start, the captain is obviously operating on a number of unexamined assumptions, including a misplaced patriotism toward his home world. Schmitz handles his thoughts about Nikkeldepain and his "true love" Illyla with ironic control: his every thought reveals a money-grubbing, puritanical, narrowminded and hypocritical society, but he fails to recognize this. Nevertheless, his basic good instincts emerge in his willingness to step in when he hears someone in trouble. Thus he takes the three young witches from their owners and offers to take them home to Karres even though their plight is none of his business.

The original story is fresh and funny because of the way it continually upsets expectations. The rest of the novel lacks the freshness of the original because it meets every expectation it sets up: each difficulty Pausert confronts he solves or has solved for him. But at the beginning Pausert continually runs into those sharp distinctions between expectations and reality which create comedy. Thus, without even quite meaning to, he offers to take Maleen home to Karres where she will be reunited with her sisters, but she tells him they are slaves on Porlumma too: "The captain's heart dropped clear through his boots. Standing there in the dark, he helplessly watched it coming: 'You could buy them awfully cheap,' she said." This is the basic method of the whole opening sequence: the captain thinks he knows where he stands and every time he thinks he has achieved equilibrium, something comes along to upset it. His ability to regain his balance each time reveals his potential as a heroic protagonist; his refusal to let Goth steal gifts for him by teleportation and his equally firm refusal to be cowed by those who blame him for her mischief reveal his moral courage.

Meanwhile, the young witches' talents provide other comic moments. Goth's teleportations twice get the captain branded as a thief. The witches' ability to use "the Sheewash Drive" takes the *Venture* out of danger when it is attacked, but also makes it the target of various dangerous interests, and the Leewit's command of languages allows her to insult and enrage others, like the Sirians whom she curses over the communicator. All of these acts serve to further alienate Pausert from "normal" society, thus pushing him closer to the break he must make in order to join the witches.

When they raise Karres, it is moving counterclockwise to the other planets in its system ("Well, it would, the captain thought"), and Pausert spends quite some time recovering and soaking up the peculiar atmosphere of this apparently idyllic and pastoral planet. Karres is similar to the ESPer planet in Joanna Russ's *And Chaos Died* (1970), but where Russ uses a pyrotechnic style and superb intelligence to create, in the very language of her novel, a model of the experience of gaining ESP on such a planet, Schmitz merely implies that certain changes have begun to occur in the captain and then bustles him off to some satisfying adventures. Russ's sociological extrapolation is also far more complex than anything Schmitz attempts.

The final comic touches of the original story occur when the people of Karres give Pausert a full cargo of immensely rich goods which, as they obviously know, he cannot legally sell in the Empire because they are from an "uncleared" world. Nevertheless, he returns to Nikkeldepain to find himself under arrest, not only for theft and slave trading but mainly because he has "a new type of space drive, which should have been brought promptly and secretly to the attention of the Republic of Nikkeldepain." By now, Pausert has realized what kind of people have power on Nikkeldepain and decided to leave that world behind him. Once he discovers Illyla has long been married to a man he despises, he attempts to escape, helped, unsurprisingly, by Goth and the Sheewash Drive which, this time, carries them clear across the Empire. Goth explains that the Karres witches feel the two of them will lead an exciting and educational life as traders in that area, and the captain feels it will be a good time.

The rest of the novel attempts to show just how good a time it will be. The captain has awakened to his own potential but he has also awakened, it seems, a power focused on him. Schmitz approaches the Psi-powers of the witches by a circuitous route, the "metaphysical concept" of "Klatha" — a cosmic energy not fully of this universe which certain people can tune in on and use. Besides this energy, there are "vatches," Klatha entities who "didn't hang around this universe much but were sometimes drawn into it by human klatha activities, and if they were amused or intrigued by what they found going on they might stay and start producing klatha phenomena themselves. They seemed to be under the impression that their experiences of the human universe were something they were dreaming." In this they are like authors, and the huge vatch the captain later draws in to his affairs is, among other things, a highly useful *deus ex machina* who, at least once, saves the captain and Goth when it seems Schmitz has plotted his story into a *cul de sac*.

Between Goth's growing ESP powers and the captain's discovery that he can control klatha energy, including vatches, the two manage to survive various attempts on their lives by people interested in the Sheewash Drive, including the notorious pirate, the Agandar, and to help defeat a malignant force of beings from another universe who threaten to enslave all humankind. Schmitz develops these adventures with ingenuity and a certain comic flair, yet they seem somewhat mechanical compared to the original story, for there is no moral or psychological growth involved. Any new interest derives from the invention of varied minor characters and exotic otherworldly landscapes.

Yet even these are essentially conventional versions of figures and landscapes long familiar in pulp fiction, however well done they may be. If Schmitz's names are good science fiction poetry — Worm Weather, grik dogs, a Sheem Spider, Nartheby Sprites, the Chaladoor — his use of essentially 1950's slang for his technology — "they would have to juice up" the *Venture*'s fuel reserves, for example — reveals an essentially noninnovative imagination at work. Schmitz occasionally appears to be aware that he is writing too close to formula. Thus he often reminds us, successfully and comically, that the captain is only human, especially when he clearly shows that Goth and the Leewit are responsible for destroying "Moander Who Speaks with a Thousand Voices," even if Pausert finally "saves the universe" by forcing his vatch to send Manaret back to its own continuum. More to the point, the conclusion of the novel implies that the danger and its removal have barely been noticed by the rest of the Empire, which is still the same; all of which suggests that the battle has been something of a pseudoevent.

Despite the various criticisms above, *The Witches of Karres* remains a highly entertaining work of fiction. Its flaws are inherent in the conventions of its genre; its accomplishments are those of a comic imagination whose best work has always been in shorter forms. Therefore, if the novel as a whole does not live up to the promise of its opening (the original story), if it is simply a fine example of good escapist science fantasy, if it presents no speculation or extrapolation of superior value in the areas of psychological, political, or sociological awareness, then it certainly has no pretensions to do so; and it *is* a genuinely enjoyable book.

THE WORD FOR WORLD IS FOREST

Author: Ursula K. Le Guin (1929-   )
First book publication: 1972
Type of work: Novel
Time: The distant future
Locale: The planet Athshe

One of science fiction's few commentaries about American involvement in Vietnam, combined with a Utopian portrait of a culture that has achieved a union of the conscious and the unconscious

Principal characters:
    SELVER THELE, a native of the planet Athshe
    CAPTAIN DON DAVIDSON, a Terran officer stationed on Athshe
    CAPTAIN RAJ LYUBOV, an anthropologist
    COLONEL DONGH, Davidson's commanding officer

Winner of a Hugo Award and nominee for a Nebula, *The Word for World Is Forest* is probably the most distinguished work to emerge from Harlan Ellison's 1972 anthology *Again, Dangerous Visions*. Despite its brevity, it is the major work of Le Guin's "Hainish" series (about worlds populated by a mysterious alien race called the Hainish) to appear between *The Left Hand of Darkness* (1969) and *The Dispossessed* (1974). Like those longer novels, it continues Le Guin's explorations of her favorite themes — the relation of social structures to ecology and biology, the responsibility of the individual in society, the interaction of psychology and environment — but it also focuses on a very specific issue of contemporary history that had not received a great deal of thoughtful attention in science fiction before: the Vietnam War. Le Guin's ability to unite all these various concerns in a tight and well-plotted piece of short fiction is no mean achievement, but there is in the work a certain amount of strain between the homiletic voice and the speculative imagination, a strain which Le Guin herself acknowledged in her afterword to the story's first appearance. On the one hand, the novel seeks to condemn the mentality of racist imperialism, represented in the story by Captain Davidson, that leads to economic exploitation and ecological irresponsibility. On the other hand, it tries to explore the possibility of a psychology based on the union of the conscious and unconscious through the deliberate control of dreams, as represented by the native Athshean culture. Both themes are drawn from real-life models — the paranoid military mind in the former case, the dream-psychology of various Indian tribes in the latter — but in order to place them in effective opposition, Le Guin is at times forced to exaggerate their characteristics. Thus Davidson sometimes appears a parody of a modern Army general, reminiscent of General Jack D. Ripper in Stanley Kubrick's *Dr. Strangelove*, and the Athshean leader Selver sometimes emerges as too much the "noble savage," reminiscent of Cochise. Between these two opposites stands the Terran anthropologist Lyubov, who seeks to understand the Athsheans and establish a ground for communication between them and the Terran settlers.

But the link is not easily forged. The Terrans are primarily interested in Athshe as a source of lumber, which has become a "necessary luxury" on Earth, and regard the Athsheans as primitives useful for domestic employment and occasional sexual gratification. The Athsheans, on the other hand, regard the Terrans as "insane," since they do not understand the significance of the forest and must go through life disconnected from their unconscious minds. The resultant conflict is what provides the story's simple plot: the systematic destruction of their environment, coupled with the oppression and exploitation of their population, forces the Athsheans to unite under Selver and initiate Guerrilla counter-warfare against the Terrans. Selver's friend Lyubov, the leading advocate for the Athsheans among the Terrans, is killed in one of the Athshean insurgency actions. Davidson tries to retaliate, but the significantly named Colonet Dongh explains that systematic warfare in a jungle environment is ineffective, and cites as evidence what happened in his ancestral region of Earth in the distant past. In the end, the Athsheans succeed in forcing the Terrans to abandon their colony, but at great cost: the Athsheans themselves have now learned the arts of murder and war.

While the parallels with Vietnam are apparent even in a brief description of the plot, these parallels should not be overemphasized. Le Guin's explorations of political, ecological, and psychological themes are far more thoughtful and complex than such simple parallels would suggest, and many of the ideas she begins to develop in this story reach their full fruition in *The Dispossessed*. In terms of political philosophy, *The Word for World Is Forest* resembles that later work by placing in opposition two cultures based on radically different economic and social values, and by illustrating the necessity for individual political action. The culture of Earth is portrayed only indirectly, through the actions of Terran characters on Athshe and by allusions to what life is like on Earth. We are told that Earth is "worn out," that wood is more valued there than gold because of the deforestation that industry and agriculture have brought about, that it is, in Davidson's eyes, a "tamed world." But most of what we know of Earth we infer from the attitudes of characters like Davidson: his belief in complete mastery of the environment, in the importance of heroic individual effort, in the oppression of "lower" life forms that extends even to a racism toward other genetic groups on Earth. Davidson is not the exclusive representative of Earth's culture and values; Lyubov and Dongh serve to modify our image of Earth a bit, but it is clear that Earth is a colonial power whose imperialism is in the service of economic gain, at least more so than some other worlds in the Hainish Federation.

Set in opposition to this capitalistic culture are the Athsheans, an anarchic forest people with no central government, who have achieved a stable society through integration with their forest environment and integration of their waking and dream-selves. Aggression and organized political action are unknown among these people, and their initial response to the invasion of the Earthmen who begin stripping their forests is tacit, if resentful cooperation. It is not until their very survival is threatened that Selver realizes the importance of resistance. In the dream-religion of the Athsheans, he temporarily becomes a god. Further motivated by the death of his wife after she is raped by Davidson, Selver organizes selective raids on Terran encampments, even witnessing the death of his human friend Lyubov in one such raid (a death whose tragedy is lessened by the Athshean ability to keep a friend "alive" in the unconscious mind). Some of the actions taken in these raids seem excessively brutal — the murder of a newly arrived group of human women, for example — but all are carefully planned to weaken Terran colonization plans and to stop the destruction of the forests. If Davidson and Lyubov come from a society that values individualism and must learn of the value of cooperation, so Selver, coming from his cooperative society, learns the value of individual action by his organization of the Athshean resistance. Neither society, then, is perfect in itself; and this theme, too, will later be expanded in *The Dispossessed*, which is subtitled "An Ambiguous Utopia."

Clearly, the ecological theme cannot be divorced from the political aspect of the story. While Davidson views the forest (and indeed, all natural environments) as raw material for the appropriation of man, the Athsheans regard it as their natural and spiritual environment, and have evolved a belief-system almost druidic in its allusions to tree-spirits and tree-clans. The forest to these people is not an undifferentiated mass of vegetation; it is both their habitat and their technology. They have achieved a union with their environment that is difficult for Terrans, more used to an adversary relationship between man and nature, to understand, and thus the Athsheans appear to men to be a part of the chaotic unknown that the forests of Athshe represent.

It is partly because of the humans' inability to understand the Athsheans or their environment that they appear insane to the Athsheans, and thus the psychological theme of the story becomes entwined with all the other strands. The major weakness of the humans in the eyes of the Athsheans, of course, is their inability to connect with their own unconscious minds — a connection as vital to the Athsheans as simple reasoning ability is to us. As a result, humans appear alienated not only from their environment and from one another, but from themselves, spending their waking hours in a kind of dream-state unaware of what is really going on in their minds. The Athsheans have overcome this split through deliberate training from childhood, and learn early in life of the respective values of "dream-time" and "world-time." Their psychology is based on integration rather than dissociation and confrontation; as a result it may seem too subtle to all but a few Terrans.

Le Guin successfully unites all these various branches of her plot through the single overriding image that dominates the entire story: the forest. The forest is virtually the entire perceptual world to the Athsheans, and in their language the word for world is the same as the word for forest. Thus the forest becomes an image not only of a specific environment, but of the phenomenal world itself, and how one deals with this world becomes an analogue of how one deals with all things outside of self: either by subduing them, as the Terrans do, or by learning from them, as the Athsheans do. But the forest is also an image of that part of the self with which the Athsheans have achieved contact: the unconscious. Like the unconscious, the forest is an emblem of the threatening unknown to Terrans who view it as uncontrolled growth, a chaos of fertility and shadows. But to the Athsheans, it is a part of themselves, an aspect of their own identity, just as the unconscious mind is. The Terran project to deforest Athshe in the service of technology thus takes on a new aspect; it becomes a fearful striking out against the threatening underside of the ordered consciousness that is represented by a "tamed planet" such as Earth.

Le Guin's forest scenes are written in a rich, poetic style that contrasts appropriately with the curt, brutal interior monologues with which she characterizes her humans; the reader is forced into a sensuous response to the chapters concerning the Athsheans, while the chapters involving human characters invite a more judgmental, intellectual response. As a result, the Athsheans, for all their alienness, seem more engaging and sympathetic than does the limited sample of humanity we are permitted to see (we do not get a chance to identify, for example, with the human females who are massacred, and while Lyubov is certainly sympathetic, his own uncertainty and confusion about the Athsheans make him a weak counterbalance to Davidson). But this lush style does not serve to sentimentalize the Athsheans, and Le Guin makes no attempt to mitigate the brutality of their acts. In the end, the real tragedy of the story is not the failure of the Terran colony on Athshe, or even the portrait of a Terran society so decadent that it must rape other worlds to maintain itself in luxury, but rather the loss of innocence of the Athsheans. In order to preserve their Edenic existence, they must paradoxically learn the lessons that drove man from the Garden in the first place.

Criticism:

Watson, Jan. "The Forest as Metaphor for Mind: *The Word for World is Forest* and *Vaster Than Empires and More Slow*," in *Science Fiction Studies*. II (1975), pp. 231-237. Watson states Le Guin uses the forest as a metaphor for world.

Alien Encounter

AUTHOR AND TITLE INDEX